Related Party Transactions and Corporate Groups

European Company Law Series

VOLUME 16

Editor

Steef M. Bartman, Attorney-at-Law, Emeritus Professor of Company Law at Leiden Law School and Professor of Corporate Group Liability at Maastricht University, the Netherlands.

Introduction

The European Company Law Series is closely linked to the bimonthly journal European Company Law, also published by Kluwer Law International.

Contents/Subjects

The series covers subjects of company law in a broad sense, including insolvency, co-determination and securities law. Topical issues such as merger control, corporate governance, and piercing the corporate veil have been covered.

Objective of Series

Analysis of topical or complex subjects in European company law.

Readership

Academics; regulators; practitioners.

The titles published in this series are listed at the end of this volume.

Related Party Transactions and Corporate Groups

When Eastern Europe Meets the West

Ivan Romashchenko

Wolters Kluwer

Published by:
Kluwer Law International B.V.
PO Box 316
2400 AH Alphen aan den Rijn
The Netherlands
E-mail: international-sales@wolterskluwer.com
Website: lrus.wolterskluwer.com

Sold and distributed in North, Central and South America by:
Wolters Kluwer Legal & Regulatory U.S.
7201 McKinney Circle
Frederick, MD 21704
United States of America
Email: customer.service@wolterskluwer.com

Sold and distributed in all other countries by:
Air Business Subscriptions
Rockwood House
Haywards Heath
West Sussex
RH16 3DH
United Kingdom
Email: international-customerservice@wolterskluwer.com

ISBN 978-94-035-1701-8

e-Book: ISBN 978-94-035-1705-6
web-PDF: ISBN 978-94-035-1713-1

To my mother, Oksana

About the Author

Ivan Romashchenko was born in 1986 in Kyiv, Ukraine, graduated from Kyiv specialized school No. 82 in 2003 and entered Taras Shevchenko National University of Kyiv, Faculty of Law, Kyiv, Ukraine, in the same year, where in 2007 he obtained bachelor's (cum laude) and in 2009 master's (cum laude). In 2009, he was appointed as an assistant professor of the Department of Civil Law in the same university. In 2011, the World Wide Studies grant from the Viktor Pinchuk Foundation allowed Ivan to enrol and pursue the Advanced LLM programme in European and International Business Law at Leiden University, Leiden, the Netherlands. In 2012, he completed his LLM and returned to work as an assistant professor at Taras Shevchenko National University of Kyiv, Kyiv, Ukraine. He started PhD research at Leiden University, Leiden, the Netherlands, in 2014 as an external PhD candidate. Within the described project he was a guest researcher at the Max Planck Institute for Comparative and International Private Law, Hamburg, Germany, in 2016 (July and August; the Institute's scholarship) and 2017 (August; the DAAD scholarship). During 2017-2018, he was a local legal education policy expert for the Independent, External, On-Site Assessment of Legal Education Quality at the National University 'Odesa Law Academy', Odesa, Ukraine, and the Yaroslav Mudryi National Law University, Kharkiv, Ukraine, implemented by the USAID New Justice Program. In 2018, he was promoted as the Associate Professor of the Department of Civil Law of Taras Shevchenko National University of Kyiv, Kyiv, Ukraine.

Ivan's research interests include corporate law, in particular RPTs and corporate groups, contract law, private international law and cultural rights. In 2016, he published a monograph on change and termination of civil legal relationships in Ukrainian law.

Table of Contents

List of Abbreviations

Accounting Directive	Directive 2013/34/EU of the European Parliament and of the Council on the annual financial statements, consolidated financial statements and related reports of certain types of undertakings
AG	Joint-stock company (Public Company) in Germany (*Aktiengeselschaft*)
AktG	German Stock Corporation Act (*Aktiengesetz*)
ALC	Additional Liability Company
BV	Private Company in the Netherlands (*Besloten Venootschap*)
BW	Civil Code of the Netherlands (*Burgerlijk Wetboek*)
CCU	Civil Code of Ukraine (*Цивільний кодекс України*)
CGC	Corporate Governance Code
Directive 2006/46/EC	Directive 2006/46/EC of the European Parliament and of the Council of 14 June 2006 amending Council Directives 78/660/EEC on the annual accounts of certain types of companies, 83/349/EEC on consolidated accounts, 86/635/EEC on the annual accounts and consolidated accounts of banks and other financial institutions and 91/674/EEC on the annual accounts and consolidated accounts of insurance undertakings
Directive 2009/102/EC	Directive 2009/102/EC of the European Parliament and of the Council of 16 September 2009 in the area of company law on single-member private limited liability companies
Directive 2017/1132	Directive 2017/1132 of the European Parliament and of the Council of 14 June 2017 relating to certain aspects of company law (codification)
EC	European Community
EMCA	European Model Company Act
EP	European Parliament

EU	European Union
Fourth Council Directive	Fourth Council Directive 78/660/EEC of 25 July 1978 based on Article 54(3)(g) of the Treaty on the annual accounts of certain types of companies
GAAP	Generally Accepted Accounting Principles
GmbH	Limited Liability Company (Private Company) in Germany (*Gesellschaft mit beschränkter Haftung*)
GmbHG	German Act on Limited Liability Companies (*Gesetz über Gesellschaften mit beschränkter Haftung*)
IAS Regulation	Regulation (EC) No. 1606/2002 of the European Parliament and the Council of 19 July 2002 on the application of international accounting standards
IAS 24	International Accounting Standard 24 'Related Party Disclosures'
IAS	International Accounting Standard
IFRS	International Financial Reporting Standard
JSC Law of Ukraine	Law of Ukraine 'On Joint Stock Companies' (*Закон України 'Про акціонерні товариства'*)
JSC	Joint-stock Company (Public Company)
KSH	Polish Code of Commercial Companies (*Kodeks spółek handlowych*)
LLC Law of Ukraine	Law of Ukraine 'On Limited and Additional Liability Compa nies' (*Закон України 'Про товариства з обмеженою та додатковою відповідальністю'*)
LLC	Limited Liability Company (Private Company)
MAR	Regulation (EU) No. 596/2014 of the European Parliament and of the Council of 16 April 2014 on market abuse (market abuse regulation) and repealing Directive 2003/6/EC of the European Parliament and of the Council and Commission Directives 2003/124/EC, 2003/125/EC and 2004/72/EC
MoMiG	German Act for the Modernization of the German Limited Liability Company Law and the Prevention of Misuse (*Modernisierung des GmbH-Rechts und zur Bekämpfung von Missbräuchen*)
NSSMC	National Securities and Stock Market Commission (*Національна комісія з цінних паперів та фондового ринку*)
NV	Public Company in the Netherlands (*Naamloze Vennootschap*)
OECD	Organisation for Economic Co-operation and Development
RPT	Related Party Transaction
S.A.	Joint-stock Company (Public Company) in Poland (*Spółka Akcyjna*)
SE	European Company (*Societas Europaea*)

Second Council Directive	Second Council Directive 77/91/EEC of 13 December 1976 on coordination of safeguards which, for the protection of the interests of members and others, are required by Member States of companies within the meaning of the second paragraph of Article 58 of the Treaty, in respect of the formation of public limited liability companies and the maintenance and alteration of their capital, with a view to making such safeguards equivalent
Seventh Council Directive	Seventh Council Directive 83/349/EEC of 13 June 1983 based on Article 54(3)(g) of the Treaty on consolidated accounts
SMIDA	Stock Market Infrastructure Development Agency
Sp.z o.o.	Limited Liability Company (Private Company) in Poland (*Spółka z ograniczoną odpowiedzialnością*)
SRD I	Directive 2007/36/EC of the European Parliament and of the Council of 11 July 2007 on the exercise of certain rights of shareholders in listed companies
SRD II	Directive (EU) 2017/828 of the European Parliament and of the Council of 17 May 2017 amending Directive 2007/36/EC as regards the encouragement of long-term shareholder engagement
Takeover Directive	Directive 2004/25/EC of the European Parliament and of the Council of 21 April 2004 on takeover bids
TFEU	Treaty on the Functioning of the European Union
Transparency Directive	Directive 2004/109/EC of the European Parliament and of the Council on the harmonization of transparency requirements in relation to information about issuers whose securities are admitted to trading on a regulated market and amending Directive 2001/34/EC
WSE Best Practice	Best Practice for GPW Listed Companies 2016

Preface

This book comes as a result of a PhD study on RPTs and corporate groups in Ukrainian corporate law, with an extensive comparative overview of Dutch, German, Polish and EU laws. The study was performed under the supervision of Steef M. Bartman, Professor of Corporate Group Liability at Maastricht University, Maastricht, the Netherlands, and Emeritus Professor of Company Law at Leiden University, the Netherlands; and Arkadiusz Radwan, Professor of Company Law at the Vytautas Magnus University, Kaunas, Lithuania, President of the Allerhand Institute, Krakow, Poland, and Director of the Scientific Centre of the Polish Academy of Sciences, Vienna, Austria.

The aim of this study is to compare the laws of Ukraine, the Netherlands, Germany, Poland and the EU and to suggest changes that would be instrumental for Ukrainian law in dealing with RPTs both inside and outside corporate groups. This requires a deep understanding of all mentioned legal systems, their legal sources, court practices and economic background.

A serious challenge while performing this study was the constant changes in legislation and case law about RPTs. During this period, the Parliament of Ukraine adopted several groundbreaking statutes in corporate law, including conceptual changes to the Law of Ukraine 'On Joint Stock Companies' and a brand-new LLC Law of Ukraine. Meantime, the EU lawmaker reconsidered the regulation of RPTs in the so-called Shareholders' Rights Directive, obliging Member States to implement these changes ultimately by 10 June 2019. These changes in statutory regulation were complemented by novelties in soft law as well, including new versions of CGCs in Poland, Germany and the Netherlands. All these events have turned this book into a manifestly topical, important and well-timed study, which might be interesting for scholars, practitioners and governments in both the jurisdictions in research focus and other countries all over the world.

Besides being at the edge of the new regulatory developments in the EU and other countries, this study has other advantages that cannot be overrated. In particular, Chapters 5 and 6 have been inspired by the strategies for RPTs described in the famous textbook *The Anatomy of Corporate Law* by Reinier Kraakman et al. The author sets out whether or not these strategies are reflected in the jurisdictions in research focus and how the Directive 2017/828 had embodied these strategies. In addition, the author looks back at the process of the Directive's drafting. This part of the book will no doubt be interesting for readers from a historical point of view and may be used by governments or lawyers to interpret the Shareholders' Rights Directive with the purpose of its implementation and further application.

Also, the author investigates alternative strategies where he, e.g., analyses how abusive 'tunnelling' may be combatted with other regulatory means. Attention is paid at how and to what extent RPTs are covered by the existing legal requirements on capital protection, group regulation, protection of minority shareholders, bankruptcy and financial regulation.

The theoretical basis of the work is interesting and useful for lawyers worldwide, including the analysis of theories on conflicts of interest and IASs. From the Ukrainian perspective, it is the first work that extensively deals with RPTs and corporate groups in such a comparative context. Further, the book offers both practical and theoretical insights, *inter alia* being the result of intensive discussions with practising lawyers from several jurisdictions. Moreover, for those who are completely unaware of Ukrainian corporate law and its peculiarities, the book offers a good introduction to the main issues of this country's legal system. Considering the fact that Ukrainian law on RPTs has a lot in common with other Eastern European jurisdictions, e.g. Belarus, Russia and other countries of the Commonwealth of Independent States, the book will find its readers among legal communities of the said countries as well. All in all, it can be stated that this book provides for a necessary bond between the Eastern European tradition of corporate law and modern corporate law of Western Europe.

Acknowledgements

The process of writing this book resembled an exciting and fascinating journey, which I have often compared to climbing a mountain. In the beginning, my goals seemed almost unattainable: the top of the mountain was clad in an impenetrable fog. My progress was continually challenged by statutory changes, both at the national level in Ukraine and at the EU level, forcing me to go back to modify some of my work and turning my path into a zigzag, rather than a straight line. A number of external obstacles also interfered with the process and affected my timing. These circumstances would have been unbearable without the constant support and inspiration that I received from my supervisors and my family.

It has been a true pleasure and honour to write this book under the supervision of Prof. Dr Steef Bartman and Prof. Dr Arkadiusz Radwan. Their advice targeted the project's core ideas and provided me with valuable insight on how to continue my research. Their feedback was always extremely substantive, deep, understandable, concise and precise. Their energy and inspiration repeatedly gave me the incentive I needed to keep pursuing my goal. I am also very grateful to Prof. Dr Alexey Kot, who kindly agreed to act as a special expert on Ukrainian law and to evaluate my book from the perspective of Ukrainian law.

The support from my family was another source of energy for my work. My mother Oksana was always ready to listen to my thoughts, to share both my worries and joys. She was with me during the most difficult moments of writing. I am also grateful to my aunt Valentyna, her husband Ihor and his sister Halyna. Their care and support gave me the incentive I needed to move forward in my academic endeavours. Our discussions around the dinner table were a wonderful opportunity to explain my book in simple terms and to better understand it myself.

My interest in corporate law was first awoken during my LLM studies at Leiden University, Leiden, the Netherlands, during 2011-2012. Dr Pavlos Masouros inspired me to work in this field and to study it more closely. It was also through Dr Masouros that I first became acquainted with *The Anatomy of Corporate Law* textbook, which was of frequent use to me while writing this work. I am profoundly grateful to Dr

Masouros for his skills and the knowledge that he shared with me and my fellow students in Leiden.

A large part of the writing and research process took place during my time at the Max Planck Institute for Comparative and International Private Law in Hamburg. I spent two months there in 2016, on a scholarship from the Institute, and one month in 2017 on a DAAD scholarship. Those periods allowed me to use the library's rich sources on the main jurisdictions in focus. More importantly, I had the rare opportunity to discuss my topic with Prof. Dr Holger Fleischer, for which I am extremely grateful. I also appreciate the considerable value of the opportunity that I had to talk about more general aspects of private law and legal research with Prof. Dr Jürgen Basedow, Dr Rainer Kulms and Eike Götz Hosemann. I am especially grateful to Prof. Dr Eugenia Kurzynsky-Singer for giving me the chance, in 2018, to present the results of my research to an audience at the Institute, where I was fortunate enough to hear many interesting questions and profound comments. During my time at the Institute, I had the opportunity to discuss my topic with many other fascinating researchers who were kind enough to open my eyes to perspectives on my topic that I had not previously considered. My thanks to Mika Aotake, Nahel Asfour, Elena Babkina, Endri Barmbek, Bernhard Burtscher, Natia Chitashvili, Mateusz Dąbroś, Hao Jiang, Akawat Laowonsiri, Renato Neto, Konrad Osajda, Donike Qerimi, Harris Tsiliotis, Monika Wałachowska, Tamas Szabados and Tamar Zarandia and others. Many thanks also to Heinrich Nemeczek for his useful advice and recommendations on German corporate law. Special thanks to Michael Scere for his help and advice.

I also want to thank the leadership of Taras Shevchenko National University of Kyiv, Faculty of Law and Department of Civil Law, Kyiv, Ukraine, for making it possible to visit Hamburg for my research and to participate in international conferences. In particular, I owe a debt of profound gratitude to Prof. Dr Leonid Hubersky, Rector of the University; Prof. Dr Volodymyr Bugrov, Vice-Rector of the University; Prof. Dr Ivan Grytsenko, Dean of the Faculty of Law; Prof. Dr Olesia Otradnova, Vice-Dean of the Faculty of Law; Prof. Dr Roman Maydanyk, Head of the Department of Civil Law; and Dr Nataliya Kuznetsova, Professor of the Department of Civil Law. I also owe a great debt of gratitude to Prof. Dr Tetyana Bodnar, who has always supported me in my academic efforts, as well as my colleagues at the Department of Civil Law: in particular Prof. Dr Iryna Dikovska, Dr Ernest Gramtskiy, Dr Kateryna Moskalenko, Dr Oleh Pervomayskiy and Dr Roman Sabodash, for our in-depth discussions on corporate law.

I would also like to express my gratitude to the Centre for European Company Law and the Allerhand Institute, Kraków, Poland, which invited me to give a presentation on RPTs in Ukraine at the conference 'Company Law Reform in Central and Eastern Europe', on 9-10 June 2016 in Warsaw (Poland). My research project also afforded me the honour of participating in other conferences on corporate law in Katowice (Poland), Ivano-Frankivsk (Ukraine) and Durham (the UK).

Lastly, I would like to thank all the practitioners and academics who responded to my anonymous survey on Google on RPTs and corporate groups.

CHAPTER 1

Introduction

§1.01 THEORETICAL BACKGROUND

The importance of legislative provisions that introduce substantive and procedural safeguards for RPTs derives from the fact that management and majority shareholders are likely to abuse their rights and harm minority shareholders or institutional investors through 'tunnelling'.[1] Creditors, employees and other stakeholders also feel the detrimental effects of a transaction that is used to extract assets from the company.[2]

Despite some obvious possible negative consequences of RPTs (i.e., that the company could be stripped of its assets, leaving minority shareholders with less likelihood of receiving dividends), types of RPTs might exist that, due to the transaction costs, could prove more beneficial for the company than other available transactions. Situations where RPTs become routine and are characterized as standard practice have been sufficiently demonstrated by Luca Enriques, using an example of an imaginary state called Tunelland:[3] a developing economy with a high risk of corruption and a poorly managed tax system, which is somehow reminiscent of Ukraine. As the author notes, once a corporate group is in place, it is harder to find RPTs suspicious, especially if corporate groups are a common organizational form for businesses within the economy.[4] Therefore, an outright prohibition on RPTs or fixing ceilings does not offer a proper solution to the shareholders' problems: this approach is too inflexible and

1. 'Tunnelling is considered to be the diversion of corporate resources from the corporation (or its minority shareholders) to the controlling shareholder', as suggested in Johnson S and others, 'Tunnelling' (2000) 90 AEA Papers and Proceedings 22, 26.
2. Antonenko L, *The Myth of Transformation Through EU Law: A Case-Study of the Company Law Reform in Ukraine*, available at SSRN: https://ssrn.com/abstract=1485607, accessed on 18 November 2018, 9.
3. Enriques L, 'Related Party Transactions: Policy Options and Real-World Challenges (with a Critique of the European Commission Proposal)' (2015) 16 European Business Organisation Law Review 1, 1-37.
4. *Ibid.*, 5.

sometimes runs contrary to the shareholders' interests.[5] It therefore remains to be investigated whether RPTs within corporate groups should receive special treatment relative to transactions outside groups.

Nevertheless, it would be a mistake to position RPTs as completely safe instruments of corporate governance. As Martin Gelter argues, the underlying concern is that, if left unconstrained, directors and officers will on the one hand squander the firm's assets or shift them into their own pockets through self-dealing transactions and on the other frequently fail to work hard enough to achieve the best possible results for the shareholders.[6] That is why imperative limitations and requirements must be established that oblige a company's officers, shareholders and other potential related parties to follow certain rules whenever they wish to enter into an RPT.

§1.02 GENERAL HISTORICAL, ECONOMIC AND LEGAL BACKGROUND TO RPTs AND CORPORATE GROUPS IN UKRAINE

[A] Introduction

This section contains a description and analysis of the general background to RPTs and corporate groups in Ukraine. It provides a brief explanation of Ukrainian corporate reality, including the existing data on corporate ownership. While the next subchapter emphasizes the statutory rules regulating RPTs of JSCs (public companies) and LLCs (private companies), the purpose of this section is to present Ukrainian corporate law and governance as a whole, and the problems it currently faces regarding RPTs.

[B] Privatization and Corporate Ownership in Ukraine

Corporate law was not on the agenda in the Soviet Union. The landscape of economic relations was populated by state enterprises, which exercised property rights through rights of operative management and control, leaving the state to fulfil the role of owner. For individuals, private property was also limited and extended to a small number of objects only. This started to change in the late 1980s, giving birth to new economic operators and leading to the collapse of the entire existing system of legal relationships.

Emerging as the successor to the Ukrainian Soviet Socialist Republic, Ukraine has existed as an independent and democratic state since 24 August 1991.[7] The year 1991 marked a time when many important laws were introduced, including the Laws of

5. Hopt KJ, 'Groups of Companies: A Comparative Study on the Economics, Law and Regulation of Corporate Groups' Law Working Paper N° 286/2015, available at: http://ssrn.com/abstract=2560935, accessed on 5 December 2018, 15.
6. Gelter M, 'Taming or Protecting the Modern Corporation? Shareholder-Stakeholder Debates in a Comparative Light' (2011) 7 New York University Journal of Law and Business 641, 657.
7. Resolution of the Verkhovna Rada of Ukrainian Soviet Socialist Republic 'On Declaration of Independence of Ukraine' [Postanova Verkhovnoyi Rady Ukrayinskoyi Radianskoyi Sotsialistychnoyi Respubliky 'Pro proholoshennia nezalezhnosti Ukrayiny'] of 24 August 1991, available at: http://zakon.rada.gov.ua/laws/show/1427-12, accessed on 31 December 2018.

Ukraine 'On Property' and 'On Economic Companies'.[8] The latter, while being recognized as progressive at the time, was in place for a few years only before revealing its evident shortcomings in protecting various stakeholders in companies, lacking mechanisms for market control and providing management with excessively broad powers.[9] The act was short (eighty-three articles covering the creation and functioning of LLCs, ALCs, JSCs and partnerships) and abstract (allowing for different interpretations) for the emerging market economy.[10]

Privatization began in 1992. The Laws of Ukraine 'On Privatization of Property of State Enterprises' and 'On Privatization of Property of Non-Large Enterprises (Small Privatization)', both repealed on 18 January 2018,[11] described the mechanisms for privatizing state enterprises. The preferred method of privatizing large enterprises was mass privatization, through the issuance of privatization certificates to employees.[12] Those certificates gave employees a preferential right to acquire securities.[13] Every citizen of Ukraine gained an entitlement to state property through the privatization certificates acquired in this manner.[14]

Mass privatization neither brought much income to the state budget nor led to improved corporate governance of the enterprises.[15] Managers and individuals close to the political elite used deficiencies in the legislation to obtain control of privatized enterprises through stock dilution or non-transparent buyout schemes, often buying shares from members of the public at prices far below market value.[16] As a result, privatized companies were initially increasingly dispersed but soon became extremely concentrated. Those minority shareholders who did not sell their shares held insufficient stock to influence company affairs. However, they remained high in number, reaching 13-15 million, depending on the source.[17] To this day, extremely dispersed ownership of small stakes in share capital continues,[18] for instance with Public JSC 'Zaporizhskiy metalurhiynyi kombinat "Zaporizhstal"'. This producer of steel and rolled iron is one of the largest Ukrainian enterprises privatized during mass privatization (revenue amounting to UAH 33.16 billion in 2016) and reportedly owned by the

8. The Law of Ukraine 'On Property' has already been repealed, while the Law of Ukraine 'On Economic Companies' has lost most of its regulatory effect due to the adoption of the JSC Law of Ukraine and LLC Law of Ukraine, which now regulate those business forms.
9. Yefymenko A, *Corporate Governance under Ukraine's New Joint Stock Company Law*, available at SSRN: http://ssrn.com/abstract=1387360, accessed on 7 December 2018, 4.
10. Antonenko L, 22.
11. Law of Ukraine 'On Privatization of State and Municipal Property' [Zakon Ukrayiny 'Pro pryvatyzatsiyu derzhavnoho ta komunalnoho mayna'] of 18 January 2018, published in Vidomosti Verkhovnoyi Rady Ukrayiny, 2018, No. 12, St. 68.
12. Law of Ukraine 'On Privatization of Property of State Enterprise' [Zakon Ukrayiny 'Pro pryvatyzatsiyu mayna derzhavnykh pidpryyemstv'] of 4 March 1992, published in Vidomosti Verkhovnoyi Rady Ukrayiny, 1992, No. 24, St. 348, Article 22.
13. *Ibid.*, Article 25.
14. *Ibid.*, Article 24.
15. Frolov P, 'Pryvatyzatsiya v Ukrayini: retrospektyvy ta perspektyvy' *Dzerkalo tyzhnia* (No. 10 (17 March-23 March)), available at: https://dt.ua/macrolevel/privatizaciya-v-ukrayini-retrospektivi-ta-perspektivi-272273_.html, accessed on 7 December 2018.
16. Yefymenko A, 2.
17. *Ibid.*, 7.
18. This could change soon, due to the extensive use of squeeze-out procedures.

'Metinvest' group, Rinat Akhmetov and Vadim Novinskiy.[19] While those individuals may be the ultimate beneficial owners, in 2018 the company officially had five shareholders[20] with stakes exceeding 5%, together holding 98.0724% of the share capital. The remaining securities, numbering more than 50 million, were dispersed among shareholders holding less than 2% of the share capital.[21]

Where the privatization process in Poland has been described as slow,[22] that qualification certainly holds true for Ukraine. More than 800 legal entities, including many state enterprises, public and private companies, still await privatization.[23] Ukraine failed to comply with the key conditions for successful privatization: speed, social purpose, effective control and access to foreign capital.[24] The only successful case of privatization of a large enterprise was the purchase of 'Kryvorizhstal' by Indian investor Arcelor Mittal in 2005: the transaction price was USD 4.8 million, which corresponds to 44% of all privatization income since 1992.[25] In 2016, calculated by revenue, private JSC 'Arcelor Mittal Kryvyi Rih' (the name was changed after the privatization) was recognized as the 4th most profitable company in Ukraine.[26] Other large state enterprises mostly fell into the hands of insiders, who preserved their controlling influence using connections with government officials and exerting influence over Parliament's legislative endeavours. One notable example of an oligarch is Rinat Akhmetov, who monopolized various spheres of the Ukrainian economy by holding shares in big companies. In 2016, he owned, either directly or indirectly, 28 of the 200 most profitable companies.[27] In 2017, he held shares in 303 legal entities in Ukraine, followed by Petro Poroshenko (76 legal entities), Dmytro Firtash (72 legal entities) and Ihor Kolomoyskyi (45 legal entities).[28] All in all, predictably,[29] privatization brought little in the way of public benefits and largely frustrated the public's expectations.

19. Holovniov S and Vinnichuk Yu, '200 naybilshykh kompaniy Ukrayiny 2016 roku' (*Business Censor (10 October 2017)*, 2017), available at: https://biz.censor.net.ua/resonance/3033764/200_nayiblshih_kompanyi_ukrani_2016_roku, accessed on 31 December 2018.
20. Companies established in Ukraine, the UK and Cyprus.
21. '00191230 – Publichne aktsionerne tovarystvo "Zaporizkyi metalurhiynyi kmbinat Zaporizhstal"' (2019), available at: https://smida.gov.ua/db/participant/00191230, accessed on 2 September 2019.
22. Boeri T and Perasso G, 'Privatization and Corporate Governance: Some Lessons for the Experience of Transitional Economies' in Balling M (ed.), *Corporate Governance, Financial Markets and Global Convergence* (Springer 1998), 83.
23. 'Perelik obyektiv derzhavnoyi vlasnosti, scho pidliahayut pryvatyzatsii u 2017-2020 rokakh, u tomu chysli tykh, scho mozhut buty pryvatyzovani pislia vnesennia zmin do aktiv zakonodavstva/peredachi v komunalnu vlasnist' (2017), available at: http://me.gov.ua/Documents/Download?id=edfd2801-0e66-40bf-9e7d-7ab6f60ad15c, accessed on 2 September 2019.
24. Frolov P.
25. *Ibid.*
26. Holovniov S and Vinnichuk Yu.
27. *Ibid.*
28. 'V Opendatabot zyavyvsia poshuk po vlasnykam kompaniy' (2017), available at: https://opendatabot.ua/blog/71-founders, accessed on 29 September 2018.
29. Black B and Kraakman R, 'A Self-Enforcing Model of Corporate Law' (1996) 109 Harvard Law Review 1911, 1925.

[C] Adoption of the JSC Law of Ukraine, Corporate Raiding and Derivative Suits

By April 2009, when the JSC Law of Ukraine took effect, the aggressive concentration of corporate ownership through privatization was already a reality. The 2003 CCU, which brought some changes in the area of corporate law, was not sufficient to prevent fraudulent business practices. Tunnelling through self-dealing became widespread.[30] Employees with increasingly dispersed minority shareholdings had no means to influence the decisions of the controlling shareholders. The agency conflict between managers and controlling shareholders was reduced to a minimum, with blockholders either threatening managers with dismissal or else 'scratching each other's backs'. Instead of being gatekeepers for the shareholders' wealth, executives became little more than servants of the blockholders.

At that point, the provisions of the JSC Law containing approval safeguards for transactions with interest, including RPTs (Article 71), were insufficient to protect minority shareholders as was their intention. Even with the system of cumulative voting to elect members of supervisory boards that was then introduced (Article 53), the small volumes of their shareholdings and the abuse of rights by blockholders meant that minority shareholders were often unable to have their interests duly represented on their supervisory boards. Compared with the current regulation, as far as RPTs are concerned, the situation with the interests of minority shareholders was aggravated by various shortcomings, including the following.

Appraisal rights were missing for dissenting shareholders opposing transactions with interest (Article 68). Where a majority of the supervisory board had an interest in a transaction, instead of placing the decision-making authority with the minority of disinterested members, the JSC Law required a vote among shareholders (Article 71(2)). No majority-of-the minority rule for transactions with interest existed; i.e., in a majority-controlled company with a shareholder as a related party, transactions with interest could be easily approved by the general meeting of shareholders.

In one important respect, minority shareholders had better protection 'on paper' than they now do. Article 72(2) of the JSC Law provided standing for shareholders to claim invalidation of transactions with interest that were incompatible with proper procedure, to claim damages and moral harm. The academic interpretation of this article confirmed the right of shareholders to use those remedies.[31] Unfortunately, however good the legislators' intentions were when they drafted this provision, the outcome was frustrating. Even before the enactment of the JSC Law, courts in Ukraine, faced numerous claims of abuse from minority shareholders, rejected the possibility of derivative claims by shareholders, and in 2003-2004 established that the company itself had to claim nullification of a transaction to which it was a party.[32] This

30. Antonenko L, 4; Yefymenko A, 4.
31. Bodnar T, 'Pravochyny aktsionernykh tovarystv, schodo vchynennia yakykh ye zainteresovannist' (2009) Yurydychna Ukrayina 36, 40.
32. Bortsevych P, 'Problemy ukladannia znachnykh pravochyniv ta pravochyniv, schodo yakykh ye zainteresovannist' (2014) Derzhava i pravo 159, 163.

controversy was ultimately resolved by the Constitutional Court of Ukraine, which interpreted a company's interests as being separate from the interests of its shareholders.[33]

The approach posited by the Constitutional Court of Ukraine and the general courts in 2003-2004 was aimed at combatting corporate raiding, most often carried out through illegal seizure of corporate assets.[34] The various court decisions had a twofold outcome. On the one hand, minority shareholders were barred from instituting manifestly baseless suits. On the other hand, they became less protected in their efforts to oppose the controlling shareholders' misdeeds.[35] Against this background, when Ukraine adopted the JSC Law, in practice Article 72(2) did not lead to new derivative suits. That same Article 72(2) was also criticized for being too abstract, as it allowed moral harm too. The commentators could not perceive how moral harm could result from transactions with interest and suggested remedies for deficient transactions with interest to be confined to invalidating such transactions and awarding damages.[36]

Instead of improving the provision in question, in 2011 the legislature slammed the door suddenly and decisively on derivative suits for shareholders, by changing the wording of the provision and removing the shareholders' standing even 'on paper'.[37] This solution was too inflexible to strike a balance between the interests of the various stakeholders. Instances of abuse by controlling shareholders were reported more often and required the introduction of a specific enforcement tool.[38]

[D] Amendments of 7 April 2015 and 16 November 2017

A new legislative trend for transactions with interest, including RPTs, and their enforcement emerged in 2015 when the Law of Ukraine 'On Amending Certain Legislative Acts of Ukraine on Protection of Investors' was adopted.[39] This act took

33. *Decision of 1 December 2004 No. 18-pn/2004 (case about legitimate interest)* Case No. 1-10/2004, Ofitsiynyi visnyk Ukrayiny of 31 December 2004, No. 50, p. 67, St. 3288 (Constitutional Court of Ukraine).
34. Radwan A, Nadzon A and Zdiruk V, *Assessment of Approximation Level of the Present Company, Corporate Governance, Accounting and Auditing Legislation and Existing Practices in Ukraine to EU Standards and Practices* (Contract N°2013/328606/2, available at SSRN: https://ssrn.com/abstract=3090335 or http://dx.doi.org/102139/ssrn3090335, 2014), 22.
35. Shareholders have retained the right to claim invalidation of decisions of corporate bodies.
36. Karchevskyi K, 'Naslidky nedotrymannia poriadku vchynennia pravochynu aktsionernoho tovarystva, schodo vchynennia yakoho isnuye zainteresovannist (porivnialno-pravovyi analiz)' (2012) Pravo i Bezpeka 281, 285.
37. Law of Ukraine 'On Amendments to the Law of Ukraine "On Joint-Stock Companies" regarding the Improvement of Functioning of Joint-Stock Companies' [Zakon Ukrayiny 'Pro vnesennia zmin do Zakonu Ukrayiny "Pro aktsionerni tovarystva" schodo vdoskonalennia mekhanizmu diyalnosti aktsionernykh tovarystv'] of 3 February 2011, published in Vidomosti Verkhovnoyi Rady Ukrayiny, 2011, No. 35, St. 344.
38. Yefymenko A, 'Pravochyny iz zainteresovanistiu' (2014) Visnyk Tsentru komertsiynoho prava 2, 4.
39. Law of Ukraine 'On Amending Certain Legislative Acts on the Protection of Investors' [Zakon Ukrayiny 'Pro vnesennia zmin do deyakykh zakonodavchykh aktiv schodo zakhystu prav investoriv'] of 7 April 2015, published in Vidomosti Verkhovnoyi Rady Ukrayiny, 2015, No. 25, St. 188.

effect on 1 May 2016 and formally allowed derivative suits for shareholders with holdings of 10% or greater in a company's share capital.[40] For derivative suits, the changes meant only one remedy: damages for the loss inflicted by company officers. The act also makes no mention of loss or damage inflicted by other related parties. However, no other category of stakeholders besides minority shareholders would be more interested in claiming invalidation of transactions with interest or compensation of damages caused to the company by controlling shareholders or affiliated persons. So far, claiming damages against company officers has not become a popular tool for shareholders to protect their rights, as the statistics on the Supreme Court's website evidence: since 1 May 2016 only forty-five cases have been initiated.[41]

Besides introducing derivative suits, as of 7 April 2015, the Law tightened the regulation of transactions with interest by adding other important new elements: the concept of an interested person, disclosure and procedural safeguards. Also, the rules on mandatory buyouts (appraisal rights) were supplemented to include additional grounds. Shareholders in JSCs were given the right to demand buyout of their shares if they voted against transactions with interest at the company's general meeting of shareholders.[42] However, the application of these provisions is not without problems. First, abuse is possible in the determination of the shares' market value.[43] The problems associated with the market value of shares are not unique to Ukraine: even developed countries experience them.[44] Second, situations may arise where a supervisory board approves a transaction with interest, despite a dissenting opinion of the supervisory board member representing the shareholder. In this case, the shareholder would not be able to demand a buyout, in spite of the fact that his or her supervisory board member voted against it.

The rules on mandatory disclosure, which were introduced by the Law of Ukraine of 7 April 2015 and became effective on 1 May 2016,[45] clearly show that transactions with interest have not been uncommon for JSCs. In 2017, JSCs in Ukraine made 603 announcements regarding approved transactions with interest. The 219 JSCs that disclosed approved transactions with interest included 116 public JSCs, 103 private JSCs, 23 banks and 5 insurance companies. Some companies disclosed multiple transactions with interest (for instance, Ukrsotsbank disclosed twenty-five), while others disclosed only one in 2017 (e.g., Naftogaz Ukrayiny).[46] Although the proportion of JSCs that disclosed decisions approving transactions with interest in 2017 was not

40. The changes were introduced in the Economic Procedural Code of Ukraine.
41. 'Opryliudnennia oholoshen u spravakh pro vidshkoduvannia zbytkiv, zavdanykh hospodarskomu tovarystvu yoho posadovoyu osoboyu' (2018), available at: https://supreme.court.gov.ua/supreme/pro_sud/opr_vid/, accessed on 2 September 2019.
42. JSC Law of Ukraine, Article 68(1).
43. *Ibid.*, Articles 8, 69.
44. Black B and Kraakman R, 1957.
45. Not to be confused with the disclosure of RPTs through financial reports, which has existed for a long time.
46. Analysis of the data from the website of the Stock Market Infrastructure Development Agency of Ukraine (SMIDA), available at: https://smida.gov.ua/, accessed on 30 September 2018.

overwhelming (219 disclosers out of more than 15,000 existing JSCs[47]), the figures nonetheless prove that transactions with interest, including RPTs, are an issue for many companies. Another fundamental change introduced by the Law of 7 April 2015 was a new concept of public JSC. Until 1 May 2016, one of the differences between public and private JSCs lay in the number of shareholders. If that number exceeded 100, private JSCs were required to convert into public JSCs. With the lifting of that requirement, many public JSCs that had been privatized in the 1990s and that had thousands of shareholders used this chance to transform into private JSCs, to be released from their 'public cage'.[48] Their main reason for transforming was that the requirements for public JSCs were stricter. Essentially, this showed that the number of shareholders was not an accurate criterion for distinguishing between public and private JSCs. It was the first step towards aligning the concept of public JSC to the concept of listed company used in EU law.

Despite the legislative efforts to bring the differences between private and public JSCs closer to how listed public companies differ from non-listed public companies in EU law, where only those public companies are listed whose shares are admitted to trading on a regulated market,[49] by 2017 many public JSCs had neither gained public listings nor succeeded in transforming into private JSCs. According to one source, in October 2017 only 6 JSCs were listed (out of more than 2000 public JSCs).[50] Open data from the SMIDA of Ukraine also show numerous cases where shares in JSCs were delisted in 2015-2016.[51]

On 16 November 2017, the Law of Ukraine 'On Amending Certain Legislative Acts on the Simplification of Business and Attraction of Investments by the Issuers of Securities' was adopted to simplify and to speed up the transformation process.[52] Under this act, most of which entered into effect on 6 January 2018, JSCs are regarded as public if they have made a public offering of their shares. The Law of 16 November 2017 also allows private JSCs to have their shares traded on stock exchanges. Before 6 January 2018, ownership of shares in private JSCs was transferred through traders outside stock exchanges. JSCs whose shares were listed on the day that the law took effect were presumed to have made a public offering of their shares. For JSCs whose shares were traded on a stock exchange, but that did not manage to become listed by

47. 'Kilkist yurydychnykh osib za organizatsiynymy formamy, stanom na 1 serpnia 2016 roku' (*State Service of Statistics of Ukraine*), available at: http://www.ukrstat.gov.ua/edrpoy/ukr/EDRPU_2016/ks_opfg/ks_opfg_0816.htm, accessed on 15 August 2016.
48. Tkachuk D, 'Publichni ta pryvatni aktsionerni tovarystva: pro zmischennia mezh' Yuryst & Zakon (February 2018), available at: http://uz.ligazakon.ua/ua/magazine_article/EA011255, accessed on 3 September 2019.
49. *See*, e.g., Directive 2007/36/EC of the European Parliament and of the Council of 11 July 2007 on the exercise of certain rights of shareholders in listed companies [2007] OJ L 184, 14.7.2007, Article 1.
50. *Ibid.*
51. https://smida.gov.ua/.
52. Law of Ukraine 'On Amending Certain Legislative Acts on the Simplification of Business and Attraction of Investments by the Issuers of Securities' [Zakon Ukrayiny 'Pro vnesennia zmin do deyakykh zakonodavchykh aktiv Ukrayiny schodo sproschennia vedennia biznesu ta zaluchennia investytsiy emitentamy tsinnykh paperiv'] of 16 November 2017, available at: http://zakon2.rada.gov.ua/laws/show/2210-viii, accessed on 27 December 2018.

6 January 2018, the Law allowed them to officially inform the NSSMC by 31 December 2018 that they wished to be treated as if they had made a public offering of their shares, in accordance with a special procedure.[53] All other public JSCs would be treated as private JSCs. All in all, only fourteen notifications were submitted by JSCs requesting treatment as public (or listed) JSCs.[54]

As a result, taking into account how few JSCs were listed on 6 January 2018 and the unwillingness among JSCs to be made subject to the strict requirements for public JSCs, today most JSCs fall under the requirements for private JSCs. Taking into account the changes described above, it is now fair to refer to public JSCs in Ukraine as listed companies. JSCs as essentially public companies may, thus, be listed or non-listed. In turn, LLCs in Ukraine may be referred to as private companies. Table 1.1 illustrates the evolution of the concepts of private and public JSCs in Ukrainian law.

Table 1.1 Evolution of the Differences Between Public and Private JSCs in Ukrainian Law

Before 1 May 2016	Only public JSCs may have their shares traded on a stock exchange and may have more than 100 shareholders. If a private JSC wishes to have more than 100 shareholders and/or to have its shares traded on a stock exchange, it must be converted into a public JSC.
From 1 May 2016 to 6 January 2018	Both public and private JSCs may have more than 100 shareholders. Only public JSCs may have their shares traded on a stock exchange. By 1 January 2018, all public JSCs were expected to become listed.
After 6 January 2018	Both public and private JSCs may have more than 100 shareholders and may have their shares traded on a stock exchange. Public JSCs are JSCs that have made or are presumed to have made the public offering of their shares. Their characteristics are such that they may also be referred to as listed companies.

53. Decision of the National Securities and Stock Market Commission 'On Approval of the Order for the Disclosure of Notification by Issuers of Securities That They Have Made a Public Offering of Securities' [Rishennia Natsionalnoyi komisii z tsinnykh paperiv ta fondovoho rynku 'Pro zatverdzhennia Poriadku opryliudnennia povidomlennia emitantamy tsinnykh paperiv pro te, scho vony vvazhayutsia takymy, scho zdiysniuvaly publichnu propozytsiyu tsinnykh paperiv'], No. 75, of 13 February 2018, published in Ofitsiynyi visnyk Ukrayiny, 2018, No. 27, St. 994.
54. According to public information of the Stock Market Infrastructure Development Agency of Ukraine (SMIDA), available at: https://smida.gov.ua/.

§1.03 REGULATION OF RPTs IN PUBLIC AND PRIVATE COMPANIES IN UKRAINE

[A] Regulation of RPTs in Public Companies in Ukraine from a Historical and Comparative Perspective

[1] Introduction

In a market environment where the economic actors conduct themselves as diligent and conscientious managers, the regulation of RPTs would be largely irrelevant. Affiliated persons would enter into transactions with each other on the same terms as with strangers. There would be no need for sophisticated rules to determine market prices in corporate transactions: the price would not depend on who the parties were and whether they were somehow related. Unfortunately, corporate reality is far from an ideal world that is innocent of market abuse and corporate fraud. The infamous corporate scandals of Enron and Parmalat showcase how managers and blockholding shareholders can misuse their power. That is why it is still necessary to protect minority shareholders from the wrongdoings of majority shareholders and to protect all shareholders from opportunistic managerial behaviour. Ukraine is no exception to this rule and needs properly balanced rules to safeguard the interests of weaker parties in corporate relationships, without becoming too detrimental and burdensome to the company's functioning.

The regulation of RPTs in Ukraine has changed several times and is not safeguarded from further legislative amendments in the immediate future. JSCs (public companies) have been affected the most by the legislative changes, while LLCs (private companies), though more heavily represented on the market (*see* Figure 1.1), have only recently become subject to extensive legislative intervention. The main difference between the regulation of RPTs in public and private companies is that public companies have a mandatory and quite detailed procedure for approval of RPTs. If the RPT represents less than 10% of the company's assets, the supervisory board becomes involved in this procedure.[55] For private companies, the shareholders must reach a unanimous decision to introduce an approval procedure in the company's articles of association.[56] Even if the shareholders agree, it is not necessarily the role of a supervisory board to approve or block RPTs, given that a supervisory board is optional for private companies.[57]

55. JSC Law of Ukraine, Article 71(7).
56. LLC Law of Ukraine, Article 45.
57. *Ibid.*, Article 38.

Figure 1.1 Number of Legal Entities in Ukraine by Business Form, as of 1 August 2019, n = 1,328,167

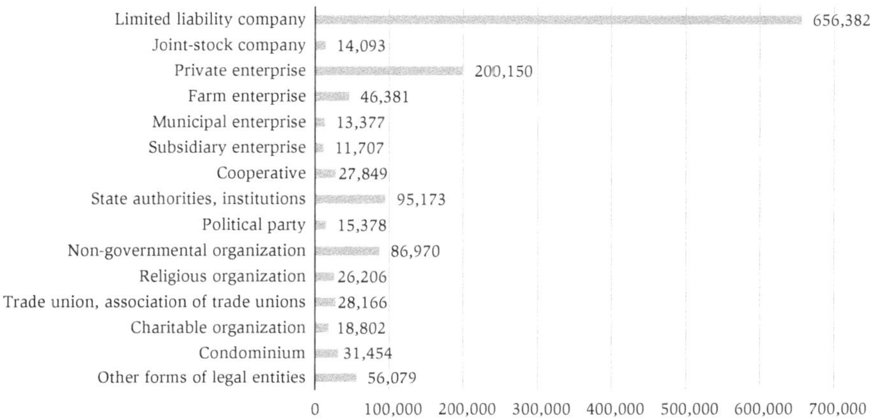

Source: Public information taken from the website of the State Service of Statistics of Ukraine: http://www.ukrstat.gov.ua/. The list of business forms shown in this figure is incomplete: only business forms used by more than 10,000 legal entities are included.

To simplify the evolution of legislation governing relationships involving RPTs in Ukrainian public companies, it can be divided into a number of time periods following the declaration of independence and emergence of Ukraine as an independent state: (a) regulation before the enactment of the JSC Law of Ukraine (before 29 April 2009); (b) regulation after the enactment of the JSC Law of Ukraine but before the enactment of the 2015 amendments (29 April 2009-30 April 2016); and (c) regulation after the enactment of the 2015 amendments (after 1 May 2016).

[2] Regulation Before the Enactment of the JSC Law of Ukraine: Before 29 April 2009

The principal event during the first period was the adoption of basic legislation governing corporate relationships. Before the CCU and the Economic Code of Ukraine (both adopted on 16 January 2003[58]) took effect on 1 January 2004, the main act in company law had been the Law of Ukraine 'On Economic Companies', adopted on 19 September 1991.[59] That law has laid the foundations for modern company law in Ukraine, by introducing the main business forms of legal entities, including JSCs and

58. Civil Code of Ukraine [Tsyvilnyi kodeks Ukrayiny] of 16 January 2003, published in Vidomosti Verkhovnoyi Rady Ukrayiny, 2003, Nos 40-44, St. 352; Economic Code of Ukraine [Hospodarksyi kodeks Ukrayiny] of 16 January 2003, published in Vidomosti Verkhovnoyi Rady Ukrayiny, 2003, No. 18, No. 19-20, No. 21-22, St. 144.
59. Law of Ukraine 'On Economic Companies' [Zakon Ukrayiny 'Pro hospodarski tovarystva'] of 19 September 1991, published in Vidomosti Verkhovnoyi Rady Ukrayiny, 1991, No. 49, St. 682.

LLCs, and creating conditions for their further formation and functioning. Hundreds of LLCs have been formed under the 1991 law, making this legal business form the most popular choice for establishing a company in the country. Today, Ukraine has more than 600,000 LLCs, against 14,000+ JSCs out of more than 1.3 million officially registered legal entities.[60]

Although the implications of the Law of Ukraine 'On Economic Companies' for the economy and legal practice should not be underestimated, as it was certainly not a 'dead law', the provisions of its eighty-three articles in total later came to be regarded as lacking sufficient detail for some major business forms, i.e. JSCs and LLCs in the first place, in that they lacked specific rules for market valuation of shares and detailed rules on conflicts of interest.

The Codes, adopted in 2003 and enacted in 2004, introduced further regulation to the area of company law. The CCU replaced the 1963 Soviet Civil Code, introducing the modern concept of legal entity to Ukrainian law and providing some basic rules on legal entities, their types and their main features. Among other provisions, Article 92 of the CCU specified the duty of management to act in the legal entity's best interests, fairly and reasonably, and not to exceed its powers.[61] Although rather abstract in nature, and subject to interpretation and debate,[62] the mere indication of this duty was a step forward in regulating corporate relationships in Ukraine. Additionally, the CCU deprived shareholders of the right to vote at the general meeting of shareholders when deciding on issues of transactions involving those same shareholders.[63] This was another step forward in dealing with RPTs, and interestingly the provisions of Article 98(3) of the CCU make no distinction between majority and minority shareholders: they cover even shareholders with insignificant percentages of the share capital. It is doubtful whether the scope of Article 98(3) needed to be so broad, given that minority shareholders are rarely able to influence the company's functioning to the same extent as majority shareholders and managers. However, the clause's broad scope has been undermined by the ease with which it can be circumvented, as Article 98 makes no mention of any other related parties besides the shareholders, rendering this rule inapplicable on matters of, for instance, transactions between a company and a shareholder's relatives.

The only exception to the broad application of this rule took effect on 17 June 2018, when the article was declared inapplicable to companies with a sole shareholder.[64] The reasons for this amendment are clear: it would be unreasonable to prohibit the absolute owner of a company to vote in corporate bodies. This might have caused unnecessary obstacles in the functioning of those bodies.

60. *See* Figure 1.1.
61. CCU, Article 92(2).
62. Poizner A and Mykhalchuk I, 'Pravochyny, v yakykh prysutnia zainteresovannist' Yurydychna hazeta (17 August 2010).
63. CCU, Article 98(3).
64. Law of Ukraine 'On Limited and Additional Liability Companies' [Zakon Ukrayiny 'Pro tovarystva z obmezhenoyu ta dodatkovoyu vidpovidalnistiu'] of 6 February 2018, published in Vidomosti Verkhovnoyi Rady Ukrayiny, 2018, No. 13, St. 69, Chapter VIII, paragraph 6, subparagraph 2.

[3] *Regulation After the Enactment of the JSC Law of Ukraine but Before the Enactment of the 2015 Amendments (29 April 2009-30 April 2016)*

Unlike the Law of Ukraine 'On Economic Companies', the JSC Law of Ukraine, adopted in 2008 and enacted on 29 April 2009, provided more detailed rules on the formation and functioning of JSCs (both private and public[65]), including a definition of an interested person and procedures for monitoring RPTs within a broader category of transactions with interest.[66] An RPT can be explained as a transaction between a company and a related party, whereas transactions with interest do not always involve an interested person. In order to be regarded as a transaction with interest, the transaction must involve an interested person in one of the following positions: (a) a party to the contract or a controller of a legal entity that is party to the contract; (b) a party receiving benefits from the transaction (beneficiary); (c) a party buying property as a result of a transaction;[67] (d) a party entering into the transaction as a representative or broker.

The existence of transactions with interest triggered the necessity to comply with the following procedure. First, the interested person was required to notify the company about the interest within three working days from the moment that the interest arose. Next, it was the management board's duty to inform the supervisory board (or the shareholders, if the company did not have a supervisory board) within five working days from the moment of receiving the information. The supervisory board then had to either approve the transaction (if it aligned with the company's interests) or prohibit it, or, alternatively, refer the issue to the general meeting of shareholders. This decision also rested with the general meeting if the company did not have a supervisory board, if a majority of the members of the supervisory board were biased or if the supervisory board failed to react in time.

Where this procedure was not followed, the transaction could be declared null and void, and the interested person could be held liable for any harm inflicted by the transaction.[68]

During this period, the concept of a transaction with interest was changed: the Law of Ukraine of 3 February 2011 exempted some categories of affiliated persons from

65. When the JSC Law of Ukraine was adopted, the understanding of private and public JSCs was based on formalistic criteria, which differed slightly from the criteria used to differentiate between listed and non-listed companies in EU law. Since the Law of Ukraine 'On Amending Certain Legislative Acts on the Simplification of Business and Attraction of Investments by the Issuers of Securities' [Zakon Ukrayiny 'Pro vnesennia zmin do deyakykh zakonodavchykh aktiv Ukrayiny schodo sproschennia vedennia biznesu ta zaluchennia investytsiy emitentamy tsinnykh paperiv'] took effect as of 16 November 2017, the difference between private and public JSCs in Ukraine has aligned more closely to the understanding of listed and non-listed companies in EU law.
66. Law of Ukraine 'On Joint Stock Companies' [Zakon Ukrayiny 'Pro aktsionerni tovarystva'] of 17 September 2008, published in Vidomosti Verkhovnoyi Rady Ukrayiny, 2008, No. 50-51, St. 384, Article 71.
67. The interpretation of the Ukrainian spelling (Ukr. – '*придбає*') used in this sentence can potentially cause a misunderstanding, meaning either 'buy' or 'acquire'.
68. *Ibid.*, Article 72.

regulation, including legal entities controlled by shareholders or controlling them, while preserving the existing system of safeguards.[69] After the 2011 amendments took effect, three categories of interested persons remained: (i) company officers, and their family members; (ii) shareholders holding 25% or more of the share capital, and their family members; (iii) legal entities where company officers or their family members owned 25% or more of the company's share capital.

The JSC Law of Ukraine also clarified who were classified as company officers and their family members. The former comprised four categories of persons: (i) the chair and members of the board of directors; (ii) the chair and members of the supervisory board; (iii) the head and members of the audit committee; and (iv) the head and members of other company bodies.[70] The latter group were defined as the interested person's spouse, parents (guardians) and their brothers, sisters, children and their spouses.[71] Although these provisions were perceived as improvements helping to protect shareholders' rights,[72] they also received some criticism from practitioners and scholars. For instance, it was noted that neither the JSC Law of Ukraine nor the CCU explained under what circumstances the supervisory board was entitled to prohibit a transaction as being incompatible with the company's interests.[73] The meaning of 'incompatible with company's interest' was considered even more ambiguous given that no legal definition was given of the company's interest, which could be freely construed.

One flaw spotted by several authors was the necessity to exclude some transactions from the scope of the law, i.e. transactions between a company and its sole shareholder if that shareholder was also the only board member.[74] The reasoning behind those critical comments, backed up by references to similar rules for public companies in some foreign jurisdictions, was that transactions where the company's sole shareholder was also its only director did not create any risks for minority shareholders: even if the company went bankrupt, that same shareholder would also be the main victim of the unsuccessful policy. Essentially, the whole company depended on a single person who combined both ownership and control, and who presumably had the greatest interest in the company's long-term sustainable operation. It was also common practice for many states to select *a more lenient approach towards shareholders, rather than managers, in regulating RPTs*, which can be explained by the fact that the former group tend to have an economic interest in the enterprise and

69. Law of Ukraine 'On Amendments to the Law of Ukraine "On Joint-Stock Companies" regarding the Improvement of Functioning of Joint-Stock Companies' [Zakon Ukrayiny 'Pro vnesennia zmin do Zakonu Ukrayiny "Pro aktsionerni tovarystva" schodo vdoskonalennia mekhanizmu diyalnosti aktsionernykh tovarystv'].
70. JSC Law of Ukraine, Article 1(15).
71. *Ibid.*, Article 71.
72. Yefymenko A, 11.
73. Bodnar T, 38.
74. Poizner A and Mykhalchuk I, 20; Shtym T, 'Aktsionerni uhody, pravochyny iz zainteresovannistiu ta znachni pravochyny v aktsionernykh tovarystvakh' (DPhil thesis, Taras Shevchenko National University of Kyiv 2014), 180; Bodnar T, 39-40.

would be less likely to have a detrimental influence on the company's functioning.[75] This flaw was subsequently removed, as the legislature seems to have taken these comments on board in the 2015 amendments (effective since 1 May 2016).

Despite this criticism about the lack of rules for transactions between a legal entity and its sole shareholder, it should be noted that the overall control of a single shareholder and the risk of mixing assets do in fact pose a threat to the interests of creditors. In the EU, these risks are addressed by Directive 2009/102/EC, which provides procedural safeguards for single-member companies.[76] Additionally, many jurisdictions, including Ukraine, use insolvency and special liability rules (e.g., veil piercing) to protect creditors' rights.

[4] Regulation after the Enactment of the 2015 Amendments (From 1 May 2016 Onwards)

The draft law regarding the protection of investors was published on the NSSMC's website in 2014.[77] It was further amended following input from representatives of the Ukrainian Bar Association, submitted to the Parliament of Ukraine, adopted on 7 April 2015 and enacted on 1 May 2016.[78]

The amendments established a series of additional conditions for applying the rules on transactions with interest contained in the JSC Law of Ukraine. In order to be covered by those rules, the value of the transaction had to exceed 100 times the minimum wage, which was around EUR 5,000 in 2016 (the minimum wage is established annually by the Law of Ukraine on the Budget[79]). The logic for the changes had derived from the necessity to exclude ordinary everyday transactions from burdensome requirements, ensuring that the procedure is not *over-inclusive and therefore burdensome*.[80] This minimum threshold for triggering the approval requirements for transactions with interest in JSCs was subsequently relaxed in 2017: according to the new amendments, approval is required only for transactions with

75. Kraakman R and others, *The Anatomy of Corporate Law: A Comparative and Functional Approach* (2nd edn, Oxford University Press 2009), 179.
76. Directive 2009/102/EC of the European Parliament and of the Council of 16 September 2009 in the area of company law on single-member private limited liability companies [2009] OJ L 258, 1.10.2009, Articles 2-5.
77. Draft Law of Ukraine 'On Amending Certain Legislative Acts regarding the Protection of Rights of Investors' [Proekt Zakonu Ukrayiny 'Pro vnesennia zmin do deyakykh zakonodavchykh aktiv schodo zakhystu prav investoriv'], available at: http://www.nssmc.gov.ua/law/19018, accessed on 15 April 2015.
78. Law of Ukraine 'On Amending Certain Legislative Acts on the Protection of Investors' [Zakon Ukrayiny 'Pro vnesennia zmin do deyakykh zakonodavchykh aktiv schodo zakhystu prav investoriv'].
79. Budgetary Code of Ukraine [Biudzhetnyi kodeks Ukrayiny] of 8 July 2010, published in Vidomosti Verkhovnoyi Rady Ukrayiny, 2010, Nos 50-51, St. 572, Article 40.
80. Enriques L, 'Related Party Transactions: Policy Options and Real-World Challenges (with a Critique of the European Commission Proposal)', 13.

interest representing more than 1% of the company's assets based on its annual report.[81]

The rules identifying interested persons were also changed, as explained in Table 1.2.

81. Law of Ukraine 'On Amending Certain Legislative Acts on the Improvement of Corporate Governance in Joint Stock Companies' [Zakon Ukrayiny 'Pro vnesennia zmin do deyakykh zakonodavchykh aktiv schodo pidvyschennia rivnia korporatyvnogo upravlinnia v aktsionernykh tovarystvakh'] of 23 March 2017, published in Vidomosti Verkhovnoyi Rady Ukrayiny, 2017, No. 25, St. 289.

Table 1.2 Categories of Interested Persons Before and After the Enactment of the 2015 Amendments to the JSC Law of Ukraine

Interested Persons	*Category 1*	*Category 2*	*Category 3*	*Category 4*
Before 1 May 2016	company officers and their family members	shareholders with 25% > share capital and their family members	legal entity that is owned 25% > by company officers and/or their family members	no regulation
After 1 May 2016	company officers and *affiliated persons*, who besides family members now also include legal entities controlled by company officers and/or their family members	shareholders with 25% > share capital and *affiliated persons*, who besides family members also include: (1) legal entities controlled by shareholders and/or their family members and (2) where the shareholder is a legal entity, affiliated persons also include: (a) a legal entity controlling the shareholder; (b) a legal entity under control of a third-party legal entity that also controls the shareholder.[82]	legal entity *where persons in Category 1 or Category 2 are company officers*	*persons identified as such in the company's articles of association*[83]

82. One exception, as mentioned previously, is that a shareholder that holds 100% of a company's share capital is not regarded as an interested person relative to that company for the purposes of the provisions on transactions with interest.
83. This new element introduced in the 2015 amendments offers greater flexibility to participants in legal relationships.

As Table 1.2 shows, the list of interested persons has mostly been extended, except in Category 3, which has been narrowed. Before the amendments, this category included legal entities where 25% or more of the shares were held by company officers and/or their family members. Now, this category is not determined by ownership, but rather by control, as differentiated by Berle and Means:[84] legal entities are regarded as interested persons if any of their company officers fall under Categories 1 and/or 2. However, legal entities in which company officers and/or their relatives own shares have not completely disappeared from the text of the law, and now fall under Category 1, under the umbrella of persons affiliated to company officers and/or their family members, i.e. legal entities controlled by them.[85] Taking into account the definition of controlling block of securities as used in the JSC Law of Ukraine, it can unequivocally be stated that the JSC Law of Ukraine interprets control foremost through ownership of an entity's share capital.[86] Therefore, a legal entity in which a company officer is a shareholder will inevitably be regarded as an interested person if the shareholder owns more than 50% of the share capital[87] or exercises control in another manner, e.g. through controlling agreements, as opposed to the previous regulation, where the deciding factor was ownership of 25% of the company's share capital.

The new amendments preserve the conditions that interested persons had to meet for transactions to be qualified as transactions with interest and the approval procedure for such transactions. The principal differences between the earlier regulation and the new one are: (a) previously, an interested person was required to notify the company about the transaction within three days after the interest arose, whereas now the specific deadline for notification has been replaced by a duty to notify the interest 'in advance'; (b) previously, no rules existed establishing what information had to be disclosed to management, whereas now the law dictates that the interested person must inform management of the interest and submit the draft agreement; (c) a new element in the law is the requirement of an independent evaluation of the transaction, with the help of an independent valuer; (d) most importantly, under the present rules, if the general meeting of shareholders decides on whether or not to approve a transaction with interest, the issue is decided by a majority of the non-interested shareholders, whereas the previous regulation referred to the general procedure of voting under which resolutions were considered to have been adopted if supported by a majority of the shareholders present at the meeting (including both

84. This distinction between ownership and control was famously made by Berle and Means, who were among the first to notice the separation between owners, who are interested in successful management of the company, and the persons who have power over an enterprise (Berle A and Means G, *The Modern Corporation and Private Property* (McMillian 1932)).
85. JSC Law of Ukraine, Articles 1(1), 71(2).
86. *Ibid.*, Article 1(6), 1(7).
87. In some cases a shareholder may hold fewer shares, but for economic and psychological reasons exercise actual control over the enterprise (Ekonomicheskiy slovar, available at: http://abc.informbureau.com/html/eiiodieuiue_iaeao_aeoee.html, http://abc.informbureau.com/html/eiiodieuiue_iaeao_aeoee.html, accessed on 11 August 2016).

interested and non-interested shareholders). However, the rule described in (d) was relaxed slightly in 2017, allowing non-listed JSCs to abandon the requirement.[88]

The consequences of non-compliance with the procedure have also been modified slightly. As already noted above, transactions with interest that did not comply with the procedural requirements could be invalidated in the old situation. Under the current version of the law, a transaction is regarded as valid only if the procedure has been followed. This raises the question of whether invalidation may be sought if the procedure is not followed. This issue is discussed in Chapter 5.

While the right of shareholders to challenge transactions with interest, including RPTs, that are not compliant with the procedure is studied in Chapter 5, the amendments are clear about additional appraisal rights of shareholders. They grant shareholders the right to demand that the company repurchase their shares if they vote against a transaction with interest at the general meeting of shareholders.[89] Although shareholders will sometimes use this right when the company is in distress, and so make the situation worse, abuse comes more frequently from the company in trying to set the price of repurchase as low as possible.

Some critical comments have been expressed with regard to the transition provisions for the 2015 amendments to the JSC Law of Ukraine. The amendments make little mention of the validity of transactions with interest that were approved before the amendments were enacted. While the most recent amendments similarly make no provision for the fate of transactions with interest that had been given supervisory board approval, as fundamental transactions (between 10% and 25% of the company's assets), before the enactment of the 2015 amendments,[90] arguably these are also subject to approval by the general meeting of shareholders under the new rules.[91]

In addition to the procedural requirements laid down in the JSC Law of Ukraine and the negative legal consequences resulting from non-compliance with the established procedure, the *ex post* disclosure obligations for public JSCs have also been changed to oblige public JSCs to inform the NSSMC about all approved transactions with interest on a quarterly and annual basis.[92] The company's notifications must include, among other details, the following information: the date of the decision approving the transaction, the material terms of the transaction, the subject of the contract, the market value of the contracted goods, the correlation between the market value and the company's assets and the voting results, with an indication of how many

88. Law of Ukraine 'On Amending Certain Legislative Acts on the Improvement of Corporate Governance in Joint Stock Companies' [Zakon Ukrayiny 'Pro vnesennia zmin do deyakykh zakonodavchykh aktiv schodo pidvyschennia rivnia korporatyvnogo upravlinnia v aktsionernykh tovarystvakh'].
89. JSC Law of Ukraine, Article 68(1).
90. *Ibid.*, Article 71(11).
91. *Ibid.*, Article 71(7).
92. Regulation on Disclosure of Information by Emitents of Securities, approved by the decision of the National Securities and Stock Market Commission of Ukraine, No. 2826 of 3 December 2013 [Polozhennia pro rozkryttia informatsii emitentamy tsinnykh paperiv, zatverdzhene rishenniam Natsionalnoyi komisii z tsinnykh paperiv ta fondovoho rynku No. 2826 vid 3 hrudnia 2013 roku], published in Ofitsiynyi visnyk Ukrayiny, 2013, No. 100, St. 3699, paragraph 1, section 3, Chapter III, paragraph 1, section 4, Chapter III.

votes were cast 'for' and 'against'.[93] A company has a duty to disclose as soon as the company, represented by the supervisory body or the general meeting of shareholders, decides on whether or not to approve a transaction with interest, but no earlier.

The most recent amendments to Article 71 of the JSC Law of Ukraine were adopted by the Parliament of Ukraine on 20 September 2019.[94] The amendments changed the definition of a transaction with interest. Previously, a transaction with interest arose if an interested person was a company officer in a legal entity that was party to a transaction. Although the definition of an interested person has not changed, and Category 3 of interested persons remains in place, as discussed above, the amendments mean that a transaction with interest now occurs if an interested person controls a legal entity that enters into a transaction with the company.

Furthermore, these changes give greater power to the general meeting of shareholders for approving transactions with interest. The general meeting will have the authority to approve transactions representing 10% or more of the company's assets, instead of 'more than 10 per cent of the company assets'. Additionally, the Law grants minority shareholders the power to initiate invalidation of transactions with interest formed on non-market terms, even if the approval procedure has been followed, and introduces joint liability of the interested person and the person who violated the requirements. One goal of these new changes is to improve Ukraine's Doing Business rating.

[B] Regulation of RPTs in Private Companies in Ukraine

Before the adoption of the JSC Law of Ukraine, the formation and functioning of JSCs was regulated similarly to LLCs, with the Law of Ukraine 'On Economic Companies' serving as the principal instrument governing corporate relationships involving economic companies. Similarly to JSCs, RPTs in LLCs are also subject to regulation by the general provisions of the 2003 CCU on legal entities that deprive shareholders of the right to vote on whether or not to approve transactions between a shareholder and the company at the general meeting of shareholders.[95] However, unlike JSCs, which in 2008 received their own separate legislation, LLCs remained within the scope of the Law of Ukraine 'On Economic Companies' until the enactment of the LLC Law of Ukraine.[96]

LLCs had not been the focus of the legislature's attention for many years. Whatever steps the Ukrainian Parliament had taken with regard to LLCs were mostly concerned with such areas as minimum share capital for companies (changing gradually from one hundred times the minimum wage, to one minimum wage, followed lastly by the abolition of all requirements for the amount of share capital,

93. *Ibid.*, paragraph 5, section 1, Chapter III.
94. Law of Ukraine 'On Amending Certain Legislative Acts of Ukraine regarding the Stimulation of Investment Activity in Ukraine' [Zakon Ukrayiny 'Pro vnesennia zmin do deyakykh zakonodavchykh aktiv Ukrayiny schodo stymuliuvannia investytsiynoyi diyalnosti v Ukrayini'] of 20 September 2019, published in Golos Ukrayiny, 2019, No. 197.
95. CCU, Article 98(3).
96. LLC Law of Ukraine.

allowing creation of 'one-UAH' companies[97]) and the maximum number of shareholders (from 10 to 100 persons[98]). However, comprehensive regulation remained lacking, as evidenced by the example of JSCs. Still, several legislative attempts were made to introduce more detailed rules for such companies, including special provisions on RPTs.

The Draft LLC Law of Ukraine had been before Ukraine's Parliament since 13 May 2016. At first, it contained rules for RPTs or, to use the Draft Law's terminology, 'transactions with interest'. Provisions in the Draft Law equated transactions with interest and RPTs as being based on the same idea: transactions with interest are formed between a company and an interested person.[99] The JSC Law of Ukraine uses a broader definition for transactions with interest than for RPTs: an interested person can either be a party to the transaction or act in a different capacity, for instance as a representative or a broker for the party in the transaction, or benefit from the transaction. The later version of the Draft LLC Law removed the detailed provisions for transactions with interest. In the finalized LLC Law of Ukraine of 6 February 2018, the provisions on transactions with interest are entirely optional.[100]

By nature, LLCs are private companies, usually owned by one or several shareholders and with a minimum amount of share capital, as opposed to JSCs, especially listed ones, which might have hundreds of minority shareholders.[101] JSCs therefore play a more public role than LLCs, as evidenced, e.g., by the difference in share capital requirements: forming a JSC requires a share capital corresponding to 1,250 times the minimum wage,[102] whereas (as explained above) no requirements currently exist for the amount of share capital in LLCs, as long as the company has share capital, even UAH 1. Due to the said difference, within this work, JSCs are often referred to as public companies, while the concept 'private company' is used to mean LLCs. The danger accompanying the functioning of listed public companies derives from the fact that their shares can be acquired by the public more easily than shares in private companies, and so outside investors buying small numbers of shares in listed companies and expecting future income in the form of dividends could suffer as a result of wrongdoings by blockholders or controlling shareholders.[103] While this also makes

97. Law of Ukraine 'On Economic Companies' [Zakon Ukrayiny 'Pro hospodarski tovarystva'], Article 52.
98. *Ibid.*, Article 50(2).
99. Draft Law of Ukraine 'On Limited and Additional Liability Companies' [Proekt Zakonu Ukrayiny 'Pro tovatystva z obmezhenoyu ta dodatkovoyu vidpovidalnistiu'], available at: http://w1.c1.rada.gov.ua/pls/zweb2/webproc4_1?pf3511 = 59093, accessed on 27 December 2018, Article 46(1).
100. LLC Law of Ukraine, Article 45(2).
101. The JSC 'Ukrayinskyi Naftogazovyi Instytut' is an example of a company with numerous minority shareholders, numbering 1,740 in total: natural persons, according to the company's disclosure in 2017 (publicly available at: http://smida.gov.ua/db/emitent/year/xml/showform/117368/130/templ, accessed on 2 September 2019).
102. JSC Law of Ukraine, Article 14(1).
103. Hopt KJ, 'Comparative Corporate Governance: The State of Art and International Regulation' in Fleckner AM and Hopt KJ (eds), *Comparative Corporate Governance: A Functional and International Analysis* (Cambridge University Press 2013), 64.

sense for large private companies with transferable shares, in which outside shareholders can also participate, the question remains whether private companies should be subject to the same strict rules as listed public companies. Introducing margins of regulation serving as thresholds or triggers for rules on transactions with interest would, therefore, be a plausible solution for purely private entities. This is what was done with the 2015 amendments to the JSC Law of Ukraine when transactions with interest representing less than 100 times the minimum wage (subsequently changed to 1% of the company's assets) were excluded from the regulation. This provision was also included in an earlier version of the Draft LLC Law of Ukraine, though with higher margins. As the authors of the Draft LLC Law of Ukraine had originally suggested, transactions with interest should not be subject to the rules on such transactions either if they involve amounts of less than 200 times the minimum wage, provided that this is also less than 10% of the company's assets, or if they exceed 10% of the company's assets but represent less than fifty times the minimum wage.[104] In addition, an earlier Draft LLC Law of Ukraine expanded the rules on transactions with interest to include all transactions regardless of the amount if they constituted a loan, financial support, pledge or surety to a company officer or affiliated person.[105] The legislators wished to concentrate the rules on transactions with interest on the types of contracts that pose the greatest risk. Ultimately, as can be seen from the Law currently in force, all these margins were abandoned and the rules on transactions with interest were made entirely optional, subject to regulation by each company's own articles of association.[106]

While some procedural safeguards, as described above, may seem useful for private companies with freely transferable shares and minority shareholders, whose rights could be violated by blockholders or management, introducing disclosure requirements for private companies in the same way as for public companies seems a bridge too far.[107] While public companies regularly report to the NSSMC, it seems unnatural for private companies, a more flexible form of business organization, to be subject to the same level of disclosure. This strategy-related issue is discussed in more detail in Chapter 5 in this book.

Last but not least, the Law of Ukraine 'On Economic Companies', which came in for criticism for not imposing sufficient regulation on private companies, did in fact provide a remedy for minority shareholders who disagreed with their company's policy on RPTs. This remedy was the right to exit, which, if exercised, triggered the company's duty to pay out assets proportionately to the exiting shareholder's share after the financial statements were approved, but within twelve months after the exit date.[108] This right was attacked heavily in Ukraine's academic circles, especially for its

104. Draft Law of Ukraine 'On Limited and Additional Liability Companies' [Proekt Zakonu Ukrayiny 'Pro tovatystva z obmezhenoyu ta dodatkovoyu vidpovidalnistiu'], Article 46(3).
105. *Ibid.*
106. LLC Law of Ukraine, Article 45(2, 3).
107. Bartman SM, 'Of Groups and Ostriches' (2007) 4 European Company Law 190.
108. Law of Ukraine 'On Economic Companies' [Zakon Ukrayiny 'Pro hospodarski tovarystva'], Article 54.

unconditional nature.[109] The LLC Law of Ukraine then modified the marginalism of the right to exit by allowing unconditional exit only for shareholders holding less than 50% of the company's share capital.[110]

§1.04 RESEARCH QUESTIONS AND METHODOLOGY

Company law in Ukraine already features rules governing RPTs in JSCs (public companies) and optional regulation for LLCs (private companies). Despite the availability of procedural safeguards in those legal entities, minority shareholders and creditors are far from being regarded as sufficiently protected from the wrongdoings of blockholders and managers. Section §1.02 showed that ownership in companies in Ukraine is concentrated, and the risk of abuse of rights by private blockholders or by the state is real. At the same time, in the past Ukrainian companies faced the possibility of corporate raiding and abusive suits by minority shareholders. It is vital to take these circumstances into account when designing the most appropriate strategy for Ukrainian corporate law as its transitions to implementing EU law. The clearest recent example of the problems with RPTs in Ukraine is the case of Privatbank JSC, one of Ukraine's systemically important banks.[111] Privatbank was nationalized by the state in December 2016. Soon afterwards, the state capitalized the bank with UAH 116.8 billion, followed by an additional UAH 38.6 billion. Overall, the state was required to infuse the bank with more than UAH 155 billion (more than EUR 5 billion) after the change of ownership.[112] The reason for the nationalization and the subsequent capital infusions was the preceding withdrawal of funds en masse through loan agreements to the companies indirectly controlled by the bank's former shareholders, Ihor Kolomoyskyi and Hennadiy Boholiubov. Before its nationalization, Privatbank restructured its loan portfolio by identifying thirty debtor companies that owed the bank more than UAH 110 billion; however, journalists were unsuccessful in uncovering the shareholders of the companies and their executives.[113] According to an independent investigation by the Organized Crime and Corruption Reporting Project, the scheme was centred around a series of insider loans to companies controlled by Kolomoyskyi and Boholiubov. The researchers alleged that *in most instances, financial records show that Ukrainian shell companies borrowed money from Privatbank in Ukraine, transferred it to Cyprus branch accounts held by offshore businesses, many of which were registered in*

109. Kibenko O and Zaleska A, 'Vykhid uchasnyka iz tovarystva z obmezhenoyu vidpovidalnistiu: problemni pytannia ta praktychni rekomendatsii' (2012) Ukrayinske komertsiyne pravo 20, 29.
110. LLC Law of Ukraine, Article 24(2).
111. 'Natsionalnyi bank vyznachyv 14 bankiv systemno vazhlyvymy' web-site of the National Bank of Ukraine, available at: https://bank.gov.ua/news/all/natsionalniy-bank-viznachiv-14-bankiv-sistemno-vajlivimi, accessed on 4 September 2019.
112. Zanuda A, 'Yak Privatbank stav temoyu vyboriv i scho bude pislia nykh' BBC Ukraine (16 April 2019), available at: https://www.bbc.com/ukrainian/features-47913100, accessed on 4 September 2019.
113. 'Pered natsionalizatsiyeyu z "Privatbanku" vyvely desiatky milyardiv hryven, – "Schemy". VIDEO' CensorNET (12 May 2017), available at: https://censor.net.ua/ua/video_news/439605/pered_natsionalizatsiyeyu_z_pryvatbanku_vyvely_desyatky_milyardiv_gryven_shemy_video, accessed on 4 September 2019.

the British Virgin Islands (BVI).[114] This case is an example of how blockholders are able to tunnel resources from their companies at the expense of other stakeholders.

A similar case of large-scale tunnelling occurred at VAB Bank JSC. That bank was declared insolvent by the National Bank of Ukraine in November 2014, and its licence was revoked in March 2015.[115] In the criminal proceedings concerning theft and corporate abuse, it was established, among other findings, that on 14 November 2014 the bank had repaid UAH 110 million to JSC 'Trostianetskiy miasokombinat' and UAH 266,455,000 to JSC 'ShP "Svitanok"' as advance payments on deposit sums, despite being prohibited at the time by the National Bank from paying advances on repayments to related parties.[116] While VAB Bank was not as large as Privatbank, these malpractices still led to violations against the bank's clients and investors.

The achievements of theoretical company law, the practice of company law and governance from the jurisdictions in the research focus and the current economic situation in Ukraine serve as important benchmarks for the present research. The inter-jurisdictional comparison of the doctrines, strategies, statutory and judicial approaches that exist in the studied jurisdictions will allow a better understanding of Ukrainian laws and lead to suggested solutions that, if implemented properly, could be useful in balancing the interests of the various groups of stakeholders as far as RPTs are concerned. The solutions will be designed with a view to making regulation more efficient from a cost-benefit perspective. The study will also examine whether different rules should be adopted for RPTs within and outside corporate groups. If RPTs require special treatment in corporate groups, proper rules should be designed in accordance with the requirements of the EU-Ukraine Association Agreement and relevant European standards and should be made separately for corporate groups and companies that do not have the characteristics of a group. Therefore, the following research question follows from the foregoing:

> What solutions can the laws of Germany, Poland, the Netherlands and the EU offer to help overcome the problems of RPTs within and outside corporate groups in Ukraine and make the current regulation in Ukraine more efficient?

Besides EU law and the company laws of Ukraine, Poland, Germany and the Netherlands, this research also examines a variety of articles, expert reports and proposals. The existing legislation of Ukraine, new legislative proposals and draft laws put forward by government authorities, the people's representatives and non-governmental organizations are analysed to identify how they correspond to European standards and best practices. The economic and social risks accompanying the

114. Stack G, *Oligarchs Weaponized Cyprus Branch of Ukraine's Largest Bank to Send $5.5 Billion Abroad*, OCCPR (19 April 2019), available at: https://www.occrp.org/en/investigations/oligarchs-weaponized-cyprus-eranch-of-ukraines-largest-bank-to-send-5-billion-abroad, accessed on 4 September 2019.
115. 'Natsionalnyi bank vitaye posylennia roboty pravookhoronnykh organiv schodo prytiagnennia do vidpovidalnosti vlasnykiv ta top-menedzheriv bankiv' Web-site of the National Bank of Ukraine (12122016), available at: https://bank.gov.ua/control/uk/publish/article?art_id=40777652&cat_id=55838, accessed on 14 September 2019.
116. *Decision of 15 August 2018* Case No. 760/21074/18 (Solomianskiy District Court of Kyiv).

introduction of new rules for non-listed and/or listed companies are also examined, as is the background to corporate enforcement in Ukraine.

One of the challenges that this research faces is that Ukrainian company law is now in a state of flux. In 2017, two bills implementing EU Directives were adopted: namely the bill on squeeze-out and sell-out procedures (implementing the Takeover Directive)[117] and the bill introducing new disclosure requirements (implementing, among others, the Transparency Directive).[118] On 6 January 2018, the LLC Law of Ukraine was adopted and subsequently enacted on 17 June 2018. The most recent amendments concerning RPTs in public companies were adopted on 20 September 2019. Further changes are expected to follow in the very near future.

Based on the key research question as outlined above, the scope of this research also includes the following secondary research questions:

What is the meaning of RPTs and how do RPTs relate to other associated terms?

What standards are used in Poland, Germany and the Netherlands to tackle the problems of RPTs? Which of those standards should be borrowed by Ukraine?

How are corporate groups regulated in Poland, Germany and the Netherlands?

Under what circumstances could the German, Polish and Dutch strategies for dealing with RPTs be successfully applied in Ukraine?

Do any non-classical strategies exist that fall outside the groups of strategies for dealing with RPTs that are described in literature, and that would be useful to borrow for Ukrainian company law?

Should regulation be provided not only for RPTs, but also for broader 'conflicted' transactions between actors surrounding companies (for example transactions between a company's subsidiary and third parties)?

What should be the scope of the rules for RPTs in Ukraine: (1) all companies limited by shares (public and private companies), (2) only public companies, (3) only listed public companies, or even (4) large companies and large groups even though they are not listed, given that their business endeavours also have a major societal impact ('national champions')?[119]

The study was mostly conducted in Ukraine, for the examination of literature, legislation and law enforcement materials, and in the Netherlands as part of an external PhD thesis. However, the fine details of Polish, German and Dutch company laws,

117. Law of Ukraine 'On Amending Certain Legislative Acts on the Improvement of Corporate Governance in Joint Stock Companies' [Zakon Ukrayiny 'Pro vnesennia zmin do deyakykh zakonodavchykh aktiv schodo pidvyschennia rivnia korporatyvnogo upravlinnia v aktsionernykh tovarystvakh'].

118. Law of Ukraine 'On Amending Certain Legislative Acts on the Simplification of Business and Attraction of Investments by the Issuers of Securities' [Zakon Ukrayiny 'Pro vnesennia zmin do deyakykh zakonodavchykh aktiv Ukrayiny schodo sproschennia vedennia biznesu ta zaluchennia investytsiy emitentamy tsinnykh paperiv'].

119. Cofferati Report of the Committee of Legal Affairs, 12 May 2015, accepted by the Legal Affairs Committee on 7 May 2015, described in Hopt KJ, 'Corporate Governance in Europe: A Critical Review of the European Commission's Initiatives on Corporate Law and Corporate Governance' European Corporate Governance Institute (ECGI) – Law Working Paper No. 296/2015, available at SSRN: https://ssrn.com/abstract=2644156 or http://dx.doi.org/102139/ssrn2644156, accessed on 5 December 2018, 14.

relevant scientific materials and other sources on the topic were studied at the Max Planck Institute for Comparative and International Private Law, where the research goals defined were also achieved.

In addition, the results of a specifically designed Google Forms survey among legal experts and practitioners enriched the research with opinions on how to improve the regulation of RPTs and corporate groups in Ukraine. Respondents were selected according to public information about top corporate law firms. Overall, 112 requests to complete the survey were sent from iromashchenko@gmail.com to email addresses found in different Internet sources, and nineteen recipients completed the survey anonymously. The questions and answers are given in the appendix to this book. The questionnaire placed less emphasis on data and facts and was instead an opinion poll. Its design was modelled after public consultations as frequently conducted by the European Commission on various aspects of company law reform in recent years. The EU has a long record of similar actions. The questionnaire, therefore, served as a means to seek opinions and as an auxiliary tool to better understand the existing issues of RPTs and corporate groups in Ukraine.

§1.05 NATIONAL JURISDICTIONS IN FOCUS

[A] Introduction

Although Ukraine possesses a legislative framework specifically designed to deal with transactions with interest, including RPTs, in public companies, this does not mean that it is unnecessary to: (i) critically assess the current legislative provisions on RPTs and provide suggestions for improvement; (ii) develop alternative RPT-related strategies that are not clearly articulated in Ukrainian legislation; (iii) borrow effective techniques from the laws of other states. Considering that Ukraine is seeking integration into the EU, it seems more practical to look at the experiences of the relevant EU Member States rather than copying legal rules from other jurisdictions. Instead of taking one country as an example for legal transplantation, it would seem wiser to adopt specific models from several countries on a case-by-case basis.[120] The Member States that have been chosen for detailed study are Poland, Germany and the Netherlands. The following section discusses corporate ownership as one of the major factors influencing any decision to transplant models from those jurisdictions.

[B] Background to Corporate Ownership in Germany, Poland and the Netherlands

It is important to be aware from the outset that each of the jurisdictions studied developed in unique circumstances and that those circumstances shaped their respective legal systems and economic situations. As a result, although all three countries belong to the civil law tradition of Continental Europe, some of the features of their

120. Radwan A, Nadzon A and Zdiruk V, 19-24.

corporate governance systems are different. The focus here is on the data that are held to be of significance for the regulation of RPTs and corporate groups.

The economies of Continental Europe are characterized by increasingly concentrated blockholdings.[121] Moreover, research by Rafael La Porta and others shows that ownership concentration is not only confined to Europe and rich countries but is also pronounced in developing countries with poor protection of minority shareholders.[122] Of the countries in focus for the present research, Germany was reported to have the highest levels of ownership concentration in listed companies, with the average shareholding of the largest blockholder at 57%.[123] Although this figure dates from 2001, the tendency towards large blockholders in big companies emerged much earlier.

Tracking the origins of corporate governance in Germany requires a brief excursion to the beginning of the twentieth century. According to Caroline Fohlin, the country had more than 5,000 stock companies (AGs) before World War I (as of 1902), including some important enterprises with dispersed managerial ownership.[124] After the war, AGs underwent a process of expansion, which, however, did not stop the emergence of more than new 19,000 AGs between 1919 and 1923.[125] Meanwhile, small enterprises also grew in number: by 1925 they constituted 90% of companies.[126] The concentration processes continued until the mid-1930s when the Nazi regime heavily centralized governance mechanisms. As a result, stock companies converted en masse into private companies, returning to similar numbers as before World War I.[127] The decline of stock companies ended after World War II, and by 1957 the 100 largest enterprises included eighty-seven public companies (AGs) and nine private companies (GmbHs).[128] In 2002, the 100 largest enterprises comprised seventy-four AGs and seven GmbHs.[129] However, the role of listed AGs is not as large as it might initially seem: in 1997, the capitalization of the German stock market constituted 31.4% of the country's gross domestic product.[130] This means that the balance of the national income was produced by non-listed AGs, GmbHs and individuals.

---

121. Becht M and Röell A, 'Blockholdings in Europe: An International Comparison' (1999) 43 European Economic Review 1049, 1055.
122. La Porta R, Lopez-de-Silanes F and Shleifer A, 'Corporate Ownership Around the World' (1999) 54 The Journal of Finance 471, 511.
123. Tamowicz P, 'Corporate Governance in Poland' in Mallin CA (ed.), *Handbook on International Corporate Governance: Country Analyses* (Edward Elgar Publishing 2011), 95.
124. Fohlin C, 'The History of Corporate Ownership and Control in Germany' in Morck RK (ed.), *A History of Corporate Governance Around the World: Family Business Groups to Professional Managers* (University of Chicago Press 2007), 227-228.
125. *Ibid.*, 229.
126. *Ibid.*, 229.
127. *Ibid.*, 230.
128. *Ibid.*, 231.
129. Von Werder A and Talaulicar T, 'Corporate Governance Developments in Germany' in Mallin CA (ed.), *Handbook on International Corporate Governance: Country Analyses* (Edward Elgar Publishing 2011), 30.
130. Jurgens U, Naumann K and Rupp J, 'Shareholder Value in an Adverse Environment: The German Case' in Clarke T (ed.), *Corporate Governance: Critical Perspectives on Business and Management* (Routledge 2005), 143.

On the subject of dominant ownership holders, banks have always been viewed as exercising significant influence on German companies.[131] This is a fair statement from a comparative perspective. For instance, compared with the Netherlands, where in 1995 banks were reported to hold 2% of all shares, in Germany at that same time banks were among the most influential institutional investors, owning around 10% of the total share capital in companies.[132] Yet it is also apparent that a share ownership of 10% is not crucial in terms of corporate decision-making. Historically, German banks have avoided acquiring large shareholdings in stock companies.[133] In the 1980s and 1990s, equity stakes in excess of 5% were held by banks and insurance companies only in companies without a majority shareholder.[134] Banks traditionally exercised control over companies through other means, namely proxy voting at general meetings, membership of supervisory boards and cross-shareholdings.[135]

However, despite the prevailing impression of the banks' power, a noticeable trend in equity ownership and participation in corporate bodies by banks has emerged since the beginning of the 1990s. Their equity ownership in listed companies went down from 12%-13% to 9% in 2003,[136] and their representation on the supervisory boards of forty large companies declined from 44% to 23% during 1992-1999.[137] In reaction to these developments, Tobias Tröger warned that by leaving their positions, banks were causing an unprecedented void due to the lack of firm-specific oversight that they had carried out previously.[138] At the same time, however, it is important not to overstate the positive effect of oversight by banks, considering the possibility of misgoverned banks and their ability to lend money without proper economic reasoning.[139]

While the banks' power seems to be in decline, other types of shareholders have been shown to hold significant stakes in German companies. According to data from 2001, non-financial firms were the largest shareholders in all types of companies (with the average share block in German companies amounting to 60.25%).[140] The median

131. *Ibid.*, 141; Morck RK and Steier L, 'The Global History of Corporate Governance: An Introduction' in Morck RK (ed.), *A History of Corporate Governance Around the World: Family Business Groups to Professional Managers* (University of Chicago Press 2007), 30.
132. Bolt W and Peeters M, 'Corporate Governance in the Netherlands' in Balling M, Hennessy E and O'Brien R (eds), *Corporate Governance, Financial Markets and Global Convergence* (Springer 1998), 95.
133. Fohlin C, 239.
134. *Ibid.*, 244.
135. *Ibid.*, 271; Becht M and Böhmer E, 'Ownership and Voting Power in Germany' in Barca F and Becht M (eds), *The Control of Corporate Europe* (Oxford University Press 2001), 142.
136. Ringe W-G, 'Changing Law and Ownership Patterns in Germany: Corporate Governance and the Erosion of Deutschland AG' in Hill JG and Thomas RS (eds), *Research Handbook on Shareholder Power* (Edward Elgar Publishing 2015), 428.
137. Beyer J and Hassel A, 'The Effects of Convergence: Internationalization and the Changing Distribution of Net Value Added in Large German Firms' in Clarke T (ed.), *Corporate Governance: Critical Perspectives on Business and Management* (Routledge 2005), 179.
138. Tröger T, 'Germany's Reluctance to Regulate Related Party Transactions: An Industrial Organization Perspective' SAFE Working Paper No. 202, available at SSRN: https://ssrn.com/abstract=3129300, accessed on 7 December 2018, 22-23.
139. Morck RK and Steier L, 6.
140. Fohlin C, 245.

stakes of other shareholders (financial enterprises, individuals, the state and non-German shareholders) are much smaller: foreign shareholders, e.g., were said to hold on average 9.61 %, whereas the balance of the share ownership was largely dispersed (averaging 20.65 %).[141] Earlier evidence from 1996[142] and 1998[143] also confirms the dominance of non-financial enterprises. At the same time, the importance of families as shareholders remains undisputed.[144] In a sample of 275 companies with shares admitted to trade on regulated markets, in the period from 1998 to 2004, family-owned companies amounted to 37.5% of the total.[145] The best performances were recorded where families exercised control through supervisory boards or acted as managers.[146] For non-listed companies, in a sample of 500 firms in 1997, families were identified as blockholders in 90.6% of the cases.[147] Although these data might have been changed since when they were collected, the status of families as influential shareholders has continued throughout the years.

Like Germany, the Netherlands has a long stock market tradition.[148] It is the country where stock market development first originated, with the first public company ever established in 1602 and remaining in operation until approximately 1799 (Vereenigde Oostindische Compagnie, the Dutch East India Company).[149] In the 1990s, the numbers of public companies in these two jurisdictions were comparable (2,164 in Germany in 1994 and 2,042 in the Netherlands in 1991).[150] However, despite the similarities, including the use of co-determination models to protect employees, the Dutch stock market has some unique features that are rarely found in other countries.

Historically, the public company (NV) was the first business form for companies in the Netherlands, and for a long time it was the only form available. In 1971, the private company (BV) was introduced, following the adoption of the First Company Law Directive in 1968; it led to the conversion of 90 % of existing NVs (nearly 50,000) into private companies.[151] In 2001, the Netherlands had around 2,000 NVs and more than 150,000 BVs.[152] Despite the large number of private firms, both listed and non-listed companies have had a considerable impact on the national economy, with a

141. *Ibid.*
142. Prigge S, 'A Survey of German Corporate Governance' in Hopt K (ed.), *Comparative Corporate Governance: The State of the Art and Emerging Research* (Oxford University Press 1998), 968.
143. Jurgens U, Naumann K and Rupp J, 144.
144. Ringe W-G, 407.
145. Andres C, 'Large Shareholders and Firm Performance: An Empirical Examination of Founding-Family Ownership' (2008) 14 Journal of Corporate Finance 431.
146. *Ibid.*, 444.
147. Faccio M and Lang LH, 'The Ultimate Ownership of Western European Corporations' (2002) 65 Journal of Financial Economics 365, 374.
148. Morck RK and Steier L, 38.
149. De Jong A and Roell A, 'Financing and Control in the Netherlands: A Historical Perspective' in Morck RK (ed.), *A History of Corporate Governance Around the World: Family Business Groups to Professional Managers* (University of Chicago Press 2007), 468.
150. Wymeersch E, 'A Status Report on Corporate Governance Rules and Practices in Some Continental European States' in Hopt K (ed.), *Comparative Corporate Governance: The State of the Art and Emerging Research* (Oxford University Press 1998), 1049.
151. De Jong A and others, 'Ownership and Control in the Netherlands' in Barca F and Becht M (eds), *The Control of Corporate Europe* (Oxford University Press 2001), 189.
152. *Ibid.*, 188.

major role reserved for a list of large and dominant companies:[153] in 1993, three quarters of the 100 largest Dutch companies were listed, while the remainder were not, including some major agricultural firms.[154]

While a concentration of capital can be observed in the Netherlands, it is not as strong as in Germany. In 1995, institutional investors possessed, on average, 24% of companies' shares (22% of shares belonging to pension funds and insurance companies and 2% belonging to banks), while foreign shareholders owned 37%.[155] Statistical evidence from Germany from the same year suggests that banks held higher stakes in companies (around 10%), yet foreign shareholders owned less capital (around 14%). In addition, private companies in Germany held twice as much stock as in the Netherlands.[156]

Although the percentage of share capital owned by foreign investors in 1995 was already rather high in the Netherlands, testifying to the openness of the Dutch securities market and its internationalization, foreign ownership increased even further during the 1995-2005 period, reaching as high as 75%, with most investors being US-based.[157] This trend was coupled with increasing dispersion at some listed companies.[158] Yet capital concentration has remained a feature of the Dutch capital market: in 2017, eighteen out of fifty listed firms had majority shareholders.[159] The trend towards increased concentration also extended to shareholders owning between 10% and 30% of all shares in 2005, reaching 19% and 36%, respectively, in 2015.[160]

Poland is another jurisdiction with concentrated corporate ownership.[161] As a country with Germanic origins, Poland has a two-tier board system of corporate governance. Unlike Germany and the Netherlands, however, it does not have any co-determination laws.[162] The average size of shareholdings in listed companies in 2015, according to a number of sources, varied between 42% and 46%, potentially exceeding 50% with unveiled indirect ownership.[163] In various studies into listed companies during that period, scholars identified the following groups as the largest shareholders: members of companies' authorities, strategic investors, the state, individuals and financial institutions.[164]

More than in Germany and the Netherlands, in Poland the state has been one of the key market players since the end of Communist rule. Privatization processes in the 1990s led to the transfer of public wealth into private hands, and the state has gradually

153. *Ibid.*, 190.
154. De Jong A and Roell A, 480.
155. Bolt W and Peeters M, 95.
156. *Ibid.*
157. Hermes N and Van Veen K, 'Corporate Governance in the Netherlands: Trends, Challenges and Opportunities (2008-2016)' in Kostyuk AN, Braendle U and Capizzi V (eds), *Corporate Governance: New Challenges and Opportunities* (Virtus Interpress 2017), 142.
158. *Ibid.*, 142.
159. *Ibid.*, 146.
160. *Ibid.*, 149.
161. Bohdanowicz L, 'Corporate Governance in Poland' in Kostyuk AN, Braendle U and Capizzi V (eds), *Corporate Governance: New Challenges and Opportunities* (Virtus Interpress 2017), 250.
162. *Ibid.*, 260.
163. *Ibid.*, 250.
164. *Ibid.*

been losing its position as a key shareholder. Privatization moved in several directions: capital privatization (selling large blocks of shares to strategic investors), mass privatization (among the general public) and insider privatization (among managers and employees of enterprises).[165] By 1995, outside shareholders increased their shareholdings considerably, and in a sample of thirty-eight companies, at least 20% of shares belonged to outside shareholders.[166] During the period between 1996 and 2000, the largest shareholders gradually acquired shares to obtain full control of their enterprises.[167] The privatization form that generated the most income was capital privatization, which concerned large units of stock, while small- and medium-sized enterprises were privatized mostly through insider schemes.[168] Although slow, capital privatization was not free of the same transparency issues and poor investor protection that also characterized mass privatization.[169] While direct sale of companies to investors were governed by legislation, the laws on mass privatization left many questions unanswered regarding the management of privatized companies.[170] As a result, companies formed under the latter procedure became concentrated without safeguarding investors' rights and maintaining transparency. In 2002, the average largest blockholding in Polish listed companies was 39%-45%.[171] Although the corresponding figures in Germany and the Netherlands at that time were higher (*see* Figure 1.2), as already discussed above, those markets became more dispersed soon afterwards due to a variety of factors, including internalization processes and changes in equity policies of institutional investors, including banks.

165. Boeri T and Perasso G, 75.
166. Tamowicz P, 93.
167. *Ibid.*
168. Boeri T and Perasso G, 79, 83.
169. *Ibid.*, 83.
170. Buxbaum RM and others, *European Economic and Business Law: Legal and Economic Analyses on Integration and Harmonization* (Walter de Gruyter 1996), 144.
171. Tamowicz P, 94-95.

Figure 1.2 1st Largest Blockholder in Listed Companies in Germany, Poland and the Netherlands (Median in %)

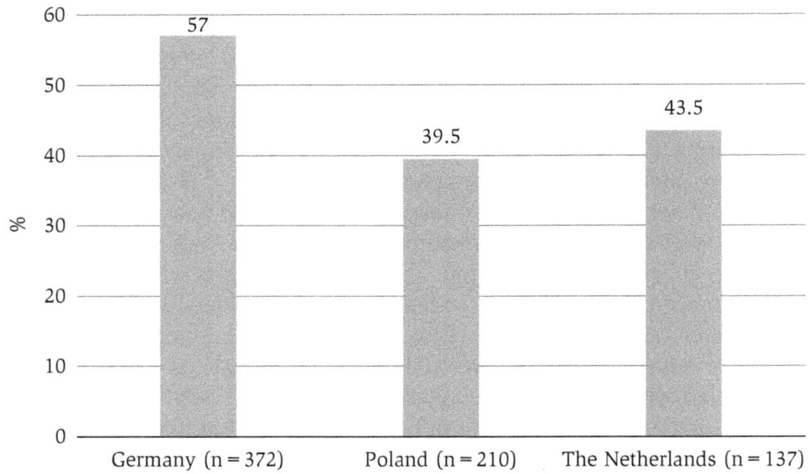

Source: Tamowicz P, 'Corporate Governance in Poland' in Mallin CA (ed.), *Handbook on International Corporate Governance: Country Analyses* (Edward Elgar Publishing 2011), 95.

The figures about the largest blockholders in Germany, Poland and the Netherlands described above primarily concern listed companies. In the case of Ukraine, corporate ownership in listed companies can be characterized only to a limited extent, due to the transition processes described in section §1.02 above.

Despite the differences in the development of the capital markets, corporate ownership in both Ukraine and the other jurisdictions discussed here is concentrated. As shown above, slow, non-transparent and destructive privatization processes led to an extremely high concentration of share capital in the largest Ukrainian companies. These processes influenced the development of market institutions and deterred foreign investors. Besides private entities and individuals that used various schemes and political influence to become controlling shareholders, the state has preserved its role as a major shareholder: in 2016, 19 of the 200 most profitable companies were state-owned.[172] Numerous state enterprises and state-owned shares in companies are still awaiting privatization. These characteristics of the Ukrainian economy must be considered in any analysis of the possibility for legal transplants from the other jurisdictions described.

172. Holovniov S and Vinnichuk Yu.

[C] Reasons for Legal Transplants from Germany, Poland, the Netherlands and the EU

The reason to analyse the laws and practices of Germany, Poland and the Netherlands centres not only on the fact that these countries belong to the tradition of civil law (as opposed to common law countries, including the United States (US) and the United Kingdom (UK)) and the prevalence of concentrated ownership there but also on their historical and geographical closeness, and their successes in creating market conditions and harmonizing national law with the requirements of EU law. The example of Poland is especially bright for Ukraine: in the 1990s, Poland managed to introduce reforms and build a strong institutional framework for company law.[173] Researching the company laws of other countries does not mean that all their provisions are transplantable, however. As Kahn-Freund so accurately noted, any attempt to use a pattern of law outside the environment of its origin will always entail the risk of rejection.[174] Kahn-Freund saw this finding as an acknowledgement and restatement in modern terms of Montesquieu's warning: *Les lois politiques et civiles de chaque nation ... doivent etre tellement propres au peuple pour lequel elles sont faites, que c'est un grand hazard si celles d'une nation peuvent convenir a un autre.*[175] Unlike Montesquieu, Berkowitz, Pistor & Richard base their theory not on conditions such as geography, culture or political regime, but rather on the notion that the law is a cognitive institution, meaning that transplants will work if they are adapted or if the population is familiar with the basic principles.[176] This means that, for borrowed company laws to be implemented, Ukrainian society must first be informed and properly prepared.

As Walton admitted with regard to German law, *there was also the great body of law – the so-called modern Roman law, or Pandektenlehre, of which certainly it could not be said that it grew out of German consciousness or that it reflected national mind and character.*[177] The authors of laws who are not directly related to the country's geography, history or culture are 'professional jurists': they possess the freedom to search for the most suitable lawmaking options and borrow them, and so adapt the country's legal system to the new circumstances. This is why it is true that borrowing plays a central part in the legal development and the adoption of rules, and although

173. Dabrowski M, Gomulka S and Rostowski J, 'Whence Reform? A Critique of the Stiglitz Perspective' (2001) 4 The Journal of Policy Reform 291, 298.
174. Kahn-Freund O, 'On Uses and Misuses of Comparative Law' (1974) 37 The Modern Law Review 1, 27.
175. Freedland M, 'Otto Kahn-Freund (1900-1979)' in Beatson J and Zimmermann R (eds), *Jurists Uprooted German-Speaking Émigré Lawyers in Twentieth-Century Britain* (Oxford University Press 2004), 311-312.
176. Berkowitz D, Pistor K and Richard J-F, 'The Transplant Effect' (2003) 51 The American Journal of Comparative Law 163, 189.
177. Walton FP, 'The Historical School of Jurisprudence and Transplantations of Law' (1927) 9 Journal of Comparative Legislation and International Law 183-184.

Ukraine has its own historical origins, its laws are not closely and intrinsically linked to its society.[178]

Before socialism, the legal systems of Central and Eastern Europe were deeply influenced by Roman-Germanic law.[179] During the Socialist era, despite the declamations on the 'originality of socialist law', Western models were borrowed.[180] After a complete emancipation from the previous ideology, some authors automatically concluded that post-socialist law would return to the Roman-Germanic legal tradition from where it had originated.[181] It is logical, therefore, that Ukraine's efforts to align its legal system more closely to German and Dutch laws should reflect the essence of its legal tradition. In addition, some attempts were already made by Ukrainian scholars to incorporate the civil law rules on legal entities from German and Dutch law while they were drafting the CCU.[182] The CCU, despite its faults and the need for improvements, has been characterized as a useful document that has considerable potential for supporting Ukraine's market economy, making investment in Ukraine more attractive and allowing business to be conducted with greater freedom.[183] In addition, the German and Dutch legal systems contain detailed rules on groups of companies, where RPTs are very common. The experiences of the selected countries are therefore worth investigating.

Besides the national jurisdictions named above, the study also investigates EU law from an evolutionary perspective. It looks closely at the recent amendments to the Shareholders' Rights Directive 2007/36/EC (SRD I) regarding RPTs[184] and the drafting process that led to that Directive in its current form. The relevance for Ukraine lies primarily in the fact that Ukraine's government needs to implement SRD I in line with the EU-Ukraine Association Agreement. Therefore, it is essential to understand the substance and the goals of the regulation underlying the Shareholders' Rights Directive 2017/828 (SRD II) in order to plan its further implementation in Ukraine.

§1.06 RESEARCH OUTLINE

This book follows a structure where general issues are studied first, after which the focus gradually shifts to more specific topics. Chapter 1 is an introduction, outlining the

178. Cairns JW, 'Watson, Walton, and the History of Legal Transplants' (2012) 41 Georgia Journal of International and Comparative Law 637, 695.
179. Ajani G, 'By Chance and Prestige: Legal Transplants in Russia and Eastern Europe' (1995) 43 The American Journal of Comparative Law 93, 94.
180. *Ibid.*, 94.
181. Zlatescu VD and Moroianu-Zlatescu I, 'Le Droit Roumain dans le Système Romano-Germanique' (1991) 43 Revue Internationale de Droit Comparé 829, 833.
182. Yefymenko A, 'Yurydychni osoby za proektom Tsyvilnoho kodeksu Ukrayiny' (2002) Yurydychnyi zhurnal 53.
183. OECD, *Legal Issues with Regard to Business Operations and Investment in Ukraine* (OECD Publishing, 2004), 15.
184. Directive 2017/828 of the European Parliament and of the Council of 17 May 2017 amending Directive 2007/36/EC as regards the encouragement of long-term shareholder engagement [2017] OJ L 132/1, 20.5.2017.

background, the research question and the methodology. Chapters 2-4 contain explanations and discussions of relevant terminology, key terms and sources on the topic. Chapters 5-6 focus more on the existing strategies for RPTs, and in particular with a view to choosing the proper strategy for Ukraine. Chapter 7, lastly, defines the main research conclusions and recommendations.

This first chapter contains a brief overview of the research, presenting the main research ideas, questions and methods used. The theoretical, economic, historical and legislative backgrounds given here provide a brief overview of the existing problems, academic discussion and sources in focus. It also helps the reader to become acquainted with the book structure.

Chapter 2 discusses what constitutes a conflict of interest and what types of such conflicts occur. The chapter consists of three sections. It starts with an introduction to the theory of conflicts of interest and outlines the main areas where conflicts of interest may occur. The conflicts that have the greatest bearing on the present research are primarily those that relate to corporate law and governance, originating in ownership and control. The second section addresses conflicts of interest and fiduciary duties, discussing the essence of fiduciary duties, with a focus on managerial duties. It also touches on the shareholder duties that some of the jurisdictions covered by this study do not accept. The final section of this chapter highlights the types of conflicts of interest, including conflicts of interest in RPTs. The ways of distinguishing types of conflicts are found in EU law, national hard and soft laws and in the court practices of some states. For instance, conflicts of interest are divided into direct and indirect conflicts based on enforcement practice.

Whereas Chapter 2 focuses on the more general issues of conflicts of interest, Chapter 3 looks more specifically at RPTs, their main features and their regulation. Given that a proper understanding of RPTs in each of the studied jurisdictions hinges on the meaning of a related party, the first three sections discuss statutes, CGCs and other sources at length to explore the notion of a related party and how that notion is construed in various sources. Special emphasis is given to IAS 24, as a point of departure for analysing the concept of a related party. Section §3.03 looks at Ukrainian statutes in more detail, for a complete picture of the regulation of RPTs in Ukraine. Section §3.04 moves away from the subjective element and shifts to the more substantive component of RPTs, by explaining the terms of RPTs. Section §3.05 elaborates on other constructions that may appear similar to RPTs, but nevertheless have features that prevent them from being equated with RPTs, require special regulation and are not covered by the scope of this study.

Chapter 4 considers the features of corporate groups to understand what constitutes a group, examining the legal and economic understanding of groups, how national and regional (i.e., EU law) statutes approach this topic, what challenges affiliation poses and what reasons exist to create corporate groups. After an analysis of how group issues are regulated in the various legal systems and whether group interest is recognized in the jurisdictions in focus, the study proceeds with the types and peculiarities of RPTs within corporate groups, i.e., intra-group transactions. Although some attention is given to the various types of intra-group transactions, this section elaborates more extensively on intra-group loans and cash pooling arrangements, as opposed to loans viewed as RPTs that have no group element. Intra-group transactions under Ukrainian law are analysed relative to the German, Dutch and Polish legal systems.

Chapter 5 takes a closer look at trends sparked by a well-known handbook,[185] primarily discussing the need to develop strategies. As previously noted, RPTs are not always regarded as perfectly safe market instruments. The need for RPT-related strategies stems from the risks that are associated with RPTs and the accompanying opportunistic practices. This chapter considers the following main strategies: procedural safeguards for RPTs; information rights and disclosure of RPTs; standard strategies for RPTs. These strategies are studied by considering the particular aspects of the existence of corporate groups and highlighting experiences in Germany, Poland and the Netherlands. Ukrainian law is described and discussed with a view to identifying the strategies that it uses to tackle RPTs and analysing whether any further change is needed. This chapter also explores other possible strategies that are not gathered under the umbrella of traditional strategies. Lastly, it examines the most recent amendments to EU law regarding RPTs, to give an understanding of how the draft of SRD II has evolved to reach its current form.

While Chapter 5 gives an overview of the strategies used in the EU, the national jurisdictions in focus and recognized more generally in corporate law theory, Chapter 6 is concerned with selecting the appropriate strategy or strategies for Ukraine. Section §6.01 explains what factors should be taken into account when selecting a strategy for RPTs, and section §6.02 describes the implementation of RPT-related strategies in Ukraine. Section §6.03 then provides a selection of legal strategies for RPTs in Ukraine, taking into account the strategies discussed in the previous chapter, the factors that need to be considered for choosing a strategy and the relevant historical, economic and legal backgrounds in Ukraine and how they influence the choice of strategy.

Chapter 7 presents the research conclusions and recommendations, seeking to strike a balance between transaction freedom and overregulation for the protection of the various groups of stakeholders in Ukraine.

185. Kraakman R and others, *The Anatomy of Corporate Law: A Comparative and Functional Approach* (3rd edn, Oxford University Press 2017), 145-169.

CHAPTER 2

Conflicts of Interest in Corporate Governance and Their Types

§2.01 CORPORATE GOVERNANCE AND OTHER AREAS WHERE INTERESTS CONFLICT

[A] Introduction to Conflicts of Interest in Law

Interests can collide in various different spheres and areas. Since the times of Roman law, private interests, initially associated with individuals, have been opposed to public interests relating to the state. These interests then came to be used to differentiate between relationships arising in private law and public law, with the two areas complementing each other and together constituting a single united legal system.[186]

Dividing interests into private and public, despite being based on simple and understandable criteria, is not enough for regulating relationships in the modern world. Defining only two types of interests is an oversimplification of the complex relationships arising in today's society with its numerous actors, each with their own interests that need to be considered. The variety of legal actors is demonstrated by the respective legislative provisions, as evidenced by Article 2 of the CCU,[187] which provides that civil relationships can be formed by natural persons, legal entities, the state, municipalities, the Autonomous Republic of Crimea and other entities governed by public law. These public-law entities are indicated exclusively for the formal purposes of legal regulation. However, taking a legal entity as a separate participant in a legal relationship, an analysis of that relationship will establish the entity's private interest as an arena for

186. Dozhdiev D, *Rimskoye chastnoye pravo* (Nersesiants V ed., 3rd edn, M.: Norma 2008), 11.
187. CCU, Article 2.

interplay between the interests of different social groups, in the terminology of Adolf Berle,[188] or social functions, according to Gunther Teubner.[189]

Reconciliation of the various parties' interests consequently poses a question for law, and company law in particular. The fact that parties in relationships pursue different goals does not in itself give rise to conflicting interests. For example, in a transaction where a player gambles in a casino, the player's interests are in opposition to the casino's interests; yet this does not constitute a conflict of interest. In order for a particular situation to involve a conflict of interest, one party must have an interest that is contrary to the interest of another party on whose behalf the first party is acting and the promotion of which *by definition* inevitably has a negative effect on the latter interest. In corporate governance, this is most common where a director attempts to derive benefits from the company in response to demands that do not coincide with the company's interests, to satisfy either the director's own interests or the interests of a third party (vertical agency conflict),[190] or where a majority shareholder acts to the detriment of minority shareholders (horizontal agency conflict).

Regulation has emerged for conflicts of interest where this is necessary to properly balance interests in relationships between parties, specifically in the functioning of investment firms and financial service providers. These are areas where the client's awareness of a conflict of interest will potentially influence his or her decision of whether or not to enter into a business relationship. The *Kick-Back I* decision of the German Federal Supreme Court is a textbook example: the bank failed to disclose to a client that it had an agreement with the client's portfolio manager, under which the bank was obliged to pay 33% of any transaction fees and custodian fees from the transaction value. The bank was found to be in breach of an organizational duty to make its employees aware of the disclosure obligations.[191] This was not in accordance with Germany's national legislation, which had been designed with a view to implementing the relevant EU directive.[192]

One of the major differences between conflicts of interest in financial services and in corporate governance lies in the respective lists of parties whose interests need to be taken into account. In financial services, the principal categories of persons that could potentially be involved in conflicting transactions include managers, employees and tied agents, any person directly or indirectly linked to them by control and their

188. Berle AA, 'Corporate Powers as Powers in Trust' (1931) 44 Harvard Law Review 1049; Berle Jr AA, 'For Whom Corporate Managers Are Trustees: A Note' (1931) 45 Harvard Law Review 1365.
189. Teubner G, 'Corporate Fiduciary Duties and Their Beneficiaries' in Hopt K and Teubner G (eds), *Corporate Governance and Directors Liabilities* (de Gruyter 1985), 151.
190. Hopt KJ, 'Trusteeship and Conflicts of Interest in Corporate, Banking, and Agency Law: Toward Common Legal Principles for Intermediaries in the Modern Service-Oriented Society' in Ferrarini G and others (eds), *Reforming Company and Takeover Law in Europe*, vol 4 (Oxford University Press 2004), 52.
191. Helm R and others, *Practitioner's Guide to Conflicts of Interest in the Financial Services Industry* (Sweet & Maxwell 2012), 279.
192. Directive 2004/39/EC of the European Parliament and of the Council of 21 April 2004 on markets in financial instruments amending Council Directives 85/611/EEC and 93/6/EEC and Directive 2000/12/EC of the European Parliament and of the Council and repealing Council Directive 93/22/EEC [2004] OJ L 145/1, 30.4.2004.

clients.[193] In corporate governance, clients are not, initially, among the groups whose interests need to be considered. This does not mean, however, that for publicly held investment banks the issues of corporate governance are left unresolved. On the contrary: regulation becomes more complicated, extending to at least two layers of conflicts of interests. On the first level (corporate governance), the issues of ownership and control come first, while on the second level (financial services), the client-manager relationship is crucial. This distinction has no bearing on companies that are not in a position to render financial services, and their executives are not burdened by an additional set of fiduciary obligations to their public-investment bank clients.[194]

Although it may seem that conflicts of interests are less complex in corporate governance than in financial services, even for corporate governance it is not always clear whether a conflict of interest exists. In situations where a director steals the company's secrets, appropriates business opportunities or receives excessive remuneration, or where a majority shareholder engages in tunnelling, it is simple to establish an outright conflict. However, besides these outright conflicts, situations exist where preferences diverge; e.g., a director can adopt one of the various different attitudes towards risk, namely risk acceptance, risk aversion or risk neutrality. This depends largely on the director's personality. The fact that the director can react differently to emerging risks makes it more difficult to identify a conflict of interest. Similarly, different actors will have different preferences depending on the allocation of the upside and downside in their relationships (equity versus debt claimants) or the diversifiability of their investments (well-diversified portfolio versus non-diversifiable human capital).

[B] Ownership and Control as Origins of Conflicts of Interest in Corporate Law

Any close examination of the issues of ownership and control supposedly separated[195] and discussed by scholars in law and economics[196] must make reference to the classic study presented by Berle and Means.[197] Ownership is explained as being apportioned to those individuals who have major interests and, before the law, those who hold legal title. Control, in turn, is in the hands of those who hold the major elements of power over an enterprise.[198] In companies, legal title is held primarily by the shareholders, while management exercises authority in the company and accordingly possesses a

193. *Ibid.*, Article 18.
194. Stark A, 'The Furore over Banker Compensation' in Peters A and Handschin L (eds), *Conflict of Interest in Global, Public and Corporate Governance* (Cambridge University Press 2012), 285.
195. Berle A and Means G, 120.
196. *See*, e.g., Bratton WW and Wachter ML, 'Shareholder Primacy's Corporatist Origins: Adolf Berle and the Modern Corporation' (2008) 34 Journal of Corporation Law 99, 118-122; Marks SG, 'The Separation of Ownership and Control' (1999) Encyclopedia of Law and Economics 692; Fama EF, 'Agency Problems and the Theory of the Firm' (1980) 88 The Journal of Political Economy 288.
197. Becht M and Mayer C, 'Introduction' in Barca F and Becht M (eds), *The Control of Corporate Europe* (Oxford University Press 2001), 1.
198. Berle A and Means G, 120.

certain amount of power. Where management is motivated solely by a desire for personal monetary gain, its interests oppose the interests of shareholders, who would rather increase the company's wealth. This then means that the interests of ownership and control are also opposed.[199]

The arguments for the separation of ownership and control as presented by Berle and Means in their celebrated book made perfect sense for the US economy at that particular stage of its development, where dispersed ownership was marked as a distinctive feature.[200] In later academic research, however, their theory was questioned, with some critics wondering whether it could be applied equally to countries where the picture of ownership was different.[201] It was even queried whether small shareholders were sufficiently numerous in the US for it to be seen as a jurisdiction with dispersed ownership.[202] Although the US is still regarded as a jurisdiction where large shareholders are relatively uncommon, the presence of family firms and wealthy investors should not be dismissed entirely.[203] In the network of shareholders, institutional investors play a special part, with shareholders pooling large sums of money to invest in companies.[204] The dramatic rise of institutional investors is a characteristic shared by all industrial economies.[205] In the US, the growth of institutional ownership has accelerated rapidly since 1980: *institutional assets grew eightfold* during the period 1990-1998.[206] The reason for the predominance of institutional investors and minority shareholders in the US might lie in the protection that their rights enjoy. The same cannot always be said for many countries with concentrated corporate ownership.[207] At the same time, it would be wrong to extend the argument of weak investor protection to developed European countries, where regulation of the financial markets has proved successful,[208] yet where controlling shareholders are prevalent. According to Becht and Böhmer's 2001 study, voting powers in German companies are highly concentrated, with over half of all listed companies being controlled by a majority block and only 17.4% of companies not having a blockholder that has a minority veto right (25%).[209] It would defy credibility to extrapolate these data to other European countries by concluding that all European companies are increasingly concentrated. As such, data reported in the Netherlands for the same year witnessed the average stake

199. *Ibid.*, 123.
200. Belcredi M and Ferrarini G, 'Corporate Boards, Incentive Pay and Shareholder Activism in Europe: Main Issues and Policy' in Belcredi M and Ferrarini G (eds), *Boards and Shareholders in European Listed Companies: Facts, Context and Post-Crisis Reforms* (Cambridge University Press 2013), 21.
201. La Porta R, Lopez-de-Silanes F and Shleifer A; La Porta R and others, 'Investor Protection and Corporate Governance' (2000) 58 Journal of Financial Economics 3.
202. La Porta R, Lopez-de-Silanes F and Shleifer A, 472.
203. Shleifer A and Vishny RW, 'A Survey of Corporate Governance' (1997) 52 The Journal of Finance 737, 754.
204. Nix P and Chen J, *The Role of Institutional Investors in Corporate Governance: An Empirical Study* (Springer 2013), 44.
205. *Ibid.*, 4.
206. Davis EP and Steil B, *Institutional Investors* (MIT Press 2001), 131.
207. La Porta R and others, 14.
208. *Ibid.*, 23.
209. Becht M and Böhmer E, 'Ownership and Voting Power in Germany', 142.

of the largest blockholder in companies listed at the Amsterdam Stock Exchange as being 27%.[210]

The established facts of concentration of capital in one party are not necessarily negative, especially taking into account the efficiency of family-owned firms and their ability to react to downturns more easily.[211] Nevertheless, they may be evidence of an absence of strong investor protection.

Despite these differences between legal systems and economies regarding the dispersion or concentration of ownership in companies, and, consequently, the issue of whether or not ownership and control are separated (at least to some degree), every company's functioning is influenced to a vast extent by both shareholders and management. Their importance to the company is beyond any doubt; however, their actions might have different effects, moving the company either towards prosperity or towards bankruptcy.

§2.02 CONFLICTS OF INTEREST AND FIDUCIARY DUTIES

[A] The Interconnection Between Interests, Rights and Duties

The concept of interest in and of itself is a necessary element in the theory of conflicts of interest. The interests of both managers and shareholders as summarized above are only one aspect of the overall picture of the corporate relationships involving these actors. The issue with the concept of interest and, consequently, with conflicts of interest is that they cannot always be measured by the law and, moreover, do not necessarily need to have any legal meaning. The fact that a person is overwhelmingly interested in personal gain for legal purposes does not matter as long as that person's actual actions are for the company's benefit. It is not the role of the law to force individuals to think in a particular manner. It would be of more significance to understand whether their acts conform to their obligations and the legal rules governing them. The interest would surely be at the root of any behaviour, an inner engine for further actions, an aspiration that is not embodied in a particular subjective right.[212]

---

210. De Jong A and others, 'Ownership and Control in the Netherlands', 205.
211. Belcredi M and Ferrarini G, 23.
212. In Ukrainian law the definition of a legitimate interest was given by the Constitutional Court of Ukraine (*Decision of 1 December 2004 No. 18-pn/2004 (case about legitimate interest)* Case No. 1-10/2004, Ofitsiynyi visnyk Ukrayiny of 31 December 2004, No. 50, p. 67, St. 3288 (Constitutional Court of Ukraine)) where it was defined as an aspiration to use a tangible or intangible asset as permission legitimated by objective law and not clearly defined in a subjective right, which is an independent object for judicial protection for the purpose of satisfying individual and collective demands that are not incompatible with the Constitution of Ukraine, Ukrainian legislation, public interest, fairness, reasonableness, good faith and other general rules. The Court was also asked to explain whether a breach of a shareholder's right could constitute a ground for protection of a legitimate interest of a company in which that shareholder owns shares. The Court replied that the company's interest cannot be equated to the sum of all the shareholders' interests and that a sole shareholder may seek judicial protection only in matters concerning his or her own rights or legitimate interests. Today, the Court's reply could be regarded as outdated, due to the fact that in 2015 the possibility of derivative suits was introduced in Ukrainian law (Law of Ukraine 'On Amending Certain Legislative Acts on the

However, for the emergence of a conflict of interest in legal terms, it is not enough to have a manager who wholeheartedly acts for the company's benefit while simultaneously thinking of stealing a car from that same company. From a psychological point of view, it can be argued that a conflict of interest exists, given that those two interests visibly conflict with each other. The latter ambivalent approach seems superfluous in jurisprudence, for at least two reasons. First, by acknowledging the legal effect of an internal conflict of interest it ignores the interests of the company's other stakeholders,[213] and second, for a person to be considered for legal purposes to be acting with a *legally relevant* conflict of interest, it requires more, namely a real violation of his or her duty of loyalty.[214]

The notions of duties and rights have more to do with actual actions than with a person's thoughts. That is why this section analyses the concept of conflict of interest primarily in connection with rights and duties of persons who are in a position to have conflicting interest.

[B] Overview of Managerial Fiduciary Duties

While conflicts of interest can occur for both managers and shareholders, managers first represent the company's interests in its dealings with others. Moreover, management is authorized to act on the company's behalf without power of attorney, but on the basis of charter documents and relevant legislative provisions.[215] This is rarely the case with shareholders: although they discuss matters that are important for the company when voting at general meetings, these actions are not representative. Rather, they are individual acts that in aggregate reflect the will of the company as a separate entity in legal relationships. Even the appointment of a shareholder as an

---

Protection of Investors' [Zakon Ukrayiny 'Pro vnesennia zmin do deyakykh zakonodavchykh aktiv schodo zakhystu prav investoriv']). At the same time, it is important to remember that the shareholder's interest may be contrary to that of the company. Following the KSH (Article 212(2)), the company's management may refuse to share information with certain shareholders if that information could be used against the company's interest.

213. Ungerer F, *Prozedurale Regulierung und Transparenz von Related Party Transactions in börsennotierten Aktiengesellschaften: eine vergleichende Untersuchung des deutschen und europäischen Aktien-und Kapitalmarktrechts unter besonderer Berücksichtigung von Art. 9c der novellierten Aktionärsrechterichtlinie* (Duncker & Humblot 2019), 43.

214. Even the breach of a duty of loyalty does not always give rise to liability. For instance, in the Netherlands, the duty not to compete with the company is covered by both general provisions of corporate law (Article 2:8, 2:9 of the BW) and articles on tort law, meaning that a breach of the non-competition duty does not automatically lead to liability (Gerner-Beuerle C, Paech P and Schuster EP, *Study on Directors' Duties and Liability* (European Commission DG Markt 2013), 155).

215. German Stock Corporation Act (Aktiengesellschaft Gesetz) (BGBl. I p. 1089) FNA 4121-1, Article 78; Civil Code of the Netherlands (Burgerlijk Wetboek) as in effect on 1 October 2008, most recently amended by the Act of [1 September 2008], Staatsblad 2008 [100], Article 2:130; Code of Commercial Companies of Poland (Kodeks Spółek Handlowych), 15 September 2000 (Dziennik Ustaw nr 94 z 8 listopada 2000 pozycje 1037), Article 201; LLC Law of Ukraine, Article 39; JSC Law of Ukraine, Article 60.

executive officer in a company does not transform share ownership into representation: it merely means that one person simultaneously is part of two different relationships in two different capacities.

In addition to the capability to act on the company's behalf, management bears another distinctive characteristic that is not shared by all corporate constituencies, namely the fiduciary duty. The existence of a fiduciary duty reflects the existence of a fiduciary relationship.[216] Scholars have made at least several attempts to define or explain the meaning of a fiduciary relationship.[217] Fiduciary relationships as defined in those works are not restricted to fiduciary duties only. Although fiduciary duties are vital for understanding fiduciary relationships, they are not rights in and of themselves. Rather, they complement the expansive discretionary powers of the company's management by counterbalancing them and establishing limitations on overly risky behaviour.[218] It is important for an obliged person to possess a certain discretion or power that affects the other party's interests.[219] In fiduciary relationships, these powers are based primarily on trust and confidence.[220] Without those basics, one party in a relationship would not give the other sufficient autonomy. While the degree of autonomy certainly varies in different countries, it must exist to at least some extent. In the Netherlands, the autonomous nature of management boards was established by the Dutch Supreme Court in the Forum Bank case in 1955.[221] In Germany, for public companies the Federal Supreme Court stated that *directors possess a wide margin of appreciation for their activities, because any business activity is inconceivable without such discretion.*[222] In Poland, the autonomy of the members of a management board in managing their company's affairs also derives from company law,[223] and the broad powers of the management board have been further confirmed by Polish case law. The judgment of the Supreme Court of the Republic of Poland of 15 April 2010 states that *Article 368 § 1 (of the KSH) provides for the general and unrestricted competence of the joint company's board to manage the affairs of the company and represent it.*[224]

216. Peters A, 'Conflict of Interest as a Cross-Cutting Problem of Governance' in Peters A and Handschin L (eds), *Conflict of Interest in Global, Public and Corporate Governance* (Cambridge University Press 2012), 13, 15.
217. Hollander C and Salzedo S, *Conflicts of Interest* (5th edn, Thomson Reuters 2016), 13-22; McCormack G, 'Fiduciary Obligations in a Changing Commercial Climate' in Rider B and Andenas M (eds), *Developments in European Company Law*, vol 1/1996 (Kluwer Law International 1997), 33-47; Akinbami F, 'The Fiduciary Duties of Institutional Investors' in Tomasic R (ed.), *Routledge Handbook of Corporate Law* (Taylor & Francis 2017), 99-100.
218. Velasco J, 'Fiduciary Duties and Fiduciary Outs' (2013) 21 George Mason Law Review 157, 168.
219. McCormack G, 33-47.
220. Hollander C and Salzedo S, 14.
221. De Savornin Lohman HA, *Duties and Liability of Directors and Shareholders under Netherlands Law: Piercing the Corporate Veil* (Kluwer Law International 1996), 9.
222. Bröhmer J, 'Germany' in Omar PJ (ed.), *Directors' Duties and Liabilities* (Ashgate/Dartmouth 2000), 55.
223. Zak T, 'Poland' in Loos A (ed.), *Directors 'Liability: A Worldwide Review'* (International Bar Association 2006), 350.
224. Judgment of the Supreme Court of the Republic of Poland II CSK 526/09, as quoted by Mitręga E, *Contemporary Enforceable Directors' Duties in Switzerland and in Poland: The Path of (GRC) Corporate Governance, Compliance and Risk Management from Soft Law to Hard Law?* (Schulthess 2016), 49.

One of the main ideas with fiduciary relationships is that they are based on trust, as the Latin origin of the word already indicates. The core obligation of the fiduciary is to act in the best interests of the beneficiary.[225] In the case of a company and its shareholders, their interests primarily involve growing their wealth, which is linked directly to the company's wealth. If inefficient corporate governance causes the company to lose money, this does not necessarily give rise to liability for breach of fiduciary obligations. In order to hold a person liable for breach of a fiduciary obligation, the judicial authorities, or another authority responsible for law enforcement, must assess whether and to what extent the fiduciary has abused his or her rights and acted in a manner incompatible with the beneficiary's interests while paying less attention to the outcome of their behaviour.[226]

The ambiguity that lies at the heart of every fiduciary relationship and makes the beneficiary vulnerable is that the fiduciary is not given specific instructions for how to act. This therefore creates the problem of how the fiduciary can be sufficiently incentivized or constrained without specifying what exact actions he or she should take.[227] At the same time, insisting on more detailed rules for fiduciaries would also have drawbacks: the more specific the director's obligations are made, the greater the possibility is that some elements will be overlooked. Practice always brings new circumstances to light that could not be predicted even by the most ingenious mind.[228] By comparison: as the incomplete contracts theory shows that all contracts are inevitably incomplete and do not observe all the variables,[229] so also would it be problematic to stipulate in law or in contract all the variables of fiduciary misconduct. In addition, the possible types of fiduciary misconduct are as numerous and unforeseeable as their counterparts, i.e. successful business decisions that lead to beneficial outcomes. Therefore, it is equally important to preserve fiduciaries' freedom and to understand how to regulate these relationships properly, taking into account that they sometimes enter the extralegal realm of ethical rules[230] and bearing in mind all the difficulties surrounding their enforcement.[231]

Opinions vary on how to group fiduciary duties. According to Bernard Black, two main duties out of four can be distinguished: a duty of care and a duty of loyalty, and additionally a duty of disclosure and a duty of 'special care', which comes into play in

225. Velasco J, 163.
226. Easterbrook FH and Fischel DR, 'Contract and Fiduciary Duty' (1993) 36 The Journal of Law & Economics 425, 426.
227. Cooter R and Freedman BJ, 'The Fiduciary Relationship: Its Economic Character and Legal Consequences' (1991) 66 New York University Law Review 1045, 1047.
228. Nolan RC, 'The Legal Control of Directors' Conflicts of Interest in the United Kingdom: Non-executive Directors Following the Higgs Report' in Armour J and McCahery JA (eds), *After Enron: Improving Corporate Law and Modernising Securities Regulation in Europe and the US* (Bloomsbury Publishing 2006), 374.
229. Scott RE and Triantis GG, 'Incomplete Contracts and the Theory of Contract Design' (2005) 56 Case Western Reserve Law Review 187, 190.
230. O'Connor MA, 'How Should We Talk about Fiduciary Duty-Directors' Conflict-of-Interest Transactions and the ALI's Principles of Corporate Governance' (1992) 61 The George Washington Law Review 954, 983.
231. Nolan RC, 377.

connection with takeovers.[232] Joseph McCahery and Erik Vermeulen separate fiduciary duties into four groups: (i) a duty of care and loyalty; (ii) a duty to disclose information; (iii) a duty to abstain from self-dealing transactions, personal use of partnership assets, usurpation of partnership opportunities and competition with the partnership; and (iv) a duty of good faith and fair dealing.[233] Julian Velasco, however, lists at least five duties, with a duty of loyalty and a duty of care forming the fiduciary 'pillars', followed by a duty of good faith, a duty of objectivity and a duty of rationality.[234] Maarten Muller equates the duty of good faith with the duty of loyalty.[235] Without evaluating the suggested groupings in detail, an endeavour that goes beyond the scope of this book, it is important to stress the interrelation between different fiduciary duties: they are all gathered under the umbrella of fiduciary relationships based on trust and confidence, where loyalty is a central part of the fiduciary's obligations.[236]

Besides recognizing the overarching nature of fiduciary duties, this research also works from the premise that the duty of care and the duty of loyalty are fundamentally different. The duty of care pertains to the standard of a diligent manager and finds its reflection in the business judgment rule, giving sufficient discretion to the company's management to act as their economic views dictate based on the available information.[237] Managers are expected to possess sufficient knowledge about the company to act in a manner that is advantageous to the company. Yet the presence of the duty of care does not necessarily mean that the business judgment rule applies. Of the jurisdictions in focus for this research, only in Germany is the business judgment rule explicitly codified;[238] in the Netherlands and Poland it is not.[239] However, the fact that the latter two jurisdictions do not have a codified business judgment rule does not mean that regulation of the duty of care is strict in all respects. For instance, in Dutch companies, the directors' duty of care stems from the broad scope of Article 2:9 of the BW, which obliges directors to be responsible for the proper performance of their duties and affords a wide margin of judicial discretion in assessing that responsibility.[240] In addition, in Germany, the existence of a codified business judgment rule is counterbalanced by the fact that the burden of proof is borne by the directors.[241]

232. Black BS, 'The Core Fiduciary Duties of Outside Directors' (2001) Asia Business Law Review 3, 2.
233. McCahery J and Vermeulen EM, 'Conflict Resolution and the Role of Courts: Empirical Study' in Neville M and Sørensen KE (eds), *Company Law and SMEs* (Thomson Reuters 2010), 228.
234. Velasco J, 165.
235. Muller MH (ed.), *Corporate Law in the Netherlands* (3rd edn, Wolters Kluwer Law & Business 2013), 139.
236. Hollander C and Salzedo S, 14.
237. Hopt KJ, 'Conflict of Interest, Secrecy and Insider Information of Directors, A Comparative Analysis' (2013) 10 European Company and Financial Law Review 167, 168.
238. Gerner-Beuerle C, Paech P and Schuster EP, 110.
239. *Ibid.*, 112.
240. *Ibid.*, 78, 110.
241. AktG, Article 93(2).

In Poland, unlike in Germany but similarly to the Netherlands, the business judgment rule is not established in statute.[242] As a result, managers in Polish companies are required to act with due care,[243] yet unlike in German public companies[244] they are not regarded as being in a 'safe harbour' of decision-making. Nevertheless, this does not diminish the fact that managers enjoy discretion when exercising their powers.[245] However, in order for a director to be held liable under Polish law, breach of the duty of care must be accompanied by a breach of a specific statutory or contractual obligation.[246]

Unlike the duty of care, the purpose of the duty of loyalty is to prevent conflicts of interest.[247] A director acting in breach of the duty of care is not necessarily in breach of the duty of loyalty, given that inefficient business decisions by directors are not always made on purpose. Such decisions may stem from poor qualification or simply planning mistakes on the directors' part. In addition, the duty of care does not affect management's duty to preserve confidentiality of information. That duty, where it is not defined in company law, is generally viewed as a part of the duty of loyalty.[248] Even if the obligation of confidentiality is enshrined in statute close to provisions on the duty of care, as in Germany,[249] doctrine nonetheless tends to include this duty in the scope of the broad notion of the duty of loyalty.[250]

What the duty of care and the duty of loyalty have in common is their 'standard' nature. Both duties are evaluated *ex post* by an independent authority.[251] Interestingly, the link between the duty of care and the duty of loyalty can be observed in the phrasing of the business judgment rule for public companies in German statute and its enforcement in practice. One of the necessary preconditions for a director of a German company to enjoy the business judgment rule is the absence of any conflict of interest:[252] a director in breach of the duty of loyalty cannot benefit from the business judgment rule.

242. Oplustil K and Radwan A, 'Company Law in Poland: Between Autonomous Development and Legal Transplants' in Jessel-Holst C, Kulms R and Trunk A (eds), *Private Law in Eastern Europe* (2010), available at: https://ssrn.com/abstract=3079494, accessed on 28 December 2018, 483.
243. KSH, Articles 293(2), 483(2).
244. AktG, Article 93(1).
245. Radwan A and Regucki T, 'The Possibilities for and Barriers to Sustainable Companies in Polish Company Law' 11 International and Comparative Corporate Law Journal, Forthcoming; University of Oslo Faculty of Law Research Paper No. 2012-32, available at: http://ssrn.com/abstract=2159217 https://ssrn.com/abstract=2159217, accessed on 6 December 2018, 20.
246. *Ibid.*, 28.
247. Hopt KJ, 'Conflict of Interest, Secrecy and Insider Information of Directors, A Comparative Analysis', 168, 175.
248. *Ibid.*, 183.
249. AktG, Article 93(1), sentence 3, Article 116.
250. Gerner-Beuerle C, Paech P and Schuster EP, A331.
251. Goshen Z, 'The Efficiency of Controlling Corporate Self-Dealing: Theory Meets Reality' (2003) 91 California Law Review 393, 403.
252. Gerner-Beuerle C, Paech P and Schuster EP, 115; AktG, Article 93(1), sentence 2.

[C] Managerial Duty of Loyalty

Among the duties described above, the duty of loyalty occupies a special place, sometimes controversially referred to as the only actual fiduciary duty.[253] This duty is most notable for this element of this research for the fact that it concerns situations involving a conflict of interest.[254] The idea on which this duty is based is easy to perceive: it merely requires the trustee to act loyally, i.e. not to place his or her own interests or the interests of third parties above the interest of the principal in relationships involving the latter. A straightforward example is a commercial transaction between a director and a company managed by that director. For this kind of transaction, the duty of loyalty is fulfilled by acting on the arm's-length conditions, meaning that the director, acting for the company, would agree on the same terms for this transaction with third parties as with himself. This is a standard requirement, which is sometimes supplemented by disclosure, approval and other obligations for the director. However, that is more an issue of strategy as determined by national company law, which is discussed in detail in the chapters that follow.

It is beyond doubt that managers are substantially regarded as agents in corporate relationships.[255] The problem lies in the fact that it is not always clear who the principal is. The easiest and the most tenable solution would be to consider the company as the principal (beneficiary).[256] As a result, the agent would be required to act in its best interests, similarly to the German concept of 'the best interests of the enterprise' (*Unternehmensinteresse*).[257] While this solution could prove effective if introduced into legislation, due to its apparent simplicity,[258] for practical reasons it needs further clarification.[259] First, companies are not black boxes, as classical economic theory teaches. They are the products of the reconciled interests of different corporate constituencies. Second, the issue of multiple loyalties rears its head if a single person performs managerial duties for various different companies, and as such has various

253. Bruner CM, 'Is the Corporate Director's Duty of Care a Fiduciary Duty: Does It Matter' (2013) 48 Wake Forest Law Review 1027; Miller PB, 'Justifying Fiduciary Duties' (2013) 58 McGill Law Journal/Revue de droit de McGill 969.
254. Pistor K and Xu C, 'Fiduciary Duty in Transitional Civil Law Jurisdictions' in Milhaupt CJ (ed.), *Global Markets, Domestic Institutions: Corporate Law and Governance in a New Era of Cross-Border Deals* (Columbia University Press 2012), 77.
255. Brudney V, 'Contract and Fiduciary Duty in Corporate Law' (1997) 38 Boston College Law Review 595, 611.
256. Andersen PK, 'Directors' Duties – and the European Model Company Act' in Neville M and Sørensen KE (eds), *Company Law and SMEs* (Thomson Reuters 2010), 78.
257. Saenger I, 'Conflicts of Interest of Supervisory Board Members in a German Stock Corporation and the Demand for Their Independence: An Investigation in the Context of the Current Corporate Governance Discussion' (2005) 1 Corporate Governance Law Review 147, 154.
258. In some cases it has already been put into law, for example in Article 2:129(5), 2:239(5) of the BW and Article 92 of the CCU.
259. The concept of a company's interests is certainly not devoid of practical content, as shown by the application of the 'ultra vires' doctrine in the Netherlands; namely, the courts will apply remedies for any conduct that is incompatible with the company's object if that conduct is not in the company's interests (*see* Muller MH (ed.), 44).

different principals.[260] Third, other internal and external stakeholders, besides shareholders, whose interests need to be considered, including employees, suppliers, customers, banks, the government and various 'pressure groups'.[261] By considering the interests of external stakeholders, including the environment and social concerns, management internalizes those interests and shifts the issue to the theory of corporate social responsibility.[262]

It can be difficult to understand which theory is more favoured in Europe: shareholder or stakeholder. On the one hand, European institutions and government representatives have frequently been enthusiastic about taking steps towards developing corporate social responsibility.[263] The dominance of stakeholder theory has been established in both Germany and the Netherlands.[264] In Germany, since 2001, pension funds have been required to report on how they integrate social and environmental factors into their investment decisions.[265] In the Netherlands, companies are encouraged to submit financial reports that also contain social and environmental information.[266] While the Polish KSH does not expressly favour any theory,[267] incidental court decisions and internal corporate documents (Polish Petroleum and Gas Mining) exist that consider the interests of various stakeholders.[268] As Anna Peters argues, a growing trend can be discerned in corporate governance and other fields of knowledge towards an expansion of fiduciary obligations to extend to a broad circle of principals.[269] For instance, in the *ASMI* case, the Enterprise Court in the Netherlands ruled in favour of activist shareholders, who claimed that the company's governance structure was outdated and defensive, in that directors were appointed based on the exclusive decision of the supervisory board, which could be overturned only by more than two-thirds of the shareholder vote. The Enterprise Court, in enquiry proceedings, ordered an investigation into the policies and affairs of ASMI. The Enterprise Court's decision was annulled by the Dutch Supreme Court, which emphasized the board's role to serve 'the interests of the company and of the enterprise it ran' and that this

---

260. Hopt KJ, 'Trusteeship and Conflicts of Interest in Corporate, Banking, and Agency Law: Toward Common Legal Principles for Intermediaries in the Modern Service-Oriented Society', 61.
261. Du Plessis JJ and others, *Principles of Contemporary Corporate Governance* (Cambridge University Press 2014), 32.
262. Sjåfjell B and Anker-Sørensen L, 'Directors' Duties and Corporate Social Responsibility (CSR)' in Birkmose HS, Neville M and Sørensen KE (eds), *Boards of Directors in European Companies: Reshaping and Harmonising Their Organisation and Duties* (Wolters Kluwer Law & Business 2013), 156.
263. Lux J, Skadegard Thorsen S and Meisling A, 'The European Initiatives' in Mullerat R (ed.), *Corporate Social Responsibility: The Corporate Governance of the 21st Century* (Kluwer Law International 2005), 279.
264. Gerner-Beuerle C, Paech P and Schuster EP, 68, 71.
265. *Ibid.*, 294-295.
266. Goldsmith J, 'Lawyers' Responsibility for Advising on Corporate Social Responsibility' in Mullerat R (ed.), *Corporate Social Responsibility: The Corporate Governance of the 21st Century* (Kluwer Law International 2005), 422.
267. Some sources argue that, of the various stakeholder groups, shareholders have the greatest influence on companies' interests in Poland (Gerner-Beuerle C, Paech P and Schuster EP, 72).
268. Radwan A and Regucki T, 'The Possibilities for and Barriers to Sustainable Companies in Polish Company Law', 18-19.
269. Peters A, 16.

involved the interests of all stakeholders, including the shareholders.[270] However, this does not imply that the board is obligated to seek the prior approval of the general meeting for strategic decisions that belong to the board's competence. The Dutch Supreme Court's judgment indicates an apparent adherence to the stakeholder theory. In the more recent case of *PPG/Akzo Nobel*, it was the Enterprise Court of Amsterdam that favoured the stakeholder theory. The Court did not agree with the minority shareholders, who wanted PPG to take over the (shares in) AkzoNobel, and the Court did not award their request for measures against the Chairman of the company's supervisory board, who resisted against the takeover. In its reasoning, the Court referred, among other considerations, to the interests of the company and all its stakeholders.[271]

The Anglo-American approach, conversely, has traditionally been one of 'shareholderism'.[272] This means that a company's shareholders are principals for its management, and so management is entrusted with the goal of maximizing share value. This theory is not commonly ascribed to the jurisdictions of Continental Europe. However, some flashes of this theory appear in European corporate law and governance in its current state. As Guido Ferrarini acknowledges, the concept suddenly emerged in Germany, traditionally referred to as a 'stakeholder' society, where the idea has now become fashionable and to a certain extent integrated into the corporate culture. To illustrate this, the author notes that listed companies have established investor relations departments and that the services of US investment banks are overwhelmingly used.[273] Yet these facts should not be interpreted as a complete shift from a stakeholder to a shareholder theory. The issue should not be characterized purely in terms of black or white. This is also true for common law jurisdictions, regarded as jurisdictions where the shareholder theory prevails, as illustrated by the UK calling for a broader consideration of societal concerns.[274] As Beate Sjåfjell states,

270. *ASMI, Decision of 9 July 2010* NJ 2010/544 (Supreme Court of the Netherlands).
271. *PPG/Akzo Nobel, Decision of 29 May 2017* JIN 2017/116 (Enterprise Court of Amsterdam). *See* R.A. Wolf, Overnameperikelen: Elliot International L.P. c.s., AkzoNobel en PPG Industries. Een analyse, TvOB 2017-5, 164.
272. The origins of shareholder theory are found in the very first part of Adolf Berle's classic article that starts with the words, *It is the thesis of this essay that all powers granted to a corporation or to the management of a corporation, or to any group within the corporation, whether derived from statute or charter or both, are necessarily and at all times exercisable only for the ratable benefit of all the shareholders …* (Berle AA, 'Corporate Powers as Powers in Trust', 1049). Even though Berle subsequently developed his approach in a direction where the company's interests further national social welfare policy (Bratton WW and Wachter ML, 118), refuting his purely shareholder stance, some scholars nonetheless regard his approach as being confined to the shareholder primacy model. Edwin Dodd, who criticized Berle for his words, preferring to consider the enterprise as *an economic institution which has a social service as well as profit-making function* (Dodd EM, 'For Whom Are Corporate Managers Trustees?' (1932) 45 Harvard Law Review 1145, 1148), is today exaggeratedly regarded as a supporter of a corporate social responsibility approach as a variation on stakeholder theory.
273. Ferrarini G, 'Shareholder Value and the Modernization of European Corporate Law' in Hopt KJ and Wymeersch E (eds), *Capital Markets and Company Law* (Oxford University Press 2003), 229-230.
274. Villiers C, 'Mapping Paper: Sustainable Companies UK Report' University of Oslo Faculty of Law Research Paper No. 2013-16 (17 June 2013), available at SSRN: https://ssrn.com/abstract =2280350, accessed on 7 December 2018.

company law across jurisdictions allows boards to implement legal externalities beyond compliance, at least as far as the business case argument allows.[275] In many countries around the world, therefore, economic players now tend to pay more attention to environmental and societal issues and regard them as part of socially and economically responsible behaviour.

What the stakeholder theory implies for conflicts of interest in corporate governance is a blurring of the line between due and undue interests pursued by managers.[276] An 'undue' interest can also be described as a secondary interest, i.e. not an interest that the agent is obliged to pursue, but, e.g., the agent's own interest, based on personal or financial relationships.[277] These are the 'grey zones of reality'[278] for conflict rules, with an ambiguity that is impossible to eliminate entirely for separating legitimate interests from illegitimate ones.

Apart from purely stakeholder and shareholder approaches, a 'third way' has been proposed for dealing with the beneficiary issue, which has been termed 'Long Governance'.[279] What does this view add to the previously expressed thoughts on shareholder or stakeholder primacy, and to whom exactly do the directors owe their duties? Long Governance essentially suggests that companies have several classes of shareholders. The interests of those who pursue long-term goals should be prioritized over those of the short-term, *deal driven merger arbitrageurs*, in the terminology of takeover law.[280] In spite of the fact that this approach seemingly favours shareholders as a class, it essentially creates a solid base for protecting various different company constituencies whose interests can be aligned by their motivation of sustainably developing the company. The reasoning behind this theory makes particular sense in the situation where a publicly held company, with a dispersed ownership of shareholders that have diverging interests, faces a takeover. It is very doubtful in that scenario that all shareholders will be facing in the same direction.[281] In fact, this theory is directed more at the company as basically the principal beneficiary for its managers, and so it provides for a more realistic implementation than the idealistic stakeholder theory or the value-driven shareholder theory. The suggested approach is similar to the enlightened shareholder value approach[282] and could correlate with the idea of the

275. Sjåfjell B, 'Achieving Corporate Sustainability: What Is the Role of the Shareholder?' in Birkmose HS (ed.), *Shareholders' Duties* (Wolters Kluwer 2017), 383.
276. Peters A, 19.
277. *Ibid.*, 20.
278. Friedberg E, 'Conflict of Interest from the Perspective of the Sociology of Organised Action' in Peters A and Handschin L (eds), *Conflict of Interest in Global, Public and Corporate Governance* (Cambridge University Press 2012), 50.
279. Masouros PE, *Corporate Law and Economic Stagnation: How Shareholder Value and Short-Termism Contribute to the Decline of the Western Economies* (Eleven International Publishing 2013), 271.
280. *Ibid.*, 278.
281. *Ibid.*, 279.
282. Ho VH, 'Enlightened Shareholder Value: Corporate Governance Beyond the Shareholder-Stakeholder Divide' (2010) 36 Journal of Corporation Law 59.

Constitutional Court of Ukraine that a company's interests are no more than the sum of the interests of all its shareholders.[283]

The idea of Long Governance has found its implementation in the recently revised Dutch CGC, most recently amended on 8 December 2016. The main goal was broadly to revise the Code to reflect the long-term value creation approach, as opposed to the short-term goals more commonly associated with detrimental events in corporate governance, including accounting fraud, corruption and cartel activity.[284] It further evidences that the long-term value creation approach and the stakeholder theory are not contradictory, but mutually complementary. This approach was further confirmed in the recent decision of the Enterprise Court of Amsterdam, in the dispute between Akzo Nobel and its shareholder PPG,[285] where the court ruled in favour of the company rather than its shareholder. In its decision, the court made explicit reference to the CGC and showed its preference for the stakeholder model by requiring that the interests of all stakeholders, including shareholders, must be taken into account. This is also in line with earlier case law in the Netherlands.[286]

[D] The Duty of Loyalty for Shareholders

Shareholders can act solely in that capacity by voting at general meetings and by exercising other rights of shareholders. In closed companies, it is moreover not uncommon for a shareholder to be appointed as a director. This then means that the shareholder owes the company a director's duty of loyalty. However, it remains controversial whether a shareholder who is not a director also has a fiduciary duty to the company. The issue causes less dispute for partnerships, where fiduciary duties most often arise, as opposed to companies. The nature of partnerships presupposes that the partners, unlike shareholders in a company, work closely together and can be held liable for their acts towards the partnership. This creates a duty of loyalty.[287] For companies, conversely, this is not a usual scenario, especially publicly held companies, where shareholders are often no more than passive investors unwilling to participate in corporate affairs or influence the decision-making. Those types of shareholders usually prefer to exercise cash flow rights either by claiming dividends or by reselling shares to capitalize on significant differences between the purchase price and the selling price. These shareholders contrast with shareholders with the capability to exercise control over the company and, consequently, to decide its destiny along with the destiny of shares belonging to the minority shareholders. Burdening controlling shareholders

283. *Decision of 1 December 2004 No. 18-pn/2004 (case about legitimate interest)* Case No. 1-10/2004, Ofitsiynyi visnyk Ukrayiny of 31 December 2004, No. 50, p. 67, St. 3288 (Constitutional Court of Ukraine).
284. *Dutch Corporate Governance Code Has Been Updated* (Monitoring Commissie Corporate Governance Code 8 December 2016).
285. *PPG/Akzo Nobel, Decision of 29 May 2017* JIN 2017/116 (Enterprise Court of Amsterdam).
286. *ABN AMRO, Decision of 13 July 2007* R07/102HR (OK 137) (Supreme Court of the Netherlands).
287. Sørensen KE, 'Duty of Loyalty of Shareholders: A Possible Remedy for Conflicts in SMEs?' in Neville M and Sørensen KE (eds), *Company Law and SMEs* (Thomson Reuters 2010), 129.

with a duty of loyalty would then play a role in protection against opportunistic behaviour from both managers and shareholders with large blocks of shares.

Opponents of the idea to increase the scope of shareholders' duties by adding the duty of loyalty admit that this approach could be counterproductive, given that shareholders should concentrate on monitoring, rather than productivity.[288] This reasoning proceeds with the argument that companies consisting of several shareholders use other devices to prevent opportunistic behaviour, namely renegotiation and reputational incentives. In general, as already noted above, the duty of loyalty is more common in partnerships, where partners do not remain hidden behind the corporate veil like shareholders in companies do. It could also be argued that for other business forms, including publicly held companies, it is less appropriate to have the same level of fiduciarity in relationships between shareholders.

Legislation in the EU is silent on this issue: no explicit rule exists that imposes a duty of loyalty towards the company on its shareholders. This area has not been harmonized, and the Court of Justice of the EU has not expressed any opinion on the matter. Governing this issue falls within the ambit of national company laws of the EU Member States. An example is Germany, where the duty of loyalty of shareholders has been recognized in case law for an extensive list of corporate forms, including private companies (GmbH) and public companies (AG).[289] The extent to which shareholders owe that duty and to which they could then be held liable depends on the structure of the company and the level of participation.[290] Historically, shareholders in Germany gradually became burdened with a duty of loyalty. It started with shareholders in closed companies (*ITT* decision, 1975), through shareholders in public companies (*Linotype* decision, 1988), reaching the introduction of a duty of loyalty for minority shareholders possessing the capability to exercise veto rights and block decisions at a general meeting (*Girmes* decision, 1995).[291]

In the Netherlands, shareholders do not have a duty of loyalty as it exists in Germany. Rather, the status of shareholders is characterized by a degree of autonomy. No direct provision is made in statute for the concept of shareholder autonomy: it comes from case law, the Dutch CGC and legal doctrine.[292] It means that shareholders are expected to pursue their own best interest on the basis of their shareholdings. This freedom is not without limitation, however. The ramifications of shareholder conduct are set out in Article 2:8 of the BW, which describes the standards of reasonableness and fairness.[293] Those standards are not an exclusive feature of the law on legal persons: the principles of fairness and reasonableness have been employed in various

288. McCahery J and Vermeulen EM, 'Conflict Resolution and the Role of Courts: Empirical Study', 230.
289. Sørensen KE, 'Duty of Loyalty of Shareholders: A Possible Remedy for Conflicts in SMEs?', 130.
290. Beinert D, Burmeister F and Tries H-J, *Mergers and Acquisitions in Germany* (Verlag C.H. Beck München 2009), 21.
291. Pistor K and Xu C, 95-96.
292. Kemp B, 'Aandeelhoudersverantwoordelijkheid: de Positieve Rol van de Aandeelhouder en Aandeelhoudersvergadering = Shareholder Responsibility: the Position and Role of the Shareholder and the Shareholders Meeting' (Dphil thesis, Wolters Kluwer 2015), 430.
293. BW, Article 2:8.

spheres, including contract law and property law,[294] and in general are attributed to Dutch legal thinking.[295] Besides the standards of reasonableness and fairness in relationships between shareholders and their company, Bastiaan Kemp outlines one additional standard: abuse of power.[296] He argues that reasonableness and fairness are positive in nature, and oblige shareholders to 'act' in a particular way, whereas abuse of power has a negative content and forces them to 'not act'. At the same time, provisions on abuse of power are similarly contained in Article 2:8, specifically in subsection 2, and where it is linked to the principles of reasonableness and fairness as outlined in the BW. The effect of Article 2:8(2) is far-reaching, as these standards can be applied by rendering law, common practice, articles of association, internal regulations or resolutions inapplicable if they are incompatible with the principles of fairness and reasonableness. Decisions of corporate bodies that are unacceptable according to standards of reasonableness and fairness are voidable under Article 2:15 of the BW.[297]

The standards of the reasonableness and fairness are by themselves vague and require further explanation. As Bastiaan Kemp clarifies, three possible scenarios exist where shareholder conduct runs contrary to the standards of reasonableness and fairness: *(a) where the conduct is intolerably disproportionate to the interest of a third party relative to the shareholder's interest, (b) where a power is exercised by the shareholder for no other purpose than to harm the interest of another stakeholder, and (c) where a shareholder exercises power for any purpose other than the purpose for which it was granted.*[298] For the first of these criteria for measuring conduct, various circumstances may be relevant, depending on the specific case,[299] including the position of the person concerned, the sector where the activities take place, the nature of the interests involved, the previous behaviour shown by the shareholder and the severity of the disadvantage.[300] These circumstances can be helpful in balancing the interests of shareholders and their company, not to mention the interests of other stakeholders. So, although the company is not strictly speaking a beneficiary for shareholders, they are not permitted to disregard its interest by acting contrary to the standards of reasonableness and fairness.

In Ukrainian company law, the duty of loyalty of shareholders does not take the same form as in Germany, for instance. Ukrainian company law does not use standards to impose a duty of loyalty: rather, it uses rules to address types of conflicted transactions. The JSC Law of Ukraine includes rules for shareholders' conflicts of interest, namely a procedure for approval of transactions between the company and

294. *Ibid.*, Articles 3:12, 6:2.
295. Cartwright J, 'Redelijkheid en billijkheid: a view from English law' (2016) 30 BW-krant Jaarboek 39.
296. Kemp B, 432.
297. Schutte T, 'Good Governance: Reasonableness and Fairness of Directors and Supervisors' Newsletter, as of 27 August 2015, available at: https://www.russell.nl/Uploaded_files/Zelf/Publicaties/good-governance-reasonableness-and-fairness-of-directors-and-supervisors6588a8pdf, accessed on 30 August 2017.
298. Kemp B, 432.
299. *Ibid.*, 433.
300. Schutte T.

any shareholder owning 25% or more of the shares or an affiliated person (for a detailed analysis of affiliated persons, *see* Chapter 3).[301] This covers only one part of the 'conflict of interest' concept, leaving all other types of conflict unaddressed: a prohibition on competing with the company and business opportunities (*see* section §2.03). Additionally, procedural safeguards established by the mentioned provisions of the Law do not cover transactions where the shareholder has an interest, but to which a company where more than 25% of share capital belongs to that shareholder is not a party – e.g., transactions between a shareholder's subsidiary and a company's competitor. In that situation, the transaction could run contrary to the company's interests. According to the context of the Law, only the company is regarded as a beneficiary here, and the interests of other stakeholders are respected as long as they align with the interest of the company in this regard. However, it is not the court's role to assess whether the company's interests have been violated on the basis of the JSC Law of Ukraine.

A similar regulation is contained in the LLC Law of Ukraine, with one significant difference: the approval requirements apply if all the company's shareholders have agreed to include them in the articles of association.[302] Interestingly, the 'conflict of interest' concept as defined in this Law is not in any way related to shareholder duties: only company officers can be affected by the 'conflict of interest' rules.[303] In other words, conflict of interest is interpreted in a narrow sense in this Law, limiting shareholder duties to optional norms about approval of transactions with interest where the shareholder holds at least 20% of the share capital or an affiliated person is the counterparty.

Therefore, even if its introduction in Ukrainian law is deemed useful, the duty of loyalty of shareholders is limited in its scope by the tenets of procedural requirements established for approval of transactions with interest in Ukrainian public and private companies where the company is regarded as a beneficiary.[304]

§2.03 REGULATORY RESPONSES TO CONFLICTS OF INTEREST

[A] Conflicts of Interest and EU Law

To identify and describe what types of conflicts of interest exist, it is necessary first to address the relevant provisions of hard and soft law directed at preventing these conflicts from occurring and, where they cannot be prevented, from causing negative consequences.

301. JSC Law of Ukraine, Article 71.
302. LLC Law of Ukraine, Article 45(3).
303. *Ibid.*, Article 42(3).
304. When the Draft LLC Law of Ukraine was submitted to Ukraine's Parliament in May 2016, it included special provisions introducing procedural safeguards for dealing with RPTs, similar to those set forth in the JSC Law of Ukraine. At a later stage, however, those provisions were substituted by a modest set of rules for conflicts of interests (Draft Law of Ukraine 'On Limited and Additional Liability Companies' [Proekt Zakonu Ukrayiny 'Pro tovatystva z obmezhenoyu ta dodatkovoyu vidpovidalnistiu']).

At the EU level, several instruments can be identified that deal with conflicts of interest. The first is the results of the successful harmonization, imposing a variety of obligations on Member States. One example is the Takeover Directive.[305] While this Directive does not in fact use the words 'conflict of interest', conflicts sometimes nevertheless arise as management of an issuer might possess information about the price of shares or other important details that could be used for his own benefit, rather than the company's. One of the explicit concerns that the Directive addresses is the possibility of bid frustration by the offeree's board.[306] The latter may obviously be influenced by the decisions of new shareholders who would gain control over the company as a result of a successful bid. Among other rules, the Directive requires that all decisions by the offeree company's board directed at bid frustration, except to seek alternative bids, should be approved by the offeree's general meeting of shareholders.[307] At the same time, while preventing the offeree's board from taking steps to block the bid, the Directive also obliges the board to prepare and make public a document about its opinion of the bid and the reasons on which that opinion is based, which must then be delivered to the employees' representatives.[308] Therefore, while bid frustration might run contrary to the interest of shareholders and the company, the board's document with its opinion of the bid by itself does not constitute frustration, and although it may contain negative, conflict-related and even unreliable information about the offeror, it is nonetheless better than nothing. If considered critically and with due understanding of the various interests involved, this document can give food for thought about whose interests the board is protecting. Still, it could also exert a negative influence on stakeholders, and overreliance on it is not recommended.

In order to improve corporate governance, which had been heavily shaken by a series of widely publicized corporate scandals,[309] the EU has also stepped in with several recommendations containing provisions aimed at dealing with conflicts of interest of directors. First, according to Commission Recommendation 2004/913/EC,[310] the remuneration policy must be disclosed through a special statement. This statement may be a part of either a remuneration report or the company's annual report, which must then be published on the company's website.[311] Remuneration schemes may easily conceal conflicts of interest due to the possibility of excessive salaries of

305. Directive 2004/25/EC of the European Parliament and of the Council of 21 April 2004 on takeover bids [2004] OJ L 142/12, 30.4.2004.
306. *Ibid.*, recital 16.
307. *Ibid.*, Article 9(2).
308. *Ibid.*, Article 9(5).
309. For example, *see*: Cuomo F, Mallin C and Zattoni A, 'Corporate Governance Codes: A Review and Research Agenda' (2016) 24 Corporate Governance: An International Review 222, 228; Haisler P, 'Codes of Conduct as a Means of Regulation: With Point of Departure in Corporate Governance Debate' in Neville M and Sørensen KE (eds), *The Regulation of Companies* (Forlaget Thompson 2003), 146.
310. Commission Recommendation of 14 December 2004 fostering an appropriate regime for the remuneration of directors of listed companies [2004] OJ L 385/55, 29.12.2004.
311. *Ibid.*, sections II, 3.1.

directors. For this reason, the Recommendation establishes mechanisms for a shareholder vote on the remuneration of individual directors[312] and share-based remuneration.[313] This means that, even if the director's remuneration is higher than average, it must first have been approved by the shareholders.

Another Commission Recommendation, 2005/162/EC,[314] is not aimed at dealing primarily with remuneration issues, but in general seeks to improve corporate governance in listed companies having either supervisory directors (always present in two-tier jurisdictions such as Germany) or non-executive directors if no supervisory board is formed. The emphasis in this Recommendation is more on the proper composition of the board, the organization of board committees and the profile and appointment of directors, including requirements for independent directors. Independent directors are required to be free from any potential conflicts of interest, as they are regarded as independent only if they do not have any business, family or other relationships with the company, its controlling shareholder or either's management.[315] The Recommendation advises companies to have independent directors in those areas where the probability of conflicts of interest is especially high, namely on remuneration, nomination and audit committees.[316]

In 2009, these two Commission Recommendations were supplemented by the new provisions to increase the focus on conflicts of interest stemming from remuneration schemes.[317] The Commission went on to suggest that directors of companies that use share-based remuneration schemes should retain their shares at the end of their mandate[318] and that the shares should not vest rights for at least three years thereafter.[319] These measures are intended to ensure that directors exercise their powers in their company's interests.

[B] Conflicts of Interest and CGCs

Where the EU's harmonized measures meet national corporate laws, a special place is occupied by CGCs and their provisions dealing specifically with directors' conflicts of interest. Since the enactment of Directive 2006/46/EC[320] and following the provisions

312. *Ibid.*, sections III, 5.
313. *Ibid.*, sections IV, 6.
314. Commission Recommendation of 15 February 2005 on the role of non-executive or supervisory directors of listed companies and on the committees of the (supervisory) board [2005] OJ L 52/51, 25.2.2005.
315. *Ibid.*, sections III, 13.1.
316. *Ibid.*, sections II, 5.
317. Commission Recommendation of 30 April 2009 complementing Recommendations 2004/913/EC and 2005/162/EC as regards the regime for the remuneration of directors of listed companies [2009] OJ L 120/28, 15.5.2009.
318. *Ibid.*, recital 8.
319. *Ibid.*, sections II, 4.1.
320. Directive 2006/46/EC of the European Parliament and of the Council of 14 June 2006 amending Council Directives 78/660/EEC on the annual accounts of certain types of companies, 83/349/EEC on consolidated accounts, 86/635/EEC on the annual accounts and consolidated accounts of banks and other financial institutions and 91/674/EEC on the annual accounts and consolidated accounts of insurance undertakings [2006] OJ L 224, 16.8.2006, 1-7.

of the Accounting Directive, which replaced the Fourth and Seventh Council Directives,[321] EU Member States have been expected to adopt CGCs. According to the phrasing of the rule in the currently enforceable Accounting Directive, the management report of any legal entity whose securities have been admitted to trade on a regulated market of one of the Member States must include a corporate governance statement, with mandatory reference to a specific CGC. If the entity does not apply the CGC in its entirety, it must explain where it deviates from the CGC and why.[322] This provision is commonly referred to as the 'comply-or-explain' principle. This principle originated in the UK Cadbury Report 1992 and has since then spread to a number of judicial corporate arrangements across Europe.[323]

The Directives mentioned above have not made CGCs into binding legal acts, limiting the imperative nature of the codes by the comply-or-explain principle. It is for the individual Member States to decide what would be the best-case scenario for regulating corporate relationships, bearing in mind the comply-or-explain principle. Regulation has therefore taken various different paths and has become country-specific, stirring up a debate on how best to qualify the nature of CGCs. Among the works that place specific emphasis on the issue of codes is the book by Annika Galle, who identifies five possible judicial corporate governance arrangements for CGCs: (i) pure self-regulation; (ii) regulation supported by non-statutory norms; (iii) facilitation by statutory rules; (iv) regulation of self-regulation (meta-regulation); and (v) pure regulation.[324] The scale presented here shows how rules in CGCs can be combined with legislative provisions. The possibilities range from independent codes that are fully separated from legislation to a regulatory approach where the provisions of CGCs are also stipulated in legislation (the Sarbanes-Oxley Act, e.g.).[325] Having examined various jurisdictions, Galle claims that the Netherlands uses arrangement (iii): the comply-or-explain principle is embedded in legislation. The situation in Germany is closer to arrangement (iv), meanwhile.[326] In the first case, the legal basis for compliance with the Dutch CGC is enshrined in the BW, where a special government regulation is set forth to govern matters regarding compliance with the code.[327] In Germany, the AktG explicitly requires compliance with the German CGC, having effect for both the past and the future.[328]

The current version of the Dutch CGC, which came into force on 1 January 2017, devotes one chapter to preventing conflicts of interest arising in management and/or supervisory board situations (principle 2.7). The previous version of the Code contained two separate sections on conflicts of interests, for management and for the

321. Directive 2013/34/EU of the European Parliament and of the Council of 26 June 2013 on the annual financial statements, consolidated financial statements and related reports of certain types of undertakings [2013] OJ L 182, 29.6.2013, Article 20.
322. *Ibid.*, Article 20(1)(b).
323. Galle JGCM, *Consensus on the Comply or Explain Principle Within the EU Corporate Governance Framework: Legal and Empirical Research* (Kluwer 2012), 90.
324. *Ibid.*, 88.
325. *Ibid.*, 89.
326. *Ibid.*, 92.
327. BW, Article 2:391(5).
328. AktG, Article 161(1).

supervisory board.[329] Among other differences, the new version vests more power in the supervisory board and increases the focus on the majority of shareholders as being subject to conflicts of interest. The types of conflicts in the new CGC are basically the same as in the previous version: (a) competing with the company; (b) demanding or receiving substantial gifts from the company; (c) taking unjustified advantage of third parties at the company's expense; (d) taking advantage of business opportunities falling to the company.[330] All these conflicts are unacceptable. In addition, the CGC contains a number of clauses establishing rules for RPTs: it defines the obligations of related parties (members of the management or supervisory boards) to disclose conflicts of interest,[331] the requirements for the terms of RPTs and their approval.[332] A further section of the CGC is devoted to a specific category of RPTs: loans, guarantees and similar arrangement that place the company in a vulnerable position.[333]

An examination of the version of the German CGC, which was most recently updated on 7 February 2017[334] quickly reveals that, similar to the previous version of the Dutch CGC, it separates conflicts of interest into conflicts of management and of the supervisory board, although in essence these conflicts have much in common. According to the 2017 German CGC, both managers and supervisors are prohibited from pursuing their personal interests in their positions and from exploiting any business opportunities that fall to the company.[335] Interestingly, only managers are subject to restrictions on competing with the company, demanding or receiving unlawful advantages from third parties in connection with their work and granting unlawful advantages to third parties; members of the supervisory board are not covered by this rule.[336] Transactions between managers, their related parties and the company must conform to standards customary in the sector. If sufficiently important, these transactions, together with managers' sideline activities and supervisors' service agreements or work contracts with the company, require approval from the supervisory board.[337] The new draft 2020 version of the German CGC devotes a separate section to conflicts of interest of members of both the management board and the supervisory board.[338] The new CGC preserves the prohibition on exploiting business opportunities, the non-compete clause for managers and the recommendation to make

329. Dutch Corporate Governance Code, as revised on 8 December 2016; the first edition of the Dutch Corporate Governance Code was drafted by the Tabaksblat Committee in 2003 and was later revised in December 2008.
330. Dutch CGC, section 2.7.1 Preventing conflicts of interest.
331. *Ibid.*, section 2.7.3 Reporting.
332. *Ibid.*, sections 2.7.4 Accountability regarding transactions: management board and supervisory board members, 2.7.5 Accountability regarding transactions: major shareholders.
333. *Ibid.*, section 2.7.6 Personal loans.
334. German Corporate Governance Code (Deutscher Corporate Governance Kodex), as amended on 7 February 2017; the Code was initially adopted in February 2002, but has since undergone revisions almost annually.
335. *Ibid.*, sections 4.3.1, 5.5.1.
336. *Ibid.*, sections 4.3.1, 4.3.2.
337. *Ibid.*, sections 4.3.3, 4.3.4, 5.5.4.
338. German draft Corporate Governance Code (Deutscher Corporate Governance Kodex) 2020, section E.

sideline activities subject to the supervisory board's approval.[339] On the issue of RPTs, the new CGC merely refers to the applicable legal regulations, rather than giving specific rules.[340]

While the CGCs in Germany and the Netherlands exist as separate instruments that are not necessarily attached to a particular institution or authority, besides the monitoring commissions that revise the codes, in Poland[341] similar rules are in the province of the Warsaw Stock Exchange, where the recent recast of the WSE Best Practice has been in effect since 1 January 2016.[342] Chapter V of the WSE Best Practice deals with conflicts of interest, naming only one type of conflict: benefits received by management or the supervisory board that could jeopardize their impartiality or objectivity in making decisions or reflect unfavourably on the assessment of the independence of their opinions or judgments.[343] The prohibitions described above, restricting competition with the company and the use of business opportunities, are not included, although arguably the broad interpretation of the concept of a conflict of interest could be said to implicitly refer to these types of conflicts as well. Other types of conflicts must be specified in the company's articles of association.[344] What the WSE Best Practice provides in return for a modest list of conflict types are various additional *ex ante* and *ex post* safeguards against conflicting behaviour. In particular, it contains the approval requirement for transactions between the company and its shareholders or related parties, with an assessment of equal treatment of shareholders and the interest of the company,[345] the duty of managers and supervisors to refrain from voting on resolutions that give rise to conflicts of interest[346] and the right of managers and supervisors to request that minutes of the management board or supervisory board show their position on the existence of a conflict.[347]

Although the title of the WSE Best Practice does not include the word 'code', nothing precludes this document from being treated as a CGC: both the authors of the WSE Best Practice and academic scholars interpret it as the basis for the comply-or-explain principle in light of relevant EU law.[348]

339. *Ibid.*, section E, Principle 19, recommendation E.3.
340. *Ibid.*, section A, Principle 6.
341. Poland had a draft Gdansk CGC, prepared by the Gdansk Institute for Market Economic in June 2002. However, it has not received any further impetus for state-wide use (Dzierzanowski M and Tamowicz P, 'The Corporate Governance Code for Polish Listed Companies (The Gdańsk Code)' (The Polish Corporate Governance Forum and The Gdansk Institute for Market Economics 15 June 2002)).
342. Best Practice of GPW Listed Companies 2016, as approved by the Exchange Supervisory Board on 13 October 2015.
343. *Ibid.*, section V.Z.3.
344. *Ibid.*, section V.Z.6.
345. *Ibid.*, section V.Z.1, V.Z.5.
346. *Ibid.*, section V.Z.2.
347. *Ibid.*, section V.Z.4.
348. *Ibid.*, Introduction; Mucha A, 'Dobre Praktyki Spółek Notowanych na GPW 2016 – kontynuacja czy rewolucja? (Best Practice for Warsaw Stock Exchange Listed Companies 2016–Continuation or Revolution?)' Allerhand Working Papers, 3 March 2016, available at SSRN: https://papers.ssrn.com/sol3/paperscfm?abstract_id = 2741585, accessed on 6 December 2018, 5.

[C] Conflicts of Interest in the Principles of Corporate Governance in Ukraine

In contrast to the European countries discussed above, Ukraine does not possess a supranational legal basis at the EU level for introducing a CGC. The Accounting Directive is not included in an annex to the EU-Ukraine Association Agreement, as it did not exist when the Agreement was being drafted. Its predecessor, the Fourth Council Directive,[349] was stipulated in the EU-Ukraine Association Agreement without the future changes introduced by Directive 2006/46/EC. Therefore, formally Ukraine has no international obligation to adopt a CGC, despite some debate on this issue. Critics who found it unnecessary to adopt a national CGC referred to the Principles of Corporate Governance adopted by the decision of the NSSMC. Those Principles are similar in content and scope (listed public companies) to the CGCs of the EU's Member States. At the same time, they essentially constitute an administrative act that is advisory in nature.[350]

Although the Principles of Corporate Governance originate from the administrative act, their usage is more limited than that of CGCs in the EU. The Principles were not adopted to implement the various EU Directives, but rather to follow paragraph 29 of Article 7 of the Law of Ukraine 'On State Regulation of Securities Market in Ukraine', which outlines the competence of the NSSMC.[351] That Law does not contain a 'comply-or-explain' rule, and the Principles add further ambiguity by referring to this rule as an alternative to the voluntary application of the Principles.[352]

In addition to the ambiguous wording of the Principles, a statutory comply-or-explain rule has recently been envisaged.[353] Issuers of securities, meaning public companies, are now obliged to prepare their annual reports in compliance either with their own CGC or with the CGC of a stock exchange or another code the company has voluntarily agreed to apply.[354] In other words, the comply-or-explain rule, having been

349. Fourth Council Directive 78/660/EEC of 25 July 1978 based on Article 54(3)(g) of the Treaty on the annual accounts of certain types of companies [1978] OJ EC L 222/11, 14.8.78.
350. Principles of Corporate Governance, approved by the Decision of the National Securities and Stock Market Commission of Ukraine of 22 July 2014, No. 955 [Pryntsypy korporatyvnoho upravlinnia, zatverdzheni rishenniam Natsionalnoyi komisii z tsinnykh paperiv ta fondovoho rynku vid 22 lypnia 2014 roku No. 955], available at: http://www.nssmc.gov.ua/law/18922, accessed on 28 December 2018.
351. Law of Ukraine 'On State Regulation of Securities Market in Ukraine' [Zakon Ukrayiny 'Pro derzhavne reguliuvannia rynku tsinnykh paperiv v Ukrayini'] of 30 October 1996, published in Vidomosti Verkhovnoyi Rady Ukrayiny, 1996, No. 51, St. 292.
352. Principles of Corporate Governance, approved by the Decision of the National Securities and Stock Market Commission of Ukraine of 22 July 2014, No. 955 [Pryntsypy korporatyvnoho upravlinnia, zatverdzheni rishenniam Natsionalnoyi komisii z tsinnykh paperiv ta fondovoho rynku vid 22 lypnia 2014 roku No. 955], section I.6.
353. Law of Ukraine 'On Amending Certain Legislative Acts on the Simplification of Business and Attraction of Investments by the Issuers of Securities' [Zakon Ukrayiny 'Pro vnesennia zmin do deyakykh zakonodavchykh aktiv Ukrayiny schodo sproschennia vedennia biznesu ta zaluchennia investytsiy emitentamy tsinnykh paperiv'], Chapter 1, paragraph 15, subparagraph 15.
354. Law of Ukraine 'On Securities and Stock Market' [Zakon Ukrayiny 'Pro tsinni papery ta fondovyi rynok'] of 23 February 2006, published in Vidomosti Verkhovnoyi Rady Ukrayiny, 2006, No. 31, St. 268, Article 40(3).

in force in the EU for some time, has only recently entered the legislative realm in Ukraine. The absence of a culture of applying this principle, coupled with the vague provisions of the Principles in practice, has made public companies reluctant to comply.

Turning to the issue of enforcement of CGCs, sufficient evidence can be found that courts in Germany and the Netherlands have applied their countries' CGCs as sources of law.[355] Conflicts of interest, as described in the codes, have also come into judicial focus in the respective jurisdictions, namely in the German case of *Kirsch v. Deutsche Bank*, where the failure by the board of a bank to deal with its chairman's false statement was established.[356] In the Dutch *Begemann* case, the Enterprise Court of Amsterdam also highlighted the need to apply the code's provisions on conflicted directors and the company's duty to publish a corporate governance statement in its annual report.[357] Another famous decision besides *Begemann* was in the *ABN AMRO* case, where the Dutch Supreme Court referred to the provisions of the Dutch CGC (the Tabaksblat Code) and applied them as giving substance to the principles of reasonableness and fairness enshrined in Article 2:8 of the BW.[358] With that decision, the Dutch Supreme Court overturned the decision of the Enterprise Court of Amsterdam, which had earlier ruled in favour of the plaintiff VEB, one of the ABN AMRO shareholders. The plaintiff had claimed that the transaction formed by ABN AMRO to sell shares in ABN AMRO North America should have been subjected, among other requirements, to prior approval by the shareholders of ABN AMRO Holding, following Article 2:8 in conjunction with Article 2:107a(1) of the BW.[359] Legal literature further argued that by ruling in this manner the Enterprise Court of Amsterdam had abandoned the stakeholder theory commonly used in the Netherlands, preferring instead to focus on the interests of shareholders.[360] Despite also basing its reasoning on Article 2:8 of the BW, by referring to the standards of reasonableness and fairness, the Supreme Court interpreted those standards differently, namely through the provisions of the CGC. One of the main arguments used by the Supreme Court was that the obligation of prior consultation of the general meeting of shareholders would have resulted in unacceptable legal uncertainty.[361] Still, CGCs cannot be equated with provisions of hard law: as Eddy Wymeersch suggests, they have not been applied as legally binding instruments.[362]

---

355. Wymeersch E, 'European Corporate Governance Codes and Their Effectiveness' in Belcredi M and Ferrarini G (eds), *Boards and Shareholders in European Listed Companies: Facts, Context and Post-Crisis Reforms* (Cambridge University Press 2013), 85-89, 98-101.
356. *Kirsch v. Deutsche Bank*, BGH, 16 February 2009, II ZR 185/07, as quoted by Wymeersch E, 'European Corporate Governance Codes and Their Effectiveness', 88.
357. *Begemann, Decision of 28 December 2006* JOR 2007/68 (Enterprise Court of Amsterdam).
358. Oostwouder W, 'Can You Trust the Dutch (Company Law System)?' (2007) 4 European Company Law 211, 212.
359. De Groot C, Van Nood A and Lambert F, 'The ABN AMRO Ruling: Some Commentaries' (2007) 4 European Company Law 168, 171.
360. *Ibid.*, 172.
361. *ABN AMRO, Decision of 13 July 2007* R07/102HR (OK 137) (Supreme Court of the Netherlands).
362. Wymeersch E, 'European Corporate Governance Codes and Their Effectiveness', 101.

Courts in Ukraine have also made reference to the Principles of Corporate Governance in their decisions.

In Case No. 20-11/421-7/514, resolved by the Supreme Economic Court of Ukraine, the claimant sought to void the director's relinquishment of the company's property for the benefit of third parties, arguing that the relinquishment had been made without the supervisory board's approval and was not on market terms. The court rejected the claim by querying the claimant's standing since at that time Ukrainian laws did not recognize shareholders submitting claims to protect their company's rights and legitimate interests (derivative action).[363] One of the sources on which the Court drew was the Principles of Corporate Governance, as in effect on the date of the judgment (2003 version), using those Principles as a secondary source, in addition to the CCU and the Land Code of Ukraine.

As an additional note on that judgment, the Economic Procedural Code of Ukraine now allows shareholders owning 10% or more of the shares to claim damages on behalf of the company.[364] This change was added in April 2015 and became effective on 1 May 2016.[365] At the same time, it does not grant shareholders the power to use legal recourse on behalf of the company other than to seek compensation for loss or damage caused by company officers.

It was a logical decision for the court to apply soft law after hard law. Moreover, in the judgment discussed here, the provisions from the Principles of Corporate Governance did not bring anything new to the rules contained in the relevant legislative acts. Without reference to the Principles, the outcome of the case would have been the same.

Even where the Principles are treated as a source of law, their effect is limited in scope, as they are generally used as an additional source to add detail and authority to statutory law, not as a source on which a lawyer can build a case. Arguably, they could be applied on their own if the court regards them as principles of law: the CCU does in fact allow applying principles of law by analogy of law if statutory provisions cannot be applied.[366] The principles specified in the CCU include the principles of fairness, good faith and reasonableness,[367] as well as a more general principle of the rule of law as declared in the Constitution of Ukraine.[368] The sphere of conflicts of interest is not excluded from the possible scope of these principles. Until recently, courts in Ukraine were reluctant to apply the principles of law. The decision by the Supreme Economic

363. *LLC 'Svarog Asset Management' v. OJSC 'Sebastopol Sea Plant', Judgment of 2 July 2008* Case No. 20-11/421-7/514 (Supreme Economic Court of Ukraine).

364. Economic Procedural Code of Ukraine [Hospodarskyi protsesualnyi kodeks Ukrayiny] of 6 November 1991, published in Vidomosti Verkhovnoyi Rady Ukrayiny, 1992, No. 6, St. 56, Articles 12(1)(4-1), 4-8, 28.

365. Law of Ukraine 'On Amending Certain Legislative Acts on the Protection of Investors' [Zakon Ukrayiny 'Pro vnesennia zmin do deyakykh zakonodavchykh aktiv schodo zakhystu prav investoriv'].

366. CCU, Article 8(2).

367. *Ibid.*, Article 3.

368. Constitution of Ukraine [Konstytutsiya Ukrayiny] of 28 June 1996, published in Vidomosti Verkhovnoyi Rady Ukrayiny, 1996, No. 30, St. 141, Article 8.

Court of Ukraine of 10 January 2012 in a Case No. 5021/1197/2011[369] is an example of a judgment where the court invalidated a transaction as being contrary to the principles of law. In this case, the transaction contract provided for fixed monthly payments for services in the amount of UAH 30,000, without stipulating any specific obligations of the other contracting party. The court annulled this contract on the basis of Articles 3, 203(1) and 509(3) of the CCU and acknowledged that it was incompatible with the principles of fairness, good faith and reasonableness. The new Supreme Court, which came into office on 15 December 2017,[370] has applied the principles of law to corporate disputes on several occasions. According to the recent digest of court practice, in corporate disputes, the Supreme Court has referred to the general principle of the rule of law, and to the principles of legal certainty and fairness as the former's constituent elements.[371]

In the cases described here, courts in Ukraine took the shortcut of applying the principles of law, usually observed within the concept of analogy of law.[372] In contrast, the concept of analogy of statute is the application of provisions of a statute regulating similar relationships, where civil relations are not governed by the Code, other civil legislation or the actual contract.[373] In corporate law, analogy of statute has been used, for instance, to apply the provisions on LLCs to private enterprises.[374] However, the Principles of Corporate Governance are by nature not an act of civil legislation and cannot be applied by analogy of statute. This therefore lessens the likelihood of independent application to corporate relationships.

Unlike the Dutch, German and Polish CGCs, the Ukrainian Principles of Corporate Governance lack a firm basis such as EU law, which consequently affects their practical significance. This is confirmed by the lack of court decisions that make reference to the 2014 Principles.

Accordingly, acknowledging the problems with the practical effect of the Principles of Corporate Governance, it is necessary to consider their substance and how it relates to conflicts of interest.

The 2014 version of the Principles that is currently in place, in fact, offers a comprehensive set of rules regarding conflicts of interest. The function of controlling the prevention, revelation and resolution of conflicts of interest is vested with the

---

369. *LLC 'Sarex' v. Open JSC 'Sumske ATP-15928', Resolution as of 10 January 2012* Case No. 5021/1197/2011 (Supreme Economic Court of Ukraine).
370. 'V Ukrayini pochav robotu novyi Verkhovnyi Sud' (2017), available at: https://ua.korrespondent.net/ukraine/3918262-v-ukraini-pochav-robotu-novyi-verkhovnyi-sud, accessed on 29 September 2019.
371. *Digest of Court Practice of the Supreme Court in Cases Arising of Corporate Relations (2018 – 15 July 2019) [Digest sudovoyi praktyky Verkhovnoho Sudu u spravakh, scho vynykayut iz korporatyvnykh vidnosyn (2018 rik – 15 lypnia 2019 roku)]* (website of the Supreme Court, available at: https://supreme.court.gov.ua/userfiles/media/Dajest_korporat_vidnosunu_1pdf?fbclid=IwAR0IBFqlG-nLKuBLtZ1is7p7h44lGyAyRoSamP3PC7X1ndYStc-c8SNFlnI, 2019), 136, 167.
372. CCU, Article 8(2).
373. *Ibid.*, Article 8(1).
374. *Osoba 6 v. Private Enterprise 'Illichivska perlyna', Judgment of 11 April 2016* Case No. 916/2855/15 (Supreme Economic Court of Ukraine).

company's supervisory board,[375] which is advised to establish separate committees from among its members to prevent conflicts of interest: an audit committee, a nomination committee, a remuneration committee and a committee on information policy.[376] Interestingly, these requirements go further than required under the JSC Law of Ukraine[377] and Commission Recommendation 2005/162/EC,[378] which make no mention of committees on information policy, while the Recommendation allows committee functions to be grouped as the supervisory board sees fit[379] – for instance, merging the nomination and remuneration committees. At the same time, it is important not to overstate how comprehensive the rules contained in the Principles are: in some respects they are vague and declarative. This is illustrated by the concept of an independent supervisory board member that the Principles offer,[380] which is considerably less detailed than the notion of an independent director, as found in the JSC Law of Ukraine[381] and Commission Recommendation 2004/913/EC.[382]

Conflicts of interest are also specifically discussed in section II, paragraph 3.3 of the Principles, which describes the duties of company officers to act in good faith and in the company's best interests,[383] to notify any conflicts of interest in connection with any company decision or transaction,[384] not to use business opportunities that fall to the company[385] and not to compete with the company.[386] The Principles also set out specific requirements for loans to company officers: these need to be recorded in the company's internal documents, approved by the supervisory board and disclosed to the shareholders.[387] Here the Dutch CGC goes a step further, by introducing additional restrictions on personal loans, namely that they need to be made in the normal course of the company's business, on the same terms that apply to the greater workforce and without the possibility of remission, so that even if approval is obtained from the

375. Principles of Corporate Governance, approved by the Decision of the National Securities and Stock Market Commission of Ukraine of 22 July 2014, No. 955 [Pryntsypy korporatyvnoho upravlinnia, zatverdzheni rishenniam Natsionalnoyi komisii z tsinnykh paperiv ta fondovoho rynku vid 22 lypnia 2014 roku No. 955], section II.3.1.3 (*r*).
376. *Ibid.*, section II.3.1.13.
377. JSC Law of Ukraine, Article 56(1).
378. Commission Recommendation of 15 February 2005 on the role of non-executive or supervisory directors of listed companies and on the committees of the (supervisory) board [2005] OJ L 52/51, 25.2.2005, sections II, 5.
379. *Ibid.*, sections II, 6.1.
380. Principles of Corporate Governance, approved by the Decision of the National Securities and Stock Market Commission of Ukraine of 22 July 2014, No. 955 [Pryntsypy korporatyvnoho upravlinnia, zatverdzheni rishenniam Natsionalnoyi komisii z tsinnykh paperiv ta fondovoho rynku vid 22 lypnia 2014 roku No. 955], sections II, 3.1.12.
381. JSC Law of Ukraine, Article 2(1)(10-1).
382. Commission Recommendation of 14 December 2004 fostering an appropriate regime for the remuneration of directors of listed companies [2004] OJ L 385/55, 29.12.2004, Annex II.
383. Principles of Corporate Governance, approved by the Decision of the National Securities and Stock Market Commission of Ukraine of 22 July 2014, No. 955 [Pryntsypy korporatyvnoho upravlinnia, zatverdzheni rishenniam Natsionalnoyi komisii z tsinnykh paperiv ta fondovoho rynku vid 22 lypnia 2014 roku No. 955], sections II, 3.3.1.
384. *Ibid.*, sections II, 3.3.2.
385. *Ibid.*, sections II, 3.3.3.
386. *Ibid.*, sections II, 3.3.4.
387. *Ibid.*, sections II, 3.3.5.

supervisory board, it must be in the company's best interests.[388] In addition, unlike the WSE Best Practice and the Principles of Corporate Governance, the Dutch CGC covers a wider range of corporate relationships by also considering conflicts of interests involving shareholders with 10% or more of the share capital: as it would be nonsensical to deny that shareholders that hold a large portion of the share capital can significantly influence the company's functioning, these elements appear to be a logical addition to the Dutch CGC.

[D] RPTs and Conflicts of Interest

If a director is said to act in conflict with the company's interests, it means that an internal contradiction exists between the interests of the director and the interests of the company (beneficiary) on whose behalf he or she is acting. This contradiction is inherent in RPTs. At the same time, the chief executive officer of a company who enters into a transaction with a relative on behalf of the company is not necessarily acting in a manner that is harmful. A related party will not necessarily behave more detrimentally to the company than a third party. Professional literature views transactions with independent third parties as being at arm's length and generally contrast them with RPTs.[389] Some sources, however, find that RPTs can be at arm's length, provided that additional procedural safeguards are used, such as India's system of prior audit committee approval.[390] Still, even if that potential approach is accepted, transactions are at arm's length from a procedural viewpoint, rather than by substance. The question is more one of parties acting independently, rather than of the fair outcome of a particular transaction. Transactions at arm's length cannot be guaranteed to arrive at a fair result. While this is also true of RPTs, the parties to RPTs are not independent actors as they would be in arm's-length transactions. Only if the RPT yields advantages to the related party does the risk inherent in conflicted transactions materialize, and is the related party acting in his or her own interest, rather than the company's. This means that even though RPTs are included among the possible types of conflicts of interest by some sources,[391] strictly speaking they are not. A conflict of interest in an RPT can be defined as an incompatibility between the interests of the related party and the interests of the company. It is then more correct to say that these 'transactions

388. Dutch CGC, section 2.7.6.
389. Cheung YL and others, 'Tunneling and Propping Up: An Analysis of Related Party Transactions by Chinese Listed Companies' (2009) 17 Pacific-Basin Finance Journal 372, 386; Gordon EA and Henry E, *Related Party Transactions and Earnings Management*, available at SSRN: https://ssrn.com/abstract=612234 or http://dx.doi.org/102139/ssrn612234, accessed on 27 November 2018, 9.
390. Mahtani U, 'An Analysis of Related-Party Transactions in India' Working Paper Series WP No: 2017/01/FN (Goa Institute of Management, Poriem, Sattari, Goa 403505), available at: https://www.gim.ac.in/newpdfs/Related-party-transactions-Group-and-Non-Group-Company-Perspective-Jan2017pdf http://www.iimb.ernet.in/sites/default/files/WP%20No.%20402_0.pdf, accessed on 6 December 2018, 2.
391. Gerner-Beuerle C and Schuster EP, 'Mapping Directors' Duties: Strategies and Trends in the EU' in Birkmose HS, Neville M and Sørensen KE (eds), *Boards of Directors in European Companies: Reshaping and Harmonising Their Organisation and Duties* (Wolters Kluwer Law & Business 2013), 23.

imply conflicts of interest',[392] as related parties can be granted additional advantages by the company. These transactions are exposed to a higher level of risk since human nature means a very high probability of related parties exploiting their position by extracting benefits from the company, and consequently giving rise to conflicts of interest.

Nevertheless, RPTs do not always lead the company to a dead end, and their use is not necessarily as deliberately harmful as anticipated. A clear example of an economy where RPTs are part of the ordinary course of business is described in an article by Luca Enriques.[393] As that author argues, in countries similar to the imaginary business-unfriendly state Tunnelland, RPTs may become a reasonable response to badly designed and poorly functioning institutions.[394] Companies in countries like Tunnelland would be forced to use RPTs to prevent their assets from flowing into the hands of corrupt officials or raiders. While this example is of course not a valid argument for continuing to use RPTs rather than changing the rules of the game for all players, even in an economy that differs from the non-existing state of Tunnelland, RPTs are not necessarily harmful to companies, especially in family-owned firms. RPTs can also have a value-creating effect for listed companies. For example, if a dominant shareholder in a company invests in a research and development project, he or she usually knows the project's chances for success better than any third party.[395] The profound understanding of the specific business and production processes makes him or her a perfect investor in this case. This is where RPTs can have a value-creating effect for numerous companies: banning them outright would rule out too many efficient transactions.[396] That is why, while in general the sense remains that behaviour that conceals conflicts of interest should be prohibited entirely, e.g. competing with the company, RPTs amount simply to risky behaviour that demands a more delicate approach through use of appropriate strategies, as amply demonstrated in the *Anatomy of Corporate Law*.[397] Like an all-out ban, a non-intervention approach is not a solution, as it would generate free-rider issues and inefficient decisions by investors.[398] The need for intermediate solutions for RPTs, rather than radical moves, matches the OECD recommendations specifically dealing with RPTs, but not with conflicts of interest in general.[399]

That having been said in regard to RPTs, and following the analysis of the CGCs described above, the types of conflicts that can be discerned are as follows: (a) use of the company's business opportunities, and competition with the company (this

392. Dotevall R, 'Is a Common Structure of Company Directors' Duties Evolving in EU?' (2016) 27 European Business Law Review 285, 6.
393. Enriques L, 'Related Party Transactions: Policy Options and Real-World Challenges (with a Critique of the European Commission Proposal)', 4.
394. *Ibid.*, 5.
395. *Ibid.*, 7.
396. Goshen Z, 'The Efficiency of Controlling Corporate Self-Dealing: Theory Meets Reality', 401.
397. Kraakman R and others, *The Anatomy of Corporate Law: A Comparative and Functional Approach* (2nd edn, Oxford University Press 2009), 155-178.
398. Goshen Z, 'The Efficiency of Controlling Corporate Self-Dealing: Theory Meets Reality', 404-407.
399. OECD, *Related Party Transactions and Minority Shareholder Rights* (OECD Publishing, 2012).

category includes transactions entering the sphere of the company's finances, but not transactions between the company and its related parties[400]); (b) use of any advantages of the company and the grant of advantages to third parties (also within RPTs).

These types of conflicts of interest inherently imply the negative consequences for the company that come with the very concept of conflicts of interest.

This list is not exhaustive: for instance, a conflict of interest also arises if a director receives excessive remuneration. At the same time, this could also be described as the use of advantages, given that the difference by which the remuneration exceeds a normal level of pay is clearly an advantage.

Lastly, a director who accepts benefits from a third party does not necessarily have conflicted interests. In fact, it does not matter for the company whether the director is granted any advantages by third parties, as long as this is not harmful to the company. Ignoring the possibility of the director receiving advantages would be overly suspicious and would have a neutral or no effect on the company's functioning. However, if the director's conduct is purposively harmful to the company, then that conduct may indubitably be argued to involve a conflict of interest, and the company would likely be entitled to damages under national laws in compensation for the director's actions.[401]

[E] Intra-group Transactions and Conflicts of Interest

Intra-group transactions occupy a special place among RPTs. Their name is, to some extent, self-explanatory: these transactions are formed between group constituencies, most commonly legal entities. The essence of corporate groups, their features and related issues are discussed at greater length in Chapter 4. This section only briefly explains how conflicts of interest occur in intra-group transactions.

Concerns arising for corporate groups are intrinsically linked to the large numbers of stakeholders whose interests need to be taken into account. At least six groups of stakeholders can be identified surrounding corporate groups, half of them insiders (management, investors and employees) and the other half external stakeholders (creditors, government and the general public).[402] While it is very well possible for the interests of internal and external stakeholders to go hand in hand, at the same time every stakeholder has their own separate interests.

Taking managers as a class of stakeholders, the first comment that must be made is that they are not saints. Their primary concern is for their liability and remuneration. These factors influence their decision-making in the same way as they do in ordinary companies. What is different in groups is that the classical agency conflict between

400. Ungerer F, 45.
401. An example of a rule entitling a company to claim such damages can be found in the Principles of Corporate Governance, approved by the Decision of the National Securities and Stock Market Commission of Ukraine of 22 July 2014, No. 955 [Pryntsypy korporatyvnoho upravlinnia, zatverdzheni rishenniam Natsionalnoyi komisii z tsinnykh paperiv ta fondovoho rynku vid 22 lypnia 2014 roku No. 955], sections II, 3.3.6.
402. Hadden T, *The Control of Corporate Groups* (Institute of Advanced Legal Studies, University of London 1983), 20.

management and shareholders is not particularly relevant for groups of companies: here, unlike for companies with dispersed ownership, the controlling shareholder has more power to decide the company's fate by voting for the preferred decisions in another company's bodies.[403] Managers in groups of companies are consequently unable to act as the guardians of corporate wealth if blockholders follow their own interests and exert their influence over board members by forcing them to follow a particular path.[404]

The second group of stakeholders is investors. Investors' interests have much in common with the interests of management. It is important for corporate reality to meet their expectations. This is possible if the company in which they have invested is sufficiently profitable, which of necessity excludes the use of any abusive tunnelling techniques by majority shareholders, management or their related parties. The unique status of the investors in groups of companies lies in the fact that they are interested in developing the group as a whole, rather than a specific branch, division or subsidiary.[405] This particular feature sets investors apart from employees, who might be more interested in the profitability and sustainability of a particular subsidiary, in safeguards to ensure working conditions and whether their salary is appropriate. Employees may have specific concerns about the company's development in connection with major corporate events, e.g. mergers and takeovers.[406]

While the interests of internal stakeholders tend to diverge, they share a desire for the company to be profitable. Of the internal stakeholders, shareholders universally have voting rights in a company, which makes them residual claimants.[407] Unlike employees and managers, they usually have sufficient incentive regarding the company's functioning, as they bear the greatest share of the risk and participate in the final distribution of income.[408] As residual claimants, shareholders tend to force managers to take greater risks.[409] Employees conversely receive only a fixed amount of company assets and bear less risk. The latter feature unites them with creditors under the umbrella of fixed claimants.[410] At the same time, creditors may become residual claimants if the risk to which they are exposed increases significantly due to the conduct of equity holders.[411]

403. Hopt KJ, 'Groups of Companies: A Comparative Study on the Economics, Law and Regulation of Corporate Groups', 4.
404. Langebucher K, 'Do We Need a Law of Corporate Groups?' in Fleischer H and others (eds), *German and Asian Perspectives on Company Law* (Mohr Siebeck 2016), 358.
405. Hadden T, 21.
406. Hopt KJ, 'Groups of Companies: A Comparative Study on the Economics, Law and Regulation of Corporate Groups', 7.
407. Easterbrook FH and Fischel DR, 'Voting in Corporate Law' (1983) 26 The Journal of Law & Economics 395, 403.
408. *Ibid.*, 403.
409. Masouros PE, 'Is the EU Taking Shareholder Rights Seriously?: An Essay on the Impotence of Shareholdership in Corporate Europe' (2010) 7 European Company Law 195, 200.
410. Enriques L, 'The Law on Company Directors' Self-Dealing: A Comparative Analysis' (2000) 2 International and Comparative Corporate Law Journal 297, 331.
411. Easterbrook FH and Fischel DR, 'Voting in Corporate Law', 404.

Creditors are by definition external stakeholders. Their main aim is to be paid for their claims.[412] This does not necessarily mean that the company will stay solvent if the creditors achieve their goal. At the same time, creditors are exposed to risks of non-payment of claims on groups of companies more than on other types of companies:[413] in corporate groups, corporate wealth is distributed between separate constituencies. Moreover, even if a company that is part of a group possesses sufficient resources at a given moment, that can change through control transactions and cash pooling agreements passed down from the group's top. These risks increase with multinational groups, where, even if the corporate veil can be pierced, creditors experience additional issues related to the cost of debt collection in different jurisdictions. That is why creditors often try to keep a close watch on the debtor company's assets by forming additional security agreements and arranging protective mechanisms.

Besides creditors, the government and the general public can also be considered separate stakeholders. Governments are stakeholders inasmuch as they are interested in collecting tax revenue. Major groups of companies usually have high levels of income and large workforces, which makes them attractive taxpayers. However, it is crucial for the government to balance its regulation to retain its taxpayers. Excessively high taxes may force companies to move to another jurisdiction. Similarly, the general public also has an interest in having large groups as taxpayers: more tax money enables the state to improve its infrastructure and to care for socially vulnerable categories of people. Yet tax considerations are not the only factors that will matter to the public: environmental concerns, e.g., constitute an important reason for the public to favour or oppose corporate groups. Groups with environmentally unsafe practices risk being red-lighted in some countries.

Last but not least, besides the interests of the separate stakeholders within and outside the group, the interests of the corporate group itself also come into play. The idea of a group's interests concerns the right and duty of the parent company to manage the group and its companies according to the group's best interests.[414] The group's interests provide the subsidiary with a 'safe harbour' of decision-making, where a particular act might be contrary to the subsidiary's own interests, but would further the interests of the group overall. In pursuit of the group's interests, a parent company might issue binding instructions that are to the detriment of the individual subsidiary. The group's interests also justify pooling transactions to withdraw funds from the subsidiary in favour of the parent or another member of the group. The issue of a group's interests has been studied by scholars in Europe, from the recommendations of the Forum Europaeum[415] to the recent findings and recommendations of the Informal

412. Hadden T, 23.
413. Langebucher K, 358.
414. Antunes JE and others, *Report of the Reflection Group on the Future of EU Company Law* (European Commission Internal Market and Services 2011), 60.
415. 'Corporate Group Law for Europe by Forum Europaeum' (2000) 1 European Business Organisation Law Review 165, 258.

Company Law Expert Group.[416] The report of that expert group emphasized that Member States have different approaches to the issue of recognizing the interests of groups, ranging from exclusively favouring the individual company's interests to a standard-based recognition of the group's interests.[417] Chapter 4 elaborates further on the differences in recognizing group interests in different Member States. For now, it is important to note that, regardless of whether a group's interests are recognized in a particular jurisdiction, it is pointless to deny the existence of certain common objectives in the functioning of multiple legal entities that are in legal and economic proximity to each other.

Bearing in mind how the group's interests impact relations between parents and subsidiaries, managers of subsidiaries may experience a dilemma in deciding which interests to follow first: those of the subsidiary or those of the group. The group's interests might run contrary to the subsidiary's interests, for instance if the subsidiary's director receives instructions to enter into a transaction that has negative consequences for the subsidiary but an overall positive effect for the group as a whole. As is evident from Dutch case law[418] and the LLC Law of Ukraine,[419] the 'conflict of interest' concept indicates that this behaviour does not amount to a conflict, given that no 'personal' interest as such is involved. Furthermore, the notion of a conflict of interest as found in those sources does not make any reference to group interests. That is why, legally, conduct by a director that satisfies his or her personal interest, to the detriment of the group's interest, but with a neutral effect on the individual company's interest, does not constitute a conflict of interest. While this implication is not surprising for the jurisdictions that do not formally recognize the concept of a group's interests (*see* Chapter 4), it has practical significance for jurisdictions where directors do not incur liability for pursuing the group's interests even if these are at odds with the interests of the separate entity.

Despite these differences between the various interests in traditional companies and in corporate groups, the concept of conflict of interest has the same negative meaning for groups of companies as it has for traditional companies.

[F] Use of Business Opportunities and Competition with the Company

The prohibition on using business opportunities and the non-compete obligation are not always clearly distinct. Here they are discussed separately partly due to the fact that the German CGC (both the 2017 version and the draft 2020 version) and the Principles of Corporate Governance in Ukraine likewise differentiate between the prohibition on

416. Armour J and others, *Report on the Recognition of the Interest of the Group (October 30, 2016)* available at: https://ssrn.com/abstract=2888863, 2016, 47.
417. *Ibid.*, 5-6.
418. *Bruil/Kombex* 29 June 2007, JOR 2007/169 (Supreme Court of the Netherlands).
419. LLC Law of Ukraine, Article 42(3).

using the company's business opportunities and the non-compete obligation.[420] Similarly, the Dutch CGC also separates its prohibitions on competing with the company and on using business opportunities.[421] However, the doctrine of corporate opportunities as found in German jurisprudence derives from the premise that the ban on using corporate opportunities covers both the duty not to compete and the non-written ban on using corporate opportunities.[422] The legislative definition of a non-compete clause is given in the AktG and provides that members of the management board may neither engage in any trade nor enter into any transaction in the company's line of business on their own behalf or on behalf of others.[423]

In Poland, the WSE Best Practices of 2002 and 2005 contained an obligation for company officers to present information on available advantageous transactions to their company. In the later versions of the WSE Best Practices, however, this provision was replaced by more abstract conflict of interest prohibitions.[424] Unlike the current version of the WSE Best Practice, the KSH provides more substance: besides preventing board members from engaging in any competitive business, it also prohibits any participation in competing legal entities, except with the company's approval.[425] Based on the wording, competition also arises if the board member is simultaneously a director of a competing entity or owns 10% or more of its share capital. If the board member engages in any of these activities, this would inevitably also mean the use of business opportunities, which constitute an interest for the company and, at the same time, bring financial benefits to the interested person.

Unlike Germany and Poland, the Netherlands does not have specific statutory rules prohibiting the use of business opportunities; it only has the relevant provisions of the Dutch CGC. Despite the lack of specific statutory regulation, courts in the Netherlands have held directors liable for abuse of business opportunities by participating in competing companies, by drawing on the general Article 2:8 and 2:9 of the BW.[426] In other words, the doctrine of corporate opportunities has found its way into Dutch jurisprudence and extends to non-compete obligations.

This being so, sufficient evidence can be found in literature and case law to justify the conclusion that use of business opportunities also includes competition with the company by the interested person – even though Germany and Poland belong to jurisdictions where the codified regulation of the corporate opportunities doctrine is limited to the non-compete obligation for directors, while the Netherlands has no

420. German CGC, as amended on 7 February 2017, section 4.3.1; German draft CGC 2020, section E; Principles of Corporate Governance, approved by the Decision of the National Securities and Stock Market Commission of Ukraine of 22 July 2014, No. 955 [Pryntsypy korporatyvnoho upravlinnia, zatverdzheni rishenniam Natsionalnoyi komisii z tsinnykh paperiv ta fondovoho rynku vid 22 lypnia 2014 roku No. 955], sections II, 3.3.3, 3.3.4.
421. Dutch CGC, section 2.7.1 Preventing conflicts of interest.
422. Gerner-Beuerle C, Paech P and Schuster EP, 132.
423. AktG, Article 88(1).
424. Oplustil K and Radwan A, 482.
425. KSH, Articles 211(1), 380(1).
426. For example, *see: Decision of 29 March 2011/1C7.002.444/01* JOR 2011/216 (Arnhem-Leeuwarden Court of Appeal); *Decision of 19 February 2014/C-16-316233 – HA ZA 11-1953* JOR 2014/124 (District Court Midden-Nederland).

binding regulation on business opportunities at all.[427] Rather, the conclusion that the non-compete rule falls within the scope of the corporate opportunities doctrine derives from the essence of the concept: competition with the company implies activity in proximity to the company's business.[428]

Two questions arise in this regard: (i) do any business opportunities exist that cannot be captured under the umbrella of non-competition and (ii) do any examples exist of competing behaviour that does not constitute the use of business opportunities?

For question (i), the answer depends largely on how broadly we define business (corporate) opportunities: if business opportunities are about business activity (narrow approach), then these acts include non-competing behaviour. In a broader approach, where this type of conflict includes using business opportunities both within and beyond the company's business,[429] then some business opportunities certainly fall beyond the scope of competing activity. This broad approach has been confirmed in German case law, where the German Supreme Court dismissed a director's demand to be restored to his directorship. The director had acquired real estate that was offered for sale by the mayor of the community where the company was located and subsequently sold the real estate to a construction company. The court disagreed with the dismissed director, notwithstanding the fact that the company had not suffered any loss or damage and did not need real estate for its own purposes.[430] For the director to avoid liability, apparently, the company should first have received and declined an offer of sale.[431]

In the Netherlands and Poland, the doctrine of corporate opportunities has a narrower application and does not extend to appropriating business opportunities for private purposes. Moreover, competition in and of itself is not sufficient for director's liability in the Netherlands, given that these relationships are governed both by general provisions on directors' conduct and by tort law.[432] Nevertheless, although the situation may appear ambiguous and lacking legal certainty, by all accounts the principles are applied with sufficient flexibility to provide suitable results.[433]

Besides the provisions regarding business opportunities in the Principles of Corporate Governance,[434] Ukraine has a threefold prohibition for supervisory board members and members of executive bodies in private companies under the recent LLC Law of Ukraine. These company officers require consent from the general meeting of shareholders or the supervisory board (for members of executive bodies) for the

427. *Ibid.*, 151.
428. *Ibid.*, 150.
429. Gerner-Beuerle C and Schuster EP, 28.
430. German building plot case (Bundesgerichsthof, WM 1967, 679), as quoted by Hopt KJ, 'Self-Dealing and Use of Corporate Opportunity and Information: Regulating Directors' Conflicts of Interest' in Hopt K and Teubner G (eds), *Corporate Governance and Directors' Liabilities* (Walter de Gruyter1985), 295.
431. Gerner-Beuerle C, Paech P and Schuster EP, 159.
432. *Ibid.*, 155-156.
433. *Ibid.*, 158.
434. Principles of Corporate Governance, approved by the Decision of the National Securities and Stock Market Commission of Ukraine of 22 July 2014, No. 955 [Pryntsypy korporatyvnoho upravlinnia, zatverdzheni rishenniam Natsionalnoyi komisii z tsinnykh paperiv ta fondovoho rynku vid 22 lypnia 2014 roku No. 955], sections II, 3.3.4, 3.3.5.

following: (a) to perform economic activity as natural persons/entrepreneurs in the sphere of the company's activity; (b) to be a partner in general or limited partnerships performing acts in the sphere of the company's activity; and (c) to be a member of a supervisory board or an executive body of another economic operator that performs acts in the sphere of the company's activity.[435] It is notable that in this provision the Ukrainian legislature codified only the narrow approach to the doctrine of corporate opportunities. The broader understanding of business opportunities, i.e. to extend beyond the non-compete rule, in the LLC Law of Ukraine is arguably covered by the rules on conflicts of interest[436] and the general provisions of tort law in the CCU.[437] However, insufficient case law has been handed down on whether the provisions on conflicts of interest and the tort law provisions should, in fact, be applied to abuse of business opportunities that extends beyond the non-compete obligation, and the practicability of the broader approach to the corporate opportunities doctrine remains doubtful.

The answer to question (ii) also depends largely on the concept of business (corporate) opportunities and how broadly it is interpreted. It can be argued that competing with the company could involve opportunities that do not necessarily 'belong' to the company and so are not business opportunities. A different approach has been suggested in literature, with Klaus Hopt suggesting that the duty not to compete with the company should be viewed as a subgroup of corporate opportunities with extraordinary features deserving special attention from the legislature.[438] The idea of the legislators drafting CGCs juxtaposing business opportunities to the non-competition duty may seem surprising, given that business opportunities are broader in scope. The endeavours of the Code's drafters could still have a logical explanation, since it is always safer to have an overinclusive provision than an underinclusive one, giving stakeholder rights more protection from the abusive behaviour of directors.

The exercise of identifying inappropriate use of business opportunities faces practical difficulties. If a company is unable or unwilling to utilize a particular opportunity, this does not automatically pave the way for the director to seize that opportunity. It is even more difficult to determine whether a given opportunity is in fact relevant to the company.[439] In Germany, this issue arose with regard to a company's former director, who had sought to exploit a new idea with a third party after leaving the company. The Federal Supreme Court prevented the director from starting a new project by using only his/her knowledge without any capital.[440] The issue was controversial: opinions on how better to qualify post-employment relationships are not unanimous. If an employment contract specifies restrictions on the use of business opportunities after the end of office, the consequences are quite clear. Otherwise, the

435. LLC Law of Ukraine, Article 40(5).
436. LLC Law of Ukraine, Article 42.
437. CCU, Article 1166.
438. Hopt KJ, 'Self-Dealing and Use of Corporate Opportunity and Information: Regulating Directors' Conflicts of Interest', 300.
439. Hopt KJ, 'Conflict of Interest, Secrecy and Insider Information of Directors, A Comparative Analysis', 179.
440. *Decision of 23 September 1985* Wertpapier-Mitteilungen, 1443 (Federal Court of Justice).

interpretation of the relationship might have a different outcome, largely depending on the jurisdiction. Unlike in Germany, the Polish, Ukrainian and Dutch laws do not require resigning directors to be subject to the non-compete obligation, unless of course the employment contract so provides.[441]

Another scenario where it is difficult to evaluate whether it would be appropriate to use a particular business opportunity is in situations where the parent company steals business opportunities from its subsidiary. To understand whether the parent's conduct is legal, it is necessary to apply both the provisions pertaining to the doctrine of corporate opportunities described above and the relevant regulations for corporate groups, including the respective standards that apply. The legislators drafting the EMCA propose resolving the issue of theft of business opportunities by a parent company by prohibiting exploitation of business opportunities in all cases where the subsidiary is not wholly owned.[442] The parent company would then be allowed to exploit opportunities of a subsidiary that is not wholly owned only if it receives approval from the disinterested directors - if that approval is withheld, the subsidiary's non-controlling shareholders must then agree to the exploitation.[443] For wholly owned subsidiaries, the EMCA does not require parent companies to seek consent from any other party to exploit business opportunities of their subsidiaries. The regulation of corporate groups in the jurisdictions in focus is discussed further in Chapter 4.

[G] Direct and Indirect Conflicts of Interest

Although conflicts of interest are a commonly discussed topic in company law theory, addressed by both statute[444] and soft law,[445] in practice some ambiguity has emerged about how to phrase the provisions that govern conflicts of interest, if they are in fact to be made legally binding at all. The extent to which rules for conflicts of interest should be formalized in law as legally binding rules is an especially controversial issue for indirect conflicts of interest. Indirect conflicts of interest arise in situations where it is not a director or a shareholder who is involved in a transaction with the company, but the director's or shareholder's related parties, for instance a controlled company.[446]

For a long time, the BW included a provision stating that, if a director had a conflict of interest with the company, the company should be represented by the

441. Gerner-Beuerle C, Paech P and Schuster EP, 139-140.
442. Andersen PK and others, 'European Model Company Act (EMCA) (September 1, 2017)' (Nordic & European Company Law Working Paper No. 16-26, available at SSRN: https://ssrn.com/abstract=2929348, 2017), section 15.13.
443. *Ibid.*
444. *See*, e.g., KSH, Articles 209, 377.
445. This includes the CGCs of Germany, Poland and the Netherlands that have been analysed above, and for the Principles of Corporate Governance, approved by the Decision of the National Securities and Stock Market Commission of Ukraine of 22 July 2014, No. 955 [Pryntsypy korporatyvnoho upravlinnia, zatverdzheni rishenniam Natsionalnoyi komisii z tsinnykh paperiv ta fondovoho rynku vid 22 lypnia 2014 roku No. 955].
446. Andersen PK and Balshøj DK, 'Directors' Conflicts of Interest: A Contribution to European Convergence' in Birkmose HS, Neville M and Sørensen KE (eds), *Boards of Directors in European Companies: Reshaping and Harmonising Their Organisation and Duties* (Wolters Kluwer Law & Business 2013), 63.

members of the supervisory board, if the company had one, and granting the general meeting of shareholders the power to intervene.[447] These rules, which were similar for both BVs and NVs, were contained in Article 2:146 and 2:256 of the BW. However, having been criticized for creating uncertainty, they were repealed.[448] Nevertheless, the discussion about the issues associated with these provisions and their enforcement has practical significance for better understanding how to draft rules for conflicts of interest. It is also important for a proper understanding of the practical consequences to distinguish between direct and indirect conflicts of interest.

Initially, Article 2:146 and 2:256 of the BW did not attract much attention from practitioners and scholars in the Netherlands, until they were studied in detail in Adriaan Dorresteijn's dissertation.[449] Almost a decade later, the Dutch Supreme Court drew attention to these rules by expanding their scope to include not only direct conflicts of interest but also indirect conflicts. This meant that even where it was not actually the director who had conflicting interests, but an intermediary company in which the director had a personal interest, the provisions could still be invoked with external effect.[450] At the same time, the Court established a number of barriers to litigation by making enforcement of these provisions contingent on the condition that the contracting party knew or should have known about the existence of the conflict of interest. Therefore, a court claim against the contract would fail if the other party could successfully prove that he or she was a bona fide contracting party.[451]

Steef Bartman described the *Bruil/Kombex* case as highly illustrative of how the implementation of legislative requirements led to undesired results.[452] The case concerned an agreement between Bruil Arnhem BV and Kombex BV under which the latter was granted an option to buy a piece of land. The agreement was signed by Mr Bruil, who at that time was both companies' sole shareholder and director. Years later, Bruil Arnhem BV sold the land to a third party and by doing so breached its obligation under the contact. Kombex BV filed for damages. The Arnhem Court of Appeal rejected the claim, referring to the breach of the conflict of interest rule by the director of Bruil Arnhem BV, who had signed the agreement.[453] However, Bruil Arnhem BV claimed that Mr Bruil at the time of granting the option had a conflicting interest and thus the company was not bound to the option. The Supreme Court of the Netherlands quashed the decision of the Court of Appeal and referred the case to another Court of Appeals to study the specific circumstances of the case more thoroughly to establish a substantive

447. Bartman SM, 'Report from the Netherlands' (2006) 3 European Company Law 33.
448. *Ibid.*, 34.
449. Dorresteijn AFM, *Tegenstrijdig Belang van Bestuurders en Commissarissen: een Rechtsvergelijkende Studie* (Kluwer 1989).
450. *Mediasafe, Decision of 22 March 1996* NJ 1996, 568 (Supreme Court of the Netherlands).
451. This opinion was subsequently confirmed and developed in other cases, where the rules enshrined in Article 2:146 and 2:256 were recognized as also being obligatory for companies with a single shareholder and requiring explicit approval from the shareholder meeting (SC 2 May 2002, *NJ* 2002, 393 (Joral), SC 9 July 2004, *NJ* 2004, 519 (Duplicado), as quoted by Bartman SM, 'Report from the Netherlands', 34).
452. Bartman SM, 'Report from the Netherlands', 34; Bartman SM, 'From Autonomy of Interests to Concurrence of Interest in Dutch Group Company Law' (2007) 4 European Company Law 207, 209-210.
453. *Decision of 11 October 2005* JOR 2005/294 (Arnhem-Leeuwarden Court of Appeal).

conflict of interest or not. In its judgment, the Supreme Court held to the substantive, rather than the formal, interpretation of a conflict of interest. Following the Supreme Court's reasoning, to establish a conflict of interest on the director's part, it was not enough to find a breach of Article 2:146 and 2:256 of the BW. The director could only be viewed as having conflicting interests if *due to the existence of a personal interest or through his involvement with another interest that is not concurrent with that of the legal entity, [the director] must be deemed incapable of safeguarding the interests of the company and its business in a manner that may be expected from a trustworthy and unprejudiced director.*[454] The 's-Hertogenbosch Court of Appeal applied the criteria outlined by the Supreme Court and did not find sufficient grounds to establish a conflict of interest that precluded the director from entering into the transaction.[455]

The *Bruil/Kombex* case revolved around a direct conflict of interest, where the director himself was an interested person. If the persons responsible for drafting and enforcing the agreement had adopted a more careful approach to the law, then these legal issues could have been avoided. It would not have been difficult at the time: the general meeting of shareholders could have appointed anyone to represent the company in the transaction. As such, it was advised that to avoid application of Article 2:146 and 2:256, the general meeting should explicitly authorize the director to represent the company regardless of the conflict of interest.[456] Although that had not been done here, eventually the 's-Hertogenbosch Court of Appeal did not establish any conflict of interest in the case at hand. By laying down the substantive criteria for the conflict of interest concept, the Supreme Court of the Netherlands limited the external negative effect of Article 2:146/2:256 and provided for additional barriers to their successful application. Although Article 2:146 and 2:256 were subsequently abolished as expected,[457] the concept of an indirect conflict of interest for management and supervisory boards was defined in the BW. Article 2:239(6) and 2:250(5) now contain rules prohibiting any conduct with conflicting interests for members of management and supervisory boards. Directors and supervisory board members are prohibited from participating in deliberations and the adoption of resolutions if a direct or indirect conflict of personal interest exists. These legislative provisions originate from pre-existing case law. For instance, in the *Versatel* case, the Supreme Court of the Netherlands prohibited both management and supervisory board members from participating in debates and decision-making where indirect conflicts of interest were involved.[458] Today this rule, as developed in *Versatel*, exists at the level of statute. The same cannot be said of the definition of an indirect conflict of interest, which is why in every single case where this arises, the Enterprise Court of Amsterdam must make reference to the phrasing of an indirect conflict of interest in previous judgments. The *Bruil/Kombex* case serves as the guideline for these purposes. The presence of an indirect conflict of interest is essential for establishing corporate malpractice or

454. *Bruil/Kombex*, 29 June 2007, JOR 2007/169 (Supreme Court of the Netherlands).
455. *Decision of 24 March 2009* JOR 2009/126 ('s-Hertogenbosch Court of Appeal).
456. Martin MR, 'Report from the Netherlands' (2008) 5 European Company Law 195.
457. De Groot C, *Corporate Governance as a Limited Legal Concept*, vol 4 (Kluwer Law International 2009), 156.
458. *Versatel, Decision of 14 September 2007* NJ 2007, 612 (Supreme Court of the Netherlands).

mismanagement (*wanbeleid*) as regularly claimed by shareholders in the course of enquiry proceedings.[459] The purpose of such proceedings is to evaluate a company's corporate governance, although this has never been an easy task for the courts, which are sometimes unaware of how corporate policy is exercised. This is further evidenced by the fact that the Supreme Court of the Netherlands has handed down multiple decisions in which it disagrees with the opinion expressed by the Enterprise Court with regard to the presence of corporate mismanagement.[460]

Some debate has arisen regarding the statutory provisions governing conflicts of interest among academics and practitioners in the Netherlands, following the Enterprise Court's *Intergamma* decision.[461] This judgment was widely criticized for not being compatible with Article 2:250(5) of the BW, by failing to consider the concept of 'personal interest', which had been added with the 2013 changes.[462] The proceedings before the Enterprise Court were initiated by a number of Intergamma's shareholders. These activist shareholders were dissatisfied with the Guinness project for which Intergamma's majority shareholders had actively lobbied. That project provided, among other elements, for the conclusion and further performance of a multimillion-euro agreement between Intergamma and CRH. CRH was the sole owner of Intergamma's shareholder VNG, indirectly possessing 48.6% of the shares in Intergamma.[463] Assessing the conduct of Intergamma's supervisory board members, who had been appointed by VNG, the Enterprise Court acknowledged the absence of any personal interest on their part in a transaction with CRH, though also finding that they should not have participated in the supervisory board's deliberations and decision-making on the Guinness project.[464] These conclusions by the Enterprise Court were criticized for being *contra legem* and failing to consider the 2013 amendments to the BW.[465] The criticism, based mostly on a literal interpretation of Article 2:239(6) and 2:250(5) of the BW, could not be accepted as the ultimate truth, however. The reasons for supporting the Court's opinion are clearly expressed in an article by Steef Bartman and Adriaan Dorresteijn.[466] Specifically, those reasons include the specific purpose of enquiry proceedings, the historical interpretation of the 2013 changes to the BW and the effect of the principles of corporate reasonableness and fairness viewed in conjunction with the directors' responsibility for proper performance of their duties.[467] It is especially the effect of those principles that prevents direct and indirect conflicts of interest from

459. Timmerman V, 'Review of Management Decisions by the Courts, Seen Partly from a Comparative Legal Perspective' in Jitta MJ (ed.), *The Companies and Business Court from a Comparative Law Perspective* (Kluwer 2004), 43.
460. *Ibid.*, 45.
461. *Intergamma, Decision of 22 December 2017* JOR 2018/210 (Enterprise Court of Amsterdam).
462. Bartman SM and Dorresteijn AF, 'Commissaris en Tegenstrijdig Belang: Handelt de Ondernemingskamer contra Legem?' (2018) Ars Aequi 913, 915.
463. *Ibid.*, 913.
464. *Intergamma, Decision of 22 December 2017* JOR 2018/210 (Enterprise Court of Amsterdam), paragraph 3.35.
465. Bartman SM and Dorresteijn AF, 913, 915.
466. *Ibid.*, 917-919.
467. BW, Article 2:8, 2:9(1).

being confined to personal interests only. The principles of fairness and reasonableness, coupled with the definition of conflicts of interest introduced in the *Bruil/Kombex* case, will therefore likely be used to deter conflicts of interest beyond the boundaries of Article 2:239(6) and 2:250(5) of the BW.

In situations involving an indirect conflict of interest, it is not always fully clear where exactly that conflict exists.[468] For the company's representatives, the duty to report conflicts of interest is perhaps not self-evident, especially considering that businesspeople are not always concerned with the legality of transactions, while indirect conflicts of interest always pose difficulties for lawyers to interpret. The problem lies in the fact that indirect conflicts of interest cannot simply be confined to related parties, i.e. to the director or major shareholder. Making lists of related parties by itself requires a significant amount of time and effort, and the completeness will depend on full disclosure of relevant information by the interested persons. In many cases, indirect conflicts of interest are not easily detected using lists of relatives or corporate control schemes, given that people also have friends and classmates. It would hardly be possible for the law to regulate this properly, as tracing relationships between (e.g.) classmates from university who have become business partners would demand creative thinking and analysis, which involves more than exhaustive lists of persons.[469] This means that indirect conflict of interest is an area that does not require strict prohibitions, but rather delicate strategies.

Interestingly, the AktG contains a provision similar to those repealed from the BW,[470] although the problems that emerged in the Netherlands have not come to light in Germany. Arguably, the reason is that Article 2:146 and 2:256 of the BW were posited to have an external effect. Article 112 of the AktG opts to regulate the relationship between the director and the company by having the company be represented by the supervisory board. A literal interpretation of this provision does not offer sufficient grounds to apply it to indirect conflicts of interests. Nevertheless, the prevailing opinion is that it extends to appointed and former managers if they are related to the management board's previous or future activity.[471] Further extension of the scope of the provision is held to be permissible as long as this is not incompatible with the principle of legal certainty, for instance if a transaction is with a company in which the manager is the sole shareholder.[472]

The GmbHG treats relationships between private companies and their management boards differently. In German private companies, it is not necessary for the

468. De Groot C, *Corporate Governance as a Limited Legal Concept*, 196.
469. An example of where indirect interests are established on the basis of intellectual examination, rather than formal requirements, can be seen in the diversified criteria for identifying bank-related parties that were introduced by the National Bank of Ukraine in 2015 (Regulation of the Board of the National Bank of Ukraine No. 315 as of 12 May 2015 'On Approval of Charter on Definition of Bank-Related Parties' [Postanova Pravlinnia Natsionalnoho banku Ukrayiny No. 315 vid 12 travnia 2015 roku 'Pro zatverdzhennia Polozhennia pro vyznachennia povyazanykh z bankom osib'], published in Offitsiynyi visnyk Ukrayiny, 2015, No. 82, Stor. 86, St. 2726).
470. AktG, Article 112.
471. Ungerer F, 99.
472. *Ibid.*

supervisory board to represent the company in its dealings with the director.[473] Article 35(3) provides that legal transactions between the director and the company are covered by Article 181 of the German Civil Code if the director is also the company's sole shareholder.[474] Given that Article 181 of the German Civil Code prohibits contracting with oneself, if the agent is involved on both sides of a transaction,[475] legal transactions in violation of Article 35(3) of the GmbHG and Article 181 of the German Civil Code may be voided.[476] For managers of German public companies, Article 181 of the German Civil Code has less effect, as Article 112 of the AktG is more specific.[477]

In Poland, Articles 210 and 379 of the KSH require that, in contracts between the management board and the company, the company must be represented either by the supervisory board or by a representative appointed by the general meeting of shareholders.[478] Unlike in Germany, where Article 112 of the AktG applies only to public companies, the wording of the Polish law means that it applies equally to both private and public companies; however, it is important to bear in mind that Polish private companies are required to have supervisory boards (as an alternative to an auditors' committee) only if the company's share capital exceeds PLN 500,000 and if the company has more than twenty-five shareholders.[479]

When comparing these provisions for direct and indirect conflicts of interest in Germany, Poland and the Netherlands with Ukrainian law, a first important factor is that the rules for Ukrainian companies are different from those of Article 112 of the AktG and Articles 210 and 379 of the KSH. Still, similarly to how Article 181 of the German Civil Code in conjunction with Article 35(3) of the GmbHG applies to relationships involving directors and their companies, the representation rules of Article 238(3) of the CCU come into play in issues of company law. In fact, Article 238(3) of the CCU is not directed primarily at governing corporate relationships; rather, it prohibits representatives from entering into transactions on behalf of the persons that they represent with themselves or with third parties that they also represented, except in matters of commercial representation or in the cases as provided by law. Essentially, two marginally different opinions exist on whether this rule should cover relationships between directors and their companies, i.e. whether the relationships between directors and their companies can be construed as representation.

In a legally binding opinion, the Supreme Court of Ukraine has expressed the view that directors do in fact act as representatives of their companies.[480] Another

473. This may be due partly to the fact that a GmbH must have a supervisory board only if the law so dictates (e.g., *see* Article 52(2) of the GmbHG).
474. German Act on Limited Liability Companies, as consolidated and published in the Federal Law Gazette III, Index No. 4123-1, as most recently amended by Article 8 of the Act of 10 May 2016 (Federal Law Gazette I p. 1142), Article 35(3).
475. German Civil Code, version published on 2 January 2002 (Federal Law Gazette [Bundesgesetzblatt] I p. 42, 2909; 2003 I p. 738), most recently amended by Article 4 paragraph 5 of the Act of 1 October 2013 (Federal Law Gazette I p. 3719), Article 181.
476. *Ibid.*, Article 134.
477. Ungerer F, 100.
478. KSH, Article 210, 379.
479. *Ibid.*, Article 213(2).
480. Legal Opinion of the Supreme Court of Ukraine in a Case about the Invalidation of Contract for Purchase of Immovable Property, Concluded between Legal and Physical Entities, due to the

approach however suggests that these relationships are quasi-representative instead.[481] The logic behind the latter view stems from the idea that the principal and the representative in classical representation are separate entities, whereas these situations lack that separation. This means that, although the director merely enjoys the authority conveyed by the law and the articles of association, he or she should be regarded as an inherent part of the company and its bodies. Still, this theory has not gained many supporters among Ukrainian and Western scholars, and the courts tend to apply the legal provisions on representation to relationships between companies and their management.[482] Little doubt remains, therefore, that Article 238(3) of the CCU can be applied to transactions between directors and their companies, regardless of whether or not the director is the company's shareholder (as in German law). This then prohibits direct conflicts of interest on the part of directors.

Second, the JSC Law of Ukraine and, to a lesser extent, the LLC Law of Ukraine contain special provisions for RPTs that are discussed in subsequent chapters[483] and that encompass both direct and indirect conflicts of interests involving directors and shareholders. At the same time, the list of related parties in the JSC and LLC Laws of Ukraine is not open to interpretation, meaning that indirect conflicts of interest have legally defined ramifications.

Third, Ukrainian company law does not include provisions similar to the rules that Dutch law formerly had in Article 2:146 and 2:256 of the BW, and currently has in Article 2:239(6) and 2:250(5). However, private companies have recently become subject to the special requirements on conflicts of interest introduced in the LLC Law of Ukraine.[484] According to the new statute, a conflict of interest arises if an officer's duty to act reasonably and in a company's interests is at odds with the private interests of the officer and/or affiliated persons.[485] The statute extends the notion of a conflict of interest to those situations if the officer or affiliated person receives gains from a third party in connection with the performance of the officer's duties.[486] By ascribing the effect of a conflict of interest to situations where an officer's affiliated person transacts with a third party, the statute not only recognizes the concept of an indirect conflict of interest but also places the undefined list of third parties on the other side of the transaction. This approach is broader than if only transactions between affiliated persons are covered by 'conflict of interest' requirements. Of course, for a transaction to be deemed to involve a conflict of interest, it must relate to the performance of the

---

Absence of Authorities of the Company's Representative (Director) [Pravovyi vysnovok Verkhovnoho Sudu Ukrayiny u spravi pro vyznannia nediysnym dohovoru kupivli-prodazhu nerukhomoho mayna, ukladenoho mizh yurydychnoyu ta fizychnoyu osobamy, z pidstav vidsutnosti u predstavnyka yurydychnoyi osoby (dyrektora tovarystva) povnovazhen] of 28 April 2016, available at: http://www.scourt.gov.ua/clients/vsu/vsu.nsf/(print)/F874308E74D9E8A5C2257FA3003B0858, accessed on 20 August 2016.

481. Tsiura V, 'Pravova pryroda predstavnytskykh povnovazhen organiv i posavodykh osib yurydychnoyi osoby' (2016) Prykarpatskyi yurydychnyi visnyk 54, 55.
482. For example, *see*: *PrJSC 'Kozeletskiy Combicorm Plant' v. LLC 'Free Group', Decision of 17 January 2017* Case No. 927/1364/15 (Kyiv Economic Court).
483. JSC Law of Ukraine, Article 71; LLC Law of Ukraine, Article 45.
484. LLC Law of Ukraine, Article 42.
485. *Ibid.*, Article 42(3).
486. *Ibid.*, Article 42(5).

officer's duties; still, the officer might not even be aware of the transaction between the affiliated persons and the third party. As a result, he or she would not be able to disclose the conflict and report the transaction to the company in time. A transaction between an affiliated person and a third party is not necessarily detrimental to the company itself if it lacks the constituent features of a conflict of interest. It would therefore seem advisable to add the element of a detrimental effect from the gain to the wording of a provision that equates gains received from third parties by company officers and their affiliated persons with conflicts of interest. Otherwise, the broad understanding of conflicts of interest as introduced by the statute places an excessive burden on the shoulders of company officers.

Besides defining conflicts of interest, the LLC Law of Ukraine prohibits company officers from accepting any advantages besides those provided under the contract between the officer and the company, and from disclosing confidential company information.[487] In addition, company officers are obliged to submit a list of their affiliated persons to the company and to disclose any conflicts of interest to the management board and (if the company has one) the supervisory board.[488] Any failure to comply with these requirements will trigger the company's right to dismiss the officer without paying compensation.[489] Taking into account the broad definition of conflicts of interest, officers could suffer negative consequences for breaching their duties even if the conflict of interest was caused by the actions of an affiliated person.

It follows from the above that indirect conflicts of interest are given less legislative attention in Germany and Poland than direct conflicts, as the legislators drafting the rules were guided by the principle of legal certainty. In the Netherlands, although indirect conflicts of interest are given a brief mention in statute, their clarification is found in cases decided by the courts. In Ukraine, the rules governing direct conflicts of interest coexist with the rules on indirect conflicts, as given shape in procedural requirements for public companies (and to a lesser extent private companies), and the broad duties of company officers of private companies under which they are obliged to be aware of any transactions of affiliated persons that might be deemed to relate to the performance of the officer's duties. The latter requirements seem to be onerous and should be relaxed.

It would be naive to claim that indirect conflicts of interest do not pose any threat to a company: it is not difficult to conceive of situations where the company's assets are tunnelled through various contract or company law vehicles to legal entities or natural persons that are closely related to directors or major shareholders. It would therefore also be wrong to close our eyes to indirect conflicts of interests and pretend that they do not exist.

487. *Ibid.*, Article 42(2, 7).
488. *Ibid.*, Article 42(4, 6).
489. *Ibid.*, Article 42(8).

This is where regulation of RPTs comes into play, as in theory RPTs are usually associated with a conflict of interest that arises for someone in the company.[490] The issues of RPTs and indirect conflicts of interest are very much intertwined: exactly who is considered to be a related party depends on how broadly (or narrowly) the concept of an indirect conflict of interest is defined. The following chapters of this book look at how extensive the list of related parties should be in terms of the fairness and reasonableness requirements from the perspectives of the different national laws.

490. McCahery JA and Vermeulen EPM, 'Corporate Governance Crises and Related Party Transactions: A Post-Parmalat Agenda' in Hopt K and others (eds), *Corporate Governance in Context: Corporations, States, and Markets in Europe, Japan, and the US* (Oxford University Press 2005), 228.

CHAPTER 3

General Features of RPTs

§3.01 THE CONCEPT OF A RELATED PARTY AS PROVIDED BY IAS 24

[A] General Features of the IASs

The meaning of an RPT varies depending on jurisdiction and what international standards apply. In company law, RPTs refer to transactions involving a party who has a link to a company's officers or shareholders and who is simultaneously transacting with that company.[491] As such, it is essential to understand what related parties are.

Though it is not completely unknown, the notion of a related party is relatively new to academic research and legislation. The national laws of a number of countries and various regional instruments include provisions that define what a related party is. EU law is no exception. In its definition of a related party, the Accounting Directive (which replaced the Fourth and the Seventh Council Directives) refers to the IASs as adopted by the IAS Regulation,[492] as did the SRD II Proposal,[493] which subsequently became the current SRD II.[494] These moves may be regarded as illustrative of the

491. For example, *see*: McCahery JA and Vermeulen EPM, 'Corporate Governance Crises and Related Party Transactions: A Post-Parmalat Agenda', 215; Mahtani U, 'An Analysis of Related-Party Transactions in India' Working Paper Series WP No: 2017/01/Fn (Goa Institute Of Management, Poriem, Sattari, Goa 403505), available at: https://www.gim.ac.in/newpdfs/Related-party-transactions-Group-and-Non-Group-Company-Perspective-Jan2017pdf, http://www.iimb.ernet.in/sites/default/files/WP%20No.%20402_0.pdf, accessed on 6 December 2018, 1.
492. Accounting Directive, 27.
493. Proposal for a Directive of the European Parliament and Council amending Directive 2007/36/EC as regards the encouragement of long-term shareholder engagement and Directive 2013/34/EU as regard certain elements of the corporate governance statement, COM (2014) 213 final 2014/0121 (COD), 9.4.2014, 17.
494. Directive 2017/828 of the European Parliament and of the Council of 17 May 2017 amending Directive 2007/36/EC as regards the encouragement of long-term shareholder engagement [2017] OJ L 132/1, 20.5.2017.

Commission's desire for uniform rules with a view to imposing consistent accounting standards.[495]

The IAS Regulation[496] to which the Accounting Directive and the SRD I refer, amended by a regulation from 2008,[497] by its nature is fully binding and directly applicable in all Member States, under the provisions of the TFEU.[498] The IAS Regulation (in its unchanged, original version) is also specified in the Annexes to the EU-Ukraine Association Agreement as an instrument that national laws should approximate.[499] Interestingly, this is a rare occasion where a regulation, despite its legally binding nature in the EU, does not automatically have a direct effect. It has already been harmonized to an extent in Ukraine. The Law of Ukraine 'On Accounting and Financial Reporting in Ukraine' establishes that enterprises with a public interest, public JSCs, enterprises extracting commercial minerals and enterprises designated by the Cabinet of Ministers of Ukraine[500] must prepare their separate and consolidated financial statements in accordance with officially published international standards that are not incompatible with the national laws of Ukraine. Other companies have only a right, rather than a duty, to do so.[501]

The IAS Regulation itself does not define the accounting standards. Rather, it outlines the framework within which the IASs are to be applied. Companies whose shares have been admitted to trade on the regulated markets in the EU are primarily subject to the duty to prepare their consolidated financial statements using the IASs.[502] For other companies, i.e. companies whose securities are not traded on the regulated markets of EU Member States or companies that do not qualify as groups of companies, the Member States have the discretionary power to permit or require use of the IASs. Accordingly, listed companies - even the ones that are part of a group - may be permitted or required to also apply the standards in their financial statements. For other companies, Member States may opt for use of the IASs and IFRS in consolidated financial statements, separate financial statements or both.[503] Member States have reacted to this option in a variety of ways. Of the jurisdictions in the focus, Germany, Poland and the Netherlands in general have refrained from making the use of the IFRSs

495. Regulation (EC) No. 1606/2002 of the European Parliament and the Council of 19 July 2002 on the application of international accounting standards [2002] OJ L 243, 11.9.2002, recital 5.
496. Grundmann S and Glasow F, *European Company Law: Organization, Finance and Capital Markets* (2nd edn, Intersentia 2012), 427.
497. Regulation (EC) No. 297/2008 of the European Parliament and the Council of 11 March 2008 amending Regulation (EC) No. 1606/2002 of the European Parliament and the Council of 19 July 2002 on the application of international accounting standards [2002] OJ L 97/62, 9.4.2008.
498. Treaty on the Functioning of the European Union [2012] OJ C 326/47, 26.10.2012, Article 288.
499. Association Agreement between the European Union and its Member States, of the one part, and Ukraine, of the other part [2014] OJ L 161/3, Annex XXXV.
500. Those other companies that are required to submit financial statements according to international standards are listed in the Order for Submission of Financial Reports, as approved by the Cabinet of Ministers of Ukraine (Resolution No. 419 of 28 February 2000), including credit unions and companies providing financial services.
501. Law of Ukraine 'On Accounting and Financial Reporting in Ukraine' [Zakon Ukrayiny 'Pro bukhgaltersyi oblik ta finansovu zvitnist'] of 8 October 1999, published in Vidomosti Verkhovnoyi Rady Ukrayiny, 1999, No. 40, St. 365, Article 12-1(2, 3).
502. IAS Regulation, Articles 1, 4.
503. *Ibid.*, Article 5.

obligatory. Only Germany mandates the use of standards for consolidated financial statements for non-listed companies, and Poland for banks. However, each of these three Member States generally allows application of the IASs with some national features. In Germany, annual financial statements must be prepared according to both national GAAP and international standards. In Poland, non-listed companies are allowed to prepare their financial statements according to the IASs and the IFRSs only if they have applied for admission to trade on a regulated market. In the Netherlands, where both separate and consolidated financial statements may follow international standards, the only exception (i.e., where companies are not permitted to use those standards for their financial statements) is for consolidated financial statements prepared under national law.[504] In general, these Member States have introduced largely discretionary regimes for application of the IASs by entities that do not include listed public companies. This is especially true for the Netherlands.[505]

In Ukraine, the use of the IASs goes further than the requirements under the IAS Regulation. When the JSC Law of Ukraine was first adopted in 2008, it provided for a change in the Law of Ukraine 'On Securities and Stock Market'. All public JSCs were obliged to disclose information about their activities on the basis of the IASs.[506] Later, in 2011, the Parliament amended the Law of Ukraine 'On Accounting and Financial Reporting in Ukraine'. The effect of the IASs was extended to include not only public JSCs but also banks, insurers and some other business forms, as established by the Cabinet of Ministers of Ukraine.[507] In the Member States discussed above, conversely, the rules are less imperative: for instance, companies rendering financial services (such as credit unions) do not fall within the scope of these mandatory rules. These moves by the Ukrainian legislature were already regarded as overly inclusive. For some companies that are not inherently public, the cost of preparing financial statements in accordance with international standards is too high (as much USD 50,000 in some cases).[508] On 1 January 2018, Ukraine introduced new rules: banks and insurers were excused from the duty to apply the IASs, while enterprises with public interest and enterprises extracting commercial minerals were added to the group of companies that must prepare their financial statements based on the IASs.[509]

504. 'Use of options of the IAS Regulation by Member States [table]', available at: (http://ec.europa.eu/finance/company-reporting/docs/legal_framework/20140718-ias-use-of-options_en.pdf, 2014).
505. *Report from the Commission to the Council and the European Parliament on the operation of Regulation (EC) No. 1606/2002 of 19 July 2002 on the application of international accounting standards* (COM (2008) 215 final, 2442008, 2008), 3.
506. Law of Ukraine 'On Securities and Stock Market' [Zakon Ukrayiny 'Pro tsinni papery ta fondovyi rynok'], Article 40(6).
507. For example, credit unions, as provided by the Order for Submission of Financial Reports, approved by the Cabinet of Ministers of Ukraine (Resolution No. 419 of 28 February 2000), paragraph 2.
508. Marenych T, 'Zaprovadzhennia mizhnarodnykh standartiv bukhgalterskoho obliku ta finansovoyi zvitnosti u vitchyznianu praktyku' (2012) Ekonomika ahropromyslovoho kompleksu 44, 47.
509. Law of Ukraine 'On Accounting and Financial Reporting in Ukraine' [Zakon Ukrayiny 'Pro bukhgaltersyi oblik ta finansovu zvitnist'], Article 12-1(2, 3).

[B] The Concept of a Related Party According to IAS 24

The specific definition of a related party is found in IAS 24, which is available in the annex to the Commission Regulation No. 1126/2008. That annex was updated in Commission Regulation (EU) 632/2010, bringing forward the most recent version of IAS 24 to supersede its 2003 version.[510]

In paragraph 9, IAS 24 defines a related party as a person or entity that is related to the entity preparing its financial statements ('the reporting entity'). The core meaning of a related party, as provided in IAS 24, is therefore concerned with a direct or indirect connection to the reporting entity. Two basic criteria are applied for identifying a related party in IAS 24.9: it is either (i) a person[511] (ii) or a legal entity.

On the subject of categories of individuals as indicated in IAS 24.9, paragraph (a) covers three types of persons: (i) those having control or joint control over the reporting entity; (ii) those having significant influence over the reporting entity; and (iii) members of the key management personnel of a reporting entity or of a parent of a reporting entity. A close member of the person's family is also regarded as a related party, even if he or she has no direct connection to the reporting entity.

Despite being detailed and elaborate, IAS 24 does not add further detail for some of its stated notions, including the notions of 'control', 'significant influence', 'key management personnel' and 'close members of the family'. As each of these concepts could itself be the subject of a separate and complex study, the present book does not discuss them all in detail.

[C] Control, Joint Control, Significant Influence and Key Management Personnel in IAS 24 and Other Sources of EU Law

The first category of persons referred to in IAS 24 (category (i)) includes individuals who have control or joint control over the entity. Both control and joint control are explained in IAS 24: *control is the power to govern the financial and operating policies of an entity so as to obtain benefits from its activities* and *joint control is defined as the contractually agreed sharing of control over an economic activity.*

These definitions of control and joint control are too abstract to provide clear limits for the terms. This is where other legal sources can be helpful for a legal interpretation of IAS 24, which is not the only legal instrument to use the notion of control in European law, let alone the national laws of the Member States.

European soft law refers to control in Commission Recommendation 2005/162/EC, stating that independent non-executive or supervisory directors may not

510. Commission Regulation (EU) No. 632/2010 of 19 July 2010 amending Regulation (EC) No. 1126/2008 adopting certain international accounting standards in accordance with Regulation (EC) No. 1606/2002 of the European Parliament and of the Council as regards International Accounting Standard (IAS) 24 and International Financial Reporting Standard (IFRS) 8 [2010] OJ L 186/1, 20.7.2010, Annex IAS 24, paragraph 29.

511. The terminology of IAS 24 has been criticized by some authors (*see* Ungerer F, 40), as persons can refer to both natural and legal persons, whereas the meaning of a person in IAS 24 is restricted to natural persons only.

be controlling shareholders. Control there is defined by reference to the cases mentioned in Article 1(1) of the Seventh Council Directive.[512] A perusal of the Seventh Council Directive, which has already been repealed by the Accounting Directive[513] but is still in place for the purposes of the EU-Ukraine Association Agreement,[514] shows that the Seventh Council Directive uses qualitative, rather than quantitative, criteria.[515] Under the Seventh Council Directive, control means more than simply having a majority of the voting rights.[516] A shareholder in a company, even one with a minority stake, can also exercise control if he or she can appoint or remove a majority of the members of an administrative, management or supervisory body;[517] exercise dominant influence over the undertaking pursuant to a contract, memorandum or the articles of association;[518] have the majority of members of an administrative, management or supervisory body appointed based solely on the shareholder's voting;[519] or exercise, either alone or in concert with other shareholders, control over a majority of the voting rights.[520] The idea behind the concept of control has not changed with the adoption of the Accounting Directive, with Article 1(1) of the Seventh Council Directive becoming Article 22(1) of the Accounting Directive. As a result, although control is based primarily on a majority of the voting rights in an undertaking, it may also have a contractual basis or be exercised even through a small shareholding.[521]

Like the Accounting Directive, SRD I similarly recognizes control and controlling shareholders.[522] Unlike the Accounting Directive, however, it does not clarify what they mean.

Another important piece of EU legislation that refers to control in companies is the Takeover Directive. According to that Directive, control is acquired by a natural person or an entity as a result of the acquisition of securities that directly or indirectly give him or her a specified percentage of the voting rights.[523] Here, the criteria are of a more quantitative nature compared with the criteria in the Accounting Directive. Based on the wording used in the Takeover Directive, the more securities a person acquires, the more control he or she obtains. From the perspective of the Takeover Directive, therefore, control is closely associated with share ownership.

---

512. Commission Recommendation of 15 February 2005 on the role of non-executive or supervisory directors of listed companies and on the committees of the (supervisory) board [2005] OJ L 52/51, 25.2.2005, Annex II, 1(d).
513. Accounting Directive, Article 52.
514. Association Agreement between the European Union and its Member States, of the one part, and Ukraine, of the other part [2014] OJ L 161/3, Annex 35.
515. Lukach I, *Teoretychni problemy pravovoho reguliuvannia korporatyvnykh vidnosyn v Ukrayini: [monographiya]* (K.: Lira-K 2015), 219.
516. Seventh Council Directive 83/349/EEC of 13 June 1983 based on the Article 54(3)(g) of the Treaty on consolidated accounts [1983] OJ L 193, 18.7.83, Article 1(1)(a).
517. *Ibid.*, Article 1(1)(b).
518. *Ibid.*, Article 1(1)(c).
519. *Ibid.*, Article 1(1)(d)(aa).
520. *Ibid.*, Article 1(1)(d)(bb).
521. Accounting Directive, recital 31.
522. Directive 2007/36/EC of the European Parliament and of the Council of 11 July 2007 on the exercise of certain rights of shareholders in listed companies [2007] OJ L 184, 14.7.2007, Article 10.
523. Takeover Directive, Article 5(1).

Article 5(3) of the Takeover Directive goes on to state that the percentage of voting rights that confer control for the purposes of paragraph 1, and the method of its calculation, must be determined by the rules of the Member State in which the company has its registered office. This means that it is within the Member States' discretion to decide how to define control for the purposes of the takeover rules.[524] No universally applicable rule exists for determining control, and Member States can choose different strategies for determining how to define it. This inevitably leads to the types of control as outlined and described in exhaustive detail by Berle and Means in their celebrated work.[525]

To elaborate, Berle and Means identify five types of control: (i) complete ownership control; (ii) majority ownership; (iii) legal device control without majority ownership; (iv) minority ownership; (v) and management control.[526] Of these five types of control, two are not necessarily based on ownership: control through a legal device and management control. Legal devices used to exercise control as mentioned by Berle and Means include multiple voting rights, pyramid structures and control through trust.[527] Management control essentially refers to cases where ownership is separated from control if a group of security holders own shares but exercise virtually no control due to their dispersed ownership.[528] This is a common feature of outsider systems more typical of the UK[529] and the US and occurs less commonly in Continental Europe. On the mainland, family-owned firms and other blockholders are widespread, making regulation more insider or control-oriented.[530] High ownership concentration, which is typical of insider systems, is often coupled with an inactive market for control and low liquidity of capital markets.[531] For instance, the concentration of voting power in German companies has previously been described as extraordinarily high for 82% of the officially listed German AGs. They are controlled by large blockholders with more than 25% of the voting rights.[532] These figures may have changed as the dynamics of voting control evolve and offer more room for dispersed ownership, yet they are still accurate due to the presence of large family-owned firms and foundation-controlled

524. Tomasz Regucki presented his comparative study of the various control mechanisms at the 6th CECL Conference in Warsaw, on 10 July 2016. Two basic approaches have been taken in these rules: defining a specific threshold for control, or applying qualitative criteria (de facto control). Both approaches have their advantages (clarity and certainty in the threshold approach, proper reflection of market dynamics in the qualitative approach) and disadvantages (the threshold approach essentially being detrimental to minority shareholders and not reflecting prevailing market conditions, and qualitative criteria not being sufficiently clear and possibly being to the detriment of majority shareholders).
525. Berle A and Means G, 70-90.
526. *Ibid.*, 70.
527. *Ibid.*, 72-80.
528. Becht M and Mayer C, 1.
529. Also described as a '*full divorce between ownership and control in a British obsession*' (*see* Searjeant G, 'Plc Is Ready to Join Mutuals in Land of the Dodo' Times (21 April 2006)).
530. Cheffins BR, *Corporate Ownership and Control: British Business Transformed* (Oxford University Press 2008), 5.
531. Keong LC, 'The Corporate Governance Debate' in Low CK (ed.), *Corporate Governance: An Asia-Pacific Critique* (Sweet & Maxwell Asia 2002), 5.
532. Becht M and Böhmer E, 'Voting Control in German Corporations' (2003) 23 International Review of Law and Economics 1, 26.

companies.[533] Situations where the largest blockholder holds more than 25% are particularly illustrative; they are known as 'working' control or, to apply the classification used by Berle and Means, cases of minority control where none of the shareholders have a majority of the voting rights, and as a consequence the primary role is occupied by the largest shareholders.

The example of 'working' control is especially controversial in light of the requirement under the Takeover Directive that a minimum ownership threshold must be established to trigger the controlling shareholder's duty to make a bid, to protect the minority shareholders.[534] Taking into account that control in these circumstances should preferably be determined on a case-by-case basis, it would be impossible to strictly impose a specific minimum shareholding that would fit every imaginable scenario. At the same time, making control subject to interpretative actions of a specific body is also impractical. Interpretation is sometimes an abusive exercise, and always a time-consuming practice. In addition, providing specific bodies with interpretative powers would not be conducive to legal certainty. That is why in these situations establishing an exact minimum shareholding required for control is a viable solution, though one that lacks universality. It would be even more ambiguous to have such a threshold established at the EU level, as share ownership could be structured differently at the national level. Consequently, despite everything, the current legislative provisions lead to a more balanced and fair legislative solution than if the issue were resolved by the EU authorities. When choosing the appropriate national model to implement Article 5 of the Takeover Directive, many Member States have opted for a 30% control threshold, such as Germany[535] and the Netherlands,[536] while in Poland the threshold is 66% of the voting rights.[537]

Regardless of how the legislature defines control, it is important to bear in mind that exercising de facto control does not necessarily require a person to have more than 30% of the share capital or voting power. As has been noted, even a 2% shareholding can confer control, if it is combined with other means of influence.[538] That is why the legal definitions of control that Member States have developed at the national level for the purposes of takeover regulation are not universally applicable in all circumstances. They have been designed specifically to deal with situations of mandatory bids, as described in Article 5 of the Takeover Directive. Using the ownership-based definition of control found in takeover laws for other means beyond Article 5 of the Takeover Directive would be taking matters too far. As evidenced by the case of Rockfeller, who

533. Fleischer H, 'A Guide to German Company Law for International Lawyers: Distinctive Features, Particularities, Idiosyncracies' in Fleischer H, Hansen JL and Ringe W-G (eds), *German and Nordic Perspectives on Company Law and Capital Markets Law* (Mohr Siebeck 2015), 9.
534. Takeover Directive, Article 5(1).
535. Beinert D, Burmeister F and Tries H-J, 67.
536. De Brauw C, Groothuis L and Stevens R, *The Netherland Takeover Guide*, available at: https://www.ibanet.org/Document/Default.aspx?DocumentUid=8E6BF591-D567-4594-BC81-00E0BA83AF39 (2014), 3.
537. Andenæs MT and Wooldridge F, *European Comparative Company Law* (Cambridge University Press 2009), 512.
538. Hopt KJ (ed.), *Groups of Companies in European Laws*, vol 2 (de Gruyter 1982), 249.

exercised control with a 14.9% shareholding only,[539] or by the provisions of the Accounting Directive that refer to 'contract-based' control, control is possible with less than the established percentage of shares.

While the Takeover Directive confers on Member States the power to take legislative steps to clarify the meaning of control in terms of Article 5, IAS 24 does not make any explicit reference to the national laws of the Member States. Rather, it presents its own vision of 'control', 'significant influence' and 'key management personnel'. To better understand the meaning of these concepts, the definitions of 'control' and 'joint control' must be compared with the definitions of 'significant influence' and 'key management personnel'. Although both 'control' and 'significant influence' constitute power, the main difference between them from the perspective of IAS 24 is that control is about the power to govern an entity's financial and operating policies, while significant influence refers to the power to participate in those policies. Significant influence may be based on share ownership, statute or agreement. Although the definitions of 'control' and 'significant influence' lack clarity and are subject to further interpretation, it can be concluded from these definitions that 'control' provides for potentially stronger ties between a related party and a reporting entity, with correspondingly more power. In turn, 'significant influence' has a more differentiated basis, including share ownership, as well as statute and agreements.[540]

One possible source of confusion in the definition of significant influence, as compared with control and joint control, is that according to IAS 24 significant influence may be based on agreements. Conversely, the definition of control does not include any reference to a contractual basis. At the same time, excluding contract-based relationships from the scope of control would be contrary to the core of the concepts of control and joint control. In Germany, the fact that control may similarly be based on agreements stems directly from Article 317 of the AktG, which explicitly provides for the possibility to enter into controlling agreements that allow the controlling enterprise to issue instructions to the subordinate company.[541] It is therefore reasonable to consider that control and joint control may be based not only on share ownership, as stated narrowly in the Takeover Directive, but also on contractual arrangements and the entity's articles of association.

Key management personnel, also identified in IAS 24 as a type of related party, are those persons who have authority and responsibility for planning, directing and controlling the entity's activities, whether directly or indirectly, including any director (whether executive or otherwise) of that entity. This definition in IAS 24 mainly covers the management boards of companies, as is evident from the very name given to this group of related parties. Whether this group also extends to members of supervisory

539. Berle A and Means G, 82-84.
540. Significant influence is treated on the same footing as the relationships between the entity and key management personnel, whereas control describes a closer relationship between a person and an entity (*see also* KPMG, *'First Impressions: Amendments to IAS 24 Related Party Disclosures', International Financial Reporting Standards, November 2009*, available at: https://home.kpmg.com/content/dam/kpmg/pdf/2010/01/First-Impressions-O-0911.pdf 2009, 10).
541. Frommel SN and Bonn A, *Company Law in Europe* (Kluwer Academic Publishers 1975), 263.

boards as used in the jurisdictions in focus (Germany and Poland enjoy the two-tier system,[542] and the Netherlands has a hybrid system of corporate governance, established after the recent 2013 amendments of corporate laws, which provides for an optional basis in the entity's articles of association[543]) is also subject to interpretation. The broad concepts of 'direct and indirect' 'direction and control of the entity's activities' do not stand in the way of them being regarded as related parties in relationships with the company.[544] Moreover, it is commonly accepted that members of management and supervisory boards should be recognized as related parties for the company. This is rooted in the provisions of the CGCs as used in Germany and the Netherlands.[545] A supervisory board member cannot be equated with the board as a separate body in a company. For this reason, it makes sense to regard transactions between a company and a member of its supervisory board as RPTs. In this respect, IAS 24 is somewhat at odds with IAS 28. The latter standard interprets representation on the board of directors or equivalent governing body of the investee as evidence of significant influence, rather than participating in an entity's key management personnel.[546] Although it has little practical significance, this difference in interpretation does not make the IASs any more helpful.

[D] IAS 24 on Legal Entities as Related Parties

While IAS 24's rules governing natural persons as related parties concern three types of relationships that give grounds to regard parties as related, the analysis of the IAS 24 provisions for legal entities in category (b) as related parties is more complicated.

542. Teichmann C and Gurman O, 'Directors' Remuneration in Germany' in Van der Elst C (ed.), *Executive Directors' Remuneration in Comparative Corporate Perspective*, vol 11 (Kluwer Law International 2015), 174; Radwan A and Regucki T, 'Legal Aspects of Executive Remuneration in Polish Listed Companies' in Van der Elst C (ed.), *Executive Directors' Remuneration in Comparative Corporate Perspective*, vol 11 (Kluwer Law International 2015), 301.
543. Lafarre A and Van der Elst C, 'Executive Pay and Say-on-Pay in the Netherlands' in Van der Elst C (ed.), *Executive Directors' Remuneration in Comparative Corporate Perspective*, vol 11 (Kluwer Law International 2015), 208-209.
544. However, IAS 24 also expressly states that legal entities that have the same persons in key management positions are not necessarily related parties. The reasoning might be that these persons are sometimes retired politicians, civil servants or celebrities serving on multiple boards at the same time (Putra LD, 'Related Party Transaction Disclosures [IAS 24]' (*Accounting, Financial and Tax*, available at: http://accounting-financial-tax.com/, April 2009) http://accounting-financial-tax.com/2009/04/related-party-transaction-disclosures-ias-24/, accessed on 25 July 2016).
545. German Corporate Governance Code (Deutscher Corporate Governance Kodex), as amended on 5 May 2015; The Dutch corporate governance code, Principles of good governance and best practices provisions, 9 December 2003.
546. International Accounting Standard 28 Investments in Associates, as adopted by Commission Regulation (EC) No. 1126/2008 of 3 November 2008 adopting certain international accounting standards in accordance with Regulation (EC) No. 1606/2002 of the European Parliament and of the Council [2008] OJ L 320/1, 29.11.2008, paragraph 7.

First, related parties as described in IAS 24 should not be confused with related companies, the term that some countries use for groups of companies.[547] Although IAS 24 largely deals with groups by referring to their constituent companies as related parties,[548] groups as such are not the only participants identified by IAS 24. Besides groups and their members,[549] IAS 24 also deals with individuals, their close family members[550] and legal entities related to each other through non-group links.

In addition to 'control', 'significant influence' and 'key management personnel' in relationships involving legal entities, IAS 24 also refers to the notions of 'associate' and 'joint venture'. Based on the provisions of IAS 24, legal entities are considered to be related if one is an associate or a joint venture of another.[551] Legal entities are also viewed as being related if two entities are joint ventures of a third party,[552] or if one entity is an associate of a third party while another one is a joint venture of that same third party.[553]

While IAS 24 refers to the notions of 'control', 'significant influence' and 'key management personnel', it does not address these terms in detail. Their meaning is mostly explained in other relevant standards, to which IAS 24 itself also makes reference.[554] IAS 31 'Interests in Joint Ventures'[555] defines a joint venture as a contractual arrangement, whereby two or more parties undertake an economic activity that is subject to joint control.[556] The definition of an associate is given in IAS 28 'Investments in Associates and Joint Ventures',[557] regarding it as an entity over which the investor has significant influence. In other words, while in a joint venture two parties exercise joint control through contractual arrangements, the relationship between an associate and an investor is one of significant influence, which is less serious and stringent than joint control. This means that 'joint venture' and 'associate' are mutually exclusive notions, reflecting a stronger connection between legal entities or 'merely' significant influence, respectively. In light of IAS 28, significant influence is interpreted as meaning, among other scenarios, 20% or more of the voting rights in the

---

547. Chong S and Dean G, 'Related Party Transactions: A Preliminary Evaluation of Sfas-57 and Ias-24 Using 4 Case Studies' (1985) 21 Abacus-A Journal of Accounting Finance and Business Studies 84, 86.
548. International Accounting Standard 24 Related Party Disclosures, as adopted by Commission Regulation (EU) No. 632/2010 of 19 July 2010 amending Regulation (EC) No. 1126/2008 adopting certain international accounting standards in accordance with Regulation (EC) No. 1606/2002 of the European Parliament and of the Council as regards International Accounting Standard (IAS) 24 and International Financial Reporting Standard (IFRS) 8 [2010] OJ L 186/1, 20.7.2010, paragraph 9(b)(i).
549. Chapter 4 examines groups and RPTs more closely.
550. *See* section §3.02.
551. IAS 24, paragraph 9(b)(ii).
552. *Ibid.*, paragraph 9(b)(iii).
553. *Ibid.*, paragraph 9(b)(iv).
554. *Ibid.*, paragraph 15.
555. Its more recent version is given shape in International Financial Reporting Standard (IFRS) 11.
556. International Accounting Standard 31 Interests in Joint Ventures, as adopted by Commission Regulation (EC) No. 1126/2008 of 3 November 2008 adopting certain international accounting standards in accordance with Regulation (EC) No. 1606/2002 of the European Parliament and of the Council [2008] OJ L 320/1, 29.11.2008, paragraph 3.
557. IAS 28 Investments in Associates, paragraph 2.

investee.[558] This does not necessarily mean that a person with less than 20% of the voting rights cannot have significant influence, however: IAS 28 establishes other factors besides voting power that can lead to significant influence.[559]

An analysis of subparagraph (ii) of paragraph 9 of IAS 24 justifies the conclusion that both the reporting entity and the legal entity in a relationship of 'control', 'joint control' or 'significant influence' are related parties. Entities that are 'associates' or 'joint ventures' are also regarded as related parties. This is an example of the principle of symmetry in action: if A is related to B for the purposes of B's financial statements, then A is also related to B in A's financial statements.[560]

For parties to be treated as related, it matters little whether the direct link between them is one of 'control' or one of 'significant influence'. However, the practical value of this distinction is obvious where paragraphs (iii), (iv), (vi) and (vii) describe situations where the link between two entities is indirect.

First, in situations where a third party exercises joint control over two entities, or even joint control over one entity and significant influence over another, those two entities are regarded as being related. Yet the same does not hold true in the case of two entities that are significantly influenced by a third party, i.e. two entities that are both associates of a third.[561]

Second, if a natural person exercises control or joint control over two entities, or joint control over one entity and significant influence over another, or controls one entity (singly or jointly) while also being a member of the key management personnel of another, those two entities are considered to be related. Again, however, if the same natural person is only a member of the key management personnel of the two entities or exercises significant influence over them both, those two entities are not related parties.[562]

It can be concluded from the above that if the distance between two parties constitutes two or more 'significant influences' or 'key management personnel' relationships, the parties are usually not related for the purposes of IAS 24. However, indirect relationships with control or joint control in one leg result in related parties.[563] That was not the case under the IASs in the 2003 edition, which included a provision that, if a member of key management personnel is in a relationship of 'significant influence' with one entity, and a close relative has significant influence over another entity, those two entities were related, as opposed to two entities under the significant influence of a corporate investor.[564] This discrepancy was changed in the current 2009 version of IAS 24, where members of key management personnel are regarded together with their close family members as one person.[565] They are treated similarly to groups

558. *Ibid.*, paragraph 8.
559. Ungerer F, 151.
560. KPMG, *'First Impressions: Amendments to IAS 24 Related Party Disclosures'*, 4.
561. Nevertheless, two venturers exercising joint control over one entity are deemed not to be related (IAS 24, paragraph 11(b)).
562. *Ibid.*, paragraph 11(a).
563. KPMG, *'First Impressions: Amendments to IAS 24 Related Party Disclosures'*, 13.
564. *Ibid.*, 12.
565. IAS 24, paragraph 9.

of companies and members of such groups,[566] meaning that every transaction between a reporting entity and a close relative of a member of its key management personnel is treated as if it were a transaction between the reporting entity and the member of its key management personnel. Under the current rules, if a member of one entity's key management personnel significantly influences another entity, those entities are not regarded as being related.

It has also been claimed that IAS 24 (2009 version) has a greater scope than its previous versions, with the elimination of the previous asymmetry in indirect relationships. For instance, from the perspective of an entity under the significant influence of an investor in another entity, they were related parties, while from the perspective of the investee the first entity was not related.[567] With the removal of this asymmetry, some entities became obliged to comply with the reporting requirements. While this certainly does not alter the fact that the changes mean that some entities no longer fall under the reporting requirements of IAS 24, as noted above,[568] in general this removal has only added to the list of potential related parties triggering duties of reporting entities and expanded the definition of a related party.[569] Though seemingly fair, the new rules have created some reporting difficulties for investees. They might not always be aware of other entities in which the investor has significant influence and the need to report properly on entities as related parties. The investor will have to share the legally relevant information with the investee to ensure that the latter can comply with its reporting obligations.[570]

Another issue that has merged in the literature on the topic is whether IAS 24 should be applied to relationships between unrelated parties. As suggested by Chong and Dean, *accountants should be concerned about all non-arm's length transactions and not merely RPTs*. The authors consider it more reasonable for IAS 24 to encompass *non-arm's length transactions between unrelated parties in addition to those between related parties*.[571] Their concern is understandable, as stakeholders are more worried about whether the transaction is on market terms than whether it is with a related party. However, the drafters of IAS 24 clearly preferred to omit transactions with unrelated parties from its scope, explaining this by admitting that *transactions between related parties may not be made at the same amounts as between unrelated parties*.[572] It is difficult to disagree with this statement. Besides the fact that transactions with unrelated parties are not numerous, other apparent reasons exist not to use them so widely. The introduction to IAS 24 for transactions with unrelated parties undoubtedly

566. *Ibid.*, paragraph 9(b)(i)(ii).
567. KPMG, '*First Impressions: Amendments to IAS 24 Related Party Disclosures*', 1, 8.
568. Under the IAS 24 (2009 version), two entities are not related by the mere fact that one entity's member of key management personnel has a close family member exercising significant influence over another entity.
569. *Endorsement of the 2009 Revised IAS 24 Related Party Disclosures, Introduction, Background and Conclusions* (European Commission, Brussels, 4 February 2010, MARKT F3, 2010), 2.
570. However, this investor's duty is of a moral nature and is not based on legally binding provisions.
571. Chong S and Dean G, 96.
572. IAS 24, paragraph 6.

poses challenges for accountants. These types of disclosures require creative professional valuation and the need for detailed disclosure criteria, and the requirements of legal certainty are clearly neglected in favour of extended and arguably more transparent disclosure. The scope of disclosure of RPTs is discussed in Chapter 5 of this book.

§3.02 THE CONCEPT OF A RELATED PARTY IN CGCs

Both Germany and the Netherlands have CGCs that prescribe rules for conflicts of interest. They cover RPTs where a member of either the management board or the supervisory board is a related party, rather than transactions between a company and its shareholders. They also address persons close to or affiliated with management or supervisory board members.

The general rule contained in the 2017 German CGC requires all transactions between an enterprise and the members of its management board and their related parties[573] to comply with standards customary in the sector.[574] Those provisions have been removed in the draft 2020 German CGC.[575]

Although the suggestion has been put forward that persons connected to management board members are not covered by the CGC,[576] the rules in the 2017 version do not exclude transactions with those parties from regulation. The regulation of parties connected to the management board differs in that managers still have more obligations than their related parties. For instance, they are required to disclose conflicts of interest to the supervisory board without delay and to inform other members of the management board accordingly. What the 2017 version of the German CGC lacks is a list of persons understood to be related parties or, in the wording of the CGC's earlier version, persons close to the members of the management board. This provision is therefore subject to interpretation.

Surprisingly, with the rules for conflicts of interest of supervisory board members, the 2017 version of the German CGC does not require transactions with persons who are not members of the supervisory board, but who are related parties or, to use older terminology: persons connected to them or companies with which they have a personal association, to comply with the standards customary in the sector[577] – despite the fact that transactions between a company and members of its supervisory board or their related parties could pose greater risks for the company. However, the AktG contains a provision stating that, where a supervisory board member enters into a contract with the company to provide professional services, in addition to his or her role on the supervisory board, the company must be represented by the entire supervisory board in its dealing with that member.[578]

573. The previous version of the CGC used a different wording: instead of 'related parties' the CGC referred to *persons that are close to or companies they have a personal association with*.
574. German CGC, as amended on 7 February 2017, § 4.3.3.
575. German draft CGC 2020, section E.
576. McCahery JA and Vermeulen EPM, 'Corporate Governance Crises and Related Party Transactions: A Post-Parmalat Agenda', 238.
577. German CGC, as amended on 7 February 2017, § 5.5.
578. AktG, Article 114.

While the 2017 version of the German CGC requires important transactions where management board members are related parties to be approved by the supervisory board,[579] the Dutch CGC (2016 version) provides for different regulations. The Dutch CGC specifies for both management and supervisory board members that decisions to enter into transactions involving conflicts of interest, including RPTs, are always subject to supervisory board approval if they are of material significance to the company or to the relevant management board member.[580] However, the Dutch CGC has the same rule for supervisory board members,[581] unlike the 2017 version of the German CGC, as noted above.

Another difference between the two CGCs lies in the provisions of the Dutch CGC specifying a list of related parties that are regarded as presenting a conflict of interest for management. The German CGC does not contain a similar rule. According to the Dutch CGC, a conflict of interest arises if a company intends to enter into transaction with a legal entity (a) in which a management or a supervisory board member has a personal material financial interest; or (b) that has a management or supervisory board member who has a relationship under family law with a management or supervisory board member of the company.[582] Additionally, the Dutch CGC prohibits members of management and supervisory boards from demanding or accepting gifts of any substance from other companies. They are also not permitted to take advantage of business opportunities falling to their company for themselves or a spouse, registered partner or other life companion, foster child or relative by blood or marriage in the first or second degree.[583]

The rules described above bring this analysis back to IAS 24, which provides the definition of a person close to a related person. IAS 24 defines them as including all family members who may be expected to influence, or to be influenced by, that person in their dealings with the entity and include: (a) the person's children and spouse or domestic partner; (b) children of the person's spouse or domestic partner; and (c) dependents of the person or the person's spouse or domestic partner.[584]

Interestingly, here the Dutch CGC provides more extensive rules to cover related parties. Besides the difference in terminology for the person's partners (*spouse, registered partner or other life companion* in the Dutch CGC and *dependents …, spouse or domestic partner* in IAS 24), the Dutch CGC also ascribes the status of a related party to 'relatives by blood or marriage in the first or second degree'. This means that the following categories are also regarded as related parties: (i) the person's grandchildren, (ii) the person's grandparents, (iii) the spouses of the person's children and (iv) the parents of the person's spouse.[585] In spite of the fact that IAS 24 contains a long list of

579. German CGC, as amended on 7 February 2017, § 4.3.4.
580. Dutch CGC, section 2.7.4 (§ II.3 in the previous version).
581. *Ibid.*, section 2.7.4 (§ III.6 in the previous version).
582. *Ibid.*, section 2.7.3 (§ II.3.2 in the previous version).
583. *Ibid.*, section 2.7.1(ii) (§ II.3.1(b)(d) in the previous version).
584. IAS 24, paragraph 9.
585. Using the instructions for determining degrees of relatedness by marriage and blood, for example as described in Borysova V and Zhylinkova I (eds), *Simeyne pravo Ukrayiny: pidruchnyk* (2nd edn, Yurinkom Inter 2009), 64.

related parties defined in vague and broad terms,[586] subject to additional interpretation by lawyers and accountants,[587] here the drafters of IAS 24 left a gap. As a result, transactions between a reporting entity and, for instance, the grandfather of a management board member will not fall under the scope of the standard, unless of course the grandfather is established to have control or significant influence over the reporting entity. It would be wrong to overstate the effect of this prohibition in the Dutch CGC:[588] as noted above, it is confined to transactions involving transfers of substantial gifts and business opportunities. Nevertheless, the difference is not so minor that it should go unnoticed. The gap in IAS 24 could be filled by the flexible rule focusing on the substance of the related party relationship, rather than on its form.[589] Interpreted broadly, this rule would allow for a sensible application of the regulations for close relatives, which would then include more than only the relatives explicitly stipulated in the standard: others who are not mentioned there but who nevertheless have close ties to the reporting entity, its shareholders or key management personnel would also be viewed as related parties. Arguably, grandparents, as second-degree relatives, could be covered by this flexible interpretation, although this flexibility does not improve clarity. Rather, it could force practitioners to analyse the substance of every single relationship between parties. For instance, a far degree of relatedness might not necessarily lead to exclusion from the rules on related parties: the person in question could have strong links to the company that also give rise to reporting obligations.

While both Germany and the Netherlands have unified single CGCs,[590] Poland uses the guidelines for companies whose securities are listed on stock exchanges. The Warsaw Stock Exchange has implemented the WSE Best Practice for WSE listed companies.[591] Like other CGCs, the WSE Best Practice employs the 'comply or explain' principle.[592]

The WSE Best Practice contains rules on conflicts of interest for members of both management and supervisory boards. Like the Dutch CGC, the WSE Best Practice requires significant agreements with related parties and also agreements with shareholders having 5% or more of the total voting rights in the company to be approved by

586. The notions of 'control', 'significant influence' and 'key management personnel' are highly illustrative examples, and the fact that the word 'includes' is used for the list of close relatives means that other close relatives are also implied. Additionally, the cultural context might influence how a 'close relative' is interpreted; for example depending on cultural origins siblings might not be regarded as close relatives (Putra LD, 'Related Party Transaction Disclosures [IAS 24]').
587. For example, in 2009, KPMG issued a report that clarified some novelties of the revised IAS 24, namely pointed at the fact that the disclosure asymmetry existing at that moment was removed (KPMG, '*First Impressions: Amendments to IAS 24 Related Party Disclosures*').
588. Dutch CGC, section 2.7.1(ii) (§ II.3.1(b)(d) in the previous version).
589. IAS 24, paragraph 10.
590. Both Germany and the Netherlands are among the countries where reporting entities are required by law to show compliance with the CGC, as opposed to countries where the listing authority officially requires disclosure (*see*: Cuomo F, Mallin C and Zattoni A, 223).
591. WSE Best Practice.
592. *Ibid.*, 2.

the supervisory board.[593] The rule about the transactions with 5% shareholders is a new addition in the current version of the WSE Best Practice – the previous version referred only to related parties.[594]

Although the terminology used in the WSE Best Practice differs from the German and the Dutch CGCs, the concept is the same: RPTs do not require approval in every situation. The approval requirements do not apply to typical transactions and transactions on market terms made between the company and members of its group in the course of the company's normal operations.[595] Similarly, the earlier version of the WSE Best Practice did not require supervisory board approval for typical transactions on market terms within the scope of a company's normal operations with a subsidiary in which the company held a majority stake.[596] Though not immediately apparent, the difference between the older and the current version seems significant. The current version does not require approval for all typical transactions. In the earlier version, typical transactions were exempted from the approval obligation only in parent-subsidiary relationships, as long as one company had a majority stake. This reflects a shift in the WSE Best Practice towards a more relaxed approach for listed companies.

The WSE Best Practice does not provide a detailed definition of a related party, instead referring simply to the IAS Regulation.[597] The previous WSE Best Practice followed the same approach. However, instead of referring directly to the IASs, it cited the relevant Regulation of the Minister of Finance, which in turn referred the reader to the IASs as approved by the IAS Regulation.[598]

Here the WSE Best Practice goes much further than the CGC currently in place in Germany. Related parties in the IASs are understood to include board members (and their close relatives) and persons having control or significant influence over the company, including shareholders with more than 20% of the shares.[599] The WSE Best Practice contains a stricter threshold than 20% and introduces a 5% share ownership threshold for approval of RPTs. This is also stricter than the 10% shareholding threshold for supervisory board approval under the revised Dutch CGC.[600] This broad interpretation of related parties in the WSE Best Practice is perhaps the reason for some Polish companies to explicitly derogate from compliance with this rule: from their perspective, it presents an obstacle to the company's functioning, and many companies

593. *Ibid.*, section V.Z.5.
594. Code of Best Practice for WSE Listed Companies (Dobre praktyki spółek notowanych na GPW), approved in 2007, amended and supplemented in 2010 and 2011, §§ II.3, III.9.
595. WSE Best Practice, section V.Z.5.
596. Code of Best Practice for WSE Listed Companies (Dobre praktyki spółek notowanych na GPW), approved in 2007, amended and supplemented in 2010 and 2011, §§ II.3.
597. WSE Best Practice, 17.
598. Regulation of the Minister of Finance on Current and Periodic Information Provided by Issuers of Securities and Conditions for Recognizing as Equivalent Information Required by the Laws of a Non-member State [Rozporządzenie Ministra Finansów, w sprawie informacji bieżących i okresowych przekazywanych przez emitentów papierów wartościowych oraz warunków uznawania za równoważne informacji wymaganych przepisami prawa państwa niebędącego państwem członkowskim], as of 19 February 2009 (Dziennik Ustaw 2014.133 z dnia 28 stycznia 2014), section 1 § 2 paragraph 32.
599. IAS 28 Investments in Associates, paragraph 8.
600. Dutch CGC, section 2.7.5.

prefer to explain the reasons for derogation instead of complying with the rules.[601] This is in line with the comply-or-explain standard demanded by the WSE Best Practice. At the same time, neither the WSE Best Practice nor the Dutch CGC covers ultimate beneficial owners, only shareholders. If shareholders are given a strict and narrow interpretation, it is not difficult to overcome the requirements. It is enough to 'not put all your eggs in the same basket', i.e. to establish multiple legal entities and acquire sufficient shareholdings through them. Those entities then exercise joint control even though each separate entity holds fewer shares than the established threshold.

The Ukrainian analogue to a CGC, despite lacking some features of the CGCs that apply in the jurisdictions in focus in this book,[602] is given shape in the Principles of Corporate Governance.[603] The Principles include a procedural safeguard for transactions involving conflicting interests.[604] If a transaction is formed that involves conflicting interests, the conflict must be disclosed and the transaction itself must be approved by the entity's supervisory board.[605] The CGCs discussed above prescribe the same mechanism for RPTs, which must obviously be regarded as falling under conflicts of interest. Unlike the CGCs discussed above, the Principles contain less clear-cut definitions and little clarification. They do not provide very much detail when explaining the nature of a conflict of interest. According to the Principles, a conflict of interest concerns a *discrepancy between personal interests of an officer or its related parties and his/her official (professional) duties to act in the best interests of the company*.[606] For instance, this may include *a contract where an officer or his/her related party acts with the company as a contracting party, as a representative or an agent in the formation conclusion and performance of the contract, receives remuneration from the company or from a person who is a party under the contract, et cetera*.[607] An analysis of these provisions of the Principles yields at least three observations.

601. In accordance with the comply-or-explain rule, the website of NEUCA S.A. lists all the instances where the company does not comply with the WSE's rules, and the accompanying reasons, available at: http://www.neuca.pl/en/investor-relations/legal_documents. To make it more appealing for investors, the company still emphasizes that transactions between the company and other subjects are scrutinized closely and that it is compliant with the Company Income Tax. NEUCA S.A. is not unique in this: Asseco South Eastern Europe S.A.'s 2012 Report on Compliance for the Corporate Governance Standards stated that this condition is applied under § 13 section 12 item 24 of its Articles of Association, available at: https://asseco.com/see/assets/Uploads/investor-relations/Legal-environment/2013/en/Group-Asseco-SEE-Corporate-Governance-Report.pdf, while the business report of Synthos S.A. for the period from 01/01/2010 to 31/12/2010, available at: https://synthosgroup.com/uploads/media/6zl-03-00496-11-ptl-sprawozdanie_z_dzia_alno_ci_synthos_sa__2010_v_5_pwc_spell_checked__2__mm_mw_ver_2_enx.pdf explicitly specified that this principle was not, and would not, be applied, as the company's existing procedures and mechanisms were sufficient, and its supervisory board was authorized to oversee the company's functioning.
602. *See* section §2.03 [C].
603. Principles of Corporate Governance, approved by the Decision of the National Securities and Stock Market Commission of Ukraine of 22 July 2014, No. 955 [Pryntsypy korporatyvnoho upravlinnia, zatverdzheni rishenniam Natsionalnoyi komisii z tsinnykh paperiv ta fondovoho rynku vid 22 lypnia 2014 roku No. 955].
604. *Ibid.*, 1.3.3, 1.3.4.
605. *Ibid.*, sections II, 3.3.2.
606. *Ibid.*, sections III, 36.
607. *Ibid.*

First, the Principles refer to only officers and their related parties as being capable of having conflicting interests. As in the German CGC (both the 2017 version and the new draft 2020 CGC), and unlike how this issue is resolved in the Dutch CGC and the WSE Best Practice, they make no mention whatsoever of shareholders.

Second, the Principles only mention related parties without offering any indication of how broadly that concept should be interpreted and based on what criteria. It remains unclear whether related parties include officers' family members, and if so to what degree of relatedness, whether legal entities controlled, jointly controlled or significantly influenced by officers are also considered to be related parties and whether further clarification may be drawn from other sources such as the IASs or acts under national law.[608]

Third, transactions involving conflicting interests include not only transactions where related parties are party, in the strict sense, to these transactions: they also cover transactions where parties act merely as representatives or agents, or receive remuneration from a party to a contract, meaning that transactions involving conflicts of interest include a broader list of transactions. They are not confined to RPTs only.[609]

Lastly, a few comments must be made on how IAS 24 and the CGCs compare. Although IAS 24, in some respect, applies a narrower concept of related parties as opposed to some provisions of the Dutch CGC as referred to above, in general IAS 24 is more detailed than the CGCs and certainly clearer than the Ukrainian Principles of Corporate Governance in defining related parties. Besides natural persons as related parties, the concept also covers legal entities that are associated with the reporting entity via various forms of connection.

§3.03 THE CONCEPT OF A RELATED PARTY UNDER UKRAINIAN LAW

[A] General Notion of a Related Party under Ukrainian Company Law

[1] Introduction

No single act in Ukraine deals comprehensively with RPTs in all their aspects. This section provides an overview of legal regulation, with a further discussion of natural persons and legal entities as related parties in the two sections that follow.

[2] Related Parties in National Accounting Standards and the Tax Code of Ukraine

As has already been mentioned above, some companies incorporated under Ukrainian laws are required to prepare both separate and consolidated financial statements according to the IASs. These requirements are laid down in the Law of Ukraine 'On

608. Related parties as meant in the national laws of Ukraine are discussed more specifically in section §3.03.
609. For more detail regarding the issues of conflicts of interest, *see* Chapter 2.

Accounting and Financial Reporting in Ukraine' and cover enterprises with a public interest, public JSCs, enterprises extracting commercial minerals and the enterprises designated by the Cabinet of Ministers of Ukraine.[610] The standards are considered to apply if they are not incompatible with the Law and are officially published on the website of the central financial authority.[611] This includes IAS 24, an official translation of which is published on the website of the Ministry of Finance of Ukraine.[612]

In addition to the applicability of IAS 24, Ukraine also has national accounting standard 23 'Related Party Disclosures'.[613] As standard 23 provides, it is not applied in cases when the IASs apply, which means budgetary enterprises are also excluded.[614] National accounting standard 23 is largely based on the same principles as IAS 24 and outlines two main categories of related parties: legal entities and natural persons. It uses the same concepts as IAS 24, including control, significant influence reflecting 20% or more of the voting rights in the investment object as defined by IAS 28,[615] key management personnel and close relatives. At the same time, standard 23 is not an exact copy of IAS 24. For instance, it makes no reference to the notion of joint control, offering instead the nebulous term of 'direct or indirect influence', so that entities are regarded as related if they exercise direct or indirect influence over the reporting entity. One basic element that both standards have in common is the prevalence of substance over form.

The concept of a related party is also defined in the Tax Code of Ukraine. The Tax Code was drafted to combat tax evasion and has a specifically taxation-oriented purpose. The tax-related definition of a related party refers to legal entities and/or natural persons with relationships that could influence the terms or economic results of their activities or the activities of persons whom they represent.[616] Being more abstract in nature, the definition is explained using specific criteria for legal entities and for natural persons, and joint criteria for both legal entities and natural persons. In general, parties can be regarded as being related in the following cases: if one party directly or indirectly owns 20% or more of the shares in the other party; if one party has the authority to appoint either the one-person senior management, or at least 50% of the collegiate senior management or supervisory board of the other party; or if one party

---

610. Law of Ukraine 'On Accounting and Financial Reporting in Ukraine' [Zakon Ukrayiny 'Pro bukhgaltersyi oblik ta finansovu zvitnist'], Article 12-1(2, 3).
611. *Ibid.*, Article 12-1(1).
612. Mizhnarodnyi standart bukhgalterskoho obliky 24 'Rozkryttia informatsii pro zvyazani osoby' (official 2016 Ukrainian translation), available at: https://minfin.gov.ua/uploads/redactor/files/IAS%2024_ukr_2016.pdf, accessed on 28 December 2018.
613. Accounting Provision (Standard) 23 'Related Party Disclosures', as approved by the order of the Ministry of Finance of Ukraine as of 18 June 2001 No. 303 [Polozhennia (standart) bukhgalterskoho obliku 23 'Rozkryttia informatsii schodo povyazanykh storin', zatverdzhene nakazom Ministerstva finansiv Ukrayiny vid 18 chervnia 2001 r. No. 3030], published in Ofitsiynyi visnyk Ukrayiny, 2001, No. 26, St. 1192.
614. *Ibid.*, paragraph 2.
615. Klymenko Ya, 'Afiliyovani osoby: Pokhodzhennia terminu, kryterii vyznachennia i zastosuvannia u vitchyznianiy ta mizhnarodniy praktykakh' (2014) Naukovi pratsi Kirovohradskoho natsionalnoho technichnoho universytetu Ekonomichni nauky 215, 223.
616. Tax Code of Ukraine [Podatkovyi kodeks Ukrayiny] of 2 December 2010, published in Vidomosti Verkhovnoyi Rady Ukrayiny, 2011, Nos 13-14, 15-16, 17, St. 112, subclause 14.1.159 clause 14.1 Article 14.

has loaned or granted sums to the other party in amounts exceeding the latter party's authorized share capital by a multiple of 3.5 (for financial institutions: by a multiple of 10). These provisions in the Tax Code share much common ground with IAS 24 – in particular with regard to the minimum shareholding (20%) necessary to establish a related party relationship. The exception is the financial support criterion, which is a unique feature of related parties under tax law. In addition, the Tax Code explains the difference between direct and indirect ownership, stipulating that the latter case involves shares owned by related parties.[617] Nevertheless, opinions are divided on whether these provisions in the Tax Code may be used to interpret the national accounting standards.

[3] Interested Persons and Transactions with Interest Within the Meaning of the JSC Law of Ukraine, the LLC Law of Ukraine and the Economic Code of Ukraine

Besides related parties, Ukrainian law also uses other notions, including the notions of interested and affiliated persons. Specifically, the JSC Law of Ukraine and the LLC Law of Ukraine both refer to the concept of a person with an interest in a transaction. Both laws contain rules providing for procedures, *ex ante* and *ex post* safeguards for transactions with interest formed between a company and an interested person; the difference lies in the legal effect. The rules under the LLC Law of Ukraine apply if shareholders so stipulate in the company's articles of association.[618] Despite their name, transactions with interest as stipulated in the JSC and LLC Laws of Ukraine do not extend to all transactions that might be of relevance to a company and cover only agreements to which the company itself is a party. This means that transactions with interest are construed through interested persons transacting with a company.[619] For public companies, in order to establish a transaction with interest, it is not necessary for an interested person to actually transact with the company: an interested person can merely be a representative or a broker, or someone who draws a gain from the transaction.[620] For private companies, transactions with interest are worded differently and include transactions with an interested person.[621] For these reasons, no obstacles preclude transactions with interest from being treated as purely RPTs in private companies.

The notion of an interested person in transactions with interest of public companies encompasses both natural persons and legal entities and consists of three categories: (i) an officer of one of the bodies of the company, or affiliated persons; (ii) a shareholder who singly or together with affiliated persons owns at least 25% of the shares in the company, or affiliated persons; (iii) a legal entity in which one of the persons defined at (i) or (ii) is an officer. For private companies, interested persons are

617. *Ibid.*, paragraphs 21-23, subclause 14.1.159 clause 14.1 Article 14.
618. JSC Law of Ukraine, Article 71(1); LLC Law of Ukraine, Article 45(1).
619. Bodnar T, 36.
620. JSC Law of Ukraine, Article 71(3).
621. LLC Law of Ukraine, Article 45(1).

construed slightly differently, in that shareholders are regarded as interested persons if they hold 20% or more of the company's share capital.

Taking into account these features of interested persons, it is also essential to understand the meaning of affiliated persons. The concept of an affiliated person as explained in the JSC Law of Ukraine[622] also applies in the case of private companies.[623] The following types of affiliated persons are identified: (a) two legal entities, where one is controlled by another or both are jointly controlled by a third party; (b) family members of a natural person - spouse, and parents (including adoptive parents), guardians, siblings, children and their spouses; (c) a natural person, with family members, and a legal entity, if the natural person and/or family members exercise control over the legal entity.

The key concept for a proper understanding of affiliated persons as meant in the JSC Law of Ukraine is 'control'. However, the concept is not actually defined in the act, but by reference to the Law of Ukraine 'On Protection of Economic Competition'.[624] It is defined as *decisive influence of one or several related parties, legal entities or individuals exercised directly or through other parties.*[625] The definition itself contains several notions that themselves are also subject to interpretation. That is why the importance of the examples of control listed in the law cannot be underestimated in providing clarity. They include, among other examples: possession or use of all or most of the company's assets; the power to decisively influence appointments, voting and decision-making by the company's management; a contract-based right to determine economic conditions or issue guidelines for the company; the right to replace the chair of the management or supervisory or another body of the company; and the right to occupy the majority of the seats on the senior management or supervisory boards or another body of the company.[626] It follows from these examples that control in the context of both the JSC Law of Ukraine and the Law of Ukraine 'On Protection of Economic Competition' has a greater scope than ownership of half of a company's share capital and may be established by force of an agreement between a company and its related parties. The forms of contract that give effect to control also include leases, though it is doubtful whether such contract should be considered the appropriate device for establishing control. The lessee under a lease will not necessarily be in a position to exercise control. Quite the contrary: the lessee might be the weaker party in a contractual relationship if the terms of the contract are so negotiated.

The rules governing transactions with interest in the JSC and LLC Laws of Ukraine do not cover RPTs in state and municipal unitary enterprises, which are forms of business activity different from public and private companies. Since 2016, these types of enterprises have also been subject to rules for transactions with interest

622. JSC Law of Ukraine, Article 1(1)(1).
623. LLC Law of Ukraine, Article 42(9).
624. Law of Ukraine 'On Protection of Economic Competition' [Zakon Ukrayiny 'Pro zakhyst ekonomichnoyi konkurentsii'] of 11 January 2001, published in Vidomosti Verkhovnoyi Rady Ukrayiny, 2001, No. 12, St. 64.
625. *Ibid.*, paragraph 4 Article 1.
626. *Ibid.*

established by the legislative authority.[627] These newly established rules in the Economic Code of Ukraine differ fundamentally from the norms described in the JSC Law of Ukraine. The distinction is intrinsically linked to public share ownership. In state and municipal enterprises, the state and the municipality exercise their rights through the appropriate governmental or local authorities. It is then not to be wondered that, besides the officers of the actual enterprises, the Economic Code regards officials of ministries or other bodies exercising authority over the enterprises as being interested persons.[628]

In addition, the Economic Code of Ukraine does not refer to the concept of an affiliated person, instead replacing it by the significantly narrower term 'ultimate beneficiary'. The consequence is that other state and municipal enterprises are not considered to be interested persons. However, this narrow legislative wording has not protected it from being criticized in some quarters for imposing excessively onerous and complicated rules for RPTs on companies in the public sector.[629]

[4] Interested Persons in Bankruptcy Statute

Besides the JSC and LLC Laws of Ukraine, one other act makes reference to interested persons and transactions with interest: the Code of Ukraine on Bankruptcy Procedures,[630] which recently replaced the Law of Ukraine 'On Restoring a Debtor's Solvency or Recognising It Bankrupt'.[631] These acts use the notion of interested person in their regulations for transactions with interest and some bankruptcy-related procedures. Similarly to how the JSC Law of Ukraine approaches the issue of transactions with interest, the Code of Ukraine on Bankruptcy Procedures and the Law of Ukraine 'On Restoring a Debtor's Solvency or Recognising It Bankrupt' are based on the subject criterion and define transactions with interest as transactions involving interested persons on the part of the debtor, the bankruptcy trustee or the creditors.[632] Taking only the manner in which the definition is worded into consideration, transactions with interest should not be confined to agreements between the debtor and the debtor's interested persons. It would also be reasonable to extend it to transactions between various interested persons (besides the debtor). At the same time, the body of statute

627. Law of Ukraine 'On Amending Certain Legislative Acts on Management of State and Municipal Property' [Zakon Ukrayiny 'Pro vnesennia zmin do deyakykh zakonodavchykh aktiv schodo upravlinnia obyektamy derzhavnoyi ta komunalnoyi vlasnosti'] of 2 June 2016, published in Vidomosti Verkhovnoyi Rady Ukrayiny, 2016, No. 228, St. 533.
628. Economic Code of Ukraine [Hospodarksyi kodeks Ukrayiny], Articles 73-1(2), 78-1(2).
629. Poyedynok V, 'Novely korporatyvnoho upravlinnia v derzhavnykh pidpryyemstvakh' (Adaptatsiya korporatyvnoho zakonodavstva Ukrayiny do prava Yevropeyskoho Soyuzu: Zbirnyk naukovykh prats za materialamy Mizhnarodnoyi naukovo-praktychnoyi konferentsii (30 veresnia – 1 zhovtnia 2016, Ivano-Frankivsk)), 185.
630. Code of Ukraine on Bankruptcy Procedures [Kodeks Ukrayiny z protsedur bankrutstva] of 18 October 2018, published in Golos Ukrayiny, 20 April 2018, No. 77.
631. Law of Ukraine 'On Restoring a Debtor's Solvency or Recognising It Bankrupt' [Zakon Ukrayiny 'Pro vidnovlennia platospromozhnosti borzhnyka abo vyznannia yoho bankrutom'] of 14 May 1992, published in Vidomosti Verkhovnoyi Rady Ukrayiny, 1992, No. 31, St. 440.
632. *Ibid.*, paragraph 12 Article 1(1); Code of Ukraine on Bankruptcy Procedures [Kodeks Ukrayiny z protsedur bankrutstva], paragraph 6 Article 1.

mostly handles transactions with interest by identifying the debtor as one of the parties – for instance, contracts that the debtor formed with interested persons during three years preceding the start of the bankruptcy proceedings may be annulled based on a complaint by a creditor or the bankruptcy trustee.[633] The previous law stipulated a similar rule for natural persons only – entrepreneurs – but with a shorter term of one year instead of three years.[634] That is why, although the definitions themselves are broad, transactions between the debtor's interested persons, not including the debtor, largely fall outside the legislator's scope of attention.

The concept of interested person under the Code of Ukraine on Bankruptcy Procedures is much broader than that described in the JSC or LLC Laws of Ukraine. Interested persons on the part of the debtor are not limited to the debtor's relatives, officers of the debtor's bodies, parties controlling the debtor, parties controlled by the debtor or parties controlled by a third party that also controls the debtor. They include all founders and shareholders of the debtor (if the debtor is a legal entity), legal entities founded or owned by the debtor and the debtor's chief accountant – both the current accountant and any chief accountant dismissed within three years leading up to the bankruptcy proceedings.[635] Most importantly, this list is not exhaustive, and if reasonable grounds exist to regard a particular person as an interested party, then they are so considered.[636] This provision is reminiscent of the rules for indirect conflicts of interest in the Dutch BW,[637] which offer the courts freedom of interpretation to consider relationships as constituting conflicts of interest. Taking into account the vague criteria for defining interested persons, Ukrainian economic courts have the authority to elaborate on the existence of interested persons. This applies in situations where bankruptcy proceedings have been instituted against a debtor, and all transactions with interest that were formed within the three years leading up to the start of the proceedings may be declared null and void.[638] While the intentions of the legislators drafting these rules were arguably good, nonetheless little doubt exists that any company officer deciding whether to make an agreement faces serious interpretation uncertainties and runs the risk that the transaction might be challenged in the future. In these circumstances, the possibility to annul a transaction is not necessarily sufficiently commensurate to unclear and excessively broad criteria that form the basis of the definition of an interested person.

633. Code of Ukraine on Bankruptcy Procedures [Kodeks Ukrayiny z protsedur bankrutstva], Article 42(2).
634. Law of Ukraine 'On Restoring a Debtor's Solvency or Recognising It Bankrupt' [Zakon Ukrayiny 'Pro vidnovlennia platospromozhnosti borzhnyka abo vyznannia yoho bankrutom'], Article 90(10).
635. The three-year term applies not only to accountants but also to officers of the debtor's bodies.
636. Code of Ukraine on Bankruptcy Procedures [Kodeks Ukrayiny z protsedur bankrutstva], paragraph 6 Article 1.
637. *See* Chapter 2.
638. Code of Ukraine on Bankruptcy Procedures [Kodeks Ukrayiny z protsedur bankrutstva], Article 42(2).

[5] Concluding Remarks on the General Notion of a Related Party in Ukraine

Ukrainian laws do not use a single uniform definition of related parties, employing instead various different notions, including interested and affiliated persons, with different meanings depending on context and purpose. The notion most closely associated with company law is that of an interested person as used in the JSC Law of Ukraine, the LLC Law of Ukraine and the law governing bankruptcy proceedings. In turn, related parties are governed by accounting and tax law regulations.

Despite the attention given to the wording used, or the form that the concepts take, their substance is of greater concern. However, uniformity is similarly lacking in terms of the substance of the notions, and some legal scholars have expressed the opinion that these laws should be aligned more closely.[639]

Notwithstanding the fact that regulations under different laws serve different goals, proper grounds do not always exist for giving a single term multiple meanings, which can only create unpredictability and complication. An example where the difference between notions is not immediately obvious is the use of quantitative criteria for establishing degrees of share ownership. The JSC Law of Ukraine stipulates 25% of the share capital as a requirement for qualification as an interested person in a transaction with interest.[640] Under the LLC Law of Ukraine, IAS 24 in conjunction with IAS 28 and the Tax Code of Ukraine, a person is considered to be a related party by holding a 20% shareholding.[641] In light of the norms of the Tax Code of Ukraine and relevant international standards, some authors have asked why the figure of 25% is used as an ownership basis for understanding the essence of transactions with interest.[642] They also suggest that the 20% threshold should be used uniformly.[643] To seize this line of argument for adopting a 20% rule and developing it further, another act could be added for a further illustration: the CCU, under which an economic company is understood to be dependent if another entity owns at least 20% of the first company's share capital,[644] triggering the owner's obligation to publicly disclose information about the acquisition.[645]

Together, these arguments contribute to the idea that the regulations require a greater degree of uniformity. However, they do not reveal the reasons for stipulating a precise shareholding (20%) in the definition of an interested person. The true economic reasons for viewing a party with a particular shareholding as a related party must lie in the powers that this exact share ownership conveys. The JSC Law of Ukraine

639. Klymenko Ya, 224.
640. JSC Law of Ukraine, Article 71(2)(2).
641. LLC Law of Ukraine, Article 45(1); IAS 28 Investments in Associates, paragraph 8; Tax Code of Ukraine [Podatkovyi kodeks Ukrayiny], subclause 14.1.159 clause 14.1 Article 14.
642. Karchevskyi K, '"Krupnyi aktsioner" yak storona pravochynu iz zainteresovanistiu' (2011) Aktualni pytannia tsyvilnoho ta hospodarskoho prava 18, 22.
643. Zasadnyi BA, 'Formuvannia oblikovoyi polityky pidpryyemstva schodo povyazanykh storin' (2015) Visnyk Kyivskoho natsionalnoho universytetu im Tarasa Shevchenka Seriya: Ekonomika 24, 29.
644. CCU, Article 118(1).
645. *Ibid.*, Article 118(2).

does not contain any rules that grant groups of shareholders with 20% or more of the share capital (and the same proportion of the voting rights) any particular or unique rights. It is then difficult to properly justify both numbers (20% and 25%). That is the reason, despite the use of 20% in some of the other legal instruments discussed, for an apparent lack of arguments, except for the need for uniformity, for lowering the existing threshold of 25% for qualification as an interested person in the JSC Law of Ukraine.

[B] Natural Persons as Related Parties in Ukrainian Law

Classification of related parties depends very much on the nature of the rights that those parties possess relative to the entity. The following types of power are distinguished in literature for categorizing related parties: ownership powers; contractual powers; management powers; and family-based influence.[646] While ownership (share-based) and contractual powers apply in cases of both legal entities and natural persons, under Ukrainian law management powers and family-based influence need to be considered only in connection with certain natural persons.[647]

The present section explores the influence that is inherently exercised by natural persons as related parties. In order to be recognized as a person with an interest in a transaction under the JSC Law of Ukraine, an individual must act in one or more of the following roles: (a) a shareholder owning at least 25% of the shares, either singly or jointly with affiliated persons; (b) an officer of one of the company's bodies; or (c) a family member of (a) or (b).

Both legal entities and individuals can own shares. For participation in corporate governance, Ukrainian law does not allow legal entities to be appointed as members of company bodies. This was not always the case, however: before 1 May 2016, legal entities could be members of the supervisory boards of public companies, where they were then represented by a natural person acting under a power of attorney. This policy changed with the introduction of the new legislative amendments that came into effect on 1 May 2016.[648] Since then, only one specific individual may occupy a position on the supervisory board. Legal entities had previously sometimes abused their rights as supervisory board members by appointing different representatives and replacing them whenever it was convenient. At present, the chairs and members of the supervisory board, the management board, the audit committee (the company's

646. Karchevskyi K, 'Porivnialno-pravova kharakterystyka poniattia "afiliyovana osoba"' (2013) Visnyk Kharkivskoho natsionalnoho universytetu vnutrishnikh sprav 217, 218; Klymenko Ya, 220; Lepel L, 'Poniattia afiliyovanykh osib u konkurentnomu zakonodavstvi Ukrayiny' (2007) Yurysprudentsiya: teoriya i praktyka 11, 18-19.
647. Although some jurisdictions allow legal entities to hold positions in company bodies, this is not the case in Ukraine, where only natural persons may be seated on the management board, the supervisory board and other company bodies.
648. Law of Ukraine 'On Amending Certain Legislative Acts on the Protection of Investors' [Zakon Ukrayiny 'Pro vnesennia zmin do deyakykh zakonodavchykh aktiv schodo zakhystu prav investoriv'].

auditor) and other company bodies are regarded as the company's officers.[649] This means that the legislature's opinion, as expressed in the Law, is that conflicts of interest can occur in situations concerning not only management and supervisory boards but also other company bodies. However, it could be argued that transactions with interest are beyond the scope of the powers of bodies that are not specified in Article 71 of the JSC Law of Ukraine. Only the management board, the supervisory board and the general meeting of shareholders have the authority to enter into RPTs and/or to approve them. Other bodies are not as closely involved in these transactions and, even if they are believed to be able to influence them, can do so only indirectly. Logically, these provisions considerably limit their reach, and valid calls have been made to remove persons whose roles have nothing to do with transactions with interest or their approval (for instance, members of the audit committee, members of the counting committee and the company secretary[650]) from the list of interested persons. These arguments also reflect the provisions of the various CGCs, where conflicts of interest are ascribed to the management and supervisory boards.[651]

It can be argued that the existing broad notion of a company's officer matches the definition of key management personnel contained in IAS 24. The latter term is also broad, as 'planning, directing and controlling the activities of the entity, directly or indirectly' can be interpreted in a variety of ways, though it still primarily concerns executive and non-executive directors.[652]

A comparison of the JSC Law of Ukraine and IAS 24 and whether they recognize natural persons as related parties yields the following basic differences.

First, as discussed above, the notions of 'control' and 'significant influence' can be interpreted against the backdrop of IAS 24 and IAS 28 as share ownership carrying at least 20% of the voting rights[653] or 20% of the share capital if the 'one share, one vote' principle as currently used in Ukraine applies.[654] In the JSC Law of Ukraine, the threshold is 25% or more of the share capital.[655]

Second, 'significant influence', as per the requirements of IAS 24, can derive not only from corporate or official duties but also from statute or contract. The JSC Law of Ukraine does not define, at least not explicitly, when a person is considered to be an interested person according to statutory requirements or under the terms of a contract.[656]

649. JSC Law of Ukraine, Article 2(1)(15).
650. Karchevskyi K, 'Problemy vyznachennia kola posadovykh osib aktsionernoho tovarystva, zainteresovannist yakykh u pravochyni tiagne za soboyu neobkhidnist zastosuvannia spetsialnoho poriadku yoho vchynennia' (2010) Aktualni pytannia tsyvilnoho ta hospodarskoho prava 91, 108.
651. For example, *see* the Dutch CGC, Principle 2.7 Preventing Conflicts of Interest, and WSE Best Practice, V. Conflict of Interest, Related Party Transactions.
652. IAS 24, paragraph 9.
653. IAS 28 Investments in Associates, paragraph 8.
654. Law of Ukraine 'On Economic Companies' [Zakon Ukrayiny 'Pro hospodarski tovarystva'], Article 44(1); Radwan A, Nadzon A and Zdiruk V, 88.
655. JSC Law of Ukraine, Article 71(2).
656. For example, as in Article 317 of the AktG, which makes specific reference to control agreements.

Third, the lists of close relatives in IAS 24 and the JSC Law of Ukraine are different. What is unique about IAS 24 is that it refers to partners, their children and dependents as close family members, but does not provide an exhaustive list. In turn, under the JSC Law of Ukraine, close family members include parents (and adoptive parents), guardians, siblings and spouses of children.

Differences in who are qualified as family members exist not only on the level of the JSC Law of Ukraine and the IASs; the meanings of related parties also differ between separate acts adopted in Ukraine. Some laws contain longer lists of related parties, while others stipulate significantly shorter ones. In general, all the acts analysed in this study commonly refer to the person's spouse (husband or wife) and children as related (i.e., interested) parties. This is a common denominator, which will probably not be contested. Both spouses and children can easily influence a person's decisions and persuade him or her to act in a particular manner. It therefore makes sense to treat transactions with spouses or children of a person as transactions with the actual person.

In other respects, opinions on whether particular persons should be regarded as related or associated are less unanimous. Although neither the national standards nor the IASs unconditionally regard parents as related parties, they are under the JSC Law of Ukraine[657] and following a decision of the Constitutional Court of Ukraine that gave the official definition on how a close family member should be interpreted.[658] The Tax Code of Ukraine also views guardians as related parties,[659] while the JSC Law of Ukraine has the same attitude towards adoptive parents.

Brothers and sisters are similarly not always considered to be related parties. Most of the acts mentioned above, except the accounting standards, include them in this notion. While siblings have blood ties to a person, those ties are in the sideways line, as opposed to direct relationships as seen in, for instance, the relationship between parent and child. Sideways relationships are horizontal, rather than vertical, in nature, which might be why fewer references are made to them in legislation. In horizontal relationships, people do not always have the authority to impose their will on the other participant in the relationship.

Another party that has no direct blood ties to the individual is the spouse of the person's child. As opposed to connections to siblings, relationships with these parties are more vertical than horizontal. They are seen as affiliated persons under the JSC Law of Ukraine, and, consequently, as persons with an interest in a transaction.[660]

The widest network of related parties is found in the Law of Ukraine 'On Banks and Banking', where related parties are not confined to direct relatives (spouses, siblings, parents, children, grandparents and grandchildren), but also include the

657. JSC Law of Ukraine, paragraph 3 Article 2(1)(1).
658. *Decision of 3 June 1999 No. 5-pn/99 (case about official interpretation of a term 'family member')* Case 1-8/99, Ofitsiynyi visnyk Ukrayiny as of 2 July 1999, No. 24, p. 180 (Constitutional Court of Ukraine).
659. Tax Code of Ukraine [Podatkovyi kodeks Ukrayiny], paragraph 7 subclause 14.1.159 clause 14.1 Article 14.
660. JSC Law of Ukraine, paragraph 3 Article 2(1)(1).

direct relatives of the person's spouse.[661] This implies that, for instance, the husband of the granddaughter of the person's wife is a related person, while in fact the individual might be wholly unaware of their existence.

Yet the web of related parties as meant in the Law of Ukraine 'On Banks and Banking' is not where it ends. What precisely the tenets of relatedness actually are becomes even more ambiguous when coupled with the discretion of the courts and other authorities to determine whether or not a specific party is related. For instance, the notion of a person's close family as provided in IAS 24 not only includes the categories of persons described above (children, spouses, etc.) but also has a larger scope: it extends to any family members who may be expected to influence or be influenced by the person in his or her dealings with the reporting entity.[662] Those other family members can include a wide range of parties, subject to the court's opinion.

The existing ambiguity is hidden in the concept of family as enshrined in the Family Code of Ukraine, which means all persons living together and sharing a common household.[663] In other words, to qualify as family members, persons must live together long enough and have the kind of relationship that is regarded as a family. This meaning has been further clarified in a decision of the Constitutional Court of Ukraine, which confirmed that family is decided not only by blood ties but also by other connections that, in combination with some additional factors (living together and sharing a household), possess all the necessary features of a family.[664] Unsurprisingly, even persons who have no blood ties can form a family, since in reality they might have a closer relationship with each other than they do with their relatives. In fact, these relationships sometimes have a solid basis, and it is understandable that some scholars have suggested that the rules on transactions with interest in the JSC Law of Ukraine should also apply to relationships between individuals who are not relatives, but who have a strong fiduciary relationship (e.g., long-standing friends and godparents).[665] At the same time, extending the list of family members to include unregistered partners and other persons living together unofficially as a family would detract from legal certainty. Lawyers would find it difficult to compose lists of related parties in the face of future transactions in public companies. In addition, some clients might be reluctant to disclose all their information about persons who do not have the paperwork to be recognized as registered partners or relatives. A delicate approach is therefore necessary for situations where non-relatives are regarded as related (or interested) parties.

661. Law of Ukraine 'On Banks and Banking' [Zakon Ukrayiny 'Pro banky i bankivsku diyalnist'] of 7 December 2000, published in Vidomosti Verkhovnoyi Rady Ukrayiny, 2001, No. 5-6, St. 30, paragraph 2 Article 2.
662. IAS 24, paragraph 9.
663. Family Code of Ukraine [Simeynyi kodeks Ukrayiny] of 10 January 2002, published in Vidomosti Verkhovnoyi Rady Ukrayiny, 2002, No. 21, St. 135, Article 2(2).
664. *Decision of 3 June 1999 No. 5-pn/99 (case about official interpretation of a term 'family member')* Case 1-8/99, Ofitsiynyi visnyk Ukrayiny of 2 July 1999, No. 24, p. 180 (Constitutional Court of Ukraine).
665. Karchevskyi K, 'Rodynnyi kryterii poniattia afiliyovana osoba (v konteksti pravovoho rezhymu pravochyniv iz zainteresovannistiu)' (2014) Visnyk Kharkivskoho natsionalnoho universytetu vnutrishnikh sprav 160, 169.

[C] Legal Entities as Related Parties under Ukrainian Law

Unlike natural persons, legal entities cannot exercise influence based on family relationships or (at least in Ukraine) positions in the company's bodies. These possibilities lie beyond the legal entity's corporate shield and demonstrate its artificial essence. Legal entities even have their own special terminology as related parties, with the following terms being used specifically to describe connections between legal entities.

The CCU refers to an LLC, an ALC or a JSC as a dependent company if 20% or more of its shares are owned by another company (its parent).[666] As a consequence, a dependent company is required to notify the authorities about the acquisition of its shares. Interestingly, the BW also employs the term 'dependent company' for both open and closed companies, though there 'dependence' has a different meaning: it is based on whether another company solely or jointly contributes at least half the issued capital of a legal person that is deemed dependent, or, where the dependent company is a partnership that has an officially registered business undertaking, the dependence arises from another company's participation in that partnership as a partner and its full liability towards third parties.[667] It is important to stress here that partnerships have a different meaning under Ukrainian law. Unlike under Dutch law, they are legal persons, namely economic companies and on the same level as private and public companies.[668] This difference, however, does not fully explain why partnerships (general and limited partnerships) are omitted from the definition of a dependent company as used in Article 118 of the CCU. Perhaps the CCU could have taken another route and recognized partnerships as dependent companies in which another company is a partner.

The consequences of being a dependent company, under the BW, should be considered in terms of large companies and their governance.[669] To qualify as large, companies must simultaneously meet three criteria: (i) the proper amount of issued capital and reserves, (ii) an established works council and (iii) at least one hundred employees in the Netherlands.[670] To be covered by the provisions for large companies, it is not necessary for the large company itself to establish a works council and employ one hundred employees: this may be accomplished by the large company's dependent company, which will have the same legal effect as though the large company had done it. Additionally, the BW prohibits large companies from appointing employees of dependent companies to their supervisory boards.[671] It also requires that some decisions by management that affect the functioning of a dependent company be subject to supervisory board approval.[672] Therefore, one of the main results of being

666. CCU, Article 118(1).
667. BW, Article 2:152, 2:262.
668. CCU, Article 113(2).
669. BW, Book 2, Title 4 section 6 and Title 5 section 6.
670. *Ibid.*, Article 2:153(2), 2:263(2).
671. *Ibid.*, Article 2:160(b), 2:270(b).
672. *Ibid.*, Article 2:164(d)(e)(j)(k), 2:274(d)(e)(j)(k).

dependent is that in some respects the large company is treated as though it forms a single person together with its dependent company.

Control, which is central to the concept of a subsidiary, is defined in several laws. The notion of control has already been discussed above[673] and by itself could serve as a separate research subject. Nevertheless, it is logical to consider it in further detail in the context of subsidiaries.

Control, as defined in the JSC Law of Ukraine and the Law of Ukraine 'On Protection of Economic Competition', is based on decisive influence on a company's governance and activity. The list of examples presented in the Law of Ukraine 'On Protection of Economic Competition' [and applying to relationships governed by the JSC Law of Ukraine] to showcase control includes, among other forms, the power to possess or use all or a considerable part of the controlled company's assets.[674] In other words, control, as described in these laws, concerns de facto latent control. It will change, depending on the circumstances of the case, and could even be held by a minority shareholder, similarly to how the Accounting Directive views control.[675]

Control is also inherent in the definition of controlled and controlling enterprises under the AktG.[676] A controlled enterprise may result from various forms of controlling influence. One of the most obvious is the existence of a majority shareholding, as expressly described in the law.[677] The notion of a subsidiary exists separately, though in fact it is also based on control: it refers to the situation where another enterprise is entitled to the majority of the voting rights in the enterprise or if another enterprise has the majority of the shares.[678] Contractual control is not in the nature of subsidiaries and parent companies, however. Other affiliated enterprises besides controlled and controlling enterprises include members of a group, members with cross-shareholdings and parties to an enterprise agreement, parent companies and subsidiaries.[679] The existence of an affiliated enterprise triggers the application of numerous articles throughout the AktG, including the provisions of Book Three, which specifically covers affiliated enterprises, namely enterprise agreements, their formation, terms, amendment and termination.[680]

The KSH makes reference to dependent and associated companies. Associated companies are companies in which another commercial company either has 20% or more of the shares or has 20% or more of the votes at the general meeting.[681] Dependent companies are primarily those in which another company holds a majority of the votes at the shareholders' meeting or can appoint more than half of the members of the management board.[682] As a consequence of being viewed as a dependent

673. *See* sections §3.01[C], §3.03[A][2].
674. Law of Ukraine 'On Protection of Economic Competition' [Zakon Ukrayiny 'Pro zakhyst ekonomichnoyi konkurentsii'], paragraph 4 Article 1.
675. Accounting Directive, recital 31.
676. AktG, Article 17.
677. *Ibid.*, Article 17(2).
678. *Ibid.*, Article 16(1).
679. *Ibid.*, Article 15.
680. *Ibid.*, Book Three, Division One.
681. KSH, clause 5 § 1 Article 4.
682. *Ibid.*, clause 4 § 1 Article 4.

company, a dependent company is regarded in some operations as inseparable from the dominant company; for instance, the dependent company is prohibited from buying the dominant company's shares.[683]

The Polish KSH contributes a peculiar feature to the concept of a dependent company: a company is dependent if more than half the members of a company's management board are represented on the management board of another company.[684] This rule is reminiscent of some provisions of Ukraine national law. First, according to the Tax Code of Ukraine, two legal entities are regarded as being related if the same persons serve as senior managers in both entities.[685] Second, the Economic Code adds an important new category of interested person to the definition of persons with an interest in a transaction: legal entities where an officer of the enterprise is an ultimate beneficiary or a member of senior management.[686] These rules are at odds with the provisions of IAS 24 in paragraph 11:[687] for IAS 24, it is not enough for parties to be related if one person is a director in two entities or significantly influences them both. The reasoning is simple: whereas the link between a director and a company is sufficient to call these two parties affiliated, the link between two companies in which one person is a director is nebulous. It is therefore doubtful whether it is necessary to establish relatedness between two companies whose only link is having the same manager; the doubts are amplified in the case of a dependent and a dominant company.

In spite of the fact that legal entities may freely participate in civil turnover by entering into transactions and by suing and being sued, it cannot be denied that ultimately natural persons are behind all corporate business forms. They own and govern them. It is not always entirely clear who is behind the corporate curtain. To reveal those persons, the laws of many states, including Ukraine, provide for techniques to identify these 'ultimate beneficiaries' (controllers) who actually control the legal entity's activity.[688] These persons might own a particular percentage of the company's share capital.[689] At the same time, they are not treated as controllers by reason of share ownership. They might exercise control through other vehicles,

683. *Ibid.*, Article 366(1).
684. *Ibid.*, subclause d) clause 4 § 1 Article 4.
685. Tax Code of Ukraine [Podatkovyi kodeks Ukrayiny], subclause 14.1.159 clause 14.1 Article 14.
686. Economic Code of Ukraine [Hospodarksyi kodeks Ukrayiny], Articles 73-1, 78-1; it should be stressed that rules on RPTs as covered by the Economic Code of Ukraine apply only to state and municipal enterprises.
687. IAS 24, paragraph 11.
688. Makhinchuk V, *Zniattia korporatyvnoyi vuali: monographia* (Ivano-Frankivsk: 'Foliant' 2017), 102.
689. The definition of an ultimate beneficiary (controller) in Ukraine can be found in the Law of Ukraine 'On Prevention of and Countering to Legalization (Laundering) of Profits Received by Committing Crimes, Financing Terrorism and Weapons of Mass Destruction' [Zakon Ukrayiny 'Pro zapobigannia ta protydiyu legalizatsii (vidmyvanniu) dokhodiv, oderzhanykh zlochynnym shliakhom, finansuvanniu teroryzmu ta finansuvanniu rozpovsiudzhennia zbroi masovogo znyschennia'] of 14 October 2014, published in Vidomosti Verkhovnoyi Rady Ukrayiny, 2014, No. 50-51, St. 3250, paragraph 20 part 1 Article 1. The minimum threshold of share ownership or votes giving a person the ability to directly or indirectly influence the company's activity is 25% of the share capital or the voting rights.

regardless of formal ownership, by possessing or using the company's assets, influencing the decision-making procedures or issuing binding recommendations to the company, either singly or jointly with other persons.[690]

Ultimate beneficiaries are not always the shareholders who have a specific proportion of the voting rights in a company. The shares that they own might belong to them on the basis of an agreement with another person. As IAS 24 indicates, the identity of the ultimate controlling party must be disclosed, if that party is not the same as the company's shareholder.[691] Under the JSC Law of Ukraine, however, only share ownership and a position as a company officer are relevant for determining whether a person has an interest or not.[692] This law does not stipulate an obligation to identify who the real ultimate beneficiaries are for the purposes of transactions approval by the appropriate company bodies (the supervisory board and the general meeting of shareholders).

One important comment must be raised here, however. For the purposes of procedural safeguards under the JSC Law of Ukraine, interested persons do not include controllers (ultimate beneficiaries).[693] At the same time, affiliated persons of interested persons do in fact include controllers.[694] The concept of control within the meaning of the Law of Ukraine 'On Protection of Economic Competition' and as used in the JSC Law of Ukraine requires identifying which persons have decisive influence over the company's governance and activity, though the principal focus is still on formal criteria. It is not obvious from the latter concept that the ultimate beneficiaries must be identified. In other words, while the concept of control is limited in scope, if given a broad interpretation it still requires knowing who the ultimate beneficiaries are. Anecdotal situations exist where one person who controls a company through other means besides share ownership is not viewed as a related party for the purposes of procedural safeguards. Meanwhile, stricter and more nebulous identification rules apply to company shareholders with 25% or more of the share capital and company officers if a broad interpretation is used for control, inherent in the concept of an interested person's affiliated person. This hypothetical evidence shows that the notion of an interested person in the JSC Law of Ukraine largely ignores controllers as related parties, except in situations where control is based on share ownership.

The circumstances described here pose a major dilemma, in whether it is necessary to establish ultimate beneficiaries as interested persons for the purposes of compliance with requirements directed at countering tunnelling and other counterproductive activities. Of course, if corporate lawyers do not have to look beyond the company structure with nominal shareholders, it makes their work much easier. The list of related parties is shorter and compliance is less onerous. At the same time, considering only the surface of corporate vehicles without delving more deeply into the

690. The view has been expressed in German jurisprudence that the power to issue binding recommendation is not sufficient to establish control between two entities (Makhinchuk V, 102).
691. IAS 24, paragraph 13.
692. JSC Law of Ukraine, Article 71(2)(2).
693. *Ibid.*, Article 71(2).
694. *Ibid.*, Article 2(1)(1).

key constituencies could undermine the very aim of RPT regulation.[695] It is vital to find the right balance between these two opposing and simultaneously significant directions in order to protect all the company's stakeholders.

§3.04 TERMS OF RPTs

Following this analysis of the parties to RPTs and the discussion of who might be involved in these transactions, the next step is to determine what is stipulated in these transactions.

In a world where it is almost impossible to name a jurisdiction that does not accept freedom of contract, at least on paper, all kinds of transactions may occur – including RPTs. It is no secret that two parties, even if they are related, still possess the freedom of contract and so may enter into various types of agreement. However, although the parties to a transaction are of primary importance for the legal qualification of a transaction as an RPT, the risks associated with RPTs are hidden in their terms. It would not be necessary to discuss RPTs if they did not pose any potential threat to the company and its stakeholders. The negative effect that RPTs bring to stakeholders does not necessarily lie in the fact that shareholders might experience issues with value creation. The whole company could eventually collapse, as happened with Adelfia, Enron and Parmalat.[696] That is why separate RPTs that, by reason of their terms, pose a potential threat to the company should be distinguished from RPTs that are very unlikely to harm the company. Above all, it is necessary to look at the existing legal instruments that describe these types of transactions and their terms.

IAS 24 gives an illustrative list of transactions with related parties that must be disclosed. These include agreements for the purchase and sale of goods, property or other assets, service contracts, leases, transfers of research and development, transfers under licence and financial agreements, contracts providing guarantees or collateral, commitments to do something in a particular event and settlement of liabilities on behalf of the entity or by the entity on behalf of a related party.[697] Participation in a defined benefit plan[698] within a group of companies, where the members of the group

695. This is discussed in greater detail in Chapter 4. For a concise explanation of the reasons to tackle RPTs, *see*: Kraakman R and others, *The Anatomy of Corporate Law: A Comparative and Functional Approach* (3rd edn, Oxford University Press 2017), 145-146.
696. Vaez SA and Banafi M, 'Prediction of Related Party Transactions Using Artificial Neural Network' (2017) 7 International Journal of Economics and Financial Issues 207.
697. IAS 24, paragraph 21.
698. The definition of a defined benefit plan can be found in paragraph 8 of IAS 19 'Employee Benefits' (International Accounting Standard 19 Employee Benefits, as amended and set out by Commission Regulation (EU) No. 475/2012 of 5 June 2012 amending Regulation (EC) No. 1126/2008 adopting certain international accounting standards in accordance with Regulation (EC) No. 1606/2002 of the European Parliament and of the Council as regards International Accounting Standard (IAS) 1 and International Accounting Standard (IAS) 19 [2012] OJ L 146/1, 6.6.2012). According to that definition, *defined benefit plans are post-employment benefit plans other than defined contribution plans*. A post-employment benefit plan is a formal or informal arrangement under which an entity provides post-employment benefits to one or more former employees. Defined contribution plans are distinguished by two key features: (i) the entity pays fixed contributions into a separate entity (a fund); and (ii) the entity is not

share all the risks, is also treated as a transaction with a related party by the IASs and accordingly must be disclosed.[699] IAS 24 does not define a minimum transaction value for triggering the duty to disclose: it simply points at the duty to disclose, even where no transactions are conducted between the parties.[700] The only factor that could be influenced by the value of transaction, according to IAS 24, is the scope of disclosure. This comes into play with government-related entities that, when preparing their financial statements, must evaluate such factors as whether the transaction is carried out on non-market terms and whether it falls outside the normal business operations.[701]

Unlike IAS 24, the JSC Law of Ukraine does not elaborate in detail on the types of transactions with related parties. It merely indicates that transactions with interest may involve transfers of assets or the rendering of services. The procedural safeguards contained in the law (approval by the supervisory board or by the general meeting of shareholders) apply only when the value of the transaction exceeds 1% of the company's assets according to the company's financial statements.[702] When a transaction is approved, it consequently triggers the disclosure obligations requiring the company to make it public[703] and to submit the 'special' information to the NSSMC in accordance with that authority's procedures.[704] This 'special' information includes the date of the decision approving the transaction with interest, the market value of the goods or services or the amount of money involved in the contract, the carrying amount of the issuer's assets according to its financial statements, the correlation between the market value of the goods or services and the carrying amount of the issuer's assets, the number of votes cast to approve the transaction and the substantial terms of the contract, including the subject of the contract, the names of the parties involved and what their interest is.[705]

The JSC Law of Ukraine and the acts of the NSSMC do not explain in detail what types of transactions are covered by their requirements, simply referring to transactions involving transfers of goods or services or payments of money. The Economic Code of Ukraine conversely explicitly specifies what transactions fall under the rules on transactions with interest where they involve state or municipal enterprises.[706] These transactions include alienations and acquisitions of property, leases of property,

obliged to pay any further contributions if the fund does have sufficient assets to pay the employee benefits relating to employee service during the current or a prior period. Any arrangement for post-employment benefits that lacks these two features is a defined benefit plan.

699. *Ibid.*, paragraph 22.
700. *Ibid.*, paragraph 13.
701. *Ibid.*, paragraph 27.
702. JSC Law of Ukraine, Article 71(1).
703. *Ibid.*, Article 71(10).
704. Regulation on Disclosure of Information by Emitents of Securities, approved by the decision of the National Securities and Stock Market Commission of Ukraine, No. 2826 of 3 December 2013 [Polozhennia pro rozkryttia informatsii emitentamy tsinnykh paperiv, zatverdzhene rishenniam Natsionalnoyi komisii z tsinnykh paperiv ta fondovoho rynku No. 2826 vid 3 hrudnia 2013 roku].
705. *Ibid.*, subclause 3 clause 5 subchapter 1 Chapter III.
706. Economic Code of Ukraine [Hospodarksyi kodeks Ukrayiny], Articles 73-1(3), 78-1(3).

transfers of property into free use, works or services, loans and other financings on a repayable or non-repayable basis, guarantees and collateral. Unlike the JSC Law of Ukraine, the Economic Code of Ukraine links these types of transactions to specific multiples of the minimum wage, ranging from 20 to 100 times the minimum wage. The earlier version of Article 71 in the JSC Law of Ukraine used the same approach for determining the minimum threshold for transactions with interest. Since the amendments of February 2017,[707] Article 71 has opted for a threshold of 1 % of the company's assets. The practical effect of this change might well be demonstrated shortly in the case of Reiffeisen Bank Aval, one of Ukraine's largest banks and public companies. Its assets, according to its 2016 annual report, had a carrying amount of UAH 57,364,637,000 (almost EUR 2 billion).[708] Using the minimum wage for 2017 of UAH 3,200 (more than EUR 100),[709] the threshold of 100 times the minimum wage as used in the Economic Code of Ukraine would be UAH 320,000 (more than EUR 10,500), whereas 1 % of Reiffeisen Bank Aval's assets was UAH 573,646,370 (more than EUR 19 million). Here, 1 % of the company's assets is considerably more than 100 times the minimum wage; however, this is not the case for all Ukraine's banks, especially those that are strictly local. For instance, the 2016 financial statements of Asvio Bank in Chernihiv[710] showed assets with a carrying amount of UAH 974,103,000 (more than EUR 32 million).[711] For Asvio, 1 % of the company's assets (UAH 9,741,030 or approximately EUR 320,000) is a different figure. These data and calculations show that the criteria for determining a minimum threshold for RPTs might impact public companies differently, depending on their size (*see* Figure 3.1). However, 1 % of a company's assets reflects the features of the company concerned, while linking procedural requirements for RPTs to the minimum wage could prove inefficient in situations where rapid inflation and economic downturns cause the minimum wage to fall behind the real economic conditions, rendering it too low to use as a fair indicator.

707. Law of Ukraine 'On Amending Certain Legislative Acts on the Improvement of Corporate Governance in Joint Stock Companies' [Zakon Ukrayiny 'Pro vnesennia zmin do deyakykh zakonodavchykh aktiv schodo pidvyschennia rivnia korporatyvnogo upravlinnia v aktsionernykh tovarystvakh'] of 23 March 2017, published in Vidomosti Verkhovnoyi Rady Ukrayiny, 2017, No. 25, St. 289.
708. *Richnyi zvit Reiffeisen Banku Aval za 2016 rik*, available at: https://www.aval.ua/f/1/about/bank_reports/AR2016_UKR_LoRes.pdf (2017).
709. Law of Ukraine 'On State Budget of Ukraine in 2017' [Zakon Ukrayiny 'Pro Derzhavnyi biudzhet Ukrayiny za 2017 rik'] of 21 December 2016, published in Vidomosti Verkhovnoyi Rady Ukrayiny, 2017, No. 3, St. 31, Article 8.
710. A city in the north of Ukraine.
711. *Finansova zvitnist PAT 'Asvio Bank' za 2016 rik*, available at: https://www.asviobank.ua/tl_files/finance/rich_zvit_2016.pdf (2017).

Figure 3.1 Comparison of the Use of Thresholds in Two Ukrainian Banks: 1% of Company Assets Versus 100 Times the Minimum Wage in 2017

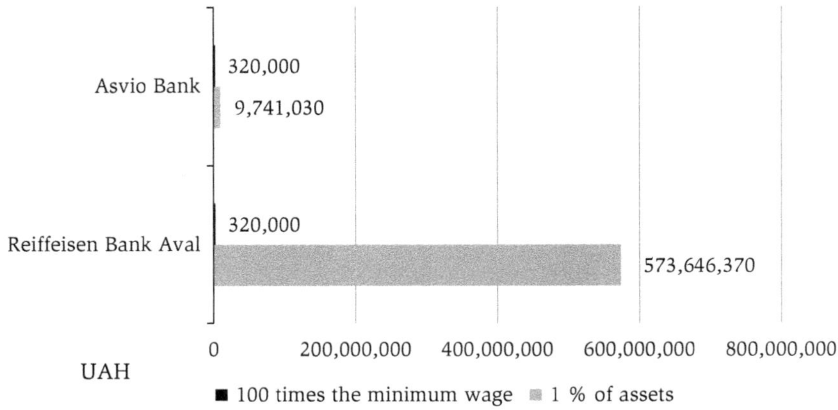

Source: 2016 annual reports of Raiffeisen Bank Aval and Asvio Bank; the Law of Ukraine 'On State Budget of Ukraine in 2017'.

Thresholds constitute an important element in regulating RPTs, and transactions of a particular weight, i.e. with the potential to harm the company to a more than trivial extent, show up on the legislative radar, while transactions with the impact of a mosquito bite are disregarded (unless, of course, they are conducted to conceal bigger transactions in aggregate). However, another significant factor from the perspective of related party monitoring is the nature of transactions.[712] Although both IAS 24 and the JSC Law of Ukraine generally refer to agreements for the provision of goods or services as the types of RPTs, it can be argued that some of these agreements, namely transactions to acquire real estate or to enjoy goods or services, that do not provide for a reciprocal performance, are in essence harmful to a company. In this regard, it is surprising that the Economic Code of Ukraine renders agreements to take receipt of irrevocable monetary aid in excess of fifty times the minimum wage subject to supervisory board approval in state-owned and municipality-owned enterprises.[713] It is highly unlikely that these transactions will have a detrimental effect on the company. The only aspect of such agreements that might give stakeholders cause for concern is if any provisions are stipulated that place additional obligations on the parties besides the rights stemming from the essence of the agreement, e.g. a non-compete clause or a clause restricting intellectual property rights. That is why even the lightest agreement for delivery of free goods or services must be subject to some form of screening. Still, it is doubtful whether these contractual arrangements should be subjected to examination by the supervisory board, instead of a more modest verification by the

712. Information about the nature of a transaction is required in the mandatory disclosure within the meaning of SRD II (Article 9c(2)).
713. Economic Code of Ukraine [Hospodarksyi kodeks Ukrayiny], Articles 73-1(3), 78-1(3).

company's legal department, compliance department or in-house counsel. The issues concerning the use of decision rights and procedural safeguards for dealing with RPTs are more strategy-related and are discussed in greater detail in Chapter 5.

§3.05 RPTs AND SIMILAR INSTRUMENTS

[A] Self-Dealing, Tunnelling, Propping and Self-Interested Transactions

RPTs are sometimes referred to by other names in literature and statute. For example, in German law a special term has emerged and received attention under the name of 'disguised distributions',[714] a concept that is concerned with the maintenance of share capital in companies.

Legal and economic scholars notably refer to 'self-dealing'[715] and 'tunnelling' in the context of RPTs.[716] Both these terms have a negative meaning and are used to describe situations where directors and/or controlling shareholders divert corporate wealth to themselves and away from other stakeholders.[717] Two main opinions have been expressed on how self-dealing and tunnelling are connected in terms of their substance.

The first opinion holds that self-dealing is a broader term. In this approach, tunnelling is most likely to take the shape of transactions.[718] Besides tunnelling, self-dealing also includes other forms of opportunism on the part of management or shareholders, in particular stock dilution through recapitalizations, mergers and squeeze-outs.[719] In the case of stock dilution, minority shareholders are deprived of benefits through corporate changes, rather than through transactions. For instance, if a company's share capital is increased by an undervalued additional contribution from a majority shareholder, the other shareholders' shares would consequently lose value. This process usually requires a decision by the general meeting of shareholders to approve amendments to the articles of association.[720] Similarly, minority shareholders

714. Fleischer H, 'Disguised Distributions and Capital Maintenance in European Company Law' in Lutter M (ed.), *Legal Capital in Europe* (Walter de Gruyter 2006).
715. Parkinson JE, *Corporate Power and Responsibility: Issues in the Theory of Company Law* (Oxford University Press Catalogue 1995), 200; Goshen Z, 'Controlling Corporate Self-Dealing: Convergence of Path Dependency?' in Milhaupt CJ (ed.), *Global Markets, Domestic Institutions: Corporate Law and Governance in a New Era of Cross-Border Deals* (Columbia University Press 2012).
716. Johnson S and others; Aharony J, Wang JW and Yuan HQ, 'Tunneling as an Incentive for Earnings Management During the IPO Process in China' (2010) 29 Journal of Accounting and Public Policy 1; Bertrand M, Mehta P and Mullainathan S, 'Ferreting out Tunneling: An Application to Indian Business Groups' NBER Working Paper No. 7952, available at: https://www.nber.org/papers/w7952, accessed on 18 November 2018.
717. Djankov S and others, 'The Law and Economics of Self-Dealing' (2008) 88 Journal of Financial Economics 430.
718. Conac P-H, Enriques L and Gelter M, 'Constraining Dominant Shareholders' Self-Dealing: The Legal Framework in France, Germany, and Italy' (2007) 4 European Company and Financial Law Review 491, 523.
719. *Ibid.*, 496.
720. *Ibid.*, 523.

and other stakeholders may suffer from corporate changes from an unfair exchange ratio between shares in merging companies or an unfair share price during a squeeze-out.

The second opinion, as set out in a celebrated article by Simon Johnson, Rafael La Porta and others, has a less restrictive view of tunnelling. The authors argue that it encompasses both direct transfers of assets (i.e., self-dealing transactions, outright theft, excessive remuneration and expropriation of business opportunities) and indirect extraction of benefits using dilutive share issuances, minority freeze-outs, insider trading and other suspicious transactions.[721] This approach ascribes a scope to tunnelling that is broad enough that it even includes insider trading based on the possession of specific information and the exploitation of inside information to the detriment of other stakeholders. This is not the case with the former opinion, which does not include insider trading in its definition of self-dealing, though even without insider trading it covers a considerable array of opportunistic acts.[722]

Both these opinions agree that tunnelling can take the form of excessive remuneration, transfer pricing, subsidized loans, non-arm's length agreements and even theft.[723] Depending on the type of siphoned property, various tunnelling techniques have been distinguished: cash flow tunnelling, asset tunnelling and equity tunnelling.[724] Tunnelling implies an extraction of assets, which is inherent in the concept. RPTs are therefore one of the tools that can be used for tunnelling.

Propping has been described as the twin of tunnelling, for its occasionally beneficial nature for the company.[725] Compared with tunnelling, propping has received less academic focus.[726] As evidenced by the Chinese economy, sometimes shareholders transfer resources to their company to support and attract minority shareholders.[727] Therefore, propping is usually a sign that a company is in need of additional funding. As Eric Friedman and others have claimed, private entrepreneurs sometimes decide to prop their firms in times of a moderate adverse shock to keep them alive.[728] If the crisis is too great, shareholders are more likely to be inclined to tunnel the assets, eventually causing the company to cease to exist.[729] Strongly performing firms are not necessarily safe from tunnelling behaviour of majority shareholders, however. Unlike propping, tunnelling is more likely to occur in companies with solid financial results;[730] in companies suffering temporary losses, propping is more probable.

---

721. Johnson S and others, 23.
722. Conac P-H, Enriques L and Gelter M, 496.
723. Chen W, Li S and Chen CX, 'How Much Control Causes Tunneling? Evidence from China' (2016) China Journal of Accounting Research, available at: http://dx.doi.org/101016/jcjar20 1610001), 3.
724. Atanasov VA, Black BS and Ciccotello CS, 'Unbundling and Measuring Tunneling' (2014) 2014 University of Illinois Law Review 1697, 1700.
725. *Ibid.*, 1704.
726. Cheung YL and others, 392.
727. Friedman E, Johnson S and Mitton T, 'Propping and Tunneling' (2003) 31 Journal of Comparative Economics 732.
728. *Ibid.*, 748.
729. *Ibid.*
730. Cheung YL and others, 374.

These two notions (tunnelling and propping) nevertheless share some common features: their essence and the legal background served as a prerequisite for their emergence. Related sales propping is said to be prevalent in regions with weaker investor protection.[731] In systems where corporate governance is more developed and that offer stronger investor protection as a consequence, both tunnelling and propping activities occur more rarely.[732]

Another term that is widely used by scholars and practitioners is 'self-interested transactions'.[733] This is one of the translations from Ukrainian to English of the notion 'transactions with interest' as used in the JSC Law of Ukraine and in the LLC Law of Ukraine.[734] Self-interested transactions should not be understood as always being formed in the interests of the related parties: a related party might enter into a transaction not only in his or her own interests but also in the interests of a close relative or another affiliated person.

The term 'transaction with interest' as used in the JSC Law of Ukraine[735] and in the LLC Law of Ukraine[736] might seem misleading at first sight. According to the JSC Law of Ukraine, it encompasses transactions in which the company is on one side of the transaction and the interested person is either on the other side or is a representative, broker or beneficiary in a transaction. The JSC Law of Ukraine also extends its rules on transactions with interest to include transactions between public companies and companies controlled by an interested person.[737] For private companies, transactions with interest have a narrower scope. Based on the literal wording of the LLC Law of Ukraine, transactions with interest are always formed between a company and its related parties, making them RPTs. The term itself also gives grounds to elaborate on other transactions that present an economic interest but to which the company itself is not a party, i.e. transactions between the company's affiliated persons such as the company's major shareholder and manager, or between the company's affiliated person and a competitor. To quote Luca Enriques, *transactions between other entities, whose welfare affects that of the company (for example, due to controlling interest of the latter in the former) and a director.*[738]

The fact that the statutory provisions can be interpreted in multiple ways is clearly an undesirable situation. Therefore, changing the terminology in the text of the act would be the appropriate course of action from an academic perspective. However, taking into account that practitioners, including judges, have already become familiar

731. Jian M and Wong TJ, 'Propping Through Related Party Transactions' (2010) 15 Review of Accounting Studies 70, 98.
732. Gupta P, *Tunneling and Propping: Indian Evidence* (Thesis within Fellowship Programme in Management, Indian Institute of Management Indore 2017), v.
733. Parkinson JE, 205; Eisenberg MA, 'Self-Interested Transactions in Corporate Law' (1987) 13 Journal of Corporation Law 997; Farrar JH, 'A Note on Dealing with Self Interested Transactions by Directors' (2000) 12 Bond Law Review 106.
734. Antonenko L, 8.
735. JSC Law of Ukraine, Article 71.
736. LLC Law of Ukraine, Article 45.
737. JSC Law of Ukraine, Article 71(3).
738. Enriques L, 'The Law on Company Directors' Self-Dealing: A Comparative Analysis', 299.

with the concept of 'transactions with interest', this superficial change would only add to the confusion.

[B] RPTs and Executive Remuneration

Executive contracts with directors constitute a special category of RPTs, dealing with labour issues in a company. These contracts differ from the sales and services transactions that the director forms on the company's behalf, in that by nature they are more internally oriented. Due to their specific features, their regulation in law is based on multiple separate sources.[739] However, despite some differences with classical tunnelling, employment contracts with executives can very well be used for asset stripping in enterprises if the remuneration is disproportionately excessive. This is where employment contracts pose a threat similar to that of other RPTs.

The relationship between pay and performance is not always clearly established. Proper remuneration does not guarantee that performance will bring substantial success to the company. In addition, even if the company's net income exceeds its outgoings, the possibility remains that the same results could have been achieved with less remuneration for or less effort from the executive. Therefore, the line between proper and excessive levels of remuneration is not always easy to see, depending largely on external factors and subjective preferences. To analyse remuneration and to understand where it is excessive, some countries employ a special strategy known as the 'constraints strategy'.[740] Germany is one of the countries where this strategy is used.

The landmark case that dealt with the issues of unreasonable remuneration in Germany was the *Mannesmann* case.[741] That case concerned the payment of millions of US dollars as 'golden parachutes' to six outgoing Mannesmann executives after the company was taken over by Vodafone.[742] The Mannesmann CEO and supervisory board members were charged under criminal law for breaching their fiduciary duties by approving the payments to executives. Legal action followed, despite the fact that Vodafone, holding 98.66% of the shares, had approved the payout.[743] All six executives were acquitted by the Regional Court in Düsseldorf in 2004, but in 2005 the

739. For example, *see*: Commission Recommendation of 14 December 2004 fostering an appropriate regime for the remuneration of directors of listed companies [2004] OJ L 385/55, 29.12.2004; Commission Recommendation of 15 February 2005 on the role of non-executive or supervisory directors of listed companies and on the committees of the (supervisory) board [2005] OJ L 52/51, 25.2.2005; Commission Recommendation of 30 April 2009 complementing Recommendations 2004/913/EC and 2005/162/EC as regards the regime for the remuneration of directors of listed companies [2009] OJ L 120/28, 15.5.2009.
740. Hill JG, 'Regulating Executive Remuneration: International Developments in the Post-Scandal Era' (2006) 3 European Company Law 64, 65.
741. *Ibid.*, 73.
742. Kraakman R and others, *The Anatomy of Corporate Law: A Comparative and Functional Approach* (3rd edn, Oxford University Press 2017), 67.
743. *Ibid.*, 68.

Federal Supreme Court disagreed with the judgment and referred the case for retrial.[744] The Supreme Court's decision established a 'tough objective' test,[745] which substantially added to the legislative provisions already in place at that time under the AktG. All extra-contractual payments for past performances, without future incentive, are now automatically considered unlawful, regardless of their amount.[746] Although a famous case, *Mannesmann* is far from the only one dealing with executive remuneration: other cases have applied and interpreted the standards introduced by the AktG too.[747] As the first sentence of Article 87(1) of the AktG states, *in determining the aggregate remuneration of any member of the supervisory board, the supervisory board must ... ensure that such aggregate remuneration is reasonable relative to the duties and performances of the member and to the company's situation, and that it does not exceed the standard remuneration without a specific reason.*[748] The word 'reasonable' or 'appropriate' has been especially problematic for applying the standard in practice.[749] For instance, in the *Mannesmann* case, an attempt was made to justify the 'appropriateness' of the bonuses by referring to the value-creating effect of the executives' conduct.[750] Although this interpretation was not upheld by the courts, it nonetheless demonstrates how a single term can have multiple interpretations depending on the circumstances.

In Ukraine, the constraints strategy is not used in connection with the remuneration of company directors, of either public or private companies. An executive's salary depends entirely on what he or she has agreed with the company and, consequently, with shareholders. Therefore, under Ukrainian company law, it is exclusively for the company's own bodies to decide whether the remuneration is excessive or not, and not for external parties such as in Germany. Nevertheless, as noted above, executive compensation is a complex matter. Although it can be identified as a tunnelling technique, it is too specific to be studied together with RPTs and their strategies.

[C] Transfer Pricing and Insider Trading

The risks that RPTs pose primarily affect private actors: minority shareholders, creditors and employees. Most commonly, a majority shareholder or a manager will act for his or her own benefit and to the detriment of minority shareholders and/or the company itself. These are the issues that company law addresses by seeking to balance the interests of the various company constituencies. What company law does not cover is the potentially negative and largely external effect of RPTs. Public welfare can also

744. Harbarth S and Kienle F, 'Director Compensation under German Law and the Mannesmann Effect' (2006) 3 European Company Law 90, 94.
745. Kraakman R and others, *The Anatomy of Corporate Law: A Comparative and Functional Approach* (3rd edn, Oxford University Press 2017), 221.
746. Harbarth S and Kienle F, 95.
747. *Ibid.*, 91.
748. AktG, Article 87(1).
749. Kolla P, 'The Mannesmann Trial and the Role of the Courts' (2004) 5 German Law Journal 829, 830.
750. *Ibid.*, 834.

be impacted by RPTs if they harm society by lowering tax proceeds through transfer pricing schemes. Although in practice transfer pricing employs RPTs as a tool, it nonetheless has its own separate set of rules, where the term 'related party transaction' is used in a different sense and for a different purpose. The general perspective is that transfer pricing mainly concerns tax liability management.[751] RPTs here serve to reduce the revenue of companies operating in unfavourable tax jurisdictions and increase the revenue of companies operating under more favourable tax conditions.[752] This is usually held to fall under public law, and this book does not discuss transfer pricing or analyse the tax aspects of RPTs in detail.

Another concept that, like the previous one, falls beyond the scope of this book is insider trading. In the economic sense, insider trading involves trades by parties who are better informed than their business partners.[753] While insider trading with the company's shares may very well be carried out by related parties, it does not necessarily involve RPTs. Insider trading can have a value-decreasing effect for the company and its shareholders, as is often the case with RPTs. However, the difference is that insider trading may cause vulnerable stakeholders to suffer due to indirect abusive enrichment by insiders, while RPTs have a more direct effect: the company's wealth is simply looted, leaving minority shareholders, creditors and employees with less chance of protecting their interests. Insider trading mostly involves transactions with investors for a company's securities, rather than its assets. The company is usually not a party to transactions characterized as insider trading. Also, opinions are divided on the efficiency of insider trading and its regulation.[754] In a way, this unites RPTs and insider trading, although it would be wrong to characterize all RPTs from one perspective (positive or negative). In essence and based on their features, however, these concepts are still substantially different. Therefore, insider trading should be studied separately.

751. Pendse SJ, 'International Transfer Pricing: A Review of Non-tax Outlook' (2012) 37 Procedia-Social and Behavioral Sciences 337, 342.
752. Talab HR, 'Transfer Pricing and Its Effect on Financial Reporting: A Theoretical Analysis of Global Tax in Multinational Companies' (2017) 11 International Business Management 921, 923.
753. Carlton DW and Fischel DR, 'The Regulation of Insider Trading' (1983) 35 Stanford Law Review 857, 860.
754. Beny LN, 'Do Insider Trading Laws Matter? Some Preliminary Comparative Evidence' (2005) 7 American Law and Economics Review 144, 145.

CHAPTER 4

RPTs in Corporate Groups

§4.01 THE CONCEPT OF A CORPORATE GROUP: REGULATION OF CORPORATE GROUPS

[A] Legal Entities as the Origins of Corporate Groups

Legal entities are the building blocks of every corporate group. Corporate groups would not exist without legal entities. In fact, legal entities existed before groups came to life. Unlike natural persons, both legal entities and groups of companies are creatures of law, as posited by the European Court of Justice in the famous *Daily Mail* case.[755] However, when legal entities were introduced into the legal realm, no clear necessity existed for anything more: they already possessed the necessary features that made them attractive to entrepreneurs: separate personality and limited liability. Today, these features are regarded as the undeniable achievements of corporate theory.[756]

Since the milestone corporate events in the nineteenth century,[757] the idea of a 'one-man' ('single-member') company has enriched both company law theory and statute. Statutory rules exist that allow for the formation and functioning of single-member companies both at the EU level and at the level of national law. Rules on single-member companies have a twofold nature. First, they provide safeguards against abusive behaviour of shareholders. For instance, Directive 2009/102/EC gives Member States discretionary power to impose special provisions for cases where either a natural person is the sole member in several companies or a single-member company or any other legal person is the sole member of a company.[758] The logic behind these

755. *The Queen v. H.M. Treasury and Commissioners of Inland Revenue ex part Daily Mail and General Trust PLC (Case 81/87)* OJ C 277 (European Court of Justice), 5511.
756. Kraakman R and others, *The Anatomy of Corporate Law: A Comparative and Functional Approach* (3rd edn, Oxford University Press 2017), 5.
757. Harris R, 'The Private Origins of the Private Company: Britain 1862-1907' (2013) 33 Oxford Journal of Legal Studies 339, 340.
758. Directive 2009/102/EC, Article 2.

safeguards is self-evident: regulations where a single natural person owns a chain of companies could create additional risks of non-performance of obligations and other related risks. In Ukraine, these safeguards were previously successfully implemented, but (for private companies) recently removed unexpectedly from the CCU by the LLC Law of Ukraine.[759]

Second and more importantly, the effect of these legislative provisions is not exclusively defensive, but also enabling. The legislation does allow persons to be the sole members of private companies. Legal regulation had to undergo a long evolution to reach this level of autonomy in the right of establishment. This right has a crucial theoretical implication: companies are not confined to simple groupings of individuals. On the contrary: membership in a company is devoid of a personal link between the individual and the company. Although a sole shareholder may of course enter into an employment contract with a company and become its director or a member of a company body, a shareholder's role in the company is characterized more by the shareholder's ability to retain a distance from direct participation in the company's operational activity and, having made a monetary contribution, only attend the general meeting of shareholders (or send a representative).

In cases where several individuals agree to become shareholders in a company, it may in fact be argued that a group of people are united by a common fund. This feature can also be described as corporateness. Otherwise, without a common fund attributed to corporateness, i.e. without an officially formed company, multiple individuals would be qualified as joint debtors or joint tortfeasors.[760] However, the very fact that a company has multiple shareholders does not automatically mean that it comprises a corporate group as defined in the scope of this research. Corporate groups cannot in any way be equated with groups of individuals. The nature and features of corporate groups are studied in greater detail in this section.

[B] The Economic and Legal Views of Corporate Groups

Corporate groups as a legal and economic phenomenon emerged in the twentieth century (and in some countries in the late-nineteenth century[761]).[762] What had previously been purely internal issues, resolved between a firm's separate constituencies, could now be decided at the group level. From an economic point of view, this does not create many problems. Economists have always regarded firms as more than a legal entity. As Harry Rajak notes, scholars and economists use the term 'firm' to

759. LLC Law of Ukraine, Chapter 8, paragraph 6(2).
760. Stoljar SJ, *Groups and Entities: An Inquiry into Corporate Theory* (Australian National University Press 1973), 189.
761. Blumberg PI, 'Limited Liability and Corporate Groups' (1985) 11 Journal of Corporation Law 573, 605.
762. Antunes JE, *Liability of Corporate Groups: Autonomy and Control in Parent-Subsidiary Relationships in US, German and EU Law: An International and Comparative Perspective* (Kluwer Law and Taxation Publisher 1994), 109.

overcome the difference between incorporated and unincorporated business entities.[763] A firm's boundaries under the economic approach are based on the distinction between the firm and the market. A firm enters the market with all its available financial and non-financial resources: tangible assets, human capital, know-how and so on. An alternative route that a firm can take is one of internal development, i.e. organizing transfers of resources or services internally.

In his celebrated article, Ronald Coase carefully studied the idea that legal entities needed to form relationships with other economic players in order to participate in turnover.[764] Coase essentially argued that, if transaction costs become too high to enter into agreements with other firms, it makes more sense to organize an internal system of relationships within the firm's own boundaries.[765] Where a transaction is organized internally, this eliminates some of the marketing costs, including contracting and enforcement cost. At a certain point, the situation may turn around, and it becomes less costly to apply to the market and utilize the price mechanism.

Before Coase initiated this discussion, firms were seen as 'black boxes'. The merit of Coase's article was that he asked profound questions; e.g., he wondered *why a firm emerges at all in a specialized exchange economy*.[766] Oliver Williamson, who further contributed to the transaction cost theory and rendered it workable, has taken Coase's ideas further. He views the firm as primarily a governance structure,[767] where governance is regarded as an overarching concept.[768]

When Alice Belcher explored Coase's doctrine in combination with the approaches taken by Knight and Weitzman, and sought to make those doctrines applicable to the law, she concluded that they were aimed at incorporating the concept of authority (to direct, to choose and to dismiss), namely authority over employees.[769] However, this suggestion contains an inherent contradiction, as it applies a specifically legal concept. For the law, authority plays a crucial role, as the law essentially asks whether or not behaviour is allowed.[770] For economics, the answer might be different. For instance, it is inappropriate from the economic perspective to assess whether a manager has the authority to enter into a transaction. Instead, economic theory asks whether it is reasonable to enter into the transaction, how far the firm can go, what it should do to maximize its profits and so on. The economic boundaries of a firm were

763. Rajak H, 'Corporate Groups and Cross-Border Bankruptcy' (2008) 44 Texas International Law Journal 521, 522.
764. Coase RH, 'The Nature of the Firm' (1937) 4 Economica 386.
765. *Ibid.*, 394.
766. *Ibid.*, 390.
767. Williamson OE, 'The Theory of the Firm as Governance Structure: From Choice to Contract' (2002) 16 The Journal of Economic Perspectives 171, 191.
768. Williamson OE, 'Transaction Cost Economics: The Natural Progression' (2010) 86 Journal of Retailing 215.
769. Belcher A, 'The Boundaries of the Firm: The Theories of Coase, Knight and Weitzman' (1997) 17 Legal Studies 22, 38.
770. McCarthy KJ, Fiolet M and Dolfsma W, *The Nature of the New Firm: Beyond the Boundaries of Organisations and Institutions* (Edward Elgar Publishing 2011), 5.

notably described by Jensen and Meckling as *the maximum attainable set of output quantities for various input quantities, given the state of technology and knowledge.*[771]

The boundaries of the firm, as defined in economic theory, are not immune to blurring. This can be caused by the existence of sophisticated inter-firm arrangements such as long-term framework agreements, franchise contracts, joint ventures and vertical network organizations. Some authors, however, have expressed the opinion that vertical network organizations actually add more specificity to the firm's boundaries and are unique constructions with their own incentive provisions and coordination devices.[772] This idea deserves further analysis. It is true that vertical integration schemes and long-term contracts cannot simply be equated with market choice. Using these devices, firms would become so closely related that it would be impossible to argue that they are 'going to the market' separately. Accordingly, a group of companies with a separate business policy and affiliates that are responsible for performing certain functions within the group will more likely be viewed as a single firm than separate legal entities within the group's structure. This is entirely fair according to Coase's theory.[773] The fact that the members of the group are individual legal entities is essential for law, but not for economics. Viewing a group of companies as a body in its own right, different from a legal entity, in and of itself contradicts the concept of company, where limited liability, meaning that a company's shareholders as a rule are not liable for the company's debts, is one of the cornerstones.

It would also be incompatible with economic theory to define the market as all other parties that are not the firm's employees or subdivisions. This legalist view of companies as separate legal entities does not suit the objectives of economic theory. In fact, it seems that economic theory has infringed on the legal realm, by adding new and previously unknown items to the agenda. In the nineteenth century, the idea of separate personality and limited liability were brilliant inventions, aimed at boosting economic turnover. No urgent necessity existed to establish corporate structures with multiple horizontally or vertically integrated companies. At the time of nineteenth century landmark case *Salomon v. Salomon* in the UK, limited liability and separate personality were viewed as the modern cure for the disease of risky entrepreneurial activity, with lack of proper protection for creditors' rights as a side effect.[774] Today, in a world of corporate groups often formed as transnational companies,[775] the formal implications of *Salomon v. Salomon* no longer reflect economic reality.[776] Classical

771. Jensen MC and Meckling WH, 'Rights and Production Functions: An Application to Labor-Managed Firms and Codetermination' (1979) 52 The Journal of Business 469.
772. Baudry B and Chassagnon V, 'The Vertical Network Organization as a Specific Governance Structure: What Are the Challenges for Incomplete Contracts Theories and What Are the Theoretical Implications for the Boundaries of the (Hub-) Firm?' (2012) 16 Journal of Management & Governance 285, 289.
773. Harper Ho VE, 'Theories of Corporate Groups: Corporate Identity Reconceived' (2012) 42 Seton Hall Law Review 879, 886.
774. Hill J, 'Corporate Groups, Creditor Protection and Cross Guarantees: Australian Perspectives' (1994) 24 Canadian Business Law Journal 321.
775. Picciotto S, *Regulating Global Corporate Capitalism* (Cambridge University Press 2011), 129.
776. Dearborn M, 'Enterprise Liability: Reviewing and Revitalizing Liability for Corporate Groups' (2009) 97 California Law Review 195, 209.

corporate theory was not designed to protect large polycorporate enterprises, the modern economic constellation of corporate groups.[777] One of the main areas where the classical tools of corporate theory have been rendered obsolete is intra-group liability.[778] Guided by group policy considerations, subsidiaries can empty their pockets and then have no possibilities to restore their finances. Limited liability and separate personality are also not the proper tools for protecting the interests of victims of torts committed by subsidiaries of a group.[779] For example, in cases of environmental pollution or consumer contamination by a subsidiary in one country based on group policy and instructions handed down from the top, it would be unfair if only the subsidiary faced liability without piercing the parent company's corporate veil.[780] Corporate groups by themselves can therefore produce risks that need to be avoided. Those risks have created new challenges for company law and a new battlefield for the legislature.[781]

[C] The Concept of Affiliation and Affiliation Challenges in Corporate Groups

A corporate group's formation is sometimes described as a company's external growth.[782] At the same time, the company's external growth is not limited to the creation of corporate groups only. Working from these premises, Ulrich Immenga wondered why businessmen *believe that the formation of company systems is the best method for promoting external growth.*[783] He asked this question in the context of his research into affiliated persons. Answering it requires a brief consideration of his study and an exploration of whether the terminology he used is relevant for the current work as well.

In fact, Immenga himself highlights the vagueness in the definitions of company systems and affiliation in some jurisdictions.[784] To follow the author's line of thought,

777. Antunes JE, 51.
778. *Ibid.*, 6.
779. Lipton P, 'The Mythology of Salomon's Case and the Law Dealing with the Tort Liabilities of Corporate Groups: An Historical Perspective' (2014) 40 Monash University Law Review 452, 487.
780. This is illustrated by the example of the Haitian Poisoning Affair, following the death of a five-year-old child from contamination in a country where the subsidiary was located. *See*: Bartman SM, 'Piercing the Corporate Veil in Haitian Poisoning Affair Rejected in First Instance: German HELM AG Not Found Liable under Dutch Corporate Law' (2016) 13 European Company Law 105.
781. Spindler G, 'Scandals, Regulation, and Supervisory Agencies: The European Perspective' in Hopt KJ (ed.), *Corporate Governance in Context: Corporations, States, and Markets in Europe, Japan, and the US* (Oxford University Press 2005), 128.
782. Immenga U, 'Company Systems and Affiliations' in Frankel T (ed.), *International Encyclopedia of Comparative Law*, vol 13 (Amer Soc Comparative Law 1988), 4.
783. *Ibid.*, 4. This is reminiscent of the classical question posed by Coase as to why a firm should emerge on the market at all. With Coase, however, the discussion was of a purely economic nature, referring to a firm as a broad concept, as has been described above.
784. *Ibid.*, 3. According to Immenga, this vagueness exists in the US and France, where the definition of affiliation is either too broad, being subject to interpretative freedom, or is not statutory-based.

this is not the case in Germany, where the law is very specific on this topic and refers to the notions of an affiliated group, parent and subsidiary relations and so on. Still, for Immenga the term 'affiliation' is broader than company systems, and includes, e.g., 'interlocking officers and directors'.[785] This stresses the need to establish types of affiliation that are relevant for corporate groups and to understand where affiliation gives rise to the emergence of corporate groups.

Affiliation describes the core characteristics of corporate groups. Without affiliation, the notion of groups would be meaningless. However, degrees of affiliation vary, and different schools of thought exist as to how close companies need to be to establish affiliation. This has caused some contention among scholars. Scholars and practitioners have developed various theories to help them understand this term, ranging from the narrow ownership-based concept to viewing even loose economic relationships through supply chains as group elements.[786] However, the narrow ownership-based group is unquestionably the most common understanding of this phenomenon. As Harper Ho admits, *this prototypical group includes a parent company and its direct and indirect subsidiaries, each with a separate legal identity and its own rights and obligations*.[787] The entities making up a group are usually private companies, but not necessarily. Both incorporated and unincorporated entities, e.g. partnerships, may become constituent elements of a group, depending on whether the legal requirements allow corporate structures with those types of entities.

The fact that ownership-based groups are the most common form of corporate groupings can be seen from the area where reaching a consensus always requires a great deal of hard work and much effort: EU law. This is where legal notions and the rules surrounding them are coined based on protracted discussion and analysis. Without going into the specifics of EU regulation,[788] a glance at the concept of a 'group' as it is now used in the Accounting Directive shows that it is worded as follows: *a parent undertaking and all its subsidiary undertakings*.[789] Similar definitions of groups can be found in IAS 24[790] and IFRS 10.[791] The definitions provided in those instruments are not, by themselves, sufficient to grant an understanding of the relationships in groups; this requires an analysis of the meaning of a 'parent undertaking'. The Accounting Directive defines a parent undertaking as an undertaking that controls one or more subsidiary undertakings.[792] Therefore, the core idea of the 'group' concept based on the provisions of the current sources of EU law mentioned above lies in control.

785. *Ibid.*
786. Harper Ho VE, 890.
787. *Ibid.*, 886.
788. This is done in section §4.01[E], below.
789. Accounting Directive, Article 2(11).
790. IAS 24, clause 9(i)(b).
791. International Financial Reporting Standard 10, as adopted by Commission Regulation (EC) No. 1126/2008 of 3 November 2008 adopting certain international accounting standards in accordance with Regulation (EC) No. 1606/2002 of the European Parliament and of the Council [2008] OJ L 320/1, 29.11.2008, clause 2.
792. *Ibid.*, Article 2(9).

Not only does the Accounting Directive (similarly to its predecessor, the Seventh Council Directive[793]) place the notion of control at the heart of the 'group' phenomenon, the concept of control is also widely used in the national laws of the EU Member States,[794] as well as in jurisdictions beyond the EU.[795] While this term has already been covered in the previous chapter and is not analysed in detail here, some group-related issues require further elaboration in the present chapter.

No definition of control is given in Article 1 of the Accounting Directive with all its other relevant definitions, despite the fact the EU legislature defines group through control. Some commentators have expressed concern about this by criticizing the Directive for lacking sufficient clarity.[796] It is not entirely clear whether, to interpret these provisions, lawyers should either search for clarification of the 'control' notion in other instruments, for instance IAS 27,[797] or else draw on the elements of control in the provisions of the same Directive. Specifically, recital 31 of the Directive reads as follows: *Control should be based on holding a majority of voting rights, but control may also exist where there are agreements with fellow shareholders or members. In certain circumstances control may be effectively exercised when the parent holds a minority or none of the shares in the subsidiary*. With this provision, the EU legislature confirms the view that a majority shareholding is the main example of control, but not the only one, describing affiliation in a group. One scenario where a shareholder has only a minority of the shares, but could exercise control nevertheless, is if a majority of the members of the administrative, management or supervisory bodies are appointed solely through the exercise of that shareholder's voting rights. At the same time, some ambiguity exists in the text of the Accounting Directive as to where exactly 'dominant influence' occurs instead of 'control': it is not entirely clear from the text of the Directive how these notions interrelate. Where everyone agrees, based on the literal interpretation of the Directive, is that these notions are mutually exclusive, meaning that 'dominant influence' by itself rules out the possibility of 'control'.[798]

Accordingly, although control is a widely accepted concept, it frequently poses difficulties for interpreting it and applying it in practice to define a group's boundaries. Essentially, two ways exist to determine control: by form and by substance.[799] The principal example of how formal techniques help to establish control is by checking whether a majority shareholding exists. Where a shareholder owns most of the voting rights in a company and, consequently, can appoint its executives, that person is a controller. However, matters become more complicated if the company has many

793. Seventh Council Directive, Article 1.
794. 'Corporate Group Law for Europe by Forum Europaeum', 187.
795. Kluver J, 'European and Australian Proposals for Corporate Group Law: A Comparative Analysis' (2000) 1 European Business Organization Law Review 287, 292.
796. Søgaard G, 'Introduction of a Group Definition in the New Accounting Directive: The Impact on Future Accounting Regulation' (2014) 11 European Company Law 232, 235.
797. *Ibid.*, 235.
798. Accounting Directive, Article 22(2)(a).
799. Adinolfi A, 'The Legal Notion of the Group Enterprise: The EEC Approach' in Sugarman D and Teubner G (eds), *Regulating Corporate Groups in Europe* (Nomos 1990), 498.

shareholders but no major shareholding. This requires an analysis of other circumstances besides the number of shares to identify the company's controller or controllers. This analysis will then be of a qualitative nature and will use other kinds of relationships besides share ownership, e.g. contractual relationships, voting results and so on. Although substantive analysis is more difficult to apply than a formal test, using purely formal criteria sometimes yields unfair results, as ownership of shares is not the only meaningful type of relationship to emerge in groups of companies. At the same time, extensively favouring substantive criteria leads to uncertainty, and it makes sense for the EU authorities to adhere mostly to formal criteria in group company law.[800]

Substantive criteria were used to determine control in the recent case of *Okpabi v. Shell*. The England and Wales Court of Appeal rendered a judgment in which it did not find proximity in the relationship between the ultimate holding company Royal Dutch Shell and its Nigerian subsidiary, as one of the conditions for the Court to have jurisdiction regarding a claim for breach of the duty of care.[801] In response to the plaintiffs' allegation that Royal Dutch Shell imposed mandatory policies, standards and guidelines for the use of pipelines by its subsidiaries, the Court emphasized the universal application of those policies.[802] In other words, according to the Court's reasoning, the relationship lacked operational control particularly for the Nigerian subsidiary.[803] This judgment might be instrumental in helping parent companies decide how to structure their corporate policies to avoid liability for loss or damage caused by their subsidiaries.

Besides loopholes and pitfalls in the substantive interpretation of control and related terms (influence, dominance and so on), in light of Article 1 of the Accounting Directive, a further issue exists, i.e. whether only vertical groups, where entities are fully dependent on each other and lack autonomous decision-making,[804] should be recognized in the definition of a group. Article 1 of the Accounting Directive concerns vertical groups only since it prefers the concept of control.[805] At the same time, however, the Accounting Directive has not fully eliminated horizontal groups; reference to them is made in the optional paragraph 7 of Article 22 of the Accounting Directive.[806] As provided by that paragraph 7, two undertakings are related by a degree of influence either through their unified management stemming from contractual or constituent documents or if the same persons occupy positions in the administrative, management or supervisory bodies of both companies. Immenga refers to the latter type of affiliation as 'interlocking officers and directors', going beyond company

800. *Ibid.*, 505.
801. Bergkamp PA, 'Parent Company Liability After Okpabi v. Shell' (2018) 15 European Company Law 112, 114.
802. *Ibid.*, 114.
803. *Ibid.*, 117.
804. Adinolfi A, 503.
805. Søgaard G, 234.
806. *Ibid.*, 34.

systems.[807] It then follows that 'company systems' in Immenga's research mean primarily 'vertical groups' based on control.

This reveals a number of challenges in formulating the boundaries of groups and answering the question of which types of affiliation are irrelevant in corporate groups. First, as has been discussed already, the idea from corporate legal theory that a group is a set of separate legal entities is no longer reflective of the growing demands of economic reality. The enterprise theory, in which an enterprise refers to a combination of parent, subsidiary and affiliated companies, has already been considered by legal scholars.[808] However, equating relationships between legal entities within a group with relationships between, for instance, the research department and the marketing department of a single company has counter-arguments of its own. One reason is that companies in a group might very well have 'outside' shareholders.[809] Those outside shareholders do not feature in vertical group relationships and might hold a small percentage of the share capital in a company belonging to a group. Their role in decision-making procedure is insignificant, yet this does not mean that their interests should be neglected.

Second, using substantive criteria to assess relationships within corporate groups lacks clarity. This approach involves using terms - control, dominance, influence and other - and the outcome may appear different in the eyes of different interpreters. That is why formal criteria are reasonably preferred, with substantive tests applied to a lesser extent, given that clarity and certainty may suffer. Recent case law also shows that courts using substantive criteria to determine control may be guided by policy considerations and the further implications of their judgments.[810]

Third, a widespread trend has emerged to view corporate groups primarily as vertical groups. The idea that a parent company exerts control in corporate groups has flooded corporate theory so widely that some authors even include this idea as one of the constituent features of all corporate groups, and by doing so exclude horizontal groups.[811] However, pretending that horizontal groups do not exist is not the solution, especially taking into account that they have emerged as a European phenomenon, as opposed to centralized multinational groups in the US and Japan.[812] In addition, Article 22 of the Accounting Directive provides for some minor optional regulation of these groups, as a legacy of the Seventh Council Directive.[813] Therefore, arrangements of horizontal groups, where, e.g., two companies own shares in each other,[814] do in fact exist and deserve consideration. At the same time, what they bring to the legal realm

807. Immenga U, 'Company Systems and Affiliations', 3.
808. Landers JM, 'A Unified Approach to Parent, Subsidiary, and Affiliate Questions in Bankruptcy' (1975) 42 The University of Chicago Law Review 590.
809. Antunes JE, 88.
810. Bergkamp PA, 117.
811. Nzafashwanayo D, 'Corporate Groups under the Laws of Rwanda: An Economic Reality Without Legal Identity' (2016) 7 Beijing Law Review 95, 98.
812. Bayer W, 'Horizontal Groups and Joint Ventures in Europe: Concepts and Reality' in Hopt KJ (ed.), *Groups of Companies in European Laws*, vol 2 (de Gruyter 1982), 3.
813. Muller W, 'Group Accounts under the Proposed Seventh EEC Directive: A Practitioner's View' in Hopt KJ (ed.), *Groups of Companies in European Laws*, vol 2 (de Gruyter 1982), 181.
814. Rajak H, 522.

is uncertainty, as formal criteria do not suit these types of groups. The question is not where the group starts, but where it ends,[815] which is how strong influence needs to be in order to identify a group. This fact, coupled with the desire of the EU authorities to prevent national governments from imposing excessive duties and burdens on groups, may be one reason why EU law favours the narrow definition of corporate groups, i.e. vertical groups consisting of entities deemed to be affiliated pursuant mainly to formal criteria.[816] As such, to maintain clarity and consistency, this book views groups primarily as control-based vertical groups, unless the text specifies otherwise.

[D] Reasons to Create Corporate Groups

To better understand the legal side of corporate groups, it is necessary to step away from the unity that is characteristic of this economic notion and instead consider their legal diversity. From the perspective of the law, corporate groups consist of multiple independent companies or other legal persons that are linked through a variety of techniques and are termed affiliates.[817] The formation of a group is different from the creation of a single company. Using the example of *Salomon v. Salomon*,[818] where Mr Salomon involved his wife and children in establishing a company, his intentions were quite clear and straightforward: to make a corporate shield that would protect his family and himself personally from excessive claims of creditors. To implement his plan, the merchant did not require more than one legal entity, since a single private company was sufficient.

Matters become more complicated if a corporate group is involved. Bearing in mind that a corporate group, by its very nature, consists of multiple legal entities, the goal pursued by Mr Salomon – to enjoy the benefits of a corporate shield in the shape of a company – is not sufficient to explain all the circumstances surrounding the creation and functioning of corporate groups. The philosophy behind corporate groups is more sophisticated than with a single legal entity. The reasons for introducing a corporate group transcend company law and may concern accounting,[819] environmental law,[820] human rights,[821] tax or anti-competition policy,[822] though tax-driven considerations are particularly prevalent.[823] However, this study does not discuss the

815. Harper Ho VE, 887.
816. Adinolfi A, 511.
817. Picciotto S, 129.
818. *Salomon v. A. Salomon and Co. Ltd.* AC 22 (United Kingdom House of Lords), 22.
819. Samaras I and Athianos S, 'Group Accounting: The Effect of IFRS Adoption. The Case of Greece' (2016) 15 Journal of Accounting and Management Information Systems 661.
820. Bergkamp L, 'The Environmental Liability Directive and Liability of Parent Companies for Damage Caused by Their Subsidiaries ("Enterprise Liability")' (2016) 13 European Company Law 183.
821. Mwaura K, 'Internalization of Costs to Corporate Groups: Part-Whole Relationships, Human Rights Norms and the Futility of the Corporate Veil' (2012) 11 Journal of International Business & Law 85, 110.
822. Avgitidis DK, *Groups of Companies: The Liability of the Parent Company for the Debts of Its Subsidiary* (Ant. N. Sakkoulas Publishers 1996), 135-140.
823. Landers JM, 589.

areas that fall beyond the issues of corporate law at length, and the importance and essence of corporate groups are analysed primarily from this perspective.

The question remains, however, why entrepreneurs need to create corporate groups. Their reasoning is not necessarily limited to the reasons for creating legal entities since groups in and of themselves indicate external growth. To summarize Immenga's thoughts on this form of external growth,[824] the following reasons can be identified. First, where a parent acquires control of an existing subsidiary, the parent has immediate access to resources, workforce and potential, without taking additional measures to develop the company internally. Second, the risks are shared by multiple separate entities, which is the next level of development in the entity doctrine. Natural persons, instead of using a single entity as a corporate shield, might try to conceal their assets and, consequently, distribute the risks behind multiple companies; groups are a safer instrument of corporate protection than ordinary companies. Third, given that control is not restricted to being a majority shareholder only, but can also stem from having de facto control with less than half the share capital, a parent company might prudently acquire control in a subsidiary by owning a small proportion of the shares and influencing the decision-making process.

These reasons are by no means exhaustive, nor do they make allowance for potential regulatory requirements that may be in force in a particular country, such as the requirement in some states that foreign companies must conduct their local business through separate subsidiaries.[825] Rather, they offer a short description of the principal corporate motives behind group formation.

[E] Development of EU Law on Corporate Groups

One of the primary sources of EU law, including EU group law, is the TFEU. While it does not make any reference to groups as a separate concept, it does provide for the freedom of establishment for legal entities to create agencies, branches and subsidiaries in the territory of any Member State.[826] This provision entered the TFEU via Article 43 of the Treaty establishing the EC. The European Court of Justice has interpreted this freedom as extending beyond the mere formation of companies in a specific Member State, and including such matters as merging with a target company.[827]

The far-reaching concept of establishment[828] may seem misleading, due to the wording of Article 48 of the TFEU. Freedom of establishment reads as belonging to nationals of Member States, i.e. natural persons. However, if these provisions are

---

824. Immenga U, 'Company Systems and Affiliations', 4-5.
825. *Corporate Groups Final Report, Prepared by Australian Companies & Securities Advisory Committee* (The Committee 2000), 4.
826. Treaty on the Functioning of the European Union [2012] OJ C 326/47, 26.10.2012, Article 43(1).
827. *SEVIC Systems AG*, Case C-411/03 European Court reports (European Court of Justice (Grand Chamber)), 10836.
828. Werlauff E, 'Group and Community? The European Court's Development of an Independent Community Law Concept of the Group and Its Significance for National Company Law' (2007) 4 European Company Law 201, 202.

interpreted in conjunction with Article 54 of the TFEU, they endow legal entities with the same rights as natural persons have. That is why it is entirely fair to say that rules on corporate groups are directly enshrined in EU primary law.[829]

For secondary law in the EU, the situation is more complicated. EU group law is not codified; acts governing relations within groups are dispersed. However, several authors have divided the various directives on EU company law into two categories: (i) directives governing the formation of corporate groups; and (ii) directives governing existing groups.[830] Opinions differ on how to better define the scope of these two categories of EU directives. For instance, in the textbook by Stefan Grundman and Falko Glasow, only the Takeover Directive is referred to as dealing with the formation of groups.[831] It is certainly logical to say that the Takeover Directive is directly related to the issue of group formations since it establishes safeguards for both blockholders ('squeeze-outs') and minority shareholders ('mandatory bids' and 'sell-outs') from abusive behaviour by the other. At the same time, the textbook by Adriaan Dorresteijn and others contains a longer list of sources of secondary EU law governing the formation of groups.[832] Among the sources, the authors refer to the Second Council Directive as facilitating the capital requirements for non-cash contributions (now codified in Directive 2017/1132[833]), the Transparency Directive containing disclosure duties triggered by the acquisition of a specific percentage of shares,[834] Directive 2009/102/EC allowing single-member companies and the Regulation on the SE Statute, which also applies to groups where an SE is formed either as a holding company[835] or as a subsidiary.[836]

In addition to more general regulation of corporate groups through secondary law, the EU also has specific and sectoral regulations that deal with group-related issues. For instance, Directive 2015/848 on insolvency proceedings includes a separate chapter devoted to insolvency proceedings of members of a group of companies.[837] That Directive provides for cooperation between insolvency practitioners appointed in proceedings involving different members of a single corporate group and contains special provisions for group coordination proceedings[838] where the group is treated as a single economic entity.

829. Teichmann C, 'Towards a European Framework for Cross-Border Group Management' (2016) 13 European Company Law 150.
830. Grundmann S and Glasow F, 756-760; Dorresteijn AF and others, *European Corporate Law* (2nd edn, Kluwer Law International 2009), 292-295.
831. Grundmann S and Glasow F, 759.
832. Dorresteijn AF and others, 292-293.
833. Directive 2017/1132 of the European Parliament and of the Council of 14 June 2017 relating to certain aspects of company law (codification) [2017] OJ L 169, 30.6.2017, Article 49(4).
834. Directive 2004/109/EC of the European Parliament and of the Council of 15 December 2004 on the harmonization of transparency requirements in relation to information about issuers whose securities are admitted to trading on a regulated market and amending Directive 2001/34/EC [2004] OJ L 390/38, 31.12.2004, Article 9.
835. Council Regulation (EC) No. 2157/2001 of 8 October 2001 on the Statute for a European company (SE), OJ L 294, 10.11.2001, Article 2(2), section 3.
836. *Ibid.*, Article 2(3), section 4.
837. Regulation (EU) No. 2015/848 of the European Parliament and of the Council of 20 May 2015 on Insolvency Proceedings [2015] OJ L 141/19, 11.9.2002, Chapter V.
838. *Ibid.*, Article 61.

Directive 2013/36/EU on access to the activity of credit institutions and the prudential supervision of credit institutions and investment firms[839] contains rules specifically directed at groups of credit institutions. Among other rules, it provides for consultation obligations of the competent authorities for members of a single group that are located in different Member States.[840] This Directive also provides for information exchanges between authorities in connection with the legal and organizational structure of groups.[841] Groups of credit institutions are also covered by regulatory requirements of Regulation 575/2013 on prudential requirements for credit institutions and investment firms.[842] The purpose of the latter instrument is to ensure that *the capital requirements apply on the basis of the consolidated situation of those institutions within the group.*[843] This is achieved through application of the requirements on a consolidated basis.[844] Under Directive 2014/59/EU, establishing a framework for the recovery and resolution of credit institutions and investment firms, a parent undertaking has a duty to draw up and submit to the consolidating supervisor a group recovery plan,[845] which must consider the financial situation of both the group as a whole and its separate group entities, especially if they are in distress.[846] As the foregoing shows, the EU legislature has undisputedly moved away from the long-standing entity approach, which follows the economic reality with shielding and separate personality,[847] and towards the enterprise approach. This also holds true for the Court of Justice of the EU, which has been said to apply both concepts for deciding cases.[848] However, the EU could have embraced the enterprise approach even more if the Ninth Directive had been adopted; however, two draft proposals for the directive were not even officially submitted.[849] The second draft of 1984 came very close to the

839. Directive 2013/36/EU of the European Parliament and of the Council of 26 June 2013 on access to the activity of credit institutions and the prudential supervision of credit institutions and investment firms, amending Directive 2002/87/EC and repealing Directives 2006/48/EC and 2006/49/EC [2013] OJ L 176, 27.6.2013.
840. *Ibid.*, Article 16(3).
841. *Ibid.*, Article 20(3).
842. Regulation (EU) No. 575/2013 of the European Parliament and of the Council of 26 June 2013 on prudential requirements for credit institutions and investment firms and amending Regulation (EU) No. 648/2012 [2013] OJ L 177, 27.6.2013.
843. *Ibid.*, recital 37.
844. *Ibid.*, Articles 11-16.
845. Directive 2014/59/EU of the European Parliament and of the Council of 15 May 2014 establishing a framework for the recovery and resolution of credit institutions and investment firms and amending Council Directive 82/891/EEC, and Directives 2001/24/EC, 2002/47/EC, 2004/25/EC, 2005/56/EC, 2007/36/EC, 2011/35/EU, 2012/30/EU and 2013/36/EU, and Regulations (EU) No. 1093/2010 and (EU) No. 648/2012, of the European Parliament and of the Council [2014] OJ L 173, 12.6.2014, Article 7(1).
846. *Ibid.*, Article 7(4).
847. Recital 6 of the SE Statute regulation finds it *essential to ensure the economic unit and the legal unit of business in the Community coincide*, though this provision exists more as an abstract idea, as every company is at liberty to choose between either forming a subsidiary in a Member State or creating a branch.
848. Sørensen KE, 'Groups of Companies in the Case Law of the Court of Justice of the European Union' (2016) 27 European Business Law Review 393, 420.
849. Grundmann S and Glasow F, 763.

German concept of group law. Having been circulated among the European Commission, it was viewed by the business community as being too cumbersome and inflexible.[850] The draft proposal contained a number of provisions that were similar to those that apply today, namely disclosure requirements for major shareholdings, yet essentially it also included the group concept. In other words, the proposal approached the perception of a company as an economic unit, giving the parent company exclusive managerial authority.[851] To balance the controlling powers, it provided for liability of the parent undertaking in respect of the subsidiary for its loss or damage and its debts. In addition, it put forward the inherently German concept of enterprise agreements. Similar to the German statutory approach, the draft Directive suggested that only dependent public companies were covered by its requirements.[852] In Germany, however, private companies are now subject to group law regulations, due to the legal enforcement practice of judicial authorities.[853]

Although the Ninth Directive failed, its idea of a group interest has not disappeared from legal debate. The turning point in the history of EU group law, when a new direction for developing law in this area was put forward, was the Forum Europaeum in 1998. The Forum essentially argued in favour of recognizing group interests, adhering to the 'Rozenblum' doctrine initially developed by the French courts. The proposal for a directive that was developed by Forum participants and was based on the seminal criminal case decided by the French Cassation Court incorporated the criteria for regarding the management of a subsidiary acting in the interests of the group as not being in breach of its duty. Essentially, those criteria were as follows: (a) a balanced and firmly established group structure; (b) incorporation of a subsidiary in a long-term and coherent policy; and (c) balanced losses/profits in the long term.[854] The Forum's recommendations drew heavily on case law, marked by greater flexibility than the earlier German-tailored draft of the Ninth Directive. This approach to dealing with group management issues met with instant resistance, being said to lack a proper basis and thus *betraying the purpose of the project*.[855]

Following the specific recommendations of the Forum Europaeum, in 2002 the High Level Group of Company Law Experts produced a report (the 'Winter Report') setting out the desired regulatory framework in Europe for tackling the burning issues of company law, including groups and pyramids.[856] Similar to the Forum's vision, the

850. Communication from the Commission to the Council and the European Parliament, Modernising Company Law and Enhancing Corporate Governance in the European Union – A Plan to Move Forward, COM (2003) 284 final, 21.5.2003, 18.
851. Gleichmann K, 'The Law of Corporate Groups in the European Community' in Sugarman D and Teubner G (eds), *Regulating Corporate Groups in Europe* (European Institute, Florence 1990), 448.
852. *Ibid.*, 447.
853. This issue is discussed elsewhere in this chapter.
854. 'Corporate Group Law for Europe by Forum Europaeum', 260.
855. Windbichler C, '"Corporate Group Law for Europe": Comments on the Forum Europaeum's Principles and Proposals for a European Corporate Group Law' (2000) 1 European Business Organization Law Review 265, 273.
856. Winter J and others, *Report of the High Level Group of Company Law Experts on a Modern Regulatory Framework for Company Law in Europe* (Office for Official Publications of the European Communities 2002), 94-101.

experts of the High Level Group advised not to adopt the Ninth Directive, but to address individual problems by modifying existing provisions.[857] On the subject of group management, it suggested allowing the adoption and implementation of coordinated group policy.[858] This recommendation was reflected in the 2003 Action Plan of the European Commission, which supported the ideas previously expressed by the High Level Group, namely the importance of group policy and the necessity of carefully designed safeguards to balance it. A directive was chosen as the appropriate instrument.[859] While that directive was scheduled to be adopted by 2008, the concerns about its timely adoption and implementation that had been expressed earlier proved justified.[860]

In 2011, the Reflection Group on the Future of EU Company Law revisited the issue of corporate groups in the EU. This time, the expert group suggested that a recommendation, rather than a directive, should be used to deal with group interests.[861] The logic behind this shift was perhaps due to *national traditions and diverging interpretations*, which are difficult to reconcile with the imperative requirements that ensue from directives. As noted by one of the commentators, this manner of legislation was *the most cautious and politically accepted proposal*, with the ability to cover a long list of group-related issues.[862] When in 2012 the EU Commission presented a new Action Plan on EU company law and governance, it supported the Reflection Group's recommendation in an abstract manner, by postponing the decision to establish a specific instrument for dealing with group interests until 2014.[863]

Between 2015 and 2017, a series of key proposals from various expert groups were introduced: the Forum Europaeum on Company Groups,[864] the Informal Company Law Expert Group[865] and European Company Law Experts.[866] These were accompanied by other significant discussions, proposals and reports from expert societies of the Club de Jurists, the Luxembourg Institute of Directors and the EMCA.[867] That model act stipulates recognition of group interests by excusing directors of

857. *Ibid.*, 99.
858. *Ibid.*, 100.
859. Communication from the Commission to the Council and the European Parliament, Modernising Company Law and Enhancing Corporate Governance in the European Union - A Plan to Move Forward, COM (2003) 284 final, 21.5.2003, 19.
860. Bartman SM, 'The Impact of Optional EU Law Making on National Company Law' (2008) 5 European Company Law 271.
861. Antunes JE and others, 65.
862. Conac P-H, 'Director's Duties in Groups of Companies: Legalizing the Interest of the Group at the European Level' (2013) 10 European Company and Financial Law Review 194, 225.
863. Communication from the Commission to the European Parliament, the Council, the European Economic and Social Committee and the Committee of the Regions, Action Plan: European Company Law and Corporate Governance - A Modern Legal Framework for More Engaged Shareholders and Sustainable Companies, COM (2012) 740 final, 12.12.2012, 15, 18.
864. Conac P-H, 'Proposal to Facilitate the Management of Cross-Border Company Groups in Europe' (2015) 12 European Company and Financial Law Review 299.
865. Armour J and others.
866. Böckli P and others, 'A Proposal for the Reform of Group Law in Europe' (2017) 18 European Business Organization Law Review 1.
867. Teichmann C, 'Towards a European Framework for Cross-Border Group Management', 154-155.

subsidiaries who act contrary to the interests of the subsidiary but in the interests of the overall group:[868] they should not be deemed to have acted in breach of their fiduciary duties in those circumstances. Besides recognition of group interests, the EMCA contains other significant rules concerning corporate groups, including group management and protection of the parent company's shareholders.[869]

Despite its stated intention to officially recognize the interests of groups, the European Commission has not yet produced any draft instruments on this topic. At present, it remains unclear what will happen next. The Commission's efforts have been contradictory. In 2014, the Informal Company Law Expert Group was composed to assist the Commission by advising on group issues, and it has already produced a report with specific and clear-cut policy recommendations. At the same time, the Commission does not mention group interests among its priorities in recent programme documents.[870] In other words, EU group law remains fragmented, being enshrined in several different instruments of secondary EU law, with the Accounting Directive in the first place.

[F] Regulation of Corporate Groups in Germany, Poland and the Netherlands

Having provided an overview of the legal regulation of corporate groups at the EU level, the next step is to examine the rules at the level of the individual Member States. Of the three jurisdictions in which this research focuses, the most complex regulation of corporate groups is found in Germany. This jurisdiction has been described as a standard-setter, possessing a unified set of legislative provisions to govern corporate groups.[871] This is also the country whose legislation was taken as a model for drafting the Ninth Directive,[872] although that draft failed to impress other Member States.[873]

Germany belongs to the category of the jurisdictions where the notion of a group interest is not recognized,[874] but instead uses a sophisticated set of statutory rules to balance the rights and duties of the various group constituencies. These rules are laid down in the AktG,[875] which applies to public companies and partnerships as dependent companies.[876] This means that the AktG applies to public companies as dependent

868. Andersen PK and others, section 15.16.
869. *Ibid.*, 369.
870. Winner M, 'Group Interest in European Company Law: An Overview' (2016) 5 Acta Universitatis Sapientiae, Legal Studies 85, 95.
871. Dearborn M, 215.
872. Tröger T, 'Corporate Groups: A German's European Perspective' in Fleischer H, Hansen JL and Ringe W-G (eds), *German and Nordic Perspectives on Company Law and Capital Markets Law* (Mohr Siebeck 2015), 166.
873. Fleischer H, 'A Guide to German Company Law for International Lawyers: Distinctive Features, Particularities, Idiosyncracies', 24.
874. Armour J and others, 24.
875. AktG, Book Three.
876. Schroeder U and Jaecks J, 'Report from Germany' (2007) 4 European Company Law 230, 231.

companies, regardless of who the shareholder is: the shareholder does not necessarily have to be a company, since a natural person may also qualify.[877]

A group, as defined under the AktG, is characterized by control and a common direction of the controlling enterprise.[878] Two types of groups are outlined: (i) de facto groups and (ii) contract-based groups.[879] The difference between these two kinds of groups can already be inferred from their names: de facto groups are where control is exercised in the absence of a control agreement, e.g. through a majority shareholding,[880] while in contract-based groups, control between entities derives from an enterprise agreement.[881] Yet the differences between the two types of groups are not confined to their names alone.

From the legal perspective, the legal consequences of these constructions are of greater relevance, and here the difference between the two groups is significant. In de facto groups, a controlling enterprise may not exercise its influence to cause the controlled company to undertake any disadvantageous actions, unless the disadvantage is compensated.[882] The precise meaning of disadvantage has been subject to interpretative exercise by the German Supreme Court and is construed to encompass *any decrease of or specific risk to the corporation's financial situation or earning position*.[883] If the disadvantage is not compensated, or no substitutional measures are provided by the end of the financial year, the controlling company is liable for any loss or damage caused to the controlled company, and to its shareholders as well, if they have suffered any additional damage besides financial loss.[884] The controlling company will only be exempted from liability if it satisfies the prudent-and-conscientious-manager test.[885] The same rules also apply to the controlling company's legal representatives.[886]

In contract-based groups, conversely, the duty of the controlling company is different and depends on the type of enterprise agreement. Two main types of enterprise agreements should be discussed here: control agreements and cash pooling agreements. Under a control agreement, the controlling company may issue instructions to the controlled company, and under a cash pooling (or 'profit transfer') agreement, one company may extract the other's funds.[887] Unlike de facto groups, in groups functioning under a control agreement the controlling company may issue instructions to the disadvantage of the controlled company, provided that those

877. Langebucher K, 363.
878. AktG, Article 18.
879. One further type of corporate group that the act identifies, an integrated company, is very uncommon and accordingly is not discussed here (Hopt KJ (ed.), *Groups of Companies in European Laws*, vol 2 (de Gruyter 1982), 232).
880. AktG, Article 17(2).
881. *Ibid.*, Articles 17(1), 18(1), § 291.
882. *Ibid.*, Article 311(1).
883. Tröger T, 'Corporate Groups: A German's European Perspective', 163.
884. AktG, Article 317(1).
885. *Ibid.*, Article 317(2).
886. *Ibid.*, Article 317(3).
887. *Ibid.*, Article 291(1).

instructions are advantageous for the controlling company or other affiliated enterprises that are members of the same group,[888] i.e. if they do not threaten the group's existence.[889] This is where the group interest notion comes into play and influences the group's decision-making. As with de facto groups, the controlling company's legal representatives will face liability for disadvantageous instructions if their actions are not those of a prudential and conscientious manager.[890] In exchange for the powers of control or to transfer profits under the control or cash pooling agreement, the controlling company has a duty to compensate any annual net loss that arises while the agreement is in place, in so far as it cannot be compensated from reserves.[891]

This difference in the effects of de facto groups and contract-based groups forms the core characteristics of group law in Germany. It represents the German legislature's approach to balancing the interests of affiliated companies.

Besides the essential rights and duties in corporate groups explained above, other provisions also safeguard a group's minority shareholders and creditors. These apply especially to contract-based groups and give special protection to creditors and outside shareholders. Creditors are protected by the rule that they must be provided with security in case the contract is terminated or cancelled.[892] Under profit-transfer agreements, outside shareholders have the right to adequate compensation by requiring payments in proportion to their shareholdings.[893] Lastly, in all contract-based groups, outside shareholders have the right to demand that their shares be purchased from them in exchange for an adequate price.[894]

De facto groups do not offer similar safeguards to creditors and outside shareholders, although the controlling company's obligation to compensate losses itself is directed at protecting those stakeholders and ensuring that transactions within the group are conducted on arm's-length terms in so far as is possible.[895] The management board of the controlled company is also obliged to publish a special report on the company's relationships with affiliated companies.[896] This document may not be treated as a mere formality and may be subjected to an audit review by an external auditor[897] or the supervisory board.[898] If the management board omits a disadvantageous transaction from the report or fails to disclose that the company suffered a disadvantage, this can constitute grounds for liability.[899]

888. *Ibid.*, Article 308(1).
889. Tröger T, 'Corporate Groups: A German's European Perspective', 164.
890. AktG, Article 309(1).
891. *Ibid.*, Article 302(1).
892. *Ibid.*, Article 303(1).
893. *Ibid.*, Article 304(1).
894. *Ibid.*, Article 305(1).
895. Dearborn M, 218.
896. AktG, Article 312(1).
897. *Ibid.*, Article 313.
898. *Ibid.*, Article 314.
899. *Ibid.*, Article 318.

Unlike public companies, which enjoy largely statutory regulation, private companies in Germany are mostly[900] governed by rules developed in case law,[901] which are often considered to be more positive than the rules for public companies.[902] The most noticeable element of the statutory provisions dealing specifically with corporate groups in private companies is the right of shareholders to issue binding instructions to directors.[903] This right is not fully shared by groups of public companies in Germany.

One rule that the AktG and the GmbHG have in common is a provision that excludes control and profit-transfer agreements from the effect of capital maintenance rules.[904] Despite this similarity, however, contract-based groups are regulated more substantially where they involve public companies. This is one of the reasons why some of the AktG's provisions apply here by analogy.[905] For instance, the requirements for shareholder consent have been viewed as suitable for approval of control transactions in private companies.[906] It has been argued if the shareholders do not give their unanimous consent, Articles 304 and 305 of the AktG may be invoked.[907] However, this is not uncontentious, and some critics have expressed the opinion that three quarters of the shareholders must approve the transaction.[908]

The analogy to groups with private companies as dependent entities is not without its limits. In the case of de facto groups, private companies have to take into account the orders of their shareholders, while for public companies following those instructions is prohibited by Article 311 of the AktG. As such, the application of Article 311 by analogy to de facto groups of private companies is considered by some to be inappropriate.[909]

Despite its abundance of detail, the German law on groups of companies nevertheless contains many notions that require clarification and need to be interpreted by the courts. An example is the meaning of a unified direction, which is a key

900. Some provisions of the GmbHG, specifically Article 30, which excludes enterprise agreements from the effect of capital maintenance rules, also concern group law, though only to a limited extent.
901. Wiedemann H, 'The German Law of Affiliated Enterprises' in Hopt KJ (ed.), *Legal and Economic Analyses on Multinational Enterprises: Groups of Companies in European Laws*, vol 2 (Gruyter, De, Rechtswissenschaften 1982), 27.
902. Immenga U, 'The Law of Groups in the Federal Republic of Germany' in Wymeersch E and Fitchew MG (eds), *Groups of Companies in the EEC* (Walter de Gruyter 1993), 112.
903. GmbHG, Article 37.
904. *Ibid.*, Article 30(1); AktG, Article 57(1).
905. Schroeder U and Jaecks J, 233.
906. For example, *see*: *Supermarket*, Case No. II ZB 7/88 105 BGHZ (Federal Court of Justice), 324; *Siemens*, Case No. II ZB 15/91 45 NJW (Federal Court of Justice), 1452.
907. Hirte H, *Kapitalgesellschaftsrecht* (RWS-Verlag 2016), 585.
908. Hommelhoff P, 'Protection of Minority Shareholders, Investors and Creditors in Corporate Groups: The Strengths and Weaknesses of German Corporate Group Law' (2001) 2 European Business Organization Law Review 61, 71.
909. *Autokran*, Case No. II ZR 275/84, 95 BGHZ (Federal Court of Justice), 340.

feature of corporate groups.[910] Another example concerns situations where the controlling company in a de facto group chooses to implement a comprehensive mechanism instead of issuing instructions.[911] These cases have been described as qualified de facto groups (*qualifiziert de facto konzern*) and are relevant to both public and private companies as dependent entities. With private companies, the German Supreme Court's stance on qualified de facto groups has not taken a straight path,[912] shifting from the use of analogy (Articles 302 and 303 of the AktG)[913] to the 'piercing the corporate veil' doctrine and tort liability for 'economic destruction' in more recent case law.[914] These examples highlight the importance of the courts' stance on German group law, which, despite its seemingly rigid and inflexible structure, includes many notions that are subject to interpretation and where the courts' views have evolved.

The next jurisdiction in focus is Poland. Although many aspects of Polish company law follow the German path of regulation,[915] *Konzernrecht* is a notable exception. Unlike the German line of legislative changes, Polish company law does not offer the same sophisticated set of uniform rules.[916] Recognition of the notion of a group interest in Poland is not directly enshrined in legislation, and the extent to which it legitimizes the actions of the management boards of subsidiaries is not entirely clear.[917] A number of Polish court judgments have managed to recognize a group interest as a justifying factor for some business decisions of subsidiaries.[918] At the same time, academic views remain divided. On the one hand, statutory law does not permit deviating from the single entity approach. On the other, commentators acknowledge the importance of a group interest and identify the following features for establishing a group: two or more related companies; permanent domination; a common interest.[919]

Attempts to legitimize the notion of a group interest have been undertaken, with the preparation of a draft resembling the French Rozenblum doctrine, with more focus on shareholders' information rights.[920] This draft was rejected, with different pressure groups favouring more marginal or more drastic changes: either introducing the Rozenblum doctrine as it is as preferred by the representatives of foreign investors or fully abandoning the idea of the legislative recognition of the group interest.[921]

---

910. Immenga U, 'The Law of Groups in the Federal Republic of Germany', 97.
911. Scheuch A, 'Konzernrecht: An Overview of the German Regulation of Corporate Groups and Resulting Liability Issues' (2016) 13 European Company Law 191, 196.
912. *Ibid.*, 197.
913. *Autokran*, Case No. II ZR 275/84, 95 BGHZ (Federal Court of Justice), 339, 345-348.
914. *See KBV*, Case No. II ZR 300/00 151 BGHZ (Federal Court of Justice), 181, 187-188; *Bremer Vulkan*, Case No. II ZR 178/99 149 BGHZ (Federal Court of Justice), 10-28; *Trihotel*, Case No. II ZR 3/04 173 BGHZ (Federal Court of Justice), 246, 252-262.
915. Sołtysiński S, 'Corporate Boards in Poland' in Davies PL and others (eds), *Corporate Boards in Law and Practice: A Comparative Analysis in Europe* (1st edn, Oxford University Press 2013), 512.
916. Armour J and others, 21.
917. Böckli P and others, 25.
918. *Judgment of 3.12.2012* V ACa 702/12 (Appellate Court in Katowice); *Judgment of 6.05.2009* II AKa 142/08 (Appellate Court in Szczecin).
919. Rządkowski M, '"Piercing the Corporate Veil Doctrine in Poland?" A Comparative Perspective' (2015) 20 Comparative Law Review 55, 80.
920. Sołtysiński S, 'Corporate Boards in Poland', 545.
921. *Ibid.*, 546.

At the same time, although statutory company law in Poland does not make any reference to the notion of a group interest, the KSH provides some rules for controlling (dominant) and dependent companies, including a broad definition of a dependent company.[922] The emergence of dominance automatically triggers various disclosure obligations of the dominant company in respect of its subsidiary, with non-compliance being penalized by the suspension of voting rights deriving from any shares representing more than 33% of the subsidiary's share capital.[923] Furthermore, if an agreement is in place for the management of the dependent company or for a profit transfer,[924] it must be filed and disclosed in the companies register.[925] Other provisions of the KSH address the group context, in particular allowing both dependent and dominant companies to be viewed, in specific situations, as a single economic unit.[926] In practice, groups are common, and in those instances, group coordination derives more formal support from group 'by-laws' (*regulamin grupy*) that are adopted by the parent company and accepted by its subsidiaries. The legal status of these by-laws is subject to some controversy.[927]

Company law in the Netherlands favours recognition of the notion of a group interest.[928] The difference between the Polish and Dutch approaches to recognition of this notion is that in the Netherlands it derives not only from established case law[929] but also directly from the provisions of the BW.

It should be noted first that Article 2:24a of the BW views a group as an economic unit, in which legal persons and partnerships are united into a single organization.[930] This definition in and of itself demonstrates that groups are not regarded in the same manner as single legal entities and that Dutch statute already goes further than this. In literature, this definition has been criticized for omitting some of the building blocks of groups, namely central management and control, which are regarded as being essential for groups.[931] However, Article 2:24a is not the only provision to recognize the concept of a group interest in the Netherlands. Book 2 of the BW contains other provisions that, although they do not use the word 'group', nonetheless implicitly refer to group

922. KSH, Article 4(1).
923. *Ibid.*, Article 6(1).
924. *Umowa o zarządzanie spółką zależną*, inspired by the German *Beherrschung- und Gewinnabführungsvertrag*, though much less complex under Polish law and with virtually no practical significance.
925. *Ibid.*, Article 7(1).
926. For example, *see*: *Ibid.*, Articles 15(2), 362(4), 394(4).
927. Oplustil K, 'Regulaminy (kodeksy) grup spółek jako instrument realizacji interesu koncernowego' in Olejniczak A, Orlicki M and Pokrzywniak J (eds), *Z badań nad prawem prywatnym: księga pamiątkowa dedykowana Profesorowi Andrzejowi Kochowi* (Poznań: Wydawnictwo Naukowe UAM 2017).
928. Armour J and others, 22.
929. *Nimox, Decision of 8 November 1991* NJ 1992, 174 (Supreme Court of the Netherlands). In this case, the distribution of profits by the sole shareholder in the company, later declared bankrupt, was considered unlawful, for violating the rights of creditors and endangering the company's continuity.
930. BW, Article 2:24b.
931. Oostrum CHAv, 'Regres bij concernfinanciering' (Dphil thesis, Wolters Kluwer 2019), 363.

relationships.[932] This derives from the wording of Article 2:140(2) and 2:250(2), which charge supervisory boards with the duty to supervise management's policy and the general course of business conducted by the company and the enterprise connected with it.[933] The concept of an enterprise as used in these articles extends beyond the boundaries of a single legal entity, i.e. a parent or a subsidiary.[934] It is also a reflection of the stakeholder model in action in the Netherlands, meaning that it is not shareholders alone whose interests must be considered.[935]

The interest of the group also finds its reflection in Article 2:129(4) and 2:239(4) of the BW, concerning the duty of management to follow instructions from another company body of the company if the articles of association so prescribe. In practice, this provision has exactly the same meaning.[936] The limits of this duty differ for private companies (BVs) and public companies (NVs): for private companies, it exists in so far as the instructions are 'in the best interests of the company and the enterprise connected with it', while for public companies the instructions must respect 'general policy'. This concept of general policy was previously also relevant for BVs and caused interpretative difficulties due to the lack of definition of the notions.[937] Following legislative amendments, BVs have experienced a change in their legal regime. At present, law requires that, provided the articles of association of the subsidiary contain the right for the general meeting to issue concrete and detailed instructions to the board, the interests of subsidiary be always considered together with the group's interests. This development signifies what Steef Bartman has called the 'concurrence of group company interests',[938] whereas an 'autonomy of interests' rule,[939] stressing the importance of the individual interests of each and every separate company, still prevails for public companies and for all private companies in the event that the articles of association do not contain any provisions on the use of instructions.[940]

The introduction of a concurrence of interests in corporate groups with the 2013 amendments should not be interpreted to mean that the concept of a group interest did

932. Timmermans CWA and Timmerman L, 'The Law on Groups of Companies in the Netherlands' in Wymeersch E (ed.), *Groups of Companies in the EEC: A Survey Report to the European Commission on the Law Relating to Corporate Groups in Various Member States* (Walter de Gruyter 1993), 233, 240.
933. BW, Article 2:250(2), 2:140(2).
934. The concept of 'the company and the enterprise connected with it' in Dutch law is reminiscent, in its stakeholder coverage, of the *Unternehmensinteresse* in German stock company law. In both cases, the concepts extend the idea of shareholder value and cannot be defined as a simple combination of interests, favouring primarily the interests of an economic unit.
935. Timmermans CWA and Timmerman L, 240.
936. *Decision of 21 December 2001* NJ 2005, 96 (Supreme Court of the Netherlands).
937. Bartman SM, 'From Autonomy of Interests to Concurrence of Interest in Dutch Group Company Law', 208.
938. *Ibid.*
939. Potjewijd G and Van der Kroon J, 'Report from the Netherlands' (2007) 4 European Company Law 235.
940. If the articles of association do not regulate instructions for management, this does not mean that the subsidiary's management is wholly free from the parent company's directions. At a minimum, the control that is inherent in parent-subsidiary relationships means that the parent can seek other ways to make the subsidiary's management implement its instructions, for instance by threatening to appoint a new management.

not exist before then. In fact, the Dutch Supreme Court had succeeded in shaping the approach to recognition of this concept long before and continued to do so afterwards, despite lacking a consistent vision of the concept.[941] The earlier *OGEM* case (1988) already stipulated the duty of the parent's directors to manage the parent and its subsidiaries to the best of their abilities.[942] Since then, the 'duty of group management' has entered the realm of Dutch case law[943] and academic sources on the topic.[944] This duty is accompanied by the 'parental duty of care',[945] as found in the *Comsys Holding* case,[946] which refers to the duty to compensate excessive risks to the subsidiaries' creditors. These developments in Dutch statute and case law on groups deal mostly with instruction-based powers of parents, while more complicated constructions of company law beyond instructions are not covered by these duties.

Therefore, in contrast to how groups are regulated in Germany, Poland and the Netherlands do not possess similar sophisticated sets of rules for corporate groups. However, as the Dutch example shows, group law is clearly in place, both in statute[947] and in case law. At present, case law in the Netherlands provides for recognition of a group interest and has elaborated the consequences of that recognition. It is important to bear in mind, though, that the extent to which the group interest is taken into account in the Netherlands largely depends on the provisions of the subsidiary's articles of association: the less detailed the corporate constituent document of the subsidiary is, the more difficult it becomes to recognize the conduct of the subsidiary's management as legitimate if it is detrimental to the subsidiary but favourable to the group.[948] In a way, this regulation is reminiscent of contract-based groups in Germany, where the parent is authorized to issue binding instructions in the group's interests. At the same time, for de facto groups both in Germany and in the Netherlands,[949] recognition of the notion of a group interest at the EU level, as proposed in the EU Commission's Action Plans,[950] would add clarity and predictability. This applies even more for Poland, where the notion of a group interest is recognized in case law.

941. Bartman SM, 'Dutch Supreme Court at a Loss over Groups' (2016) 13 European Company Law 123.
942. *OGEM, Decision of 10 January 1990* NJ 1990/465 (Supreme Court of the Netherlands).
943. For example, *see*: *Decision of 21 December 2001* NJ 2005, 96 (Supreme Court of the Netherlands).
944. For example, *see*: Bartman SM, Dorresteijn AFM and Olaerts M, *Van Het Concern* (Wolters Kluwer 2016).
945. Bartman SM, 'Dutch Supreme Court at a Loss over Groups', 125.
946. *Comsys Holding, Decision of 11 September 2009* NJ 2009, 565 (Supreme Court of the Netherlands).
947. For example, Article 2:24b, 2:129, 2:150, 2:239 and 2:250 of the BW.
948. Bartman SM, 'Dutch Supreme Court at a Loss over Groups', 128.
949. The latter jurisdiction does not officially use this concept. It is used here for academic purposes only.
950. Communication from the Commission to the European Parliament, the Council, the European Economic and Social Committee and the Committee of the Regions, Action Plan: European Company Law and Corporate Governance – A Modern Legal Framework for More Engaged Shareholders and Sustainable Companies, COM (2012) 740 final, 12.12.2012, 15.

[G] Regulation of Corporate Groups in Ukraine

The issue that has occupied the minds of corporate law scholars since at least the Forum Europaeum in 1998 is missing from the regulation of corporate groups in Ukraine. However, this does not mean that no group regulation whatsoever is in place – some regulatory acts in fact deal with the group-related issues and are presented below.

First, some general notions and rules are included in the CCU[951] and the Economic Code of Ukraine,[952] namely the meaning of dependent companies and the different types of dependency (simple or decisive). However, these rules lack a true legal effect. The fact that a company is dependent essentially triggers only a disclosure obligation: it does not mean that the parent company may or may not issue certain types of instruction, or that management of the dependent company must be indemnified for losses. The same holds true for holding companies and associations of enterprises.[953] Holding companies only have an obligation to bear additional liability if a company that is owned by a holding company goes bankrupt as a result of the holding company's actions.[954] This provision, however, is too abstract to be applied consistently.

Second, Ukrainian laws contain reporting requirements. The Law of Ukraine 'On Accounting and Financial Reporting in Ukraine' provides the definition of consolidated financial statements, i.e. containing the accounts of both the controlled and controlling entities, which it then views as a single economic unit.[955] Parent companies are obliged to submit consolidated financial statements in accordance with the national standards or the IASs, in addition to their separate financial statements. They are exempt from the obligation to submit consolidated financial statements if their indicators meet two of the following conditions: (i) the value of their assets is EUR 4 million or less; (ii) their net income is EUR 8 million or less; (iii) the workforce is fifty persons or fewer.[956]

Lastly, rules on corporate groups are also found in the JSC Law of Ukraine, though they do not include a definition of a corporate group. Rather, group-related issues are addressed in relation to simplified mergers between parents and 90% owned subsidiaries,[957] single-member companies[958] and RPTs. For instance, on the subject of RPTs, if a shareholder directly or indirectly owns 100% of an entity's share capital and forms the transaction with the public company directly or through an affiliated person, this fact does not trigger the procedural requirements for RPTs.[959] The idea behind this regulation is that onerous regulation of RPTs is unnecessary if the company does not

951. CCU, Article 118(2).
952. Economic Code of Ukraine [Hospodarksyi kodeks Ukrayiny], Article 126(4).
953. *Ibid.*, Articles 118-124, 126.
954. *Ibid.*, Article 126(6).
955. Law of Ukraine 'On Accounting and Financial Reporting in Ukraine' [Zakon Ukrayiny 'Pro bukhgaltersyi oblik ta finansovu zvitnist'], paragraph 8, Article 1(1).
956. *Ibid.*, Article 12(1).
957. JSC Law of Ukraine, Article 84(4).
958. *Ibid.*, Article 4.
959. *Ibid.*, Article 71(2)(2).

have any minority shareholders whose rights might be violated. This is most common with groups of companies in which a subsidiary is wholly owned by its parent.

That being said, Ukraine visibly does not have the same sophisticated rules for corporate groups as Germany does. This means, first, that contract-based groups are not relevant for the Ukrainian jurisdiction. Even if two companies enter into an agreement that is reminiscent, in all its separate features, of a control agreement or a profit-transfer agreement,[960] no rules on enterprise agreements exist in Ukrainian company law, nor any legal consequences similar to those described in the AktG. That is why these agreements, if they are formed in Ukrainian territory, are governed by general laws on obligations, including the provisions on the formation, performance and validity of contracts. Second, rules on de facto groups as are found in Germany[961] are also missing from Ukrainian law, so even though it would be futile to deny the existence of corporate groups in Ukraine, their formation does not trigger the same compensation obligations as in Germany.

The situation is more complicated for recognition of the group interest notion in Ukraine. The country does not have any provisions similar to those in the Dutch BW that oblige a company's management to follow instructions from another corporate body,[962] including its parent, if the company's articles of association so dictate. Ukrainian law by comparison does not have the same discretionary rules. For both public and private companies, lists exist of legally required provisions that must be inserted in the entity's articles of association[963] and a general rule allowing other provisions that 'are not unlawful'.[964] Two obstacles arise here: first, it is difficult to say whether provisions in a company's articles under which the management and supervisory boards are permitted to follow instructions from an external company body 'are not unlawful'; second, even if a court finds that the provisions are indeed lawful, this does not automatically lead to adverse legal consequences, as case law shows. These two issues are discussed in detail below.

First, on whether including a duty for management to follow instructions issued by an external corporate body is unlawful, it is important to note that some legal practitioners in Ukraine do in fact include such provisions in companies' articles of association and manage to successfully submit them for registration. Given that the registration authorities may refuse to register the articles if they are incompatible with the Constitution and the laws of Ukraine,[965] the fact that these documents are

960. AktG, Article 291.
961. *Ibid.*, Article 308.
962. BW, Articles 129(4), 239(4).
963. JSC Law of Ukraine, Article 13(2); LLC Law of Ukraine, Article 11(5).
964. JSC Law of Ukraine, Article 13(4); LLC Law of Ukraine, Article 11(6).
965. Law of Ukraine 'On State Registration of Legal Entities, Natural Persons – Entrepreneurs and Public Associations' [Zakon Ukrayiny 'Pro derzhavnu reyestratsiyu yurydychnykh osib, fizychnykh osib – pidpryyemtsiv ta hromadskykh formuvan'] of 15 May 2003, published in Vidomosti Verkhovnoyi Rady Ukrayiny, 2003, No. 31, St. 263, Article 28(1)(5).

registered indirectly evidences that the authorities agree to have these provisions included.[966]

When evaluating the risk that provisions in a company's articles of association will be declared invalid for being unlawful, it is important to remember that the Ukrainian courts have invalidated provisions in articles of association on a purely formal basis. For example, the Economic Court of Kyiv previously invalidated provisions in the articles of association in a private company, by reason that they were 'self-contradictory'. On the one hand, the articles included a provision on the company's one-person executive body, yet at the same time that body was given the title of 'general director'. The court held that the title 'general director' referred to an individual in a collegial body ('directorate'), and in this case the body should have been simply called 'director', without 'general'. The court acknowledged the breach of shareholder rights and invalidated the provisions of the articles stipulating the management's authority.[967]

In a different case, the court ruled that the provisions of a company's articles were not unlawful. The contested provisions provided for a two-stage appointment of management: first by the supervisory board and then by the general meeting of shareholders. Although the JSC Law of Ukraine stipulates a one-stage process only, the court found that it was not incompatible with statutory requirements.[968] In this case, the result might have been different, had the court applied the same formal criteria as in the case discussed above. That is the source of confusion surrounding the probability of invalidation of articles of association that confer on company bodies of a parent company the right to issue instructions to subsidiary bodies. Even if the officer registering the articles of association overlooks the provision, the risk of their future annulment nevertheless remains. This statement is especially true in the case of public companies, where it is prohibited to grant the founders more powers than the law provides.[969] This rule may be interpreted by law enforcement authorities as prohibiting instructions from a parent's bodies.

Second, if a company's articles of association are found to be unlawful, this gives more to prove during the resolution of corporate disputes if the constituent documents contain deficiencies. According to Resolution No. 13 of the Plenum of the Supreme Court of Ukraine of 24 October 2008, three conditions must be satisfied for a company's constituent documents to be invalidated: the documents do not meet to the legislative requirements; breaches in the approval of the documents cannot be eliminated; and provisions of the documents violate the plaintiff's rights and legitimate interests.[970] In

966. The importance of the 'human factor' should not be underestimated here, either: registration officers might simply overlook the provisions in question, either intentionally or through negligence.
967. *Decision of 16 November 2017* Case No. 910/10759/17 (Kyiv Economic Court).
968. *Decision of 30 March 2015* Case No. 910/23044/14 (Kyiv Appellate Economic Court).
969. JSC Law of Ukraine, Article 13(3).
970. Regulation of the Plenum of the Supreme Court of Ukraine 'On Resolution of Civil Disputes on Annulment of Transactions' No. 9 [Postanova plenumu Verzhovnoho Sudu Ukrayiny 'Pro sudovu praktyku rozgliadu tsyvilnykh sprav pro vyznannia pravochyniv nediysnymy'] of 6 November 2009, available at: http://zakon2.rada.gov.ua/laws/show/v0009700-09/print1501964340775284, accessed on 30 December 2018.

the absence of all three conditions, courts have refrained from invalidating the constituent documents, instead preferring other remedies, such as ordering the articles of association to be amended and those amendments to be registered.[971] However, in some cases, the courts have established violations of the legislative requirements and the other conditions necessary to annul articles of association, in whole or in part. For instance, in one case the court invalidated a provision in an entity's articles that required a qualified majority of more than three-fourths (75% + 1) of all the shareholder votes for amendment of the articles, instead of 'more than three-fourths' (75% + 1) of the votes of the shareholders present at the meeting, as required by Article 42(5) of the JSC Law of Ukraine. The court ruled that this provision deprived the shareholders of their rights, potentially leading to a situation where even with the quorum (60% + 1 at that moment[972]) the general meeting would be unable to pass a resolution to amend the articles of association.[973] Among other considerations, the court referred to Article 13(3) of the Law, which states that the articles of association may not deprive shareholders of their rights. This provision adds more substance to the argument that the group interest notion is generally not recognized in Ukraine.

Table 4.1 presents a comparison of the rules on a parent company's right to issue instructions to its subsidiaries across the studied jurisdictions.

Table 4.1 Right of Parent Companies to Issue Instructions to Their Subsidiaries

Germany	*The Netherlands*	*Poland*	*Ukraine*
GmbH and contract-based AG, provided that instructions are to the advantage of one of the group companies	A company body of an NV or BV may issue instructions if the subsidiary's articles of association so provide	No explicit regulation, but specific regulation for contract-based groups pursuant to Article 7 of the KSH	No explicit regulation

Returning to the comparison between Ukrainian and Dutch company law on the recognition of the notion of a group interest, it is important to consider that in the Netherlands, even if the articles of association do not include any reference to the duty of a company's management to follow instructions from another corporate body, the BW nevertheless obliges the company's directors/management and supervisory board to be guided by the best interests of the legal person and the enterprise connected with it,[974] as discussed above. Ukrainian law does not contain the same rule on the competition of interests, but rather holds exclusively to the interest of the sole company, regardless of whether it is a parent or a subsidiary. This rule is applied

971. *Decision of 12 February 2015* Case No. 910/27663/14 (Kyiv Economic Court).
972. Currently the quorum in JSCs is 50% + 1 of the entity's share capital. For LLCs, the quorum has been repealed.
973. *Decision of 19 March 2014* Case No. 910/16760/13 (Kyiv Economic Court).
974. BW, Article 2:129(5) and 2:239(5).

equally to public companies,[975] private companies[976] and other legal entities when they are represented in civil turnover.[977] In other words, current regulation in Ukraine legitimates the legal entity doctrine and offers no possibility of adopting an alternative approach in a company's constituent documents.

However, although Ukrainian company law favours the legal entity doctrine and requires directors to act in the exclusive interests of the company, this does not necessarily mean that an external body cannot issue instructions to the subsidiary's management or board and these bodies can be held liable for following those instructions. First, the instructions may be in the company's interests, meaning that no conflict exists between the parent and the subsidiary, or between the subsidiary and its creditors. Second, if the management or the supervisory board acts in a manner that is incompatible with the company's interests by following the instructions of an external body, any company claiming damages from the company's officers would have to satisfy several conditions. The grounds for damages are set out in the Kyiv Appellate Economic Court's decision on a shareholders' derivative action, namely that four conditions must be satisfied: (i) wrongful conduct on the part of the debtor against company's interests; (ii) harm in the form of damage to the company; (iii) a link between the debtor's conduct and the damage; and (iv) fault on the debtor's part.[978] In that case, the debtor's wrongful conduct against the company's interests did not stem from following the parent's instructions, but rather from spending company funds without properly reporting the spending or from forming contracts. However, the conditions for the director's liability, borrowed directly from tort law, would be the same in the case of damage from following the parent's instructions. At the same time, from the legal perspective, it is important to establish whether the company acted in or against the company's interests, and the instructions from the external corporate body are merely one factor for establishing the latter.

Therefore, Ukraine neither has provisions similar to those in Germany, where parent companies possess the right to issue instructions to their subsidiaries, coupled with a duty of compensation, nor does it recognize the group interest notion as in the Netherlands. Moreover, Ukraine has no rules for contract-based groups as in Poland. Nevertheless, certain features of recognition of the group interest notion can be inferred from the practice of the registration authorities; however, these are insufficient for establishing a properly defined recognition of the notion of a group interest.

§4.02 RPTs WITHIN CORPORATE GROUPS

[A] Types of RPTs Within Corporate Groups

RPTs are an inherent concept in corporate groups. The risks attaching to these types of instruments in ordinary companies also apply to groups of companies. Although this

975. JSC Law of Ukraine, Article 63(1).
976. LLC Law of Ukraine, Article 40(1).
977. CCU, Article 92(3).
978. *Decision of 10 October 2017* Case No. 922/2187/16 (Kyiv Appellate Economic Court).

does not mean that transactions between companies and non-affiliated parties are always fair and advantageous, as the European Reporting Advisory Group has highlighted, the effect of an RPT on an entity's financial performance and position derives from how much influence a related party can exercise over its transactions with the entity.[979] It is more likely that a related party will enter into a transaction with a controlling shareholder that is not on market terms.[980]

The specific concern arising for subsidiaries from RPTs is when they are required to act in the interests of the group, but to their own detriment.[981] These situations include payments of fees or dividends by the subsidiary to another subsidiary/group member, or financial assistance to a group member in need. Internal transactions are divided into two main categories, based on their effect: unjustified and ordinary internal transactions.[982] Detrimental inefficient tunnelling transactions can be further divided, depending on what is tunnelled, into cash flow tunnelling, asset tunnelling and equity tunnelling.[983] Although this distinction sounds right in general terms, it is important to bear in mind that it is based on the standard of review. If the standard of review is too strict, then even efficient transactions might be prohibited or penalized.[984] This level way of regulation would create excessive obstacles for the market economy, forcing enterprises either to seek out other jurisdictions or else choose other ways to implement their group policies. This distinction is therefore a conditional one.

The presumption of inefficiency of RPTs is based on the conflict of interest hypothesis, meaning that related parties will act in their own interest, disregarding the company's objectives.[985] This theory contrasts with the efficient-transaction hypothesis, which is based on the advantages that RPTs carry, including facilitation of coordination and prevention of hold-up problems.[986] Taking one theory and rejecting the other clashes with the findings of Michele Pizzo, who describes RPTs as capable of either fulfilling sound business needs or being used for fraudulent purposes.[987] The author suggests an obviously attractive idea of a contingency framework that unites both theories in so far as the 'organizational context and institutional environment' allow.[988]

979. *Endorsement of the 2009 Revised IAS 24 Related Party Disclosures, Introduction, Background and Conclusions* (European Commission, Brussels, 4 February 2010, MARKT F3, 2010), 6.
980. Sørensen KE, 'Shareholders' Duty to Disclose' in Birkmose HS (ed.), *Shareholders' Duties* (Wolters Kluwer 2017), 315.
981. Yasui T, 'Corporate Governance of Financial Groups' OECD Corporate Governance Working Papers, available at: http://dx.doi.org/101787/5jlv1m6zq3nx-en, accessed on 7 December 2018, 24.
982. Kang SY, 'Rethinking Self-Dealing and the Fairness Standard: A Law and Economics Framework for Internal Transactions in Corporate Groups' (2016) 11 Virginia Law and Business Review 95, 109.
983. Atanasov VA, Black BS and Ciccotello CS, 1700.
984. *Ibid.*, 109.
985. Van der Elst C, 'The Duties of Significant Shareholders in Transactions with the Company' in Birkmose HS (ed.), *Shareholders' Duties* (Wolters Kluwer 2017), 203.
986. *Ibid.*, 204.
987. Pizzo M, 'Related Party Transactions under a Contingency Perspective' (2013) 17 Journal of Management & Governance 309, 326.
988. *Ibid.*, 326.

Intra-group transactions unquestionably have the potential to damage the company's functioning and the welfare of corporate stakeholders through misappropriation.[989] Famous corporate scandals confirm this, such as Privatbank in Ukraine.[990] However, it is vital for corporate groups to use RPTs. As Steef Bartman acknowledges,[991] these transactions are the reason for many groups to exist, by generating most of their corporate wealth. Zohar Goshen also notes that RPTs are sometimes the best option available to the enterprise.[992] In other words, although conflicted transactions may have a negative effect on enterprises, this does not necessarily mean that the same is true for all RPTs. The final evaluation of a transaction's efficiency depends on the circumstances, including the organizational context and the institutional environment.

While intra-group transactions can be divided into the categories of ordinary and unjustified transactions, other, less ambiguous, criteria might also be available for classifying internal transactions. For instance, Rwandan scholar Dieudonne Nzafashwanayo identifies the following types of intra-group transactions: (a) intra-group dealing/trading; (b) intra-group lending; and (c) intra-group guarantees.[993] The first category of internal transactions comprises transfers of goods and services between group affiliates and is most often based on 'transfer pricing' considerations, namely to shift profits from high-tax to low-tax jurisdictions.[994] The second type is intra-group lending, used to capitalize group members. This type of intra-group transaction is closely linked to the third instrument, intra-group guarantees, which are used to secure the liability of debtors under contracts with principals. In group situations, at least three types of guarantee can be distinguished: upstream (issued by subsidiaries to guarantee loans of parents), downstream (issued by parents to guarantee loans of subsidiaries) and cross-stream (issued to guarantee loans of sister companies).[995]

Based on transaction objects, two main categories of intra-group transactions can be identified: (i) cash payments, loans and provisions of guarantees, where monetary funds or rights to these funds form the object of a transaction; and (ii) transfers of assets, including goods, and provision of services, through swaps or fully payable transactions, where monetary funds are used only as a payment device rather than the actual object of the transaction. This classification of intra-group transactions can be further complicated by the variety of objects in civil turnover, while for tax purposes it is irrelevant whether a transaction involves a transfer of tangible or intangible property, for instance.[996] However, for the purposes of company and group law, in particular, it is more important to distinguish between transactions in which funds are the principal object and other transactions involving non-monetary transfers. First,

989. Ahmad E, 'Dilemma of Subsidiary Directors' (Master thesis, University of Groningen 2015), 34.
990. 'Ukraine's Biggest Lender PrivatBank Nationalised' (*BBC News*, 2016), available at: http://www.bbc.com/news/business-38365579, accessed on 1 May 2018.
991. Bartman SM, 'The Obligation to Contribute in the Case of Group Financing under Dutch Law: How to Allocate the Pain among Group Members?' (2013) 10 European Company Law 15, 19.
992. Goshen Z, 'The Efficiency of Controlling Corporate Self-Dealing: Theory Meets Reality', 400.
993. Nzafashwanayo D, 102-104.
994. *Ibid.*, 102.
995. *Ibid.*, 104.
996. PwC, *International Transfer Pricing 2015/16*, available at: https://www.pwc.com/gx/en/international-transfer-pricing/assets/itp-2015-2016-final.pdf, 2015), 9.

loans and similar transactions have attracted more regulation than other intra-group transactions. Second, with monetary transfers, no clear need exists to perform an additional evaluation of the transaction's market value, given that the value is already expressed in monetary terms. Third, monetary transactions always involve transfers of liquid assets, whereas goods and services are not necessarily liquid.

Further classification criteria can be put forward based on existing regulations for RPTs. According to IAS 24, RPTs are defined as transfers of resources, services or obligations.[997] This broad economic view of RPTs might not be applicable to some purely legal transactions that do not involve a performance, such as termination of a contract.[998] Based on this definition, RPTs are purely material transactions.[999] The immateriality of transactions constitutes grounds not to disclose the acts, as they fall outside the scope.[1000] The materiality of RPTs implies that abstract objects (ideas, for instance) do not qualify as objects of transfers for accounting purposes.[1001] While these objects can of course be transferred from one company to another within a group, and still fall under the term 'related party transaction' depending on the participants, from an accounting perspective they are viewed as immaterial. From the perspective of the IASs, transactions are material if they are significant, i.e. if they represent value. The commentary adds that the materiality of transactions should be defined on a case-by-case basis, using both qualitative and quantitative criteria.[1002] This manner of regulation offers grounds to separate material and immaterial transactions.

[B] Intra-group Loans and Cash Pooling

Loan agreements are a commonly used instrument for many corporate groups. Like other contractual ties between parent companies and subsidiaries, which are divided into upstream (backwards) agreements to sources of supply and downstream (forwards) agreements to distribution,[1003] loan transactions can also be upstream, downstream and cross-stream. Cross-stream loans, also referred to as lateral loans, are loans between companies that are not subordinate to each other, but are components of the same corporate group.[1004]

From the perspective of their effect, loan agreements can be either on market terms and, consequently, advantageous for the company, or else disadvantageous. The risk of a detrimental effect is especially high where loans are RPTs. CGCs are designed specifically with these types of transactions in mind, which by itself is a sign that they should be treated with caution. As the Dutch CGC warns, loans may only be granted to

997. IAS 24, paragraph 9.
998. Ungerer F, 315.
999. Baums T and Scott KE, 'Taking Shareholder Protection Seriously? Corporate Governance in the United States and Germany' (2005) 53 The American Journal of Comparative Law 31, 42.
1000. KPMG, *'First Impressions: Amendments to IAS 24 Related Party Disclosures'*, 16.
1001. Enriques L, 'Related Party Transactions: Policy Options and Real-World Challenges (with a Critique of the European Commission Proposal)', 11.
1002. Ungerer F, 160.
1003. Picciotto S, 133.
1004. Cahn A, 'Intra-group Loans under German Law' (2010) 7 European Company Law 44.

members of the management and supervisory boards if they are part of the normal course of business, on the same terms that apply to the rest of the workforce and subject to supervisory board approval.[1005] This section analyses loans from the perspective of group law. The need for this analysis is based on their widespread use in corporate groups for what is commonly known as 'cash pooling'. Cash pooling is considered to be a technique that does not present an immediate danger,[1006] and intra-group loan agreements are regarded as relatively safe cash pooling, as long as no assets are siphoned out of the company.

The standards for cash pooling differ between jurisdictions. The first and most frequently cited situation is in Germany, where cash pooling arrangements are subject to capital maintenance rules and liquidity protection.[1007]

The capital maintenance rules for public and private companies are similar in some respects. Both for public companies,[1008] as per Directive 2017/1132,[1009] and for private companies[1010] shareholders' contributions may not be refunded. In Germany, this requirement was subject to a strict regime, launched by the so-called 2003 November judgment of the Federal Supreme Court; it was later relaxed by the MoMiG.[1011]

The MoMiG provisions marked the return of German law to the 'balance sheet' test,[1012] meaning that contributions may, in fact, be repaid if a shareholder provides a fully enforceable entitlement in exchange, as viewed at the drawdown.[1013] This change is especially important for corporate groups, as it means that, for both public and private companies, the rules on capital maintenance do not apply in situations involving enterprise agreements in the form of a control or a profit-transfer agreement.[1014] In exchange for this exemption, the contracting party in the control or profit-transfer agreement must compensate the other company for any annual net loss that it incurs while the agreement is in effect.[1015] However, it is uncertain whether it is necessary to have a fully enforceable entitlement based on the enterprise agreement in order to avoid the prohibition on repaying contributions. According to the wording of the act, and accepting the idea that this way one party would be burdened by an obligation to obtain more information from its parent company, it seems more

1005. Dutch CGC, Principle 2.7 Preventing Conflicts of Interest, 2.7.6.
1006. Conac P-H, 'Director's Duties in Groups of Companies: Legalising the Interest of the Group at the European Level' in Birkmose HS, Neville M and Sørensen KE (eds), *Boards of Directors in European Companies: Reshaping and Harmonising Their Organisation and Duties* (Wolters Kluwer Law & Business 2013), 100.
1007. Mader D and Schümann-Kleber K, 'Germany' in Willems M (ed.), *Cash Pooling and Insolvency: A Practical Global Handbook* (Globe Business Publishing Ltd 2012), 187.
1008. AktG, Article 571(1).
1009. Directive 2017/1132, Article 56(1).
1010. GmbHG, Article 30(1).
1011. Cahn A, 'Intra-group Loans under German Law', 50.
1012. Mader D and Schümann-Kleber K, 188.
1013. Heerstraßen F and Nebe F, *Cash Pooling after the Reform of the German Act on Limited Liability Companies (GmbHG)*, Loschelder Rechtsanwälte, available at: https://loschelder.de/fileadmin/user_upload/downloads/pdf/aktuelles/2009/2009-01_DetailsAktuell.pdf, accessed on 5 December 2018, 4.
1014. AktG, Article 571(1); GmbHG, Article 30(1).
1015. AktG, Article 302(1).

plausible to agree with Andreas Cahn, who argues that forcing the subsidiary to perform this duty is incompatible with the principle of legal certainty.[1016] In general, managers of subsidiaries have a fiduciary duty to check their parent companies' creditworthiness on a regular basis and, if any doubt emerges, launch a claim for termination of the upstream agreement or for collateral under the agreement.[1017] However, this duty should not be confused with the duty to evaluate a debtor's situation at the moment of drawdown in order to determine whether the claim is unimpaired.

Where de facto groups are concerned, the rules on distributions by public and private companies require separate analysis, as private companies are subject to different rules.

In de facto groups with public companies as subsidiaries, the parent company has an obligation to compensate the subsidiary for all disadvantages caused, and to observe the period of compensation: during the financial year when the disadvantage was caused; otherwise the time and means may be determined at any moment no later than the end of the financial year.[1018] Unlike with contract-based groups, where funds distributed as loans or cash pooling schemes are explicitly exempt from the prohibition on repaying distributions under the capital maintenance provisions, no explicit provision applies to de facto groups. German scholars debated whether upstream loans in de facto groups should be made subject to the capital maintenance requirements. Strong arguments were made both for and against such a move, from the actual need for these rules to references to capital requirements under EU law.[1019] The debate was settled by a judgment of the Federal Supreme Court, which held that the requirements of Article 311 on de facto groups superseded the capital maintenance rules.[1020] The only nuance was that the Court required the claim for compensation to be unimpaired.[1021] In this ruling, the Court brought compensation claims under the general requirements as applicable to all shareholder loans under the capital maintenance rules.

While for de facto groups consisting of public companies (AGs) the rules on group law manifestly infringe on the realm of capital maintenance, loans in de facto groups with private companies (GmbHs) as subsidiaries enjoy simpler regulation, being subject only to the capital maintenance regulations.

When establishing cash pooling facilities in Germany, companies are required not only to comply with the capital maintenance rules, which are significantly influenced by group law provisions, but also to observe the liquidity protection rules, which are designed to protect creditors. This does not only mean that for upstream loans the manager of a subsidiary must check the parent company's creditworthiness on a regular basis;[1022] another consequence is that the actions of managers may not

1016. Cahn A, 'Intra-group Loans under German Law', 46.
1017. Spahlinger A and Kortz H, 'Germany' in Baer G and Karen OF (eds), *Financing Company Group Restructurings* (Oxford University Press 2015), 209.
1018. AktG, Article 311.
1019. Cahn A, 'Intra-group Loans under German Law', 46.
1020. *MPS*, Case No. II ZR 102/07 179 BGHZ (Federal Court of Justice), 71.
1021. *Ibid.*, 71, 77.
1022. Mader D and Schümann-Kleber K, 190.

render the company illiquid or over-extended.[1023] Additionally, for downstream loans, repayments made one year before insolvency proceedings may be voided by the insolvency administrator.[1024] Unlike the previous regime of converting all loans transferred in times of crisis into equity, this serious trigger, which was introduced with the MoMiG and is enshrined in the German Bankruptcy Code,[1025] forces the parent's management to carefully evaluate the economic state of the subsidiary, however difficult that might be.[1026]

Lastly, where cross-stream (lateral) loans are concerned, the rules described above would be incomplete if they could be avoided by simply replacing a parent or a subsidiary with another member of the group, rendering this regulation economically inefficient. As such, the courts in Germany chose the path of establishing the same legal consequences for loans between two members of a group as in relationships between parents and subsidiaries. In other words, 'shareholder loans' are interpreted broadly, by involving direct and indirect shareholders.[1027] The only situation where it is doubtful whether lateral loans will fall under the capital maintenance regulations is with enterprise (control and cash pooling) agreements. Given that the rules for the capital preservation do not apply to these types of agreements, it is unlikely that the parties could catch every possible option for cross-stream loans in their contractual covenants. According to Andreas Cahn, this regulatory gap *appears to have been neglected* by the proponents of contractual solutions to corporate groups.[1028]

Upstream, downstream and cross-stream loans are not unknown to Dutch law. These instruments are also used for cash pooling techniques within groups of companies. Additionally, given that zero-balancing is said to be used as one of the cash pooling options in the Netherlands,[1029] the Dutch approach does not initially seem to be as strict and complex as in Germany. At the same time, the requirements in the Netherlands are far from being ineffective. For public companies (NVs), this stems primarily from the fact that the Second Council Directive has been implemented in the Netherlands: distributions, including loans, to shareholders may be made only to the extent that the company's net assets exceed the sum of the amount of the called-up and paid capital and the reserves required by law (balance sheet test).[1030]

1023. AktG, Article 92; GmbHG, Article 64.
1024. Spahlinger A and Kortz H, 205.
1025. Insolvency Statute of 5 October 1994 (Federal Law Gazette I p. 2866), most recently amended by Article 19 of the Act of 20 December 2011 (Federal Law Gazette I p. 2854), Article 135(1)(2).
1026. Heerstraßen F and Nebe F, 6.
1027. Vetter J and Schwandtner C, 'Cash Pooling under the Revised German Private Limited Companies Act (GmbHG)' (2008) 9 German Law Journal 1155, 1175.
1028. Cahn A, 'Capital Maintenance' in Fleischer H and others (eds), *German and Asian Perspectives on Company Law* (Mohr Siebeck 2016), 179.
1029. Van Horzen J, 'Netherlands' in Willems M (ed.), *Cash Pooling and Insolvency: A Practical Global Handbook* (Globe Business Publishing Ltd 2012), 333.
1030. BW, Article 2:105(2).

The Dutch capital maintenance regime for private companies (BVs) is slightly different and underwent change in 2009.[1031] Essentially, it combines two tests: (i) the balance sheet test and (ii) the distribution test.[1032] The distribution test requires the company's management to ensure that the company will be able to pay its due and payable debts after it has made a distribution.[1033] Only if this requirement is met, may management approve the distribution. If it subsequently emerges that the company is unable to pay its due and payable debts, then the managers are jointly and severally liable to compensate any shortfall resulting from the distribution, plus the statutory interest on that shortfall from the date of the distribution.[1034] Managers may consider a number of circumstances to assess the lawfulness of the distribution, e.g. *solvability and profitability, off balance obligations, payment dates and life span of company's properties*.[1035] This test does not apply to NVs.[1036]

Besides these capital maintenance provisions and the burden they place on financial transactions, more generalized corporate requirements apply that serve to preserve the company's capital from disproportionate distributions. When making distributions, members of the management and supervisory boards must be guided by the interests of the company and the enterprise connected with it, i.e. by the group interest.[1037] While an upstream loan or a payment under a downstream loan may of course be justified by the group's interests, this is not necessarily the case. In addition, the ultra vires doctrine may come into play and provide for the avoidance of legal acts that are contrary to the company's objects if the other party knows that the transaction is at odds with those objects.[1038] The effectiveness of this instrument varies considerably, as companies phrase their articles of association differently. If loans to shareholders are explicitly prohibited under the articles of association, then it will be very likely that a claim for avoidance will be successful. At the same time, it is important to remember that the ultra vires doctrine is unlikely to be invoked if the loan agreement aligns with the group's interests. The judgment rendered by the Supreme Court of the Netherlands in the *Rivier de Lek* case shows that cash pooling facilities installed in the interests of all the group's undertakings are generally allowed.[1039] As such, the use of the ultra vires doctrine for intra-group loan agreements is limited, though it should not be rejected entirely.

In addition to the restrictions described above, bankruptcy law in the Netherlands imposes further restrictions on the execution of intra-group transactions during

---

1031. Verkerk B, 'Modernizing of Dutch Company Law: Reform of the Law Applicable to the BV and a New Legal Framework for the One-Tier Board Within NVs and BVs' (2010) 7 European Company Law 113.
1032. *Ibid.*, 115.
1033. BW, Article 2:216(2).
1034. *Ibid.*, Article 2:216(3).
1035. Verkerk B, 115.
1036. Jong BJD, 'The Distinction Between Public and Private Companies and Its Relevance for Company Law: Observations from the United Kingdom and the Netherlands' (2016) 27 European Business Law Review 1, 12.
1037. BW, Article 2:129(5) and 2:239(5).
1038. *Ibid.*, Article 2:7.
1039. *Rivier de Lek, Decision of 18 April 2003* JOR 2003/160 (Supreme Court of the Netherlands).

the one-year period prior to the commencement of insolvency proceedings and performed without any prior obligation to do so. Such transactions are presumed to prejudice the company's creditors and may therefore be voided at the insolvency administrator's claim.[1040]

Other safeguards are also in place that are often used in business practice in the Netherlands and that may be employed by subsidiaries. For instance, according to agreements within corporate groups, companies may have joint and several liability for the debts of other group members.[1041] However, this and other instruments are optional and are subject to the willingness of the parties concerned.

The Polish regulation of intra-group loan agreements differs first and foremost in that Polish law does not recognize corporate groups, except for some provisions on dominant companies and related parties in the KSH.[1042] As explained above, rules on the group interest notion are also missing from Poland's statutory provisions, despite some attempts to regulate the issue and some law enforcement practice.[1043] It cannot be guaranteed that Poland's judicial authorities will regard upstream loans and payments under downstream loans as being in the group's interests.

As a Member State of the EU, Poland has implemented the provisions of the former Second Council Directive, now codified in Directive 2017/1132. This includes the prohibition on reimbursing contributions for both private companies (sp.z o.o.) and public companies (S.A.).[1044] However, the regime is not as sophisticated as in Germany, where group law has an enormous impact on these relationships. Polish law has even been claimed to have stricter capital maintenance rules than Germany, as it does not offer the same exemptions.[1045]

Similar to German and Dutch law, Polish law also includes special safeguards in its bankruptcy regulations. The rule is that transactions between the debtor and another company dominated by the debtor that were made during the six months prior to the start of bankruptcy proceedings are invalid.[1046] The consequences of this provision are limited to directly related companies within a group, and financing through sister companies is not covered by these regulations and so provides a way to avoid these requirements.

Compared with the other jurisdictions examined here, the rules on distributions in Ukraine do not possess any capital maintenance requirements at the same level. Restrictions on distributions are confined to constraints on payments of dividends.

1040. Gispen G and Van Gangelen B, *Insolvency and Directors' Duties in the Netherlands: Overview* (Thomson Reuters Practical Law 2018), available at: https://uk.practicallaw.thomsonreuters.com/1-635-9172?transitionType=Default&contextData=(sc.Default)&firstPage=true&bhcp=1, accessed on 17 May 2018.
1041. Van Galen R, 'The Netherlands' in Baer G and Karen OF (eds), *Financing Company Group Restructurings* (Oxford University Press 2015), 351.
1042. Barlowski M, 'Poland' in Baer G and Karen OF (eds), *Financing Company Group Restructurings* (Oxford University Press 2015), 367.
1043. Rządkowski M, 80.
1044. KSH, Articles 189, 344.
1045. Opalski A, 'Transakcje między podmiotami powiązanymi w prawie spółek' (2012) Przegląd Prawa Handlowego 4, 16.
1046. Barlowski M, 386.

Both public and private companies must include the appropriation of undistributed income and dividend distribution on the agenda for their annual shareholders' meetings.[1047] For private companies, dividends are paid to shareholders based on a decision to that effect by the general meeting of shareholders.[1048] This is the same for public companies as far as ordinary shares are concerned (no decision is required for privileged shares).[1049]

The restrictions on dividend payments by Ukrainian public companies are substantially different from the restrictions that apply to private companies. For public companies, the decision to pay a dividend may not be made if the company's net assets are lower than the sum of its share capital, reserves and the amount by which the liquidation value of privileged shares exceeds their nominal value.[1050] Private companies may stipulate dividend payment restrictions in their articles of association.[1051] Statutory restrictions on dividends by private companies come into play in two cases: (i) if the company has unsettled obligations towards shareholders; and (ii) if the company's assets are insufficient to pay its creditors' claims, or would be insufficient as a result of the dividend;[1052] this restriction is similar to the distribution test used in the Netherlands, though here it applies to distributions in a narrow sense, i.e. dividends only.

The situation in Ukraine is also different for group law regulations: Ukraine is not under any internationally recognized legal obligation to implement rules on the recognition of group interest or related concepts, nor has Ukraine undertaken to include this concept in its national laws. However, it has detailed rules for RPTs ('transactions with interest'), which are optional for private companies[1053] and mandatory for public companies.[1054] These rules are discussed in Chapters 1 and 5 of this book, not in the present section.

Of the concepts discussed above in regard to Germany, Poland and the Netherlands, Ukraine possesses similar pre-insolvency regulations. Before the Code of Ukraine on Bankruptcy Procedures was adopted, the Law of Ukraine 'On Restoring a Debtor's Insolvency or Recognizing It Bankrupt' provided for avoidance of transactions conducted one year before insolvency proceedings if they were not on market terms, e.g. without monetary compensation or where monetary obligations were performed earlier than expected.[1055] The avoidance of these transactions did not depend on whether they were made within a group or not. The new Code of Ukraine on

1047. JSC Law of Ukraine, Article 32(2); LLC Law of Ukraine, Article 31(2).
1048. LLC Law of Ukraine, Article 30(2)(12).
1049. JSC Law of Ukraine, Article 30(3, 4).
1050. *Ibid.*, Article 31(1)(2).
1051. LLC Law of Ukraine, Article 27(2).
1052. *Ibid.*, Article 27(1).
1053. *Ibid.*, Article 45.
1054. JSC Law of Ukraine, Article 71.
1055. Law of Ukraine 'On Restoring a Debtor's Solvency or Recognising It Bankrupt' [Zakon Ukrayiny 'Pro vidnovlennia platospromozhnosti borzhnyka abo vyznannia yoho bankrutom'], Article 20(1).

Bankruptcy Procedures preserves the latter provision,[1056] while also adding further provisions specifically targeting RPTs. Under those provisions, contracts formed between a debtor and an interested person during the three years immediately prior to insolvency proceedings may be voided by an economic court if the bankruptcy administrator or a creditor so requests.[1057] Under the Code of Ukraine on Bankruptcy Procedures, this approach is far stricter than that in the Law of Ukraine 'On Restoring a Debtor's Solvency or Recognising It Bankrupt' and the rules in the other jurisdictions studied here.

As demonstrated above, capital maintenance rules influence the regulation of intra-group monetary transactions. This regulation is heavily influenced by the implementation of the Second Council Directive, now codified in Directive 2017/1132, which prohibits distributions if (a) either the value of the entity's net assets is lower than the company's subscribed capital and reserves (balance sheet test), or (b) the amount of a distribution exceeds the company's balance sheet profits (net profits test).[1058] The extent to which the various Member States have implemented this provision depends on their national laws, in particular how broadly they interpret the meaning of distribution.[1059] A common factor shared by all the jurisdictions in focus in this research (Germany, Poland and the Netherlands) is that they extend the requirements governing unlawful distributions not only to public companies (AG, NV and S.A.) but also to private companies (GmbH, BV and sp.z o.o.), only with slightly more flexible requirements.[1060]

Table 4.2 presents the main regulatory aspects of distributions through loans in the studied jurisdictions.

1056. Code of Ukraine on Bankruptcy Procedures [Kodeks Ukrayiny z protsedur bankrutstva], Article 42(1).
1057. *Ibid.*, Article 42(2).
1058. Directive 2017/1132, Article 56(1, 3).
1059. Armour J and others, 14.
1060. Cahn A, 'Intra-group Loans under German Law', 45.

Table 4.2 Regulation of Intra-Group Distributions (Loans) to Shareholders in the Jurisdictions in Focus, for Public and Private Companies

Jurisdiction *Type of Regulation*	*Germany*	*The Netherlands*	*Poland*	*Ukraine*
Capital maintenance,in particular the prohibition on repayment of contributions	AG and GmbH, except contract-based groups and de facto AG groups	No prohibition on reimbursing contributions, restrictions apply to distributions by NV and BV	S.A. and sp.z o.o.	No prohibition on reimbursing contributions, restrictions apply only to payments of dividends by JSCs and LLCs
Group law regulation, through the recognition of group interests and/or alternative intra-group obligations	AG and GmbH contract-based groups (*Vertragskonzern*): duty to compensate losses AG de facto groups: duty to compensate disadvantages	NV and BV: managers may enter into transactions if they satisfy the group interest + ultra vires doctrine applicable	Group interest recognized by the courts, specific regulation for contract-based groups under Article 7 of the KSH	Group interest is not recognized, no regulation similar to *Konzernrecht*, but detailed rules on RPTs (mandatory for JSCs and optional for LLCs)
'Before insolvency' period, for avoidance of intra-group transactions by the insolvency administrator	One year for shareholder loans, where repayment was made during that year	One year for intra-group transactions	Six months for transactions between a debtor and a debtor-dominated company	Three years for contracts between a debtor and a related party, and one year for transactions, including intra-group transactions, on non-market terms

The table demonstrates that Ukraine does not have the same degree of capital maintenance and group law rules as the other jurisdictions in focus in this research. Distributions based on upstream or downstream loans are subject to more relaxed regulation in Ukraine. At the same time, pre-insolvency statutory requirements show a significant level of correlation with the other national laws. Moreover, the most recent amendments to the bankruptcy regulations in Ukraine make it possible to void RPTs concluded within a three-year 'before insolvency' period, which is far stricter than the one year used in Germany and the Netherlands, or the six months in Poland.

CHAPTER 5

Strategies for RPTs

§5.01 GENERAL OVERVIEW OF RPT RISKS AND STRATEGIES

[A] Risks of RPTs

One of the most important issues that minority shareholders and creditors face with RPTs is tunnelling: the practice of extracting assets from a company. Tunnelling has already been explained in Chapter 3, together with the concepts of self-dealing and propping. Although tunnelling has largely negative connotations, the author who introduced the concept of tunnelling in legal research,[1061] Simon Johnson, wrote in his celebrated article, *much of the tunnelling is legal.*[1062] Tunnelling techniques can be exercised 'below the radar' and do not carry any liability or other penalties as established by statute or case law for persons practising them. Still, its legality does not necessarily mean that tunnelling is beneficial for the company. For instance, if a company sells goods to a related party below market value in a jurisdiction lacking liability rules for undervalued dealing, that company would suffer a loss, despite the legitimate nature of the transactions. This situation not only is an example of a detrimental RPT but also highlights the complexity of applying standards, where the outcome of an assessment often depends on how the authority concerned interprets RPTs. The standards strategy is discussed in section §5.04.

No one will dispute that tunnelling occurs in both developed and developing countries.[1063] Empirical evidence from China, with its vast representation in literature, suggests that the following types of RPTs involving apparent tunnelling have been reported: corporate loans to parent companies in the period after the Initial Public Offering;[1064] sales of assets below market value and acquisition of overpriced assets in

1061. Atanasov VA, Black BS and Ciccotello CS, 1698.
1062. Johnson S and others, 26.
1063. *Ibid.*
1064. Aharony J, Wang JW and Yuan HQ, 25.

companies listed on Honk Kong Stock Exchange;[1065] equity sales, trades of goods and services and cash payments in listed companies after the 2012 anti-corruption campaign.[1066] In the US, the most prominent example of tunnelling is Enron, where multiple transactions were used to loot wealth and then hide the catastrophic results of this managerial opportunism.[1067] In Russia, the tunnelling practices at Gazprom, an oil and gas company with a major state shareholding, combined all the types of tunnelling mentioned above, including illicit sales of gas, pipeline stations, procurements of overvalued services, etc.[1068] Considerable value diversions due to tunnelling have also been found in Indian pyramid groups.[1069] The OECD has drawn attention to the risks of tunnelling in Indian firms associated with many family-owned companies.[1070] The negative impact of tunnelling RPTs and their effect on firm valuation was observed in Malaysian firms during the period 2014-2015.[1071] In Italy, Parmalat, notoriously known as the European Enron, employed a range of tunnelling schemes to enrich related parties while conducting numerous loss-making operations, which eventually resulted in its collapse in 2003.[1072]

Drawbacks of RPTs are not confined to tunnelling only. Michele Pizzo summarizes them as follows: weaker corporate governance, poorer earnings management, employment of relatives in family firms and misleading statements.[1073] Some of these issues are unlikely to be viewed as manifest drawbacks, such as the employment of relatives in family firms, which by itself does not raise explicit concerns, as long as those relatives do not abuse their positions. Nevertheless, evidence exists that in certain jurisdictions RPTs seem to serve as an instrument to manage earnings.[1074]

Some scholars have expressed the opinion that value diversion from RPTs with directors as related parties may be advantageous, as it eliminates incentives for directors to manage earnings and serves as an alternative form of compensation.[1075] This view has been convincingly challenged by other academics, arguing that, in order to balance company value against its diversion, the countervailing positive effect must

1065. Cheung YL, 'Buy High, Sell Low: How Listed Firms Price Asset Transfers in Related Party Transactions' (2009) 33 Journal of Banking & Finance (Netherlands) 914, 924.
1066. Evidence also suggests that the 2012 anti-corruption campaign was a successful deterrent to tunnelling practices (Xu G and others, 'Public Governance and Tunneling: Evidence from a Quasi-Experiment in China' Working Paper, available at: http://ied-wbef.hkbu.edu.hk/conference-proceedings/doc/S001-Full.pdf, accessed on 7 December 2018, 25).
1067. Atanasov VA, Black BS and Ciccotello CS, 1699.
1068. *Ibid.*, 1701.
1069. Bertrand M, Mehta P and Mullainathan S, 35.
1070. OECD, *Improving Corporate Governance in India: Related Party Transactions and Minority Shareholder Protection* (OECD Publishing, 2014), 35.
1071. Gan V, *The Impact of Related Party Transactions on Performance and Valuation of Malaysian Listed Firms: Testing the Influence of Corporate Governance* (Thesis for the Degree of Master of Commerce, Swinburne University of Technology 2017), 117.
1072. McCahery JA and Vermeulen EP, *Corporate Governance of Non-listed Companies* (Oxford University Press 2010), 228-229.
1073. *Ibid.*, 312.
1074. Moscariello N, 'Related Party Transactions in Continental European Countries: Evidence from Italy' (2012) 9 International Journal of Disclosure and Governance 126, 129.
1075. Gordon EA and Henry E, *Related Party Transactions and Earnings Management*, available at SSRN: https://ssrn.com/abstract=612234 or http://dx.doi.org/102139/ssrn612234, accessed on 27 November 2018, 2.

be sufficient to outweigh the cost,[1076] including, e.g., the diminished effect of performance-based executive pay.[1077]

This critical approach underscores the detrimental nature of RPTs and provides incentives for introducing protective mechanisms to deal with them. In other words, it promotes the conflict of interest hypothesis, treating RPTs as potentially harmful instruments.[1078] In contrast to this theory, the efficient-transaction hypothesis regards RPTs as safe economic instruments, providing for better coordination between market participants and deeper reciprocal knowledge.[1079] The latter theory derives its arguments from the fact that some RPTs have an effect opposite to tunnelling. According to studies of the Chinese market, RPTs have been used as propping techniques to allocate resources and minimize the risks of subsidiaries.[1080] In addition, evidence from economic studies on Nigeria and Indonesia refutes the absolute disadvantageous nature of RPTs: in those countries, no obvious links were reported between RPTs and poor performance or expropriation.[1081]

Given the complex nature of RPTs, and the differences in their interpretation by various actors, it is impossible to fully accept one of the two contradicting theories for RPTs (conflict of interest hypothesis or efficient-transaction hypothesis) and reject the other. RPTs have the potential to both destroy and increase corporate value.[1082] That is why it is vital for regulation to consider their risks and advantages. Based on the contribution by Michele Pizzo, who strongly opposed favouring one theory only, the following factors should be taken into account in designing strategies for dealing with RPTs: organizational context; institutional environment; and complementarities/substitution.[1083] In other words, successful implementation of a particular strategy in a jurisdiction, where it has prevented related parties in listed companies from diverting value (as might occur in China), does not necessarily mean that the same strategy will be equally effective in another jurisdiction, and even less that it will work for non-listed companies. These circumstances render it necessary to study the various organizational and institutional factors before legal strategies can be suggested. What factors need to be considered in the context of designing strategies for RPTs is discussed in section §6.01.

Despite the differences across jurisdictions and in scholarly thinking on the effect of RPTs and their interpretative discrepancies, the existence of risks inherent in RPTs does not undermine the idea that some RPTs are sound business exchanges.[1084] As

1076. Bebchuk LA and Jolls C, 'Managerial Value Diversion and Shareholder Wealth' (1999) 15 Journal of Law, Economics, and Organization 487, 501.
1077. McCahery JA and Vermeulen EP, *Corporate Governance of Non-listed Companies*, 227.
1078. Pizzo M, 313.
1079. *Ibid.*, 317.
1080. Moscariello N, 130.
1081. Edesiri Okoro G and Jeroh E, 'Does Related-Party Transactions Affect Financial Performance of Firms in Nigeria' (2016) 6 Business Trends 47, 52; Mita AF and Utama S, 'The Influence of Corporate Governance Mechanism on the Relationship Between Related Party Transactions and Earnings Management' (2015) 7 International Research Journal of Business Studies 1, 11.
1082. Maigoshi ZS, Latif RA and Kamardin H, 'Earnings Management: A Case of Related Party Transactions' (2016) 6 International Journal of Economics and Financial Issues 51, 53.
1083. Pizzo M, 325-326.
1084. *Ibid.*, 317.

such, it reflects best practices, as outlined by the OECD, not to prohibit these transactions, but to properly address the associated conflicts of interests.[1085] The basic strategies that are used in the studied jurisdictions or that have been developed based on best practices are discussed below.

[B] Basic Strategies for RPTs

The famous book *The Anatomy of Corporate Law: The Comparative and Functional Approach* outlines the following strategies for dealing with RPTs: affiliation terms, agent incentives, decision rights, rules strategy and standards strategy.[1086] This celebrated textbook is not the only source shaping the discussion of RPT-related strategies; further references on the available tools for RPTs can be found in other sources as well, grouped into 'ex ante' and 'ex post' tools, or property rules and liability rules,[1087] allowing for slight differences in the language used and the lists of strategies.[1088] However, despite those differences, what matters most is the substance hidden behind the names given to the strategies, tools and techniques.

Affiliation terms refer primarily to the strategy of mandatory disclosure. In literature, this strategy is also referred to as 'information rights'.[1089] Disclosure may apply either to the annual or quarterly publication of information on RPTs or to targeted disclosure at the request of minority shareholders or other stakeholders.[1090] This strategy is widely used for listed companies, where investors are required to be aware of major corporate events and should be able to react accordingly. Section §5.03 describes this strategy more extensively, and section §5.05 describes the system of RPT disclosure at the EU level.

1085. OECD, *G20/OECD Principles of Corporate Governance* (OECD Publishing 2015), 25.
1086. Enriques L, Hertig G and Kanda H, 'Related-Party Transactions' in Kraakman R and others (eds), *The Anatomy of Corporate Law: A Comparative and Functional Approach* (2nd edn, Oxford University Press 2009), 155.
1087. Davies P and Hopt K, 'Corporate Boards in Europe: Accountability and Convergence' (2013) 61 American Journal of Comparative Law 301, 398.
1088. For example, Samuel Issacharoff describes three methods for dealing with conflicts of interest: (i) substantial regulation, (ii) process regulation and (iii) liability regulation (Issacharoff S, 'Legal Responses to Conflicts of Interest' in Moore DA and others (eds), *Conflicts of Interest: Challenges and Solutions in Business, Law, Medicine, and Public Policy* (Cambridge University Press 2005), 191-197). The author's grouping of strategies is neither uncontentious nor exhaustive. Where he refers to substantial regulation, he essentially means the rules strategy, while liability regulation is said to mean the standards strategy. However, nothing stands in the way classifying the standards strategy as a substantial strategy, as it polices RPTs by considering the fairness characteristics of transactions between related parties. Conversely, information obligations, which the author omits, and the process strategy are both formal in nature and, rather than clarifying the meaning of fairness, impose requirements that, if observed, are expected to ensure fairness in reality.
1089. McCahery JA and Vermeulen EPM, 'Corporate Governance Crises and Related Party Transactions: A Post-Parmalat Agenda', 233.
1090. Enriques L and others, 'Related-Party Transactions' in Kraakman R and others (eds), *The Anatomy of Corporate Law: A Comparative and Functional Approach* (3rd edn, Oxford University Press 2017), 151.

The strategies of agent incentives and decision rights are related, in that they both refer to the internal governance structure.[1091] Both strategies are built around the company's decision-making procedures. The difference lies in which body is authorized to approve or block RPTs. The agent incentives strategy relies on the board's discretion to decide on RPTs, authorizing disinterested directors, or a supervisory board, or a committee within the existing board. The decision rights strategy assigns shareholders rights of input on RPTs through general meetings. These strategies are discussed in more detail in section §5.02, under the heading of procedural safeguards.

The principal example of the rules strategy is a prohibition on RPTs. An outright prohibition of RPTs would certainly remove the implied conflicts of interest associated with them. Related parties would not be permitted to conduct value-destroying transactions. However, this seemingly rock-solid argument is defeated by several serious disadvantages. First, another consequence is that a prohibition would prevent numerous efficient transactions. This holds especially true for intra-group transactions, which in some cases are in fact the reason for forming a group.[1092] Second, the risk of detrimental transactions would still remain: directors or controlling shareholders would switch to substituting techniques to extract assets.[1093] For instance, related parties might turn to special purpose vehicles, which would then act as intermediaries, receiving a consideration from a related party in exchange for their services. This practice gained infamy as a result of the Parmalat scandal and later became subject to EU accounting regulation.[1094] Lastly, in some situations, the benefits of RPTs increasingly overcome their drawbacks, in particular if a company is in bankruptcy and has no persons (except related parties) with which to deal.[1095]

Due to its self-defeating nature, where it is used at all, the prohibition strategy is included in national laws in part, to cover essentially the most suspicious transactions: usually loan agreements and credit transactions with directors,[1096] or similarly dangerous contracts such as guarantees.[1097] The danger associated with these transactions lies in the risk of non-repayment of the loan by the director or his or her related persons.[1098]

A form of a partial ban on self-dealing was stipulated in the 2017 version of the German CGC.[1099] Members of the management board and employees were not

1091. McCahery JA and Vermeulen EPM, 'Corporate Governance Crises and Related Party Transactions: A Post-Parmalat Agenda', 236.
1092. Bartman SM, 'The Obligation to Contribute in the Case of Group Financing under Dutch Law: How to Allocate the Pain among Group Members?', 19.
1093. Enriques L, 'Related Party Transactions: Policy Options and Real-World Challenges (with a Critique of the European Commission Proposal)', 14.
1094. McCahery JA and Vermeulen EP, *Corporate Governance of Non-listed Companies*, 233.
1095. Enriques L, 'Related Party Transactions: Policy Options and Real-World Challenges (with a Critique of the European Commission Proposal)', 14.
1096. *Ibid.*, 14; Enriques L and others, 'Related-Party Transactions' in Kraakman R and others (eds), *The Anatomy of Corporate Law: A Comparative and Functional Approach* (3rd edn, Oxford University Press 2017), 158; OECD, *Related Party Transactions and Minority Shareholder Rights* (OECD Publishing, 2012), 11.
1097. Hopt KJ, 'Conflict of Interest, Secrecy and Insider Information of Directors, A Comparative Analysis', 177.
1098. Enriques L, 'The Law on Company Directors' Self-Dealing: A Comparative Analysis', 307.
1099. The draft 2020 version of the German CGC no longer includes this provision.

permitted, in connection with their work, to demand or accept from third parties payments or other advantages for themselves or for any other person, nor to grant third parties unlawful advantages.[1100] Unlawful advantages can be granted through RPTs if a manager, acting on the company's behalf, sells goods for less than their market value or buys goods for more than their market value. Interpreted literally, this provision entailed that, even with supervisory board approval, members of the management board could not take receipt of any advantages. This interpretation was further confirmed by §4.3.4 of the 2017 version of the German CGC, which stated that management board members might take on sideline activities, especially supervisory board mandates outside the enterprise, only with approval from the supervisory board. Therefore, while accepting payments or other advantages and granting unlawful advantages are prohibited, sideline activities are not forbidden, only subject to approval from the supervisory board.

Discussing the prohibition strategy, Zohar Goshen claims this approach to be identical to unanimous approval by shareholders.[1101] The rationale behind this is apparent: obtaining unanimous approval from all the shareholders, especially in companies with dispersed ownership, will require substantial efforts. For listed companies with thousands of shareholders, it is almost unattainable. Even in a closed company with diverging shareholder interests, it is no simple task to obtain approval for an RPT.

It is not strange, therefore, that many jurisdictions demand that major corporate events be approved either by a qualified majority or unanimously. Mergers, dissolutions and sales of major assets affect the rights of all shareholders. They are too important to be left unregulated. However, the prohibition strategy cannot conceivably have the same effect as the approval requirement. The core idea of the prohibition strategy is to prevent certain transactions from happening. If any leeway were to be given for nevertheless conducting one of those transactions, the regulation would instead apply other mechanisms. In addition, equating the prohibition strategy with the unanimous approval entails the risk of disregarding the interests of creditors and other stakeholders: even if all the shareholders approve a transaction, other stakeholders might have different opinions on the matter. Therefore, to avoid overlaps between various techniques, these prohibitions are best viewed as being separate from approval obligations.

Compared with the rules strategy, the standards strategy is not as unsophisticated and straightforward. Instead of inflexible instructions that permit or ban particular forms of conduct, standards afford directors a degree of discretion, imposing instructions to act in a particular way within established boundaries, and setting a margin of appreciation for enforcement authorities.[1102] The standards strategy always involves application of *ex post* remedies. In a perfect world, the rules strategy would prevent RPTs and thus be applied *ex ante*. In the real world, however, parties do not always act in accordance with the law, and efficient RPTs are common, and the rules strategy

1100. German CGC, as amended on 7 February 2017, §4.3.2.
1101. Goshen Z, 'The Efficiency of Controlling Corporate Self-Dealing: Theory Meets Reality', 401.
1102. Issacharoff S, 198.

would largely be applied *ex post* instead.[1103] The standards strategy is discussed in section §5.04.

The five strategies mentioned exhaust the list of potential instruments from the *Anatomy of Corporate Law* textbook. Within the existing legal tools to combat tunnelling via RPTs, Luca Enriques tends to highlight third-party advice and fairness opinions.[1104] Enriques does not afford this strategy the same independent status as the others. An advisor's opinion, by itself, accomplishes little without decision-making procedures or relevant information disclosure. It may also be prepared in the course of special legal proceedings, to assist the court in assessing the fairness of an RPT or to help shareholders collect information about the company, as observed in enquiry proceedings in the Netherlands.[1105] The practice of appointing a special auditor (audit firm) by the court at the request of shareholders who together represent a certain percentage of the shares has a legal basis in Germany[1106] and Poland.[1107] In Ukraine, an audit review may be requested by shareholders representing 10% or more of the share capital.[1108] However, in Ukraine this procedure is far less sophisticated and institutionalized than in the Netherlands. The main difficulty with appointing a special auditor and other gatekeepers lies in their professionalism and reputation.[1109] The more accurate and deeper the analysis in the advisory opinion is, the more capable it is of influencing the outcome of a given strategy. The report or another document has practical effect to the extent that the relevant strategy for which it is employed is enforceable. Nevertheless, the OECD has underlined the key role played by external experts/auditors/advisors in a range of jurisdictions.[1110]

Zohar Goshen, writing about possible solutions for self-dealing, puts forward a multifaceted analysis for non-intervention. This strategy would be an effective solution in a perfectly efficient market. Securities would be valued based on the associated safeguards, forcing investors to contribute more to companies possessing better protective mechanisms.[1111] This is difficult to picture in the real world, with all its numerous deficiencies and derogations, information costs and asymmetry. If acquiring a safeguarded security involves high information costs, investors are likely to instead

1103. Enriques L, 'Related Party Transactions: Policy Options and Real-World Challenges (with a Critique of the European Commission Proposal)', 14.
1104. *Ibid.*, 22.
1105. Van Bekkum J and others, 'Corporate Governance in the Netherlands' in Fleckner AM and Hopt KJ (eds), *Comparative Corporate Governance: A Functional and International Analysis* (Cambridge University Press 2013), 294.
1106. AktG, Article 142.
1107. KSH, Article 223 for limited liability companies (*sp. z o.o.*), Article 85 of the Act on the Public Offer and the Conditions for Introducing Financial Instruments to the Organized Trading System and Public Companies (Ustawa o ofercie publicznej i warunkach wprowadzania instrumentów finansowych do zorganizowanego systemu obrotu oraz o spółkach publicznych), 29 July 2005 (Dziennik Ustaw z 16 września 2016 pozycje 1639) for listed JSCs (*spółka akcyjna*).
1108. JSC Law of Ukraine, Article 75.
1109. Hopt KJ, 'Comparative Corporate Governance: The State of Art and International Regulation', 80.
1110. OECD, *Related Party Transactions and Minority Shareholder Rights* (OECD Publishing, 2012), 33.
1111. Goshen Z, 'The Efficiency of Controlling Corporate Self-Dealing: Theory Meets Reality', 405.

buy a security without those safeguards, incentivizing companies to issue securities without spending much to protect investors from self-dealing. The result would be unpredictable and, therefore, inefficient.[1112]

Takahiro Yasui adds to the traditional strategies aimed specifically at RPTs (disclosure, board approval, shareholder approval, prohibition of transactions) by suggesting financial regulation.[1113] By financial regulation, Yasui means special provisions for transfers of funds between members of financial groups. These special provisions would apply only to corporate groups, as discussed in Chapter 4, and financial regulation is not viable as a universal strategy for RPTs, but rather as a unique tool for intra-group transactions. Group law and other specific measures are discussed in section §5.01.

[C] Identification of Other Strategies

[1] Beyond RPT-Related Strategies

Besides the basic strategies for dealing with RPTs that either place powers of approval in the hands of the company's decision-making bodies or of the courts or else afford government authorities the discretion to collect information from companies, other techniques might also exist to prevent abusive RPTs and incentivize efficient ones. While these techniques might not necessarily be designed in and of themselves specifically to tackle RPTs, they could have the effect of successfully deterring wrongful practices or promotion of beneficial conduct. The *Anatomy for Corporate Law* purposely omitted these strategies from the chapter on RPT-related strategies,[1114] for being either too general or too narrowly focused on particular issues such as insolvency.

[2] Capital Maintenance and RPT-Related Strategies

One of the legal blocks that has a major impact on RPTs lies in the provisions on capital maintenance, as discussed in Chapter 4. This area of regulation is highly developed in German jurisprudence, backed up by statutory provisions and case law. The German rules on preserving share capital are highly relevant for RPTs, owing primarily to the concept of hidden distributions.

Viewed as a product of German legal thinking,[1115] the idea of hidden or disguised distributions concerns restrictions on distributions from share capital as applying not only to dividends and similar payments. Distributions through excessive salaries, loan agreements, credit contracts, guarantees, collateral and other transactions also fall

1112. *Ibid.*, 406.
1113. Yasui T, 26.
1114. Enriques L and others, 'Related-Party Transactions' in Kraakman R and others (eds), *The Anatomy of Corporate Law: A Comparative and Functional Approach* (3rd edn, Oxford University Press 2017), 146.
1115. Fleischer H, 'Disguised Distributions and Capital Maintenance in European Company Law', 95.

under these restrictions.[1116] By laying down these provisions, German law has gone beyond the requirements of the Second Council Directive (now codified). Instead of restricting only dividend/interest payments and covering exclusively listed companies, the German regulation on hidden distributions extends to both public companies (AGs)[1117] and private companies (GmbHs).[1118] The basic principle is the same for both types of companies: shareholders cannot be refunded for their capital contributions if the payments are not unimpaired.[1119] The amounts allowed for distribution from an AG's profit is determined as the difference between the company's assets, in the broad sense, and its share capital, liabilities and mandatory reserves.[1120] For GmbHs, the regime is more relaxed, in that it prohibits reducing the balance sheet value of the company's assets below the sum of its liabilities and share capital.[1121] With the increased reliance on the rules on balance sheet data, the amount that may be distributed varies, depending on how the accounting standards are applied, which then raises the issue of subjective asset valuation. This critical point is slightly mitigated by the fact that the national accounting principles are held to ensure objective valuation of assets and liabilities.[1122] In addition, this rule is not the only capital maintenance requirement for dealing with disguised distributions by German companies, which are also subject to the prohibition on payments that result in a deficit on the company's balance sheet,[1123] the rules on restitution of loans[1124] and the rules on director's liability for rendering the company insolvent.[1125]

An important point needs to be stressed here: while shareholder loans and loans to directors both carry a risk of corporate value diversion, they are governed by different rules. Loans to directors are not subject to the prohibition on reimbursing contributions, unless of course the director is also a shareholder. Loans to members of management and supervisory boards in German public companies (AGs) are subject to sophisticated and largely procedural rules, which are covered in section §5.02.[1126] For private companies (GmbHs), a director's ability to enter into loan agreements with the company is also limited, though no procedural safeguards exist. Instead, the law bars directors from receiving loans from the funds necessary to maintain their company's share capital.[1127] It is commonly held that, unlike with shareholder loans, claims for

1116. Rosengarten J, Burmeister F and Klein M, *The German Limited Liability Company: An Introduction to the Act on Limited Liability Companies with German/English Text, Synoptically Arranged, of the Act, a Sample of Articles of Association, Samples of the Other Formation Documents of the Company, the Classification of the Balance Sheet and the Profit and Loss Statement of a Company and an Extract from the Commercial Register* (CH Beck 2015), 42, 43; Ungerer F, 75-76.
1117. AktG, Article 57(1).
1118. GmbHG, Article 30(1).
1119. Cahn A and Donald DC, *Comparative Company Law: Text and Cases on the Laws Governing Corporations in Germany, the UK and the USA* (Cambridge University Press 2010), 222.
1120. *Ibid.*, 223.
1121. Cahn A, 'Capital Maintenance', 164.
1122. *Ibid.*, 162.
1123. Müller KJ, *The GmbH: A Guide to the German Limited Liability Company* (CH Beck 2016), 78.
1124. Cahn A, 'Capital Maintenance', 174.
1125. Cahn A and Donald DC, 225.
1126. AktG, Article 89, 115.
1127. GmbHG, Article 43a.

repayment are disregarded for the purposes of evaluating whether the entity has a deficit on its balance sheet.[1128]

The concept of disguised distributions is also known in Poland.[1129] Both private companies (sp. z o.o.) and public companies (S.A.) are prohibited from refunding contributions to shareholders.[1130] Despite the fact that the doctrine of disguised contributions found its way into Polish law from German law, in Poland this doctrine is applied even more strictly than in Germany and accordingly has received more criticism.[1131] The reasons include the fact that Polish law lacks the same broad exemptions as are contained in German company and group law for full value distributions and distributions under enterprise agreements.

In the Netherlands, it is unlikely to find the concept of disguised distributions in the same form as in German or Polish law. Increases and reductions of capital in Dutch public companies (NVs) are subject to strict rules, based on the EU capital maintenance regime.[1132] In addition to the balance sheet test, to assess whether the company's assets are at the required level, the liquidity test was introduced for BVs.[1133] Related to the duty of loyalty,[1134] and also referred to as the distribution test,[1135] it requires management to assess whether the company is capable of paying its due and outstanding debts.[1136] If the board fails to conduct a proper assessment, the consequences may be harsh for both the directors and the recipients if they knew or should reasonably have foreseen that the company would be unable to meet its obligations.[1137]

In Ukraine, no provision is made for the concept of disguised distributions. The rules on distributions to shareholders in public and private companies are limited to dividends only. These rules have been described in Chapter 4. Distributions by private and public companies that are not members of a corporate group are subject to the same restrictions as distributions within corporate groups. In other words, the principal findings of Chapter 4 are fair for RPTs outside corporate groups.

The Second Council Directive, now codified in Directive 2017/1132 and subject to implementation by Ukraine, under the EU-Ukraine Association Agreement, provides for two tests for rules governing distributions to shareholders: the asset-based (balance sheet) solvency test and the net profits test.[1138] The asset-based test prevents companies from paying out dividends if its net assets as recognized in its financial statement are less, or following the distribution would become less, than the company's

1128. Müller KJ, 86.
1129. Böckli P and others, 24; KSH, Article 355(3).
1130. KSH, Articles 189(1) and 344(1).
1131. Opalski A, 16.
1132. Van den Braak S, 'Creditor Protection at the Crossroads of Company and Insolvency Law: The Dutch Example' (2008) 5 European Company Law 229, 230; BW, Article 2:98, 2:98c, 2:99 and 2:100.
1133. Smits H and Portengen HJ, 'Report from the Netherlands' (2007) 4 European Company Law 128, 129.
1134. Van den Braak S, 230.
1135. Verkerk B, 115.
1136. BW, Article 2:207(2).
1137. Vreeman NL, 'Trading the Straightjacket for a Leotard: Introducing the New Dutch BV Law' (2012) 9 European Company Law 305, 308.
1138. Antonenko L, 27.

subscribed capital plus non-distributable reserves.[1139] The net profit test establishes a limit on distributions: profits at the end of the year, plus retained profits and withdrawals from the reserves, less prior-year losses and additions to the reserves.[1140] Both tests fall short of reaching their goals in the JSC Law of Ukraine, under which the asset-based test applies at the date of the decision to make the distribution, but not when or after the distribution is made.[1141] The effect of the net profit test is also limited, with the law not requiring losses and additions to the reserves to be taken into consideration for the purposes of determining the distributable base.[1142]

Besides only partially implementing the asset-based and net profits tests, the Ukrainian legislature has failed to supplement the capital maintenance rules for public companies with the liquidity test, as posited by Black and Kraakman as being part of the self-enforcing model of company law.[1143] Regulation for private companies mirrors that for public companies: while the liquidity test to ensure that assets are sufficient to satisfy the claims of the company's creditors is enshrined in statute,[1144] the net profits test and the asset-based test from the Second Council Directive are omitted.[1145] Instead of the asset-based test and the net profits test, the LLC Law of Ukraine imposes a different restriction on payments of dividends: the law restricts payments if the company has not settled its positions with former shareholders.[1146]

Overall, Ukraine has not fully implemented the capital maintenance rules as they are laid down in the Second Council Directive, nor the liquidity test for public companies. Although the liquidity test is in place for private companies, the asset-based and the net profits tests are missing. For companies, their management and shareholders in Ukraine, the current regulation of capital maintenance in general seems more satisfactory than it would be if the missing tests were implemented. With stricter statutory capital maintenance rules, management and shareholders would need to be more careful with dividend payments. For instance, if a liquidity test is required for public companies, it would force management to evaluate the company's obligations more precisely before making any distributions.

Management and shareholders would be further discomfited if the doctrine of disguised distributions were implemented in Ukraine. If it were, the restrictions would apply not only to dividends but also to other concealed distributions, including loans and excessive purchases of goods. Stricter capital maintenance rules might then sometimes deter managers and shareholders from entering into even profit-generating

1139. Directive 2017/1132, Article 56(1).
1140. *Ibid.*, Article 56(3).
1141. JSC Law of Ukraine, Article 31(1)(2).
1142. *Ibid.*, Article 30(2).
1143. Black B and Kraakman R, 1968.
1144. LLC Law of Ukraine, Article 27(1)(2).
1145. As justification for this step, it could be argued that the Second Council Directive does not extend to private companies, and Member States are not obliged to implement these requirements for companies besides public companies. Still, this argument can hardly apply universally, given that in various EU Member States private companies often enjoy the same regulation as their counterparts.
1146. LLC Law of Ukraine, Article 27(1)(1).

transactions, for fear of being prosecuted further down the road for potential wrongdoings. Moreover, if the doctrine of disguised distributions were applied formally, meaning that any distributions to shareholders are frowned upon, then management would be unwilling to enter into any transactions whatsoever with shareholders or their related parties. These risks must be taken into account, given the potential influence on the business judgment of company officers.

However, as the corporate scandals at Privatbank and VAB Bank (*see* Chapter 1) have shown, disguised distributions are often used to tunnel resources from companies. With abusive disguised distributions, it is primarily the company making distributions that suffers, followed by the minority shareholders, creditors and employees. That is why the current approach of restricting only dividend distributions by public and private companies to shareholders in Ukraine falls short. Greater efforts are needed from the legislature, the courts and practitioners to tackle abusive and destructive disguised distributions to shareholders and their related parties.

[3] Group Law and RPT-Related Strategies

Besides, in ordinary entities without relationships of control, RPTs also are common in corporate groups. There RPTs are less visible; it is more difficult for minority shareholders to detect them and to assess whether they are on market terms[1147] and, if they are not on market terms, whether a company actually needs the transactions. That is why group law occupies a major place in the regulation of RPTs, which have been described in Chapter 4.

RPTs in corporate groups take the form of intra-group transactions, either between parents and subsidiaries or between group members that are not necessarily vertically related. For intra-group transactions, the regulation of RPTs and group law sometimes works in opposite directions. Group law is aimed at maintaining the group's existence, in particular by allowing management of a subsidiary to act contrary to the subsidiary's interest if this is in the interests of the group as a whole, without fear of being prosecuted further down the road. Unlike group regulation, the strategies designed to deal with RPTs by providing safeguards against tunnelling, if applied in rigid manner and without allowing exemptions, sometimes work as a deterrent to transactions in the group's interests. As such, the idea of applying the rules for RPTs to the group interest notion is one worth exploring.[1148] If the rules for RPTs are applied without regard for the group's interests, the functioning of corporate groups would suffer from excessive regulation.

Of the jurisdictions in focus in this research, the notion of a group interest is recognized in case law or academic writing in the Netherlands and Poland.[1149] Germany does not recognize group interests,[1150] though it has sophisticated provisions

1147. Hopt KJ, 'Groups of Companies: A Comparative Study on the Economics, Law and Regulation of Corporate Groups', 14.
1148. Böckli P and others, 42.
1149. Armour J and others, 22.
1150. *Ibid.*, 24.

for groups of companies that intersect with the capital maintenance rules. The analysis in Chapter 4 shows that Ukraine does not recognize the group interest notion, though this is somewhat contentious. Most of the respondents to the survey carried out using Google Forms (twelve of the nineteen respondents) were in favour of recognizing group interests for all types of companies, three respondents supported recognition of group interests for public companies, one respondent favoured it for financial institutions and one respondent for banks and public companies and two were against recognition. When asked what could be done to improve recognition, seventeen of the nineteen answered that the group interest notion should be implemented through legislative amendments and subsequent case law, rather than through case law based on legal principles. These results show that the respondents have more faith in statute than in other sources of law. The concept of the group interest is still unfamiliar in Ukraine's corporate law theory and corporate governance, and as such will need to be explained in the statutory provisions. In order to bring about a positive effect, it will need to be clarified further and properly interpreted in theory and practice.

For German groups, various types of rules potentially have an RPT-related perspective. First, if a controlled company conducts an RPT at the instruction of its controlling company and suffers a loss as a result, safeguards exist as to protect the former's interests. The practical problem lies in understanding whether a company experienced the disadvantage due to that particular RPT.[1151] At the same time, it is unlikely, or at least hard to imagine, that not a single RPT performed between the controlling company and the controlled company will have a negative effect.[1152] If it is possible under the given circumstances to establish that the controlled company suffered a disadvantage due to a particular RPT, different forms of protection are available, depending on the relationship and the type of controlled company: a contract-based group or a de facto group, and an AG or a GmbH. In contract-based groups, dominant AGs have the authority to issue disadvantageous instructions, as long as they are advantageous to the controlling enterprise or its affiliated enterprises.[1153] In return, the enterprise agreement dictates that annual losses must be compensated.[1154] In the absence of an enterprise agreement, de facto AG groups are prohibited from issuing disadvantageous instructions, unless they provide compensation.[1155] Disadvantages that are not compensated by the end of financial year trigger liability on the part of the controlling company, and the controlled company may then claim damages.[1156] Again, however, the damages are difficult to calculate with precision.[1157] Private companies are governed by less statutory regulation, and most of

1151. Stecher MW and others, *Protection of Minority Shareholders*, vol 4 (Kluwer Law International 1997), 19.
1152. Schiessl M, 'The Liability of Corporations and Shareholders for the Capitalization and Obligations of Subsidiaries under German Law' (1985) 7 Northwestern Journal of International Law & Business 480, 505.
1153. AktG, Article 308(1).
1154. *Ibid.*, Article 302(1).
1155. *Ibid.*, Article 311(1).
1156. *Ibid.*, Article 317(1).
1157. Stecher MW, 'Germany' in Stecher MW (ed.), *Protection of Minority Shareholders*, vol 4 (Kluwer Law International 1997), 101.

their regulation is found in case law, where the interests of controlled GmbHs are championed and harm to the dependent company is prohibited.[1158]

Second, German group law contains provisions protecting minority shareholders and creditors of controlled companies against abusive RPTs within groups. Protection is provided primarily through the general compensation mechanism as described above, though these groups also have access to individual remedies. In the contract-based AG groups (*Vertragskonzern*), minority shareholders are entitled to annual compensation as stipulated in the enterprise agreement, or alternatively to the right to exit (*Abfindunsgrecht*),[1159] while creditors with outstanding claims have the right to demand security.[1160] In de facto AG groups, the subsidiary's management is obliged to report on all intra-group dealings.[1161] Criticism has been levelled at this system of reporting on the grounds that the reports are confidential,[1162] subject to disclosure only to the company's auditor and supervisory board. In defence of these provisions, it can be argued that the company's external auditor and supervisory board do in fact have access to the document,[1163] which indirectly ensures that minority shareholders will have more information.

Third, group law takes priority over capital maintenance rules, including those on RPTs. Specifically, shareholder loans and other disguised distributions are not subject to the prohibition on repayments of contributions in groups of companies where a profit-transfer agreement or enterprise agreement is in place.[1164] Besides enterprise agreements, a general exemption from the capital maintenance provisions on claims for full repayment applies, while the provisions on the duty of loyalty are arguably also supplanted.[1165]

[4] Bankruptcy Regulation and RPT-Related Strategies

Further complicating the situation, bankruptcy-related issues also come into play with the regulation of RPTs and corporate groups. The need to balance the interests of the various corporate stakeholders, in particular minority shareholders and creditors, and the group's overall interest, becomes distorted if a company approaches insolvency and enters the realm of bankruptcy regulation. The chief purpose of bankruptcy law is to protect creditors, which gain in prominence over the interests of other stakeholders as the company moves closer to entering insolvency proceedings. This is logical since allowing other categories of stakeholders to benefit at the expense of creditors is not a

1158. *Ibid.*
1159. AktG, Article 304(1), 305(1). For more on exercising rights of exit in the Netherlands, *see*: De Vries PP, 'Exit Rights of Minority Shareholders in a Private Limited Company' (Dphil thesis, University of Groningen 2010); Wang Q, 'Exit Remedies for Minority Shareholders in Close Companies' (Dphil thesis, University of Groningen 2011).
1160. AktG, Article 303(1).
1161. *Ibid.*, Article 312(1).
1162. Sargent N, 'Beyond the Legal Entity Doctrine: Parent-Subsidiary Relations under the West German Konzernrecht' (1985) 10 Canadian Business Law Journal 327, 351.
1163. AktG, Article 312, 314.
1164. *Ibid.*, Article 57(1); GmbHG, Article 30(1).
1165. Langebucher K, 364.

viable solution. Among other tasks, bankruptcy law seeks to prevent the directors of a company that is on the verge of bankruptcy from opportunistically transferring assets to related parties, rather than waiting for the assets to be allocated.[1166] However, as with the need to balance RPT-related strategies against the group's interests, allowing transactions that are disadvantageous to a subsidiary but that are necessary for the group in the long run, it is also necessary to consider the value-creating benefits of intra-group transactions for bankruptcy law purposes.[1167] In order to achieve this balance, other remedies have been suggested, with substantive measures prevailing over formal ones.[1168]

One of the solutions put forward to overcome the drawbacks of collective insolvency proceedings, especially in jurisdictions with weaker judiciaries, is to endow creditors with an individual right to challenge transactions outside the insolvency proceedings.[1169] So far, this solution has not found root in the bankruptcy regulations for RPTs in Ukraine. In addition to the general 'before insolvency' period, i.e. how far back the court-appointed administrator may void transactions[1170] (discussed in Chapter 4, where it is compared with similar rules in other jurisdictions[1171]), Ukraine's bankruptcy statute contains other provisions that deal specifically with RPTs, where they concern companies. For example, transactions with interest[1172] in rehabilitation proceedings are concluded by the rehabilitation administrators, subject to approval from a committee of creditors.[1173] This rule applies only to rehabilitation proceedings, i.e. one part of the bankruptcy proceedings, where an economic court hearing a bankruptcy case might not even have the power to intervene. This is an example of

1166. Van Zwieten K, 'Related Party Transactions in Insolvency' ECGI – Law Working Paper No. 401/2018, available at SSRN: http://ssrn.com/abstract_id=3173629, accessed on 7 December 2018, 2.
1167. Mevorach I, 'Transaction Avoidance in Bankruptcy of Corporate Groups' (2011) 8 European Company and Financial Law Review 235, 248-249.
1168. *Ibid.*, 246.
1169. Van Zwieten K, 21.
1170. Law of Ukraine 'On Restoring a Debtor's Solvency or Recognising It Bankrupt' [Zakon Ukrayiny 'Pro vidnovlennia platospromozhnosti borzhnyka abo vyznannia yoho bankrutom'], Article 20(1); Code of Ukraine on Bankruptcy Procedures [Kodeks Ukrayiny z protsedur bankrutstva], Article 42.
1171. Some comments should be made here in connection with the general period for voiding transactions in bankruptcy proceedings. First, where the bankrupt is a natural person, specific provisions govern the avoidance of RPTs concluded within one year before the beginning of the insolvency proceedings (Article 90(10)). Second, the opinion has been expressed in literature that providing a general period for voiding all transactions is not the best solution. Given the increased risks of RPTs, the possibility has been raised of introducing longer periods for these types of transactions (Mevorach I, 243). However, this solution has shortcomings of its own, as it is not evidence-based: no valid reason exists to expect that extending a contentious period would have a positive effect; on the contrary, this requirement seems to be a step towards a more formal treatment of RPTs and away from more balanced substantive regulation.
1172. This is the word used for RPTs in Ukrainian bankruptcy statute. Related parties in transactions with interest are defined in Chapter 3.
1173. Law of Ukraine 'On Restoring a Debtor's Solvency or Recognising It Bankrupt' [Zakon Ukrayiny 'Pro vidnovlennia platospromozhnosti borzhnyka abo vyznannia yoho bankrutom'], Article 28(9); Code of Ukraine on Bankruptcy Procedures [Kodeks Ukrayiny z protsedur bankrutstva], Article 50(8).

how procedural safeguards for RPTs are used in bankruptcy proceedings. Besides the approval procedure, statutory law on bankruptcy also provides for information rights for RPTs. A bankruptcy administrator has a duty to disclose all information about RPTs conducted by the debtor on the website of the state bankruptcy authority at least once per month, ensuring that all the company's creditors can access the information.[1174] This duty was enshrined in statute with the adoption of the Code of Ukraine on Bankruptcy Procedures.

Another direction in which bankruptcy regulation of RPTs has developed is by expanding directors' liability for acts committed before the insolvency.[1175] For German private companies (GmbHs), a provision was introduced in 2009 under which directors are obliged to repay shareholder loans if they led to the company's illiquidity, unless they manifestly observed due care in connection with those loans.[1176] Again, this rule straddles the point where RPT-strategies, capital maintenance provisions, group law and bankruptcy regulation meet.

[5] Protection of Minority Shareholders and RPT-Related Strategies

RPT-related strategies are largely concerned with shareholder rights. The decision rights strategy, in particular, highlights the importance of shareholder rights, by giving them the right to approve or block RPTs. Although this right is extremely important, other rights also enable shareholders to obtain a response and find practical meaning in situations involving value-destroying RPTs. Some of these rights are connected to some of the strategies outlined above, including the procedural and information strategies. The World Bank outlines three dimensions of minority shareholder protection: transparency of RPTs, the ability of shareholders to sue directors and hold them liable for self-dealing and access to evidence and to allocation of legal expenses in shareholder litigation.[1177] Additionally, the company law regimes in the studied jurisdictions grant shareholders these mentioned rights in circumstances that do not necessarily involve RPTs but have a more general character. For instance, the Dutch system provides for enquiry proceedings before the Enterprise Court of Amsterdam. The right to file for these proceedings vests with shareholders representing at least one-tenth of the share capital and to beneficiaries to shares or depositary receipts for shares representing a nominal value of EUR 225,000, if the company's share capital is no more than EUR 22.5 million, or less if so determined in its articles of association. For companies whose share capital is greater than EUR 22.5 million, this right is vested in investors holding a stake of at least one-hundredth of the outstanding share capital or, if the company is listed on a stock exchange, a stake representing at least EUR 20

1174. Code of Ukraine on Bankruptcy Procedures [Kodeks Ukrayiny z protsedur bankrutstva], Article 12(2)(5).
1175. Teichmann C, 'Modernizing the GmbH: Germany's Move in Regulatory Competition' (2010) 7 European Company Law 20, 24.
1176. GmbHG, Article 64.
1177. *Doing Business 2019: Training for Reform* (International Bank for Reconstruction and Development/The World Bank 2019), 98.

million at the close of the final business day before the request is filed.[1178] Before the petition is filed, certain preliminary requirements need to be met: the management and supervisory boards must be notified about the objections and given the opportunity to act in response,[1179] or the petition will be dismissed.[1180] If the petition is accepted, this is an indication that the court has doubts about whether the corporate policy pursued by the company is appropriate, and the first phase of the proceedings begins. This first phase involves a court-appointed expert preparing a report,[1181] which must provide the court with sufficient material to answer one key question: whether any mismanagement (*wanbeleid*) has occurred in the company. In other words, the court must be able to determine whether or not a constituent body acted negligently or culpably.[1182] Among other examples, this might concern entering into RPTs that are incompatible with the basics of responsible business management.[1183] If the court establishes mismanagement, and if either the petitioning shareholder or another interested person so requests, the court may apply remedies to address this mismanagement and its consequences in the second phase of the enquiry proceedings.[1184] Throughout the proceedings, the court may impose provisional measures with immediate but time-limited effect, such as suspending directors, deviating from the company's articles of association or placing all or part of the outstanding shares in trust.[1185]

Enquiry proceedings do not exist in the legal systems of Germany, Poland and Ukraine. Instead, these jurisdictions use a different instrument, namely the appointment of a special auditor.[1186] In German public companies (AGs), the right to request the court to appoint a special auditor vests with one or more shareholders holding one-tenth of the share capital or shares with a nominal value of at least EUR 100,000.[1187] If that special auditor finds that the company suffered damage due to the actions of the management or supervisory board, e.g., the court will appoint a special representative to represent the company's interests in court.[1188] In Poland, similarly, listed public companies are subject to the right to request a special auditor, which vests with shareholders representing at least 5% of the company's share capital.[1189] If the meeting of shareholders does not appoint an auditor, then the shareholders who initiated the request may apply to the register court. The auditor's report must be

1178. BW, Article 2:346.
1179. *Ibid.*, Article 2:349.
1180. Sanders P, *Dutch Company Law* (Oyez Publishing 1977), 63.
1181. Tuijtel MM, 'The Dutch Inquiry Proceedings: A Unique Instrument for Minority Protection from a Comparative Law Perspective' (2005) 2 European Company Law 90, 91.
1182. *Ibid.*, 91.
1183. *Ibid.*; *OGEM, Decision of 10 January 1990* NJ 1990/465 (Supreme Court of the Netherlands), subsection 7.2.
1184. BW, Article 2:356.
1185. BW, Article 2:349a.
1186. McCahery JA and Vermeulen EPM, 'Corporate Governance Crises and Related Party Transactions: A Post-Parmalat Agenda', 239.
1187. AktG, Article 142.
1188. Hasselbach K and Spengler M, 'Report from Germany' (2005) 4 European Company Law 113, 115.
1189. Iwanicki J and Nowacki A, 'Report from Poland' (2007) 4 European Company Law 90, 92.

presented to the management and supervisory board, and be publicly disclosed.[1190] The costs of the audit are paid by the company.[1191] However, if the listed company's management board applies to the register court, the court may make its ruling on the appointment of a special auditor conditional, requiring the persons who brought the motion to deposit appropriate security. If the register court finds that no breaches occurred, it may then rule that the security is forfeited for the company's benefit.[1192] Lastly, in Ukraine the right to appoint a special auditor vests with shareholders holding 10% or more of the share capital in their public companies.[1193] In contrast to how other jurisdictions deal with this issue, the assumption is that these shareholders enter into a contract with the auditor directly and therefore bear the cost of the audit.[1194] Article 75 of the JSC Law of Ukraine, which governs these matters, does not provide for any enforcement mechanisms for inspection proceedings; instead, it mainly sets forth the inspection procedure and refrains from dictating how the report findings should be implemented or what should be done if the company's bodies refuse to share materials or information with the auditor.

Besides the mechanism of appointing special auditors/experts, which by themselves do not serve as a remedy[1195] and add value only in so far as the resulting report sheds light on the corporate culture, other rights are also available in response to detrimental RPTs, in particular the right to exit the company.[1196] Dutch law specifies a special procedure allowing shareholders to exit their companies if they cannot within reason be expected to continue their shareholdings due to the conduct of one or more other shareholders;[1197] it is not necessary in this connection for that conduct to be harmful to the company's interests.[1198] Dutch law is unique in this regard, as this exit procedure relies heavily on the judicial authorities. Germany does not offer a general exit right for shareholders, except the rights within groups of companies discussed above.[1199] In Ukraine, shareholders in private companies have an exit right.[1200] Unlike

1190. *Ibid.*, 92.
1191. Act on Public Offers and the Conditions for Introducing Financial Instruments to the Organized Trading System and Public Companies (Ustawa o ofercie publicznej i warunkach wprowadzania instrumentów finansowych do zorganizowanego systemu obrotu oraz o spółkach publicznych), 29 July 2005 (Dziennik Ustaw z 16 września 2016 pozycje 1639), Article 85(6).
1192. *Ibid.*, Article 85(2).
1193. JSC Law of Ukraine, Article 75(5).
1194. The purpose of this regulation in Ukraine is to prevent abuse by minority shareholders who might otherwise seek to overwhelm the company's operational activities with unnecessary audits.
1195. Perakes E, 'Rights of Minority Shareholders General Report' in Perakes E (ed.), *Rights of Minority Shareholders: XVIth Congress of the International Academy of Comparative Law* (Brisbane (Australia) 2002); General and National Reports (Bruylant 2004), 71.
1196. *Ibid.*, 62.
1197. BW, Article 2:343.
1198. Timmerman L and Doorman A, 'Rights of Minority Shareholders in the Netherlands' in Perakes E (ed.), *Rights of Minority Shareholders: XVIth Congress of the International Academy of Comparative Law* (Brisbane (Australia) 2002); General and National Reports (Bruylant 2004), 592.
1199. Hopt KJ, 'Rights of Minority Shareholders under German Law' in Perakes E (ed.), *Rights of Minority Shareholders: XVIth Congress of the International Academy of Comparative Law* (Brisbane (Australia) 2002); General and National Reports (Bruylant 2004), 409.

in the Netherlands, they may exercise that right unilaterally, without applying to the judicial authorities and without being required to state their reasons for leaving the company.[1201] Although this right to exit is unconditional, it is limited under the LLC Law of Ukraine, in that it applies only to shareholders with less than 50% of the company's share capital. If a shareholder holding 50% or more of the share capital wishes to exit the company, a special approval procedure is triggered. One apparent drawback of this regulation is that it makes allowance for situations where related parties separately have minority stakes but together hold more than 50% of the share capital; as such, while appearing strict, this requirement suffers from its formal shortcomings and is easily bypassed by shrewd shareholders.

Shareholders in Ukrainian public companies do not have the same unconditional right to exit as for private companies. To terminate a shareholding in a public company, the shareholder must sell his or her securities or, if the shareholder voted against certain major resolutions, demand that the company repurchase them. This appraisal right may be triggered in various scenarios, including if the shareholder votes against a transaction with interest, including RPTs, at the general meeting of shareholders.[1202] The issue then is to determine a fair price for repurchasing the shares to satisfy the shareholder's claim.

This summary of the rights of minority shareholders is by no means an exhaustive overview of the available mechanisms in response to RPTs. A recent study by the European Commission into the protection of minority shareholders describes further shareholder rights, including economic, control, information, litigation and equality rights, that can serve as effective means to address the issues of RPTs.[1203] At the same time, to prevent the concept of RPTs from being diluted and to preserve the focus on the principal minority shareholder rights in connection with RPTs, it is reasonable to consider the rights that can be classified as control rights and to divide them into three categories, in the same manner as in the report: (i) the right to access information regarding RPTs; (ii) the right to block/approve RPTs; and (iii) the right to oversee RPTs.[1204] These are discussed in the following section.

1200. LLC Law of Ukraine, Article 24.

1201. The roots of the unconditional nature of these provisions go back to the idea of a self-enforcing model of company law that was suggested by Reinier Kraakman and Bernard Black in the 1990s for Russia and other post-Soviet countries with weak enforcement mechanisms (*see*: Black B and Kraakman R, 1978).

1202. JSC Law of Ukraine, Article 68(1).

1203. *Study on Minority Shareholders Protection, Final Report* (Prepared by TGS Baltic 2018).

1204. *Ibid.*, 141-147.

§5.02 PROCEDURAL SAFEGUARDS FOR RPTs

[A] The Agent's Incentives Strategy

[1] Introduction

The agent's incentives strategy stems from the rule that a company's board is a trustee of the shareholders, is authorized to act on behalf of the shareholders and for the company's benefit. The principal undisputed advantage of this strategy, compared with the strategy of approval by the general meeting of shareholders, is that it is far less costly. Its manner of application depends, among other factors, on the system of corporate governance used in the jurisdiction (a one-tier, two-tier or mixed system).

[2] Board Approval in Germany

The German jurisdiction is famous for its two-tier system of a management board (*Vorstand*)[1205] and a supervisory board (*Aufsichtsrat*),[1206] as opposed to the one-tier system, as used in the UK, which features a single board of directors.[1207] The two-tier system of corporate governance was proposed as a solution to industrial crises, and as a way to balance the interests of managers, owners and employees.[1208] As a result, the management board is strictly separated from the supervisory board.[1209] This set-up applies only to public companies (AGs), where the supervisory board plays the pivotal role,[1210] and those private companies (GmbHs) where it is mandatory to have a supervisory board.[1211]

The supervisory board represents the company in its relationship with management:[1212] it is the supervisory board that signs contracts with management board members and determines their remuneration.[1213] If a supervisory board member wishes to enter into a transaction with the company, then he or she is excluded under Article 134 of the German Civil Code from voting on that transaction.[1214] In addition, if a supervisory board member forms a service agreement or a contract to undertake a special assignment with the company, that agreement or contract requires approval

1205. AktG, Articles 76, 77 and 105(1).
1206. *Ibid.*, Article 111.
1207. Teichmann C and Gurman O, 174.
1208. *Ibid.*, 174-175.
1209. For example, *see* AktG, Article 105(1).
1210. McCahery JA and Vermeulen EPM, 'Corporate Governance Crises and Related Party Transactions: A Post-Parmalat Agenda', 238.
1211. GmbHG. Article 52(2).
1212. AktG, Article 112. This provision is a special clause, based on the general prohibition for agents to be involved on both sides of a transactions, as stipulated in Article 181 of German BGB (German Civil Code).
1213. *Ibid.*, Articles 84, 87.
1214. German Civil Code, Article 34.

from the supervisory board.[1215] The prevailing opinion in literature is that Article 114 of the AktG also applies to persons close to the supervisory board members.[1216]

The AktG also requires approval for RPTs with company officers that present a significant threat to the company, i.e. loan agreements.[1217] Besides loan agreements, which are explicitly mentioned in the law, transfers of property, including their collateral and preliminary contracts, are considered to be covered by Article 89 in the same way as loans are.[1218] Approval is required for one or more specific RPTs, and no more than three months in advance.[1219] Members of the management and supervisory boards must seek approval for loan agreements, whether they themselves are involved in the transactions or where the contracting party is an affiliated person, in particular a spouse, a minor child, any third person acting on their behalf or a company of which they are a legal representative.[1220] Loan agreements are exempt from the approval requirement if the loan is supplied in exchange for goods or if the borrower is a company affiliated with the lender.

For AGs, the approval requirement for loan agreements extends beyond the boundaries of the individual company. If a member of the management or supervisory board of a controlled company seeks a loan from the controlling company, the same approval is required, though this time from the supervisory board of the controlling company, rather than the controlled company.[1221]

As shown, the statute extends the board approval requirement to related parties only for loan agreements,[1222] and the general rule that subjects managerial self-dealing to the supervisory board's agreement makes no reference to other related parties besides managers.[1223] This narrow view has been endorsed by some scholars,[1224] while others have taken the path of a broader understanding of Article 112, by including a person's relatives and even shadow directors.[1225] Some commentators have put forward the view that, contrary to Article 112, Article 89 does not apply to former members of the management board,[1226] which derives from the broad scope of Article 112.

The provisions described above do not explicitly subject transactions with shareholders to a vote by the supervisory board. Nevertheless, Article 111(4) of the

1215. *Ibid.*, Article 114.
1216. Ungerer F, 112.
1217. AktG, Articles 89, 115.
1218. Ungerer F, 103.
1219. AktG, Article 89(1) sentence 2, 115(1) sentence 3.
1220. *Ibid.*, Articles 89(3), 89(4), 115(2), 115(3).
1221. *Ibid.*, Articles 89(2), 115(1).
1222. Still, the list of related parties under Articles 89 and 115 AktG is modest compared with the broad definition of a related party in the IASs, as discussed in Chapter 3. Some authors have criticized the notion of a related party as used there as being underinclusive or overinclusive (Wiedemann H, *Organverantwortung und Gesellschafterklagen in der Aktiengesellschaft: 296. Sitzung am 16. Oktober 1985 in Düsseldorf (Fassung vom 1. 1. 1989)* (Springer-Verlag 2013), 20).
1223. AktG, Article 112.
1224. Baums T and Scott KE, 41.
1225. Enriques L, 'Related Party Transactions: Policy Options and Real-World Challenges (with a Critique of the European Commission Proposal)', 15.
1226. Ungerer F, 104.

AktG may be invoked to include transactions with shareholders in the articles of association as being subject to a vote by the supervisory board.[1227]

If the rules on self-dealing are breached, the negative consequences depend on which specific obligation and article were breached. For managerial self-dealing conducted without supervisory board approval, as required by Article 112, the consequence is that the RPT is void if it is harmful to the company and if the party concerned acted in bad faith.[1228] If a member of the supervisory board has formed a service contract on top of his or her employment, without board approval, the remuneration for those services must be repaid.[1229] This is also the consequence of loan agreements with management and supervisory board members that are concluded without board approval.[1230] The repayment obligation under Articles 114(2), 89(5) and 115(4) does not arise if the supervisory board subsequently consents to the transaction.[1231] In addition, members of the management and supervisory boards may be held personally liable for breaching their duty of care, as well as possibly suffering criminal sanctions if this involved wilful conduct to cause harm.[1232] In practice, however, the liability of directors for wrongful conduct has its limitations and should not be overemphasized.[1233]

Besides at the level of statute (the AktG) the agent's incentives strategy has been implemented at the level of soft law (the 2017 version of the German CGC). Provisions in these two sources are not viewed as contradictory: the German CGC either reiterates the wording of the statute or adds recommendations.[1234] For instance, according to the 2017 version of the German CGC, loans from the enterprise to members of the management or supervisory board or their relatives require approval from the supervisory board (this rule has been removed in the draft 2020 German CGC).[1235] This provision follows the idea enshrined in Articles 89 and 115 of the AktG with reference to loan agreements. However, the provisions of the AktG are more detailed and indicate the specific family relationships that are covered by the AktG and extend the rules to legal entities, subject to various exemptions. Conversely, the German CGC provisions are more abstract in nature and, if interpreted broadly (such as the concept of a relative), significantly increase the requirements for listed companies. This reflects the advisory nature of the German CGC and its sweeping aim to promote confidence in the management and supervision of German listed companies.[1236]

1227. *Ibid.*, 122.
1228. Enriques L, 'The Law on Company Directors' Self-Dealing: A Comparative Analysis', 317.
1229. AktG, Article 114(2).
1230. *Ibid.*, Articles 89(5) and 115(4).
1231. *Ibid.*, Articles 114(2), 89(5) and 115(4).
1232. *Ibid.*, Articles 93 and 116; McCahery JA and Vermeulen EPM, 'Corporate Governance Crises and Related Party Transactions: A Post-Parmalat Agenda', 238.
1233. Merkt H, 'Germany: Internal and External Corporate Governance' in Fleckner AM and Hopt KJ (eds), *Comparative Corporate Governance: A Functional and International Analysis* (Cambridge University Press 2013), 566.
1234. Teichmann C and Gurman O, 176.
1235. German CGC, as amended on 7 February 2017, § 3.9.
1236. *Ibid.*, 1.

Other provisions in the 2017 version of the German CGC governing RPTs between the company and the members of its management and supervisory boards similarly have a broader scope than their statutory counterparts in the AktG. The 2017 version of the German CGC contains a requirement that important transactions involving a conflict of interest among the management board must be approved by the supervisory board.[1237] This wording implies that unimportant conflicted transactions are not subject to this approval by the supervisory board and poses the question of what the adjective 'important' means in this context. The wording of Article 112 of the AktG, conversely, which deals with the representation of the company in relationships with management, does not make any distinction between 'important' and 'unimportant' RPTs.

For transactions conducted by members of the supervisory board, the current (i.e., 2017) version of the German CGC contains different provisions. It states that advisory and other service agreements and contracts for work between the company and a member of its supervisory board require the supervisory board's approval.[1238] Advisory and service agreements and contracts for work by supervisory board members therefore always require approval from the supervisory board, regardless of whether or not they are important, while no direct mention is made of other forms of agreements and contracts that supervisory board members might conclude.

In general terms, in Germany statutory provisions are often interpreted in a broad sense, to imply longer lists of related parties than literally provided. This observation ties back in with the concept of a related party discussed in Chapter 3 and the concept of an indirect conflict of interest considered in Chapter 2. The possibility of broad interpretation does not seem defunct, as long as the criteria for interpreting the notion of a related party are sufficiently clear and precise; if they are not, the system creates a risk of undermining certainty and overregulating the functioning of companies.

In the Google Forms survey carried out as part of the present research, the respondents were asked one question as to whether courts should have the authority to interpret the meaning of an interested person more extensively and extend liability to interested persons who are not directly specified in Article 71 of the JSC Law of Ukraine but share all the features necessary for a sufficiently strong link to the company. Although most respondents answered 'yes' (thirteen out of nineteen), one answer was difficult to disagree with: that it is first necessary to define a clear description of what features these persons possess. The problem with closed lists of related parties, however, is that a way can always be found to circumvent them. As such, the proper criteria for related parties cannot mean either vague guidelines or a short list of related parties.

1237. *Ibid.*, § 4.3.3.
1238. *Ibid.*, § 5.5.4.

[3] Board Approval in Poland

Similar to the German approach, Polish law as a general rule[1239] allocates the decision-making power for RPTs between a director and his or her company to the supervisory board.[1240] This regulation follows the adherence in Polish law to the two-tier system of corporate governance for public companies (S.A.), meaning that these companies have a structure including both a management board and a supervisory board.[1241] These rules evidence the fact that Poland belongs to the Germanic legal tradition, despite suggestions to allow one-tier boards, as being more shareholder-oriented.[1242] For the present, Poland allows one-tier for a different business form, namely European Companies (*Societas Europea*).[1243]

Polish supervisory boards (*rada nadzorcza*) are responsible for monitoring management and the company's overall functioning.[1244] This set-up is mandatory for Polish public companies (S.A.)[1245] and optional for private companies (sp. z o.o.) unless they have more than twenty-five shareholders and a share capital in excess of PLN 500,000. The law offers an alternative to the optional and mandatory supervisory boards for the sp. z o.o. form: shareholders may opt to establish an audit committee instead (a system that goes back to well before the corporate governance movement brought about the introduction of audit committees for the boards of listed companies).[1246] In practice, however, if the shareholders decide to establish a monitoring body, it is almost always a supervisory board, not an audit committee. Allowing for the fact that supervisory boards are not always mandatory for private companies, the rules governing conflicts of interest, drafted with the German statute in mind, are largely the same for private and public companies. With both types of companies, in a contract between a company and a member of its management board, the company is represented by the supervisory board or a legal representative appointed by the shareholders' meeting.[1247] Although the wording is reminiscent of that of Article 112 of the AktG, the substance is in fact different. First, the rule applies to private companies, whereas in German GmbHs these conflicts of interest are subject to the general prohibition on self-contracting contained in the German Civil Code.[1248] Second, it

1239. The exception, where the decision lies with the general meeting of shareholders rather than the supervisory board, applies to credit, loan, suretyship and similar contracts with members of the management or supervisory board, members of the audit committee, the procurator or liquidator, under Article 15 of the KSH. This rule extends to agreements where these company officers are the beneficiaries or where their transaction is with a subsidiary.
1240. Gerner-Beuerle C, Paech P and Schuster EP, 147.
1241. Radwan A and Regucki T, 'Legal Aspects of Executive Remuneration in Polish Listed Companies', 301.
1242. Samól K, 'One-Or Two-Tier Board System? A Comparative Analysis of the British and Polish Systems of Corporate Governance' (2016) 13 European Company Law 67, 77.
1243. Council Regulation (EC) No. 2157/2001 of 8 October 2001 on the Statute for a European company (SE), OJ L 294, 10.11.2001.
1244. KSH, Articles 219 and 382.
1245. *Ibid.*, Article 381.
1246. *Ibid.*, Article 213(2).
1247. *Ibid.*, Articles 210(1), 379(1).
1248. GmbHG, Article 35(3); German Civil Code, Article 181.

provides for an alternative to the supervisory board, namely a specially appointed representative. Such a representative is also appointed in all situations where the company does not have a supervisory board.[1249] However, the issue is less clear where the company does in fact have a supervisory board: if the shareholders appoint a special representative, this might lead to potential competition between the separate bodies.

In addition to the rule for how companies are represented in their relationships with management, the KSH obliges members of management boards of both types of companies to abstain in matters concerning the settlement of issues involving the manager and his or her related parties[1250] and entitles them to request that this be recorded in the minutes.[1251] In Germany, this obligation is not codified, or arguably even recognized.[1252] In practice, however, this rule does not have much value in Poland, following the ruling by the Supreme Court of Poland that violation of Article 377 of the KSH does not constitute grounds for annulling a transaction with a board member who failed to abstain.[1253] This judgment was criticized, as it meant that no sanction was applied to a transaction with a close relative of a manager.[1254] Nevertheless, an ambiguous possibility exists to claim damages from the conflicted manager.[1255]

Besides the general provisions authorizing supervisory boards to represent their companies in dealings with managers, the KSH dictates that credit, loan, suretyship and similar contracts with a member of the management board, the supervisory board or the audit committee or a procurator or liquidator, or for the benefit of any of these persons, must be approved by the general meeting of shareholders.[1256] For contracts between these persons and a subsidiary of the company, approval is required from the dominant company.[1257] This provision is reminiscent of the rules governing service agreements and loans with supervisory board members under the AktG,[1258] although some differences can be identified. First, Article 15 of the KSH applies to both private companies (sp. z o.o.) and public companies (S.A.), whereas the AktG covers only public companies (AGs), and the GmbHG does not have a similar requirement. Second, the scope of Article 15 of the KSH is different: unlike Article 114 of the AktG, it does not govern service contracts, though it covers contracts similar to credit, loans and

1249. In LLCs (sp. z o.o.) fewer than twenty-five shareholders or with a share capital less than PLN 500,000.

1250. A 'related party' under the KSH here refers to a spouse, relative by blood in the first or second degree of affinity or a person with whom the member has a personal relationship. This list of related parties is longer than the lists under Articles 89 and 115 of the AktG, though it makes no mention of legal entities as related parties and, in general, applies a much narrower concept of a related party than that used in the IASs and as discussed in Chapter 3.

1251. KSH, Articles 209, 377.

1252. Enriques L, 'The Law on Company Directors' Self-Dealing: A Comparative Analysis', 317.

1253. *Judgment of 11.01.2002* IV CKN 1903/00, OSN 2002 (Supreme Court of Poland), No. 11, item 137.

1254. Sołtysiński S, 'Poland: Corporate Governance of Joint-Stock Companies' in Fleckner AM and Hopt KJ (eds), *Comparative Corporate Governance: A Functional and International Analysis* (Cambridge University Press 2013), 772.

1255. KSH, Articles 293, 483.

1256. *Ibid.*, Article 15(1).

1257. *Ibid.*, Article 15(2).

1258. AktG, Articles 114 and 115.

suretyship, and a broad interpretation of the concept of a 'similar contract' would mean that some service contracts also qualify. In addition, Article 15 of the KSH applies not only to members of the management board and the supervisory board but also to audit committee members, procurators and liquidators and also governs contracts under which these persons are the beneficiaries. This wording implies that contracts with family members also fall under the scope of Article 15 of the KSH, though it is not clear exactly how far it reaches. Third, and most important, the legal effect of Article 15 of the KSH is that approval from the general meeting of shareholders is required, rather than simply approval from the supervisory board. This consequence shifts Article 15 from the agent incentives strategy to the decision rights strategy, which is analysed below.

Besides these statutory laws, some aspects of conflicts of interest of members of management and supervisory boards are regulated by soft law. According to the WSE Best Practice, members of management and supervisory boards have a duty to refrain from voting on resolutions that might give rise to a conflict of interest, and an associated right to request that this be noted in the minutes.[1259] One possible problem with this clause is the same as with the analogous statutory provision: its lack of enforceability. This is emphasized by the recommendatory nature of the WSE Best Practice, which is commonly described as a code of corporate governance.[1260]

The WSE Best Practice also confers on management the power to seek approval from the supervisory board for a transaction with a shareholder who owns at least 5% of the votes, or with a related party.[1261] A few observations must be made in this connection. First, in Germany neither the CGC (whether the 2017 or the draft 2020 version) nor statutory law dictates supervisory board approval for RPTs with shareholders – Polish law is unique here. Second, the WSE Best Practice defines related parties in the same manner as IAS 24 and therefore governs RPTs with a company's key management personnel, including management and board members of subsidiaries. Third, board approval is not mandatory: it *may* be requested by management, meaning that a biased management would be reluctant to make such a request. Taken literally, this provision prevents supervisory boards from initiating the approval procedure for a contentious RPT without a formal request from management. It is therefore doubtful that this legal provision should be regarded as flawless.

[4] Approval by a Disinterested Body in the Netherlands

Unlike Germany and Poland, the Netherlands does not place the entire weight of deciding on RPTs on the supervisory board's shoulders. At least, it does not do so initially, having introduced other procedural safeguards to protect companies against self-dealing. The Netherlands is one of the group of jurisdictions where conflicted transactions are conditional mainly on disclosure and a decision by a disinterested

1259. WSE Best Practice, V.Z.2, V.Z.4.
1260. *Ibid.*, 2.
1261. *Ibid.*, V.Z.5.

company body.[1262] This means that if an officer has a direct or indirect conflict of personal interest, he or she is prohibited from participating in the decision-making process regarding the RPT.[1263] As opposed to Polish statutory company law, in the Netherlands, the rule prohibiting officers from participating in the deliberation and adoption of conflicted resolutions applies equally to BVs and NVs, and not only for management[1264] but also for the supervisory board.[1265] If management is incapable of adopting the resolution, or if the conflict of interest is with a member of the supervisory board, the decision rests with the supervisory board. If the company does not have a supervisory board, or if the supervisory board is incapable of deciding, the authority lies with the shareholders, unless the company's articles of association state otherwise. A breach of this procedure will potentially lead to the annulment of the resolution approving the transaction[1266] and an order to compensate any loss or damage inflicted by the harmful conduct of the officers or a counterparty benefitting from the RPT.[1267] Some of the commentaries on these provisions in the BW opts for a literal interpretation, emphasizing the importance of the words 'personal interest' in their application.[1268] Under this interpretation, officers are permitted to participate in the deliberations and decisions of their respective bodies if, for instance, they only perform a certain function within the legal entity, without having any personal interest. However, in light of recent case law of the Enterprise Court of Amsterdam, and taking into account the overarching effect of the principle of reasonableness and fairness in corporate disputes, a broader approach seems appropriate.[1269] It might be incompatible with the principles of law for the notion of a personal interest to carry so much weight that it allows deliberations and decision-making if the officer concerned is acting in conflict with his or her non-private qualitative interests. It seems that the Enterprise Court's views on conflicts of interest, which is heavily influenced by the overarching effect of the principle of reasonableness and fairness in company relationships (Article 2:8 BW), have a wider scope than a strict statute-based interpretation.

The use of the mechanism of approval by disinterested officers reflects how corporate governance works in the Netherlands. Most companies in the Netherlands have a classical two-tier board structure, although the legislature recently introduced the option of a one-tier board.[1270] A series of new provisions under Book 2 of the BW came into effect on 1 January 2013, allowing companies to choose between the one-tier and the two-tier system in their articles of association.[1271] If the company opts for the

1262. Gerner-Beuerle C, Paech P and Schuster EP, 146.
1263. BW, Article 2:129(6), 2:140(5), 2:239(6), and 2:250(5); for the definition of a conflict of interest and the distinction between direct and indirect conflicts of interest, *see* Chapter 2.
1264. BW, Article 2:129(6) and 2:239(6).
1265. *Ibid.*, Article 2:140(5) and 2:250(5).
1266. *Ibid.*, Article 2:15(1)(a).
1267. *Ibid.*, Articles 2:9 and 6:162.
1268. Bartman SM and Dorresteijn AF, 913, 916.
1269. *Ibid.*, 919; BW, Article 2:8, 2:9(1); *Intergamma, Decision of 22 December 2017* JOR 2018/210 (Enterprise Court of Amsterdam), paragraph 3:35.
1270. BW, Article 2:129a and 2:239a; Bill amending Book 2 of the BW, Parliamentary Proceedings II 2009/10, 31 763, No. A.
1271. BW, Article 2:129a, 2:164a, 2:239a and 2:274a.

one-tier board, the executive directors do not decide on all issues: they are subject to monitoring by the non-executive directors, who also make nominations and determine the officers' remuneration.[1272]

If a company decides to adopt the two-tier system, it must form a supervisory board. However, only large companies have an actual obligation to form a supervisory board or include non-executive directors on the board. Both private companies (BVs) and public companies (NVs) are viewed as large companies if they meet certain legislative criteria in terms of issued capital and reserves, the existence of a works council and number of employees (more than one hundred), and must file a statement to that effect with the commercial register.[1273] Companies that do not meet those requirements are not required to file a statement with the commercial register to change their status and, accordingly, are exempt from the duty to establish a supervisory board or appoint non-executive directors.[1274]

As the foregoing illustrates, the Dutch system of placing the authority to decide on RPTs with the supervisory board is not a universal solution. Companies that have opted for the one-tier system or (for non-large companies) have decided not to introduce either model simply do not have a supervisory board. Granting decision-making powers to disinterested members of the management or supervisory board is therefore a more appropriate rule in a mixed system of corporate governance. Nevertheless, the codifiers of the Dutch CGC have stressed that the Netherlands has traditionally adhered to the dual system and have drafted the CGC to reflect the demands of the two-tier board model.[1275] Only one of the CGC's five chapters addresses the one-tier board structure, while the others contain recommendations for companies with a supervisory board. The concept chosen for the Dutch CGC has influenced the regulation of RPTs, and supervisory boards therefore have the authority to rule on decisions to enter into the following types of RPT: (i) transactions with conflicts of interest involving management or supervisory board members that are of material significance to the company and/or the board member concerned;[1276] (ii) transactions with natural persons or legal entities holding at least 10% of shares that are materially significant to the company and/or to the shareholder concerned;[1277] and (iii) loans, guarantees and similar transactions with management and supervisory board members.[1278] These regulations for RPTs reinforce the role of the supervisory board and have done nothing to diminish the influence of the one-tier system of corporate governance in the Netherlands. Data on appointments of former managers to their companies' supervisory boards provide evidence that one-tier boards are becoming more common in Dutch corporate reality.[1279]

1272. *Ibid.*, Article 2:129a(1) and 2:239a(1).
1273. *Ibid.*, Article 2:153(2) and 2:263(2).
1274. *Ibid.*, Article 2:140(1) and 2:250(1).
1275. Dutch CGC, 8.
1276. *Ibid.*, 2.7.4.
1277. *Ibid.*, 2.7.5.
1278. *Ibid.*, 2.7.6.
1279. Maassen G and Van Den Bosch F, 'On the Supposed Independence of Two-Tier Boards: Formal Structure and Reality in the Netherlands' (1999) 7 Corporate Governance: An International Review 31, 36-37.

As this research shows, Germany uses the system of board approval to prevent or mitigate conflicts of interest involving officers only:[1280] conflicts of interest of shareholders are not addressed by this strategy. The same is true for Polish law, as far as the statutory provisions (the KSH) are concerned. However, under the WSE Best Practice, supervisory board approval may be requested for significant RPTs with shareholders holding more than 5% of the share capital. No such provision is included in the 2017 and 2020 versions of the German CGC, whose scope is confined only to conflicts of interest of management and supervisory board members. Regulation of RPTs in the Netherlands, in turn, is similar to the system used in Poland. While the BW uses procedural safeguards only for the conflicts of interest involving management and supervisory board members, the provisions of the Dutch CGC expand the scope of the requirement of supervisory board approval to include RPTs with shareholders holding at least 10% of the share capital.[1281]

[5] Board Approval and Related Procedure in Ukraine

Unlike in Germany, Poland and the Netherlands, in Ukraine it is statutory law that dictates supervisory board approval for RPTs with shareholders. As a rule, in public companies it is the supervisory board that possesses the authority to approve transactions with interest, including RPTs, representing more than 1% of the company's assets, where the transaction is conducted with any of the following categories of persons: company officers, including members of the management or supervisory board or another company body; their affiliated persons; shareholders holding 25% or more of the share capital; their affiliated persons; legal entities in which any of the persons listed above is a company officer; other persons as identified in the articles of association.[1282] For private companies, shareholders may include similar approval provisions in the articles of association, subject to unanimous shareholder approval.[1283]

Similarly to some of the other jurisdictions in this study, Ukraine uses a set-up closer to the two-tier system of corporate governance, in that all listed public companies and non-listed public companies with ten or more shareholders are required to have a supervisory board.[1284] If a public company does not have a supervisory

1280. The term 'officer' is used here to refer to members of the management and supervisory boards.
1281. On the one hand, the provision in the Dutch CGC is stricter than its counterpart in the WSE Best Practice, as it uses more imperative wording: the supervisory board does not require a request from management to start the approval proceedings. On the other hand, the shareholding threshold is higher in the Dutch CGC (*10% v. 5%* in the WSE Best Practice), and the Dutch CGC does not make RPTs with other related parties subject to board approval.
1282. JSC Law of Ukraine, Article 71(2); for a more detailed description of related parties under the JSC Law of Ukraine and other Ukrainian statute, *see* Chapters 1 and 2.
1283. LLC Law of Ukraine, Article 45.
1284. The suggestion was expressed to extend the requirement to all types of JSCs, because Ukraine belongs to a two-tier system of corporate governance (Radwan A, Nadzon A and Zdiruk V, 37).

board, the supervisory board functions are performed by the shareholders' meeting,[1285] rather than by non-executive directors as in the Netherlands. Consequently, approval from disinterested directors, as described in the Dutch BW, is not a feature of the management of Ukrainian public companies. The role of management is reduced to taking receipt of information concerning transactions with interest from potential related parties and passing it on to the supervisory board.[1286] However, the absence of a majority-of-the-minority approval rule for the management board (due to the acceptance of a two-tier board model) does not mean that the supervisory board has the authority to decide if it is composed of interested members. For a transaction to be approved, a majority of the disinterested members of the supervisory board must vote in favour of the resolution, or even one disinterested member if no other members are disinterested.[1287] In addition, the supervisory board is required to bring in a third party (an independent auditor or another sufficiently qualified expert) to help review the transaction.[1288] If the company does not have a supervisory board, if all the supervisory board members are interested or if the transaction value is 10% or more of the company's assets according to its financial statements, the shareholders must decide on its approval.[1289] The shareholders' meeting may also rule on the issue if the supervisory board does not do so within thirty days or if it refuses to approve the transaction. The Principles of Corporate Governance, which serve as a substitute for a CGC,[1290] also prevent interested supervisory board members from deliberating and voting on a resolution or transaction.[1291]

As the foregoing shows, the JSC Law of Ukraine contains highly detailed rules for the procedure of board approval for RPTs compared with the rules for RPTs in statutory law in the other jurisdictions analysed here, and with the Principles of Corporate Governance that are in effect in Ukraine. Besides introducing the system of approval for transactions with interest by disinterested supervisory board members, it also provides for other procedural aspects that must be taken into account, including disclosure to management, a fairness opinion from a third party and a time period (thirty days) within which the supervisory board must decide on the transaction. The question then is what the consequences are of breaching these rules. According to the JSC Law of Ukraine, if the correct procedure is not followed, the transaction will create, change or terminate rights and duties of the JSC only if the company subsequently approves it using in the same procedure.[1292] This version of the clause became effective on 1 May

1285. JSC Law of Ukraine, Article 51(2). In LLCs, the supervisory board may be formed if shareholders wish so (LLC Law of Ukraine, Article 38(1)).
1286. JSC Law of Ukraine, Article 71(4).
1287. *Ibid.*, Article 71(6).
1288. *Ibid.*, Article 71(5).
1289. *Ibid.*, Article 71(7).
1290. *See* Chapter 2 for a detailed description and analysis of the Principles.
1291. Principles of Corporate Governance, approved by the Decision of the National Securities and Stock Market Commission of Ukraine of 22 July 2014, No. 955 [Pryntsypy korporatyvnoho upravlinnia, zatverdzheni rishenniam Natsionalnoyi komisii z tsinnykh paperiv ta fondovoho rynku vid 22 lypnia 2014 roku No. 955], 3.3.2(B).
1292. JSC Law of Ukraine, Article 72(1).

2016;[1293] previously, Article 72 of the JSC Law of Ukraine allowed any transaction concluded in breach of the procedural requirements to be invalidated. Following the legislative provisions that were in place previously, the economic courts in Ukraine have invalidated transactions with interest that were in breach of the procedural rules under the JSC Law of Ukraine. For instance, the Supreme Court of Ukraine has confirmed decisions of the Court of First Instance and the appellate court that a purchase contract between two companies, where a legal representative of one contracting company was simultaneously a member of the audit committee of another contracting company, qualified as a transaction with interest. The contract was invalidated by reason of non-compliance with the procedure outlined in Article 71 of the JSC Law of Ukraine.[1294] Similarly, a collateral agreement was invalidated on the grounds that the guarantor's representative was simultaneously a co-owner and member of the management of the debtor and had failed to inform the shareholders and obtain supervisory board approval, as required.[1295]

Only few judgments have been handed down on claims to invalidate transactions with interest concluded after 1 May 2016, and not all of those claims have reached the Supreme Court. In one case that was decided by the Court of First Instance and subsequently by the appellate court, a contract between a public company and a private company for a real estate transaction was regarded as a transaction with interest, by reason that the wife of a member of the public company's supervisory board signed it on behalf of the private company. Considering that the transaction value represented more than 10% of the company's assets, approval should have been sought from the general meeting of shareholders, which was not done. As a result, the transaction was invalidated based on Articles 71 and 72 of the JSC Law of Ukraine.[1296] In other words, despite the altered wording of Article 72, the manner in which courts interpret this provision is little different from how they interpreted previously. It still serves as a legal basis for annulment claims. Most of the experts surveyed through Google Forms (eleven of nineteen) shared this opinion and selected this remedy as the proper remedy for tackling RPTs. In a recent judgment of the Supreme Court, a transaction with interest was invalidated in a similar fashion: a purchase contract was concluded between a public company and a private company, which was represented by a member of the public company's supervisory board. The Court held that the supervisory board's approval was not sufficient, as all the members of the board had an interest in the transaction, and consequently it should have been referred to the shareholders' meeting for approval.[1297]

An alternative to the remedy of annulling the RPT that parties have applied in court proceedings is to claim invalidation of the decisions of company bodies to approve the RPT. In one case, a supervisory board was held to be incompetent to

1293. Law of Ukraine 'On Amending Certain Legislative Acts on the Protection of Investors' [Zakon Ukrayiny 'Pro vnesennia zmin do deyakykh zakonodavchykh aktiv schodo zakhystu prav investoriv'].
1294. *Judgment of 28 February 2018* Case No. 910/2822/16 (Supreme Court).
1295. *Judgment of 16 February 2016* Case No. 948/845/15 (Supreme Economic Court of Ukraine).
1296. *Judgment of 25 July 2017* Case No. 912/4264/16 (Dnipropetrovsk Appellate Economic Court).
1297. *Judgment of 16 May 2018* Case No. 910/2872/16 (Supreme Court).

decide, by reason of lacking a quorum: of the board's five members, only two disinterested members were present.[1298] In addition, the interested member of the supervisory board had failed to inform the management and supervisory boards of the interest in the transaction. The court invalidated the supervisory board's decision without invalidating the transaction.[1299] While annulment of the board's decision does not automatically mean that the approved transaction is instantly void, successful invalidation of a decision by a company body may lead to a further claim to invalidate the transaction.

In the studied judgments of the Ukrainian courts, transactions with interest were invalidated on compelling grounds, namely that the whole procedure was not followed. What is unclear, however, is whether a transaction with interest can be invalidated if only part of the procedure was followed. This might be the case, for instance, if management was not informed about the conflict of interest in an RPT and did not refer the RPT to the supervisory board for approval, but the supervisory board learned about the RPT from a third party and a majority of the disinterested members approved it, yet failed to request a fairness opinion and gave its approval after the thirty-day deadline had passed. The law does not have any straightforward answers to these situations. Article 72 of the JSC Law of Ukraine, if read literally, attaches the negative consequences to any procedural non-compliance. However, it would be undesirable for RPTs to be invalidated in every single instance, even where no actual harm has been caused to any stakeholders. The system should react mainly to 'significant procedural defects'.[1300] The most important factor is that approval must be given by the competent body composed of disinterested members, based on full disclosure.[1301] An approach that adheres too closely to the formalities and penalizes even the smallest breach of procedure would have a cost, acting as a deterrent to many efficient transactions. As such, no reasonable justification exists for annulling RPTs that are approved outside the formal period. This is amplified by the fact that supervisory board approval may be obtained *ex post*, as in other jurisdictions, notably Germany.[1302] At the same time, the requirement of a fairness opinion should not be ignored so easily. The law now assigns a key role to the external expert engaged by the supervisory board.[1303] Without a fairness opinion, the supervisory board's approval might be held to lack a proper basis of full disclosure. In the hierarchy of procedural breaches, therefore, failure to obtain a fairness opinion cannot be viewed as immaterial but should trigger negative consequences.

1298. The case was decided according to the law that was effective before 1 May 2016, under which the supervisory board was competent only if a majority of its members were disinterested. This was changed on 1 May 2016, and now, even if only one member is disinterested, the issue may be decided by that one member.
1299. *Judgment of 7 September 2016* Case No. 910/29782/15 (Kyiv Appellate Economic Court).
1300. Sáez MI and Riaño D, 'Corporate Governance and the Shareholders' Meeting: Voting and Litigation' (2013) 14 European Business Organization Law Review 343, 361.
1301. Jacobson MA, 'Interested Director Transactions and the (Equivocal) Effects of Shareholder Ratification' (1996) 21 Delawer Journal of Corporate Law 981, 1024.
1302. AktG, Articles 89(5), 114(2), 115(4).
1303. Except for non-listed public companies, where a fairness opinion is only mandatory if the company's articles of association so require.

While the law should obviously react only to serious procedural breaches, some RPTs might cause the company losses despite formal compliance with the procedural safeguards. Unquestioning reliance on formal board approval is therefore not always the proper route for every RPT. In the Google Forms survey, the experts' opinions on whether or not to subject approved RPTs to additional review were divided almost equally (*10 v. 9*). Those who were against annulling approved RPTs most likely felt that these changes would bring an unacceptable degree of uncertainty, and so preferred to preserve the status quo instead of changing the system. Still, it would be wrong to entirely rule out the possibility that an RPT approved by a company's company bodies might have detrimental consequences. Perhaps it was the latter argument that inspired the Parliament of Ukraine to amend the JSC Law of Ukraine to allow approved transactions with interest to be invalidated based on a shareholder's application if an independent review confirms that their terms are less favourable than usual market terms. This amendment was adopted on 20 September 2019 and entered into force on 17 October 2019.[1304]

Besides the invalidation of RPTs or decisions of company bodies, Ukrainian corporate law allows damages to be claimed from interested persons if the public company suffered harm as a result of a breach of the procedural requirements.[1305] According to the amendments of 20 September 2019, the interested person would also be jointly and severally liable to pay the damages, together with the person who breached the procedures. While these claims are subject to the general requirements for damages,[1306] unlike invalidation claims their use is currently not widespread. The recent addition of derivative actions to Ukraine's procedural economic law, granting shareholders with 10% or more of the share capital the power to sue on behalf of the company, applies only to claims for damages against company officers.[1307] If the loss or damage was caused by other interested persons, the shareholders would have no standing to claim damages on behalf of the company. Surprisingly, under the 20 September 2019 amendment, shareholders are entitled to seek invalidation of a transaction with interest that is concluded on non-market terms, yet no explicit provision exists that authorizes them to claim damages on behalf of the company. In reality, this means two claims will need to be brought to claim damages for a transaction with interest on non-market terms: first, an invalidation claim by the shareholder, followed by a claim for damages by the company, represented by management. Moreover, based on the wording of the statute, shareholders are not permitted, or at least not explicitly, to claim invalidation of transactions with interest on grounds that they were concluded in breach of the procedural requirements. In order to ensure better protection of minority shareholders and to close the existing

1304. Law of Ukraine 'On Amending Certain Legislative Acts of Ukraine regarding the Stimulation of Investment Activity in Ukraine' [Zakon Ukrayiny 'Pro vnesennia zmin do deyakykh zakonodavchykh aktiv Ukrayiny schodo stymuliuvannia investytsiynoyi diyalnosti v Ukrayini'].
1305. JSC Law of Ukraine, Article 71(11).
1306. CCU, Article 1166.
1307. Economic Procedural Code of Ukraine [Hospodarskyi protsesualnyi kodeks Ukrayiny], Article 54.

regulatory gap, therefore, an obvious need exists to authorize shareholders to claim invalidation of transactions with interest that breached the procedural requirements, and to expand the scope of derivative suits to include other remedies, e.g. the right to claim damages from interested persons.

In general, the idea of granting shareholders the right to initiate invalidation of RPTs is laudable, especially where managers or their affiliated persons are the interested persons: they will be disincentivized to claim annulment of RPTs on behalf of the company.[1308] Instead, minority shareholders would be the appropriate group to file the invalidation claim, and it makes sense to give shareholders standing in claims regarding wrongful RPTs.[1309] At the same time, this demands a careful approach, since abusive enforcement of remedies against RPTs could destabilize the company's activity.[1310] The legislative amendments need to consider the high risk of corporate raiding and the possibility of repeated abuse of rights by willing shareholders, and it is hard to disagree with Tetiana Shtym's argument that the introduction of derivative suits in Ukraine should be combined with meaningful preventive safeguards against potential abuses.[1311] One way of strengthening the regulation of derivative suits is to introduce a minimum share ownership duration in order for a shareholder to have standing, e.g. the six-month minimum applied in Japan, as described by Yuliya Khort.[1312] Still, these risks do not by themselves negate the need to increase protection of minority shareholders. Proper implementation of the right of shareholders to challenge RPTs might improve Ukraine's Doing Business ranking, as it did for Afghanistan.[1313] In addition, as has been argued in literature, depriving shareholders of the possibility to protect their rights is incompatible with the views of the European Court of Human Rights.[1314] Here, the effect of abuse is mitigated by the fact that shareholders would be regarded as acting on behalf of the company, rather than for themselves.

[B] The Decision Rights Strategy

The decision rights strategy shifts the approval requirement from the company's officers to the general meeting of shareholders. The result is a more costly and cumbersome procedure. Nevertheless, it would be negligent to completely reject this form of safeguard: it is particularly useful for situations where the board either consists of interested members only or is reluctant to decide on a transaction.

1308. Cheung YL, 5.
1309. Boyarchuk K, 'Pravovi naslidky porushennia poriadku vchynennia pravochyniv iz zatsikavlenistiu' (2014) Nashe pravo 168, 170.
1310. Chyzhyk H, 'Pravochyny iz zainteresovannistiu ta znachni pravochyny v aktsionernykh tovarystvakh Ukrayiny' (2013) Studentskyi yurydychnyi zhurnal: dodatok do zhurnalu 'Pravo Ukrayiny' 45, 46.
1311. Shtym T, 189.
1312. Khort YV, 'Company Law in Ukraine: Recent Regulatory Developments' (2018) 80 **Актуальні проблеми держави і права** 179, 181.
1313. *Doing Business 2019: Training for Reform*, 6.
1314. Murashko N, 'Some Aspects of Shareholders' Rights Protection: Legal Practice Review' (2013) Studentskyi yurydychnyi zhurnal: dodatok do zhurnalu 'Pravo Ukrayiny' 69, 72.

The shareholder approval system is comparatively less widespread than board approval and is confined to significant transactions where, most commonly, the related parties are controllers,[1315] or where the shareholders' rights have suffered an impairment.[1316] Germany, Poland and the Netherlands are among the jurisdictions where shareholders in public companies have the right to block or approve any RPT conducted within two years after the company's incorporation if it represents more than one-tenth of the company's assets.[1317] In those countries, the procedure for these transactions is complicated and is based on Article 9 of the former Second Council Directive, now Article 52 of the Directive 2017/1132. Named *Nachgründung*, meaning 'after-establishment', its roots lie in creditor protection, and its purpose is to curb circumvention efforts, i.e. circumvention of capital formation requirements.

In Germany, any agreement under which a company acquires existing or future facilities for a consideration that is greater than one-tenth of its share capital must be approved by the shareholders and recorded in the commercial register;[1318] otherwise, the agreement is unenforceable. Before the general meeting of shareholders consents to the agreement, the text of the agreement must be made available to all shareholders, and its meaning should be explained before the meeting.[1319] Moreover, the supervisory board and the formation auditors must analyse it prior to the meeting and report on their findings.[1320] At the meeting of shareholders, no less than three quarters of the shares must be represented to pass the resolution.[1321] Lastly, even if these formalities are observed, the courts may deny registration of the agreement, if the report prepared by the supervisory board is found to be inaccurate, incomplete or incompatible with statutory provisions, or if the consideration for the assets is unreasonably high.[1322] In other words, these agreements are subject to both *ex ante* (by the supervisory board, auditors and shareholders) and *ex post* reviews (by the courts). Moreover, the court review is both substantive and procedural, and its analysis goes beyond the scope of the agreement's procedural fairness.

In the Netherlands, the test for these agreements involves a similarly high threshold. Transactions to acquire property belonging to a founder of the company, or that belonged to a founder within one year prior to the incorporation, that are performed before two years have passed since the incorporation and without the consent of the general meeting can be declared null and void.[1323] The agreement must be made available at the company's offices for inspection by all its shareholders;[1324] it

1315. Enriques L and others, 'Related-Party Transactions' in Kraakman R and others (eds), *The Anatomy of Corporate Law: A Comparative and Functional Approach* (3rd edn, Oxford University Press 2017), 156; OECD, *Related Party Transactions and Minority Shareholder Rights* (OECD Publishing, 2012), 34.
1316. Ungerer F, 119.
1317. *Study on Minority Shareholders Protection, Final Report* (prepared by TGS Baltic 2018), 143.
1318. AktG, Article 52(1).
1319. *Ibid.*, Article 52(2).
1320. *Ibid.*, Article 52(3), 52(4).
1321. *Ibid.*, Article 52(5).
1322. *Ibid.*, Article 52(7).
1323. BW, Article 2:94c(1).
1324. *Ibid.*, Article 2:94c(5).

must also include a description stating the value, the consideration and the valuation method applied, the officers' signatures[1325] and a statement by a registered auditor.[1326] The original or a copy of the statement must be deposited with the commercial register within eight days after the transaction is effected or approved.[1327]

Poland has a similar requirement. Any agreement to acquire facilities from a founder or shareholder in excess of one-tenth of the company's assets, before two years have passed since the incorporation, must be approved by two-thirds of the votes in a public company (S.A.).[1328] Polish law is stricter than other regimes, in that the requirement of shareholder consent also extends to agreements where a dependent company, partnership or cooperative of the company is either the beneficiary or the seller of the assets. This makes it more difficult to perform intra-group transactions.[1329] Management is obliged to provide a report on the agreement, which is then scrutinized by a specially appointed auditor and presented to the general meeting.[1330] This procedure is not used for acquisitions in public procurement, liquidation, bankruptcy or foreclosure proceedings.[1331]

Besides these provisions targeted at post-formation agreements by public companies, the KSH also contains a similar requirement for Polish private companies (sp. z o.o.). Under Article 229 of the KSH, a vote of approval from the shareholders is required for any agreement to acquire real estate or a share in real estate or to acquire fixed assets for a price greater than one quarter of the company's initial capital, but no less than PLN 50,000, if the agreement is formed before two years have passed since the company was registered, unless the articles of association already made reference to the agreement. While this provision does not concern RPTs, the two-year period is reminiscent of the rules for public companies described above.

Reference to the decision rights strategy in Polish companies, for both private and public companies, is also made in Article 15 of the KSH. As discussed above, this provision covers the types of RPTs that pose the greatest risks (credit, loans, suretyships and similar contracts) with members of the management board, the supervisory board or the audit committee, a procurator or a liquidator as contracting parties or beneficiaries. In contrast to how the KSH deals with these transactions, under Articles 89 and 115 of the German AktG, loan agreements with members of the management board or the supervisory board must be approved by the supervisory board, meaning that the agent incentives strategy is employed, rather the decision rights strategy.

In addition to the statutory use of the decision rights strategy, Polish law also employs this strategy at the level of the WSE Best Practice. Under the WSE Best Practice, significant agreements with related parties are subject to a vote of the general meeting.[1332] Despite their broad scope, especially considering that the WSE Best

1325. *Ibid.*, Article 2:94c(2).
1326. *Ibid.*, Article 2:94c(3).
1327. *Ibid.*, Article 2:94c(6).
1328. KSH, Article 394(1).
1329. *Ibid.*, Article 394(1), 394(2).
1330. *Ibid.*, Article 394(3).
1331. *Ibid.*, Article 394(4).
1332. WSE Best Practice, V.Z.5.

Practice views related parties in the same way as the IASs do, the code's provisions are worded in abstract terms, affording a wide range of discretion to the companies implementing the code.

Besides the option of approval of RPTs by the supervisory board, a disinterested body or the general meeting of shareholders alone, another possibility is to render RPTs subject to the approval of multiple company bodies. For example, in the Netherlands, the idea has been put forward that Article 2:107a of the BW entitles the general meeting of shareholders to have input on management resolutions regarding RPTs.[1333] This article grants the general meeting the authority to decide on management resolutions that involve a material change in the identity or character of the company or its undertaking. While its broad scope means that its provisions may also extend to RPT-related resolutions, the actual text makes no reference to RPTs, and as such it is not aimed specifically at RPTs, but serves more as a general legal basis for various types of decisions.

In Ukraine, the use of the decision rights strategy is set forth directly in the JSC Law of Ukraine for transactions with interest representing 10% or more of a company's assets according to its financial statements, or where the company either does not have a supervisory board or where supervisory board is composed of interested members only.[1334] This requirement is an extension of the board approval rule that subjects material RPTs to a shareholder vote and carries the same negative consequences for breaches of these procedural safeguards. The JSC Law of Ukraine explicitly places the decision-making authority in the hands of disinterested shareholders, codifying the 'majority-of-the-minority' rule.[1335] Its effect is slightly curtailed by the fact that shareholders in non-listed public companies are not permitted to stipulate this restriction in the company's articles of association.[1336] However, this is a reasonable rule, given that non-listed public companies are essentially private entities with a limited number of minority shareholders. Controllers of these companies often act as related parties in transactions, and consequently would be barred from approving many transactions. The same reasoning holds true for private companies, where rules on RPT approval are optional.

In light of the foregoing, it is important to stress that the optional nature of the rules for RPTs by private companies is not universally supported. The majority of experts who responded to the Google Forms survey expressed the opinion that rules are needed for RPTs of private companies similar to those that apply to public companies. This opinion can be explained by the fact that many large enterprises are registered as private companies, and consequently private companies should not necessarily be viewed as unimportant or as having no minority shareholders. If a private company is sufficiently large to have an impact on the economy or if it has minority shareholders, it would therefore be necessary to introduce additional safeguards to protect its

1333. Kamerstuk 35058 nr. 3, available at: https://zoek.officielebekendmakingen.nl/dossier/35058/kst-35058-3?resultIndex=3&sorttype=1&sortorder=4.
1334. JSC Law of Ukraine, Article 71(4).
1335. Goshen Z, 'The Efficiency of Controlling Corporate Self-Dealing: Theory Meets Reality', 402.
1336. JSC Law of Ukraine, Article 71(4).

stakeholders' rights. For private companies that have the potential to significantly impact the economy or that have minority shareholders, therefore, optional procedural safeguards do not always represent the best approach.

In addition, in 2018 the JSC Law of Ukraine added a new provision for RPTs that a company conducts with its founders within two years after its incorporation and that have a market value of 10% or more of the company's assets as measured in its most recent financial statements (or its share capital, if it has not yet prepared any financial statements).[1337] Interestingly, the provision appeared in Article 70, governing fundamental transactions, yet it is covered by the same regime that applies to transactions with interest (Article 71), being subject to a vote by shareholders and carrying disclosure requirements.

[C] General Notes on Board Independence and Procedural Safeguards

As can be inferred from the matters described above, each of the studied jurisdictions uses procedural safeguards to govern RPTs, with process regulation carrying weight in Ukraine in particular. Both the agent incentives and decision rights strategies for RPTs have been developed for Ukrainian public companies. Strict rules on approval of transactions with interest go hand in hand with the formal approach taken by courts to invalidate transactions with interest concluded in breach of the procedural requirements, without any deep analysis of the economic effect of those transactions. The fact that the courts do not evaluate the effects of RPTs where RPTs are subsequently approved seems remarkable in some cases. Obviously, the company's position might suffer from RPTs that are concluded in accordance with the procedural requirements, but manifestly on non-market terms. The most recent changes, of 20 September 2019, seek to rectify this situation, by allowing invalidation of transactions with interest that are compliant with the procedural requirements, but are on non-market terms. Logically, these statutory and judicial approaches pose a fundamental question: whether the current process regulation of RPTs is efficient enough.

Procedural safeguards can be regarded as efficient if they successfully prevent tunnelling, as the major destructive consequence of abusive RPTs, without deterring value-creating transactions. Accomplishing these goals is subject to two conditions. First, the mechanism must subject only high-risk transactions to the procedural safeguards, while leaving beneficial or unimportant transactions untouched. This is given shape through the definition of a related party and by establishing appropriate materiality criteria (thresholds), though it is vital to strike a balance between underinclusive and overinclusive definitions. The definition of a related party and materiality criteria have been discussed at length in Chapter 3. Second, once a transaction is subject to the screening by a company's internal bodies, those bodies must possess characteristics that make the result efficient. One of those necessary characteristics is independence.

1337. *Ibid.*, Article 70(6).

Ukrainian law places a great deal of value on the presence of independent directors on the supervisory board. For listed public companies and in non-listed public companies where more than 50% of the shares are owned by the state or by wholly state-owned companies, one-third of the supervisory board's members (with a minimum of two) must be independent directors.[1338] These natural persons are subject to demanding requirements on the absence of conflicts of interest, inspired by the best practice provisions.[1339] Independent directors qualify as disinterested members of a supervisory board in terms of the approval rule if they have no interest in the transaction under review. If they do, they must abstain from the supervisory board's vote. This means that the notion of independence cannot be equated with the notion of an independent director. Unfortunately, it is impossible to fully guarantee the independence of supervisory board members;[1340] even if an independent director who at the time of his or her appointment had no ties to the company or its related parties, and who met all other formal criteria, might not, in the real world, always act in the best interests of the company. It is therefore not unsurprising that a trend has emerged, following the corporate scandals in Europe, to apply stricter standards for the independence of directors.[1341]

Of course, empirical evidence in some jurisdictions suggests that independent directors have been used to great effect in privatized companies.[1342] However, one size does not fit all, and it is doubtful whether the guardians of public investors would perform their duties effectively in a blockholder corporate environment.[1343] For instance, the highly innovative solution of granting minority shareholders the right to veto appointments, reappointments and termination of directors, combined with the lack of input for controllers in the reappointment and termination of directors,[1344] is hardly appropriate for family-controlled businesses with almost no outside shareholders. Even for listed companies, independent directors are not a panacea. In spite of the fact that arguments are still made to increase the numbers of independent directors on supervisory boards to improve corporate governance,[1345] evidence to the contrary shows that directors can circumvent these safeguards, e.g. by holding joint meetings.[1346]

It is beyond question that procedures for appointing and reappointing supervisory board members must be phrased in a way that ensures that only diligent and

1338. *Ibid.*, Article 53(4).
1339. *Ibid.*, Article 53-1.
1340. Enriques L, 'Bad Apples, Bad Oranges: A Comment from Old Europe on Post-Enron Corporate Governance Reforms' (2003) 38 Wake Forest Law Review 911, 927.
1341. Hopt KJ and Leyens PC, 'Board Models in Europe: Recent Developments of Internal Corporate Governance Structures in Germany, the United Kingdom, France, and Italy' (2004) 1 European Company and Financial Law Review 135, 164.
1342. Enriques L, 'Bad Apples, Bad Oranges: A Comment from Old Europe on Post-Enron Corporate Governance Reforms', 928.
1343. *Ibid.*, 934.
1344. Bebchuk LA and Hamdani A, 'Independent Directors and Controlling Shareholders' (2017) 165 University of Pennsylvania Law Review 1271, 1293.
1345. Peck S and Ruigrok W, 'Hiding Behind the Flag? Prospects for Change in German Corporate Governance' (2000) 18 European Management Journal 420, 424.
1346. Maassen G and Van Den Bosch F, 36-37.

responsible persons are elected: persons who would protect the interests of company rather than those of the persons who appointed them and the persons close to them. However, a discussion of such procedures goes beyond the scope of this work, and moreover 'independence as it relates to RPTs' is a situational concept that needs to be considered separately for each transaction.[1347] In order to maintain situational independence, it is necessary to prevent interested persons from participating in the deliberations and votes on transactions in listed companies and to attach enforceable sanctions to any breach of those rules. For non-listed companies, the solution is more firm-specific, given the various possible corporate ownership scenarios. For non-listed companies with large numbers of shareholders (more than 100[1348]), the idea of a supervisory board effectively protecting the interests of the company's various stakeholders, e.g. by approving or blocking RPTs, sounds reasonable. However, where the company is in the hands of one or more blockholders who wish to exercise effective control over the company's transactions, regarding them as interested persons and depriving them of the right to vote on some transactions is not an efficient solution. In the absence of minority shareholders, controlling shareholders should not be burdened with unnecessary regulations that stand in the way of them governing their own business. The business model in these cases should be designed to promote business activity and deter managerial self-dealing. Most often, this is achieved by creating a specific body to rule on self-interested transactions.[1349] That being said, it is vital not to lose sight of the interests of other stakeholders, including creditors and employees.

§5.03 INFORMATION RIGHTS AND DISCLOSURE OF RPTs

[A] Types of Disclosure Duties

In EU Member States, disclosure of RPTs is required pursuant to two sets of rules: (i) national rules and (ii) the rules of EU law. The rules of EU law on mandatory disclosure of RPTs, which are described in length in the Accounting Directive, the IAS Regulation and the Transparency Directive,[1350] are discussed in section §5.05. The present section covers the national rules on disclosure of RPTs, including statute and CGCs, i.e. what specific Member States have to offer in addition to the requirements. Disclosure rules come in two types: (i) duties of related parties to disclose information about RPTs (often as part of a more general obligation to disclose conflicts of interest) and (ii)

1347. Hill CA and McDonnell B, 'Sanitizing Interested Transactions' (2011) 36 Delaware Journal of Corporate Law 12, 931.

1348. This figure is not occasional, because before 1 May 2016 it served as a criterion for distinguishing between non-listed and listed JSCs in Ukraine. Now, the use of pre-emptive rights is prohibited for Ukrainian JSCs with more than 100 shareholders.

1349. Parkinson JE, 236.

1350. The provisions of the EU instruments are often applied in combination with relevant implementing provisions of national legislation. For example, *see* Article 132 of the German Securities Trading Act in the version of 9 September 1998 (Federal Law Gazette [Bundesgesetzblatt] I p. 2708), most recently amended by Article 12 of the Law of 25 March 2019 (Federal Law Gazette I p. 357), implementing the Transparency Directive.

duties of the company to make information on RPTs public or available to particular stakeholders, including the duties of disclosure assigned to specific company bodies.

[B] Disclosure Duty of Related Parties

Disclosure duties of related parties are intrinsically linked to the procedural regulations outlined above, in that disclosure is often followed by relevant RPT being approved or blocked. Under the 2017 version of the German CGC, a member of management is required to inform the supervisory board and the other management board members without undue delay.[1351] This disclosure duty is supplemented by supervisory board approval for significant RPTs.[1352] Under the new draft 2020 CGC, managers are obliged to also inform the chair of the management board.[1353] Some authors have inferred this informational duty of management board members from the statutory provision authorizing the supervisory board to represent the company's interests in its dealings with the management board.[1354] Supervisory board members also have a duty to inform the other members of an RPT (under both the 2017 version and the draft 2020 version of the German CGC),[1355] followed by the approval requirement in the case of advisory or other service agreements or contracts for work (under the 2017 version only).[1356] These duties stem from the general duty of loyalty of officers.[1357]

In Poland, similarly, the WSE Best Practice imposes a duty on members of management and supervisory boards to notify the management or the supervisory board of any conflicts of interest, including conflicted transactions.[1358] The only difference is that this provision, if read literally, makes it possible to choose who is notified, i.e. members of the supervisory board may fulfil their duty by informing either the management or the supervisory board. In actuality, this alternative has little practical significance, given that the supervisory board's approval is still required for RPTs.[1359]

The Dutch CGC contains detailed rules for reporting conflicts of interest by related parties, specifying exactly who must be notified. Members of the management board are required to report their conflicts of interest in transactions of significance to the chairman and other members of the management board without delay. A conflicted member of the supervisory board needs to report only to the chairman of the board; if the chairman is also an interested person, however, he or she must disclose all the

1351. German CGC, as amended on 7 February 2017, § 4.3.3.
1352. The qualitative approach is used to define RPTs subject to disclosure and approval (Bava F and Gromis di Trana M, 'Disclosure on Related Party Transactions: Evidence from Italian Listed Companies' (2016) 6 Accounting, Economics and Law-A Convivium 119, 133).
1353. German draft CGC 2020, section E.
1354. Hopt KJ, 'Self-Dealing and Use of Corporate Opportunity and Information: Regulating Directors' Conflicts of Interest', 290.
1355. German CGC, as amended on 7 February 2017, § 5.5.2; German CGC 2019, section E.
1356. German CGC, as amended on 7 February 2017, § 5.5.4.
1357. Enriques L, 'The Law on Company Directors' Self-Dealing: A Comparative Analysis', 314.
1358. WSE Best Practice, V.Z.2.
1359. *Ibid.*, V.Z.5.

relevant information to the board's deputy chairman.[1360] In addition to the provisions of the Dutch CGC, it has been suggested that Dutch case law is moving in the direction of requesting officers to disclose their conflicts of interest to shareholders.[1361]

In Ukraine, the duty of related parties to disclose information on RPTs is both codified in statute and included in the Principles of Corporate Governance. Under the Principles of Corporate Governance, company officers must disclose any conflicts of interest of which they are aware to the company's supervisory board.[1362] Interestingly, the JSC Law of Ukraine specifies another recipient of the information: the management board. The information to be provided by the interested person should explain the details of the interest and the draft transaction.[1363] Performing this duty is the first step towards the approval procedure and triggers the duty of the management board to refer the draft transaction and comments on the associated interest to the supervisory board or, if the company does not have a supervisory board, to the individual shareholders.[1364] Failing to comply with this duty may be viewed as a breach of procedure, as discussed at length in the previous section.

The duty of a related party to disclose conflicts of interest, including information concerning RPTs, was recently codified for LLCs (private companies). Company officers of private companies, including members of the management and supervisory boards and other persons as stipulated in the articles of association, are required to give written notification to both the management and supervisory boards (if the company has one) within two days after they become aware of the conflict of interest.[1365] Disclosing the conflict triggers the duty of management to inform all the company's shareholders within two days after receiving the information.[1366] Unlike for public companies, for private companies disclosure of conflicts of interest does not trigger the procedure of approval by company bodies. For such a disclosure of a conflict of interest (i.e., an RPT) to trigger the approval procedure, the shareholders must agree to include the relevant procedure in the company's articles of association.[1367] Nevertheless, failure to comply with the disclosure is not without consequence: a company officer who fails to disclose a conflict of interest may be dismissed without compensation.[1368]

As the foregoing shows, the jurisdictions in focus mostly require company officers to disclose their conflicts of interest, including conflicts that stem from RPTs. Shareholders do not usually have a duty to inform company bodies about any RPTs, except as dictated by the regulation of transactions with interest in the JSC Law of

1360. Dutch CGC, 2.7.3.
1361. McCahery JA and Vermeulen EPM, 'Corporate Governance Crises and Related Party Transactions: A Post-Parmalat Agenda', 242.
1362. Principles of Corporate Governance, approved by the Decision of the National Securities and Stock Market Commission of Ukraine of 22 July 2014, No. 955 [Pryntsypy korporatyvnoho upravlinnia, zatverdzheni rishenniam Natsionalnoyi komisii z tsinnykh paperiv ta fondovoho rynku vid 22 lypnia 2014 roku No. 955], 3.3.2.
1363. JSC Law of Ukraine, Article 71(4).
1364. *Ibid.*, Article 71(4).
1365. LLC Law of Ukraine, Article 42(6).
1366. *Ibid.*, Article 42(6).
1367. *Ibid.*, Article 45(2).
1368. *Ibid.*, Article 42(8).

Ukraine. Under the JSC Law of Ukraine, shareholders holding 25% or more of the company's share capital and their affiliated persons are required to inform management of future RPTs and submit the relevant information and documents.

[C] Disclosure Duty of Companies

Where a company has a duty to make certain information about RPTs public or available to stakeholders, that duty is often assigned to a specific company body. For instance, the 2017 and 2020 versions of the German CGC dictate that the supervisory board must inform the shareholders' meeting of all conflicts of interest and how they are addressed in the board's report.[1369] At the same time, examples to the contrary also exist, where no specific body is specified. In Poland, under the WSE Best Practice, if the general meeting's approval is required for a significant RPT, the company must provide all shareholders with access to the information needed to assess the impact of the transaction on the company's interests.[1370] In these cases, it does not matter which body performs this duty, though it would probably be the body charged with convening the meeting.

In Germany, for groups of companies that do not have a control agreement, the management boards of public companies (AGs) have a duty to prepare a report on all relationships with affiliated persons within three months after the end of the financial year.[1371] That report must include information about intra-group RPTs, stating any consideration given or received, together with comments from management explaining whether or not the transactions were advantageous.[1372] Although an external auditor must express an opinion on the report,[1373] and the supervisory board must review it,[1374] the report as a whole is not made public. This means that minority shareholders have only indirect access to the report, through the auditors or the supervisory board.[1375]

Another special type of report that is required in connection with RPTs in Germany is the post-formation report, which is prepared by the supervisory board before any post-formation acquisition can be approved, as described in the previous section.[1376] One of the key elements of the procedure for approving this special category of RPTs is sharing information with shareholders about the agreement for the acquisition, which even involves publishing it on the homepage of the company's website.[1377] Unlike in Germany, Poland requires reports on post-formation acquisitions to be prepared by management, verified by auditors and presented to the general

1369. German CGC, as amended on 7 February 2017, § 5.5.3; German draft CGC 2020, section E.
1370. WSE Best Practice, V.Z.5.
1371. AktG, Article 312(1).
1372. *Ibid.*, Article 312(1)(3).
1373. *Ibid.*, Article 313.
1374. *Ibid.*, Article 314.
1375. Enriques L and others, 'Related-Party Transactions' in Kraakman R and others (eds), *The Anatomy of Corporate Law: A Comparative and Functional Approach* (3rd edn, Oxford University Press 2017), 149.
1376. AktG, Article 52.
1377. *Ibid.*, Article 52(2).

meeting of shareholders.[1378] In the Netherlands, rather than a report as in the other jurisdictions, management is charged with a duty to describe the property to be acquired and the consideration to be paid. That description must be signed by the officers and must be made available to the shareholders at the company's offices for reading and making copies.[1379]

In Ukraine, approval from the general meeting of shareholders, based on prior notification, is required for transactions with interest that represent 10% or more of the company's assets according to its financial statements.[1380] By itself, the requirement under Ukrainian law has a broader scope than the rules in other jurisdictions, as it covers all transactions with interest, including (since their recent addition) post-formation transactions with founders. However, in some respects, the notification and approval obligations for post-formation agreements in other jurisdictions are stricter, such as the voting and registration requirements.

On the subject of management reports, the Dutch CGC dictates that they must contain the details of all RPTs with members of the management and supervisory boards and shareholders holding at least 10% of the shares in the company.[1381]

A special note must be made of the mandatory disclosure as required by the IASs, as described in Chapter 3 and mentioned below in section §5.05. Under EU law, the management and supervisory boards of listed companies are collectively responsible for the company's financial statements, the annual report and the corporate governance statement.[1382] These documents generally contain a variety of information regarding the company's status and the prospects for its future development, including, among other information, details of RPTs.[1383] Germany requires two types of periodic disclosure of RPTs: disclosure pursuant to the IASs and disclosure based on the German Commercial Code (for companies that are not oriented on the capital markets).[1384] The main difference between these two types of disclosure is that the Commercial Code requires disclosure only for RPTs that are concluded on non-market terms.[1385] In the Netherlands, companies must present information about material RPTs that are not on market conditions, including the volume of the transaction, the nature of the relationship with the related party and whatever other information concerning the transaction is necessary to provide a clear view of the company's financial condition,[1386] in their financial statements.[1387] In Poland, all listed companies

1378. KSH, Article 394(3).
1379. BW, Article 2:94c(2)(5).
1380. JSC Law of Ukraine, Article 71(7).
1381. Dutch CGC, 2.7.4 and 2.7.5.
1382. Du Plessis JJ and others, *German Corporate Governance in International and European Context* (Springer Science & Business Media 2012), 279.
1383. Schmidt P-J, 'Disclosure and Auditing: A German Auditor's Perspective' in Hopt KJ and others (eds), *Comparative Corporate Governance, Clarendon, Oxford* (Oxford University Press 1998), 747.
1384. German Commercial Code, revised version published in the Federal Law Gazetter [Bundesgesetzblatt], Part III, section 4100-1, most recently amended by Article 3 of the Law of 10 July 2018 (Federal Law Gazette I p. 1102), Articles 285, 314(1).
1385. Ungerer F, 174.
1386. BW, Article 2:381(3).
1387. *Study on Minority Shareholders Protection, Final Report* (Prepared by TGS Baltic 2018), 378.

and banks must apply the IASs when preparing their financial statements. Even non-listed companies must include a section in their financial statements containing additional information and explanatory notes, where any information about RPTs concluded on non-market terms must be presented.[1388]

In Ukraine, the Principles of Corporate Governance dictate that companies must regularly disclose information about decisions concerning the conclusion of RPTs.[1389] Various mechanisms are used for these disclosures. First, enterprises with a public interest, listed public companies, enterprises extracting commercial minerals and enterprises specified by the Cabinet of Ministers of Ukraine are obliged to prepare financial statements in accordance with the IASs, including IAS 24.[1390] Second, companies must use the local accounting standards for related parties, even if they do not apply IASs.[1391] Third, listed public companies must disclose annual, quarterly and special information to the NSSMC of Ukraine and to its general informational database, including information regarding transactions with interest, interested persons and the circumstances creating the interest.[1392] Non-listed public companies are required to disclose those circumstances only in special information (i.e., they do not have a duty to disclose this information periodically).[1393] In other words, all public companies must disclose information regarding approved transactions with interest as special information, which means that this information is disclosed shortly after the triggering event (approval of the transaction). It is recorded in the open database within one day after the event.[1394] These changes were introduced with the amendments that took effect on 1 May 2016.[1395] The first disclosure was carried out on 17 June 2016, by Public JSC National JSC 'Naftogaz Ukrainy', following a transaction for gas supplies on 16 June 2016.[1396] Since then, special information regarding transactions with interest has been

1388. *Ibid.*, 316.
1389. Principles of Corporate Governance, approved by the Decision of the National Securities and Stock Market Commission of Ukraine of 22 July 2014, No. 955 [Pryntsypy korporatyvnoho upravlinnia, zatverdzheni rishenniam Natsionalnoyi komisii z tsinnykh paperiv ta fondovoho rynku vid 22 lypnia 2014 roku No. 955], 4.1.1.
1390. Law of Ukraine 'On Accounting and Financial Reporting in Ukraine' [Zakon Ukrayiny 'Pro bukhgaltersyi oblik ta finansovu zvitnist'], Article 12-1(2, 3).
1391. Accounting Provision (Standard) 23 'Related Party Disclosures', as approved by the order of the Ministry of Finance of Ukraine as of 18 June 2001 No. 303 [Polozhennia (standart) bukhgalterskoho obliku 23 'Rozkryttia informatsii schodo povyazanykh storin', zatverdzhene nakazom Ministerstva finansiv Ukrayiny vid 18 chervnia 2001 r. No. 3030], published in Ofitsiynyi visnyk Ukrayiny, 2001, No. 26, St. 1192.
1392. Law of Ukraine 'On Securities and Stock Market' [Zakon Ukrayiny 'Pro tsinni papery ta fondovyi rynok'], Articles 40(3)(7, 8), 40(5)(8, 9) and 41(1)(5, 6).
1393. *Ibid.*, Articles 40(8), 41(1)(5, 6).
1394. Regulation on Disclosure of Information by Emitents of Securities, approved by the decision of the National Securities and Stock Market Commission of Ukraine, No. 2826 of 3 December 2013 [Polozhennia pro rozkryttia informatsii emitentamy tsinnykh paperiv, zatverdzhene rishenniam Natsionalnoyi komisii z tsinnykh paperiv ta fondovoho rynku No. 2826 vid 3 hrudnia 2013 roku], Chapter II section 1 clause 5.
1395. Law of Ukraine 'On Amending Certain Legislative Acts on the Protection of Investors' [Zakon Ukrayiny 'Pro vnesennia zmin do deyakykh zakonodavchykh aktiv schodo zakhystu prav investoriv'].
1396. Information about the transactions is available at: https://smida.gov.ua/db/xml/irregular/75583, accessed on 17 October 2018.

disclosed on numerous occasions.[1397] The NSSMC's website has an easy-to-use tool for checking information about approved transactions; the only drawback is that it is meant for monitoring approved transactions with interest of public companies only, while non-approved transactions remain concealed and are difficult to examine with other available tools.

Some comments must be made here in connection with the disclosure of special information as described above. First, these requirements apply only to JSCs (public companies), and other business forms are excluded from the disclosure obligation, including LLCs (private companies), where RPTs are common. Second, the requirements demand disclosure of decisions approving transactions with interest. In other words, RPTs that, for whatever reason, do not fall under the procedural regulations (such RPTs with persons who are not formally regarded as related parties) and RPTs that have not been approved, in breach of the procedural regulations, do not have to be disclosed. Third, these requirements apply to decisions on the approval of transactions with interest, but not to the actual transactions. Overall, the ramifications of the disclosure are limited in scope. Minority shareholders would benefit more from disclosure of RPTs that have not undergone approval scrutiny, in breach of the requirements, since those RPTs present a clear threat to the company. Nonetheless, this mandatory disclosure offers a valuable, user-friendly (compared with disclosure in financial reports) and fully accessible source.[1398] Among other benefits, it provides details of the body that approved the transaction and the market value of the transaction. Interested stakeholders can then use that information to verify whether the RPT was approved by the proper body, taking into account its market value. It is therefore not strange that the increased transparency of RPTs was noted in the World Bank's report.[1399] The risk that harmful RPTs are not disclosed remains, however. Evidence from the Chinese economy shows that value-destroying RPTs are accompanied by a drop in disclosure.[1400] This may happen in Ukraine as well since a controlling shareholder could manipulate the requirements. At the same time, the disclosed RPTs might also include value-destroying transactions. In order to tackle this issue properly, shareholders need more powers in connection with derivative suits, based on the statutory changes outlined above.

This research would be incomplete without highlighting the disclosure duties of company bodies that are triggered when shareholders exercise their rights. Those rights are usually not RPT-specific; rather, disclosure of RPTs is exercised within a general framework right and a corresponding duty – e.g., the right of shareholders in German private companies to receive information concerning the company's affairs,[1401] or the right to information during general meetings of shareholders in German public companies.[1402] As one of the key information rights of shareholders, it has limitations and is restricted by the ramifications of shareholder interests in the

1397. In 2017, Ukrainian JSCs disclosed 603 approved RPTs.
1398. The authorization process is a simple one.
1399. *Doing Business 2019: Training for Reform*, 19.
1400. Cheung YL and others, 374.
1401. GmbHG, Article 51a(1).
1402. AktG, Article 131(1).

company.[1403] While those interests obviously also involve RPTs, they are not limited to such transactions. Therefore, information about RPTs can be disclosed when shareholders exercise their general rights. Some of these rights have been described in §5.01[C], in the discussion of regulation beyond RPT-related strategies.

[D] General Notes on the Limits of Disclosure

As the analysis of statutory law and soft law in the studied jurisdictions shows, none of the jurisdictions in focus vest shareholders with a special right to access information about RPTs.[1404] This absence of specific enabling provisions is compensated by the fact that some RPTs are subject to informational scrutiny in these jurisdictions.[1405] The question that then arises is whether this degree of regulation is sufficient to ensure efficiency of RPTs or, conversely, whether it goes too far.

Opinions on the influence of disclosure differ. Some scholars have been highly critical of its effect, blaming it for distortions in perception and increase of scrutiny,[1406] leading to more biased advice from advisors.[1407] Others have emphasized the importance of disclosure, by arguing that it can alter managerial conduct.[1408] Both these views come across as largely exaggerated.

The idea that disclosure might lead to less efficacy in transactions in fact has a logical basis. Related parties and company bodies that disclose RPTs might present the information in a manner that does not make them vulnerable. If management must report on RPTs, it would most likely refrain from showing those in an unfavourable manner, as they might otherwise be used against management and its policies. Moreover, related parties with abusive intentions, who are aware of the safeguards and wish to avoid the spotlight, could circumvent the rules by drawing on other schemes that do not require disclosure. Another frustrating factor is that disclosure is not a remedy in and of itself, but rather an empowerment right: if applied *ex post*, it is often a prelude to further claims and enforcement. With *ex ante* disclosure, it is a way to warn interested persons about the potential negative effect of RPTs. In either case, disclosure lacks any remedial effect, without directly leading to a restoration of rights and interests.

Although these facts present an accurate depiction of the reality of RPTs, they should rather be described as deficiencies in corporate relationships, rather than drawbacks of the affiliation terms strategy. Agency costs and moral hazards are not easy to govern and, of course, the disclosure duty alone is not enough to prevent

1403. Cahn A and Donald DC, 512.
1404. *Study on Minority Shareholders Protection, Final Report* (Prepared by TGS Baltic 2018), 141.
1405. *Ibid.*, 141.
1406. Cain DM, Loewenstein G and Moore DA, 'Coming Clean but Playing Dirtier: The Shortcomings of Disclosure as a Solution to Conflicts of Interest' in Moore DA and others (eds), *Conflicts of Interest: Challenges and Solutions in Business, Law, Medicine, and Public Policy* (Cambridge University Press 2005), 114.
1407. *Ibid.*, 116.
1408. Fox MB, 'Required Disclosure and Corporate Governance' in Hopt KJ and others (eds), *Comparative Corporate Governance: The State of the Art and Emerging Research* (Oxford University Press 1998), 713.

detrimental RPTs or to help the damaged parties to obtain compensation. Similarly, it would be wrong to blame the informational failure for allowing Parmalat to collapse.[1409] Rather, it was a failure of the corporate governance regime as mediated by various gatekeepers.[1410] The disclosure regime should not be viewed in isolation from other safeguards and strategies; on the contrary, without proper disclosure it is impossible to achieve a fair view.[1411] Disclosure is essential to manage conflicts of interest and to handle RPTs. The issue therefore does not lie in the need for disclosure, but in the limits of disclosure.[1412] Disclosure should not be excessively onerous and demand too much scrutiny. For example, non-listed companies should not be regarded in the same way as listed companies for disclosure purposes. Listed companies should bear the duty of increased disclosure, taking into account the special category of minority shareholders. For non-listed companies, disclosure of RPTs as a potentially harmful technique is justified only for companies that, by their size or workforce, present a public interest. This demands balancing the bureaucracy of excessive disclosure against sufficient information for all stakeholders, and the formal application of disclosure requirements for listed companies against the need for a special disclosure duty for other companies that, by their characteristics, present a public interest.

§5.04 STANDARDS STRATEGY FOR RPTs

[A] The Duty of Loyalty as a Core Element of the Standards Strategy

Largely, the standards strategy for RPTs is centred around the doctrine of fiduciary duties, in particular the duty of loyalty. As discussed at length in Chapter 2, it applies to managers and, in some jurisdictions, to shareholders. Traditionally, company officers, controlling shareholders and parent companies are the potential holders of a duty of loyalty.[1413]

Besides describing the holders of a duty of loyalty, section §2.02 explained the main beneficiaries of that duty, provided a comparison between the shareholder and stakeholder theories, how they relate to the duty of care and what the business judgment rule means. The present section offers a more specific analysis of standards

1409. Melis G and Melis A, 'Financial Reporting, Corporate Governance and Parmalat: Was It a Financial Reporting Failure?' in O'Brien J (ed.), *Governing the Corporation: Regulation and Corporate Governance in an Age of Scandal and Global Markets* (John Wiley & Sons 2005), 253.
1410. Coffee Jr JC, 'Understanding Enron: "It's About the Gatekeepers, Stupid"' (2002) 57 The Business Lawyer 1403.
1411. Feleaga L and Neacsu I, 'Disclosure of Related Party Transactions and Information Regarding Transfer Pricing by the Companies Listed on Bucharest Stock Exchange' (2016) 15 Journal of Accounting and Management Information Systems 785, 804.
1412. Kraakman R, 'Disclosure of Corporate Governance: An Overview Essay' in Ferrarini G and others (eds), *Reforming Company and Takeover Law in Europe* (Oxford University Press 2004), 110.
1413. Enriques L and others, 'Related-Party Transactions' in Kraakman R and others (eds), *The Anatomy of Corporate Law: A Comparative and Functional Approach* (3rd edn, Oxford University Press 2017), 162-163.

as a means of dealing with RPTs, without the focus on other expressions of conflicts of interest that Chapter 2 had.

[B] RPT-Related Standards and Their Enforcement

[1] The Duty of Loyalty as a Standard in Germany and Poland

Although it is described as a standard, the duty of loyalty does not carry specific clear-cut rules. This is the key difference between this strategy and the procedural and informational safeguards discussed above. If an approval procedure is breached, the facts are not subject to the same close and detailed scrutiny as they would be if a standards strategy applied,[1414] where the courts must approach the breach by delving into the substance. The standard does not provide any straightforward answers to the problem of RPTs, but serves instead as a guide to identifying the most appropriate solution.[1415]

In Germany, the duty of loyalty has several dimensions. Primarily, it is ascribed to managers of companies, who are obliged to behave in the company's best interests, without any conflicts of interest.[1416] German statutory law does not contain an explicit definition of this duty as it applies to officers of listed and non-listed companies. Instead of describing it in general terms, the legislature specifically provides for its expression in public companies (AGs), namely the non-compete obligation[1417] and the duty of confidentiality,[1418] which are not particularly relevant for RPTs. The resulting gap is filled by the provisions of the German CGC (both the 2017 and the 2020 versions), which contain a general prohibition on pursuing personal interests,[1419] and by legal doctrine.[1420]

The fact that officers have a duty of loyalty does not bar them from entering into RPTs. An officer is regarded as acting in accordance with that duty if he or she enters into a transaction that is on market terms[1421] or, for listed companies, that is compliant with customary standards for the sector (according to the 2017 version of the German CGC).[1422] If an officer of a German company acts contrary to the company's interests in favour of his or her own interests, he or she is liable in respect of the company for the loss or damage arising from that breach.[1423] In exceptional cases, e.g. gross negligence,

1414. Cahn A and Donald DC, 334.
1415. Fan C, *Bringing Controlling Shareholders to Court: Standard-Based Strategies and Controlling Shareholder Opportunism* (Eleven International Publishing 2013), 39.
1416. Bröhmer J, 60.
1417. AktG, Article 88.
1418. *Ibid.*, Article 93(1).
1419. German CGC, as amended on 7 February 2017, 4.3.1; German draft CGC 2020, section E.
1420. Mäntysaari P, *Comparative Corporate Governance: Shareholders as a Rule-Maker* (Springer Science & Business Media 2005), 340.
1421. Cahn A and Donald DC, 340.
1422. *Ibid.*, 446; German CGC, as amended on 7 February 2017, 4.3.3.
1423. AktG, Article 93(2); GmbHG, Article 43(2).

the officer's liability also extends to external parties.[1424] If the shareholders in an AG suffer from the negative consequences, in addition to the loss incurred by the company, they are also entitled to pursue claims against its managers.[1425]

In accordance with the foregoing, and with the thoughts of other scholars, that RPTs must comply with the procedural requirements and must also be fair, i.e., they must conform to the standards.[1426] Supervisory board approval alone does not protect an officer who has entered into an RPT from a claim for damages. This idea has its basis in statutory law.[1427] However, approval of an officer's act by the general meeting of shareholders carries more weight in the eyes of law and exculpates the officer from liability.[1428] Still, a resolution by the shareholders' meeting is not a panacea. For instance, for post-formation acquisitions, the courts may deny registration of the acquisition if the consideration paid for the assets was unreasonably high.[1429] The court has this discretion notwithstanding even if the resolution was adopted by a majority of at least three quarters of the share capital.[1430] This illustrates how important the standards strategy is in Germany.

Compared with managers, members of the supervisory board are not charged with the company's day-to-day affairs. Their principal function is to oversee management,[1431] and this directly influences the scope of their liability. Although supervisory board members are subject to the same provisions regarding the duty of care and responsibility,[1432] it goes without saying that liability for the company's decisions lies primarily with its managers. However, this may change if a member of the supervisory board exerts influence on the manager to act in a manner that is detrimental to the company; in these situations, the supervisory board member is also liable for damages.[1433] These provisions of corporate law in Germany reflect the theory of *faktischen Organen*, meaning that persons acting as members of management bear the same responsibility as if they were legally appointed.[1434]

Besides managers and supervisory board members, shareholders also have a duty of loyalty.[1435] Again, this duty has no statutory basis, but evolved in case law, first

1424. AktG, Article 93(5); Drygala T, 'Directors Liability in the Member States of the European Union' in Lutter M (ed.), *Legal Capital in Europe* (Walter de Gruyter 2006), 241.
1425. AktG, Articles 117(5), 147(2).
1426. Fleischer H, 'The Responsibility of the Management and Its Enforcement' in Ferrarini G and others (eds), *Reforming Company and Takeover Law in Europe* (Oxford University Press 2004), 385.
1427. AktG, Articles 93(4), 117(2).
1428. *Ibid.*, Articles 93(4), 117(2); Grigoleit HC, 'Directors' Liability and Enforcement Mechanisms from the German Perspective: General Structure and Key Issues' in Fleischer H and others (eds), *German and Asian Perspectives on Company Law* (Mohr Siebeck 2016), 115.
1429. AktG, Article 52(7).
1430. *Ibid.*, Article 52(5).
1431. *Ibid.*, Article 111(1).
1432. *Ibid.*, Article 116.
1433. *Ibid.*, Article 117(1).
1434. Sørensen KE, 'Duty of Loyalty of Shareholders: A Possible Remedy for Conflicts in SMEs?', 146.
1435. Bachmann G and others, *Regulating the Closed Corporation*, vol 4 (Walter de Gruyter 2013), 53.

covering shareholders in GmbHs and ending with minority shareholders in AGs.[1436] While it is still debatable whether this duty does in fact extend to minority shareholders,[1437] they are more likely to be liable for detrimental acts if they can exert significant influence by blocking decisions of the general meeting.[1438]

Shareholders owe a fiduciary duty to both the company and their fellow shareholders.[1439] Consequently, if a shareholder displays detrimental conduct, both the company and fellow shareholders may claim compensation for the loss or damage caused by the breach of this duty. If only the company suffered, and not the other shareholders, then the breaching shareholder must pay damages to the company, even if the other shareholders brought the claim.[1440] For a claim for damages to succeed, clear intent, rather than simple negligence, on the part of the breaching shareholder must be established.[1441]

Besides court injunctions and declarations,[1442] another remedy that is available in response to a breach of the shareholders' duty of loyalty is nullification of a resolution taken by the general meeting.[1443] The right to claim nullification vests with the other shareholders and has its legal basis in the AktG; it makes it possible to set aside resolutions of the general meeting by reason of a breach of the law or the company's articles,[1444] or a shareholder's harmful conduct.[1445] The right of shareholders to challenge resolutions of private companies (GmbH) is recognized by analogy,[1446] although it is not without limits. First, abuse of the right to challenge the company's resolutions is not allowed.[1447] Second, even if a shareholder breaches the duty of loyalty, if he or she does not have sufficient votes to sway the outcome of the shareholder vote, insufficient grounds exist to set aside the resolution.[1448]

Under German group law, where abusive intra-group transactions are easily imaginable and the need to strike a balance between the various stakeholder groups is clear, the shareholder's duty of loyalty transforms into a duty of loyalty on the part of the parent (i.e., the controlling company). Controlling companies have a duty of loyalty in both de facto groups and contract-based groups.[1449]

1436. Sørensen KE, 'Duty of Loyalty of Shareholders: A Possible Remedy for Conflicts in SMEs?', 130-131.
1437. *Ibid.*, 131.
1438. Spindler G, 'The Role of Shareholders in Public Companies' in Fleischer H and others (eds), *German and Asian Perspectives on Company Law* (Mohr Siebeck 2016), 211.
1439. Mäntysaari P, *Comparative Corporate Governance: Shareholders as a Rule-Maker*, 380.
1440. Cahn A, 'The Shareholders' Fiduciary Duty in German Company Law' in Birkmose HS (ed.), *Shareholders' Duties* (Wolters Kluwer 2017), 357.
1441. *Ibid.*, 357.
1442. *Ibid.*, 356-358.
1443. Roth GH and Kindler P, *The Spirit of Corporate Law: Core Principles of Corporate Law in Continental Europe* (Beck/Hart 2013), 138.
1444. AktG, Article 243(1).
1445. *Ibid.*, Article 243(2).
1446. Kespohl A, 'Germany' in Campbell D (ed.), *Shareholders' Liability (The Comparative Law Yearbook of International Business)*, vol Special Issue (Graham & Trotman/Martinus Nijhoff 2017), 136.
1447. Mäntysaari P, *Comparative Corporate Governance: Shareholders as a Rule-Maker*, 380.
1448. Cahn A, 'The Shareholders' Fiduciary Duty in German Company Law', 358.
1449. *Ibid.*, 353.

In AG groups that are based on control agreements, the controlling company may issue instructions that are disadvantageous to the controlled company, but beneficial for the group as a whole or one of its members.[1450] In exchange, the controlling company has a duty to compensate any annual net loss (to the extent the loss cannot be compensated by withdrawals from other profit reserves[1451]), combined with a duty to ensure adequate compensation for minority shareholders.[1452] In de facto groups, the balance between the interests of different group members is safeguarded by the controlling company's obligation to compensate any disadvantageous instructions.[1453] This obligation is relaxed somewhat by allowing compensation to be made beyond the end of the financial year, provided that the time and means of compensation are established by the time the financial year ends.[1454] If the controlling company fails to compensate a disadvantage, it is liable towards the controlled company and its shareholders for damages.[1455] In substance, regulation of de facto AG ultimately relies on a fairness standard that dictates that RPTs must be on market terms.[1456]

Special group provisions for public companies (AGs) mean that the general rules on shareholders' liability for breaching the duty of loyalty apply to the extent that they are compatible with the statutory regime. The situation is different for private companies (GmbHs), which are governed by more modest statutory regulation. The approach developed by the courts and in literature is based on the idea that the obligations and powers of parents in contract-based GmbH groups follow the same rules as set forth in the AktG.[1457] However, the approach for de facto GmbH groups is not the same as for de facto AG groups, in that Articles 311 and 317 of the AktG on compensation for disadvantages and loss or damage do not apply.[1458] This means that, for de facto GmbH groups, the general rules on liability in the form of damages apply to breaches of the duty of loyalty, rather than the statutory regulations for de facto AG groups.

In addition to claims by subsidiaries and their shareholders in a group context, German case law shows that creditors of a subsidiary may sue its controlling company for improper asset transfers, according to the rules of tort law.[1459] This example of piercing the corporate veil stems from the fiduciary relationship between the parent and the subsidiary;[1460] the reasoning behind it is that a parent has the potential to harm creditors with claims on the subsidiary through disadvantageous RPTs.

1450. AktG, Article 308(1).
1451. *Ibid.*, Article 302(1).
1452. *Ibid.*, Article 304(1).
1453. *Ibid.*, Article 311(1).
1454. *Ibid.*, Article 311(2).
1455. *Ibid.*, Article 317(1).
1456. Enriques L, Hertig G and Kanda H, 'Related-Party Transactions' in Kraakman R and others (eds), *The Anatomy of Corporate Law A Comparative and Functional Approach* (2nd edn, Oxford University Press 2009), 176.
1457. Alting C, 'Piercing the Corporate Veil in American and German Law-Liability of Individuals and Entities: A Comparative View' (1995) 2 Tulsa Journal of Comparative and International Law 187, 237.
1458. *Ibid.*, 239.
1459. Vandekerckhove K, *Piercing the Corporate Veil* (Wolters Kluwer 2007), 261.
1460. *Ibid.*, 260.

The duty of loyalty for company officers in Poland derives from civil law and legal doctrine.[1461] The KSH contains provisions that govern the duty of loyalty, including an obligation to abstain from the settlement of issues involving conflicts of interest,[1462] representation of the company by its supervisory board in dealings with conflicted members,[1463] and the non-compete clause.[1464] As in Germany, Polish statute does not give a general definition of the duty of loyalty; this absence is somewhat compensated by the provisions of the WSE Best Practice, however, under which management and supervisory board members are obliged to refrain from any activity that might cause a conflict of interest.[1465]

If the company suffers loss or damage as a result of the acts or omissions of management or supervisory board members, those members must compensate the company for that loss or damage.[1466] This applies equally to breaches of the duty of loyalty.[1467] These situations are governed by the general rules on tortious liability, although the approach that the courts take to liability of officers is casuistic by nature and difficult to predict.[1468] It is therefore uncertain that shareholders and third parties could claim damages directly from the company's officers.

Shareholders also have a duty of loyalty, pursuant to the general principle of equal treatment, based on the provisions of statute and CGC,[1469] though it is debatable whether this extends to shareholders in listed companies.[1470] However, for public companies (S.A.), statutory law provides a comparable standard: the remuneration received by shareholders may not exceed the average remuneration for such business transactions.[1471] This means that transactions with shareholders that involve remuneration must be on market terms.[1472] Given how the concept of hidden payments is viewed under Polish company law, transactions with shareholders for remuneration in excess of this standard might be regarded as disguised distributions, which would then have to be refunded to the company. It would be for the courts to establish what an average remuneration is and what would be equally fair in transactions with third parties. This standard has been criticized for not offering sufficient flexibility, by ignoring group relationships, and is in need of an update.[1473] It is difficult for third parties (i.e., the company's creditors) to claim damages from shareholders under this standard.

1461. Radwan A and Regucki T, 'The Possibilities for and Barriers to Sustainable Companies in Polish Company Law', 28-29.
1462. KSH, Articles 209 and 377.
1463. *Ibid.*, Articles 210 and 379.
1464. *Ibid.*, Articles 211 and 380.
1465. WSE Best Practice, V.R.1.
1466. KSH, Articles 293 and 483.
1467. Drygala T, 250.
1468. Radwan A and Regucki T, 'The Possibilities for and Barriers to Sustainable Companies in Polish Company Law', 29, 48.
1469. KSH, Article 20; WSE Best Practice, V.Z.1.
1470. Radwan A and Regucki T, 'The Possibilities for and Barriers to Sustainable Companies in Polish Company Law', 22.
1471. KSH, Article 355(3).
1472. Opalski A, 5.
1473. *Ibid.*, 6.

[2] *The Standards Strategy for RPTs in the Netherlands*

Instead of imposing a duty of loyalty, Dutch law operates on the principles of reasonableness and fairness to determine standards of conduct of company officers and other persons involved in the organization of a legal entity.[1474] These principles are characteristic of the legal system in the Netherlands and apply beyond company law as well.[1475] In the hierarchy of legal sources, they carry greater weight than statute, custom, articles of association and company-specific regulations[1476] and offer a legal basis for annulling resolutions of a company's constituent bodies.[1477]

In spite of the fact that the principles of reasonableness and fairness have replaced the duty of loyalty in the Dutch doctrine,[1478] it would be wrong to think that the law in the Netherlands relies only on principles to guide company officers. Members of management and supervisory boards are subject to various specific provisions: they must act in the best interests of the company and the enterprise connected with it.[1479] Courts have interpreted this provision to mean that officers should promote the continued success of the company and its connected enterprise, taking into account the company's organizational specifics.[1480] Although this provision essentially affords company officers a broad discretion, it also provides important guidance about the long-term goals that they must pursue, with due observance of the firm's specific features.

Although reasonableness and fairness are important factors in questions of an officer's loyal conduct, coupled with a duty to be guided by the best interests of the specific company and its connected enterprise, in terms of liability Article 2:9 of the BW is most frequently put forward as the basis for proper performance of officers' duties.[1481] That clause is also the key legal ground for internal liability of company officers towards the company. For Article 2:9 to be invoked, and an officer to be held liable, that officer must be seriously at fault in his or her performance.[1482] A variety of factors should be considered in connection with this issue, including whether the officer acted on an informed basis, how the duties are shared between the company's officers, what standard of knowledge and due diligence are expected from this person, etc.[1483] If a company's business fails, this does not automatically mean that the officer is in breach: this duty is primarily one of effort.[1484]

1474. Muller MH (ed.), 139, Article 2:8 BW.
1475. Cartwright J, 39.
1476. BW, Article 2:8(2).
1477. *Ibid.*, Article 15(1)(b).
1478. De Savornin Lohman HA, 30.
1479. BW, Article 2:129(5), 2:140(2), 2:239(5) and 2:250(2).
1480. De Groot C, 'The Duty of Directors to Be Guided by the Best Interests of the Company' in Breedveld C and others (eds), *Core Concepts in the Dutch Civil Code: Continuously in Motion* (BW-krant Jaarboek 2016), 209.
1481. Muller MH (ed.), 140; De Savornin Lohman HA, 35; Borrius Y, 'Directors' Liability: The Netherlands' (2011) 8 European Company Law 246, 248.
1482. Muller MH (ed.), 141.
1483. *Ibid.*
1484. Drygala T, 243.

A high threshold for internal liability explains why officers have not been held liable for damages in many published cases.[1485] Other possible reasons include obstacles to overcoming loyalty issues and the time and cost involved in court proceedings.[1486] Still, Article 2:9 is not a dead letter, and it has been invoked to effect in some publicly accessible cases. The following instances involving RPTs are described as entailing breaches of Article 2:9: a transaction that favours an officer and is detrimental to the company,[1487] a loan to an insolvent relative of a company officer and an unsecured loan to the chair of a company's supervisory board.[1488] In each of these cases, officers were blamed for entering into detrimental RPTs despite the absence of statutory requirements for RPTs. Except for the provisions described above, today Dutch statute remains largely silent on the issue of when RPTs are efficient, although some guidelines can be found at the level of soft law. According to the Dutch CGC, transactions with managers, supervisory board members and shareholders holding more than 10% of the company's share capital must be agreed on terms that are customary in the market.[1489] The standard for providing loans, guarantees and similar instruments to management and supervisory board members is different: these transactions may be made only in the company's normal course of business and on the same terms that apply to the company's workforce as a whole.[1490] Bearing in mind that Dutch courts may draw on the provisions of the CGC for interpreting the principles of reasonableness and fairness,[1491] the RPT requirements contained in the Dutch CGC may be expected to apply in practice.

Court action against board members for their conduct by external parties, including individual shareholders and creditors, is based on tort (Article 6:162 BW). Both situations, viz. internal liability based on Article 2:9 BW and external liability based on Article 2:162 BW, carry a high threshold, namely the requirement of serious blame/fault on the officer's part.[1492]

The conduct of shareholders, like the actions of officers, is also subject to the principles of reasonableness and fairness. The extent to which these principles, combined with rules on abuses of power, influence the standards of conduct and responsibility of shareholders depends on the specific circumstances, including the size of the shareholding.[1493] If the shareholder exercises control over the company, he or she might be held liable for the company's acts in respect of creditors, under the provisions of tort law (Article 2:162 of the BW).[1494] The landmark case, where creditors succeeded in their claims for damages against the shareholder, was *Osby*,[1495] in which

1485. De Savornin Lohman HA, 40-41.
1486. Borrius Y, 248.
1487. *Deen v. Perlak* 17 June 1921, NJ 1921, 737 (Supreme Court of the Netherlands).
1488. De Savornin Lohman HA, 41.
1489. Dutch CGC, 2.7.4, 2.7.5.
1490. *Ibid.*, 2.7.6.
1491. For further details, *see* Chapter 2.
1492. *Tulip Air, Decision of 5 September 2014* NJ 2015/21, annotated by P van Schilfgaarde (Supreme Court of the Netherlands).
1493. Kemp B, 432-433.
1494. De Savornin Lohman HA, 129.
1495. *Osby, Decision of 25 September 1981* NJ 1982 (Supreme Court of the Netherlands).

the majority shareholder had used RPTs to transfer (fiduciary) ownership to subsidiary assets to themselves and to their affiliates. The court *inter alia* considered that the shareholder was aware, or should have been aware, that such RPTs would damage the subsidiary's creditors. This case illustrates the use of tort law to pierce the corporate veil in the Netherlands.[1496] Another situation in which shareholders might be held liable for damages on the same footing as company officers is if they act as de facto managers;[1497] in these situations, their liability is based on the same articles as if they were appointed as company officers.

[3] The Standards Strategy for RPTs in Ukraine

Compared with Germany, Poland and the Netherlands, Ukraine's use of standards is less developed. As shown in the previous sections, RPTs by public companies in Ukraine are subject to detailed procedural and informational scrutiny. Courts tend to invalidate RPTs that are concluded in breach of the procedural requirements. This holds true for the nullification of resolutions by company bodies to approve RPTs. However, two caveats must be made here.

First, Ukraine's Supreme Court has recently started to apply legal principles in corporate disputes. For instance, in a judgment of 27 February 2018, the Supreme Court annulled a decision by the general meeting of shareholders of a private company by reason that it was incompatible with legal principles. The case involved a company whose share capital had been increased by a shareholder owning more than 60% of votes, diluting the shares of the other shareholder from approximately 30% of the share capital to about 0.3%. The Supreme Court reasoned that the decision of the general meeting of shareholders to allow a shareholder to increase the company's share capital without considering the other shareholders, resulting in their dilution, was contrary to statutory rules, the principle of the rule of law and the Convention for the protection of human rights and fundamental freedoms.[1498] While this case did not concern RPTs, the fact that the Supreme Court applied legal principles to invalidate a decision of a company body means that future cases could appear in which the Court invalidates other decisions of a company body to approve an RPT.

Second, on 20 September 2019, the Parliament of Ukraine adopted a series of amendments to the JSC Law of Ukraine, making it possible to invalidate transactions with interest that are concluded on less favourable terms than the usual market terms. Under these amendments, market terms are based on a report of an independent

---

1496. Vandekerckhove K, 226. *See also*: Bartman SM, *Concernbeleid en aansprakelijkheid: over (oa) convergentie in rechtsdenken op het gebied van concernverhoudingen tussen Nederland en de Bondsrepubliek Duitsland* (Kluwer 1989).

1497. De Savornin Lohman HA, 139-140; BW, Article 2:151 and 2:261.

1498. *Digest of Court Practice of the Supreme Court in Cases Arising of Corporate Relations (2018 – 15 July 2019) [Digest sudovoyi praktyky Verkhovnoho Sudu u spravakh, scho vynykayut iz korporatyvnykh vidnosyn (2018 rik – 15 lypnia 2019 roku)]* (website of the Supreme Court, available at: https://supreme.court.gov.ua/userfiles/media/Dajest_korporat_vidnosunu_1 pdf?fbclid=IwAR0IBFqlG-nLKuBLtZ1is7p7h44lGyAyRoSamP3PC7X1ndYStc-c8SNFlnI, 2019), 26-27.

evaluator, and shareholders have standing to challenge transactions with interest on non-market terms. Damages can be claimed on behalf of the company for the difference between the market price and the actual price, owed jointly by the interested person and the supervisory board members who voted in favour of the transaction (if it was approved by the supervisory board).[1499]

In addition to the 20 September 2019 amendments, statutory law provides an almost invisible route for invalidating RPTs on general grounds, as set forth in the CCU. As Article 215 of the CCU suggests, read in conjunction with Article 203, transactions that are incompatible with this Code, other acts of civil legislation, the interests of the state or society or moral grounds may be annulled.[1500] Examples exist in case law where the courts annulled a transaction with interest by drawing on both the JSC Law of Ukraine and the general provisions of the CCU on invalidating transactions.[1501] The courts have acknowledged, e.g., that shareholders were deprived of their right to participate in the company's bodies.

An alternative interpretation of Article 203(1) of the CCU might give a slight degree of leeway to invalidate transactions involving conflicting interests. One of the requirements of Article 203(1) is that transactions may not be incompatible with the CCU. Article 509(3) of the CCU moreover requires that obligations, including contractual obligations, must be based on standards of reasonableness, bona fide conduct and fairness. These grounds are also described as the general principles of civil legislation, according to Article 3 of the CCU. It could therefore be argued that a transaction that is incompatible with these three general principles may be annulled pursuant to Article 203(1) of the CCU. The Supreme Economic Court of Ukraine has already drawn on these provisions to invalidate transactions, specifically in its judgment of 10 January 2012.[1502] However, in that judgment, the transaction was found not only to be in breach of the general principles under Articles 3 and 509(3): the transaction was established to be sham, which offers separate grounds for annulment under Articles 203(5) and 234 of the CCU. As such, although the court referred to the general principles, they were not applied independently, but rather to strengthen the court's reasoning. If a court decides to invalidate a transaction involving a conflict of interest, it would probably not find a firm basis for that invalidation in statute, and its only solution would be to interpret the conflict of interest in light of the general principles of civil legislation. So far, only the Supreme Court has been seen to apply these legal principles to corporate disputes;[1503] on the whole, the courts prefer to use their broad discretionary powers in truly exceptional circumstances.[1504]

1499. Law of Ukraine 'On Amending Certain Legislative Acts of Ukraine regarding the Stimulation of Investment Activity in Ukraine' [Zakon Ukrayiny 'Pro vnesennia zmin do deyakykh zakonodavchykh aktiv Ukrayiny schodo stymuliuvannia investytsiynoyi diyalnosti v Ukrayini'].
1500. CCU, Articles 203(1), 215(1).
1501. *OSOBA4 (Kropyvnytskiy) v. PrJSC 'Vesna', LLC 'KDC', Kirovohrad city council, Judgment of 2 July 2008* Case No. 20-11/421-7/514 (Dnipropetrovsk Appellate Economic Court).
1502. *LLC 'Sarex' v. Open JSC 'Sumske ATP-15928', Judgment of 10 January 2012* Case No. 5021/1197/2011 (Supreme Economic Court of Ukraine).
1503. *Digest of Court Practice of the Supreme Court in Cases Arising of Corporate Relations (2018 – 15 July 2019) [Digest sudovoyi praktyky Verkhovnoho Sudu u spravakh, scho vynykayut iz*

The final possibility for invalidating transactions is on moral grounds. This notion makes a number of appearances in the CCU,[1505] though its meaning has never been explained. Even the Plenum of the Supreme Court of Ukraine, in its regulation devoted to the annulment of transactions in civil cases, has not clarified what this nebulous term means precisely.[1506] No widely known cases are currently available where the courts drew on moral grounds to annul a transaction, let alone cases where conflicts of interest were considered to be part of the moral reasoning. Most courts prefer to stick to the literal wording of legislative provisions and are reluctant to use their powers to interpret facts creatively. While it is possible to find judgments in which the court quoted the provisions of Article 203 of the CCU (being one of the clauses to make reference to moral grounds),[1507] those decisions would stand even if they did not include any mention of moral grounds. In one judgment, the court in fact claimed that transactions could be invalidated only if they were incompatible with statute, rather than with the principles of morality, and so placed the emphasis on statute as its main source of law.[1508] This category, therefore, has little practical significance. Nevertheless, some scholars have expressed thoughts on how to interpret these moral grounds; e.g., some argue that this category could include the prohibition on abusing rights and the principles of property independence and legal equality.[1509]

In the Netherlands, a definition of a conflict of interest can be found in the well-known *Bruil/Kombex* case.[1510] The court explained that a conflict of interest exists if an officer having *a direct or indirect personal interest which is not congruent with the interest of a company, taking into account all circumstances of the case at hand, could not have deemed himself capable to safeguard the interest of the company with the*

---

korporatyvnykh vidnosyn (2018 rik – 15 lypnia 2019 roku)] (website of the Supreme Court, available at: https://supreme.court.gov.ua/userfiles/media/Dajest_korporat_vidnosunu_1pdf?fbclid=IwAR0IBFqlG-nLKuBLtZ1is7p7h44lGyAyRoSamP3PC7X1ndYStc-c8SNFlnI, 2019).

1504. One illustrative example is a largely political decision of the Supreme Court of Ukraine, in which it cancelled the results of the election of Viktor Yanukovych by reason of a breach of the election principles as outlined in Articles 38, 71 and 103 of the Constitution of Ukraine and in Article 11(2) of the Law of Ukraine 'On Elections of the President of Ukraine' (*see President V.A.Yuschenko v. Central Election Commission of Ukraine, Decision of 3 December 2004*, available at: http://zakon2.rada.gov.ua/laws/show/n0090700-04/print1487111999168257 (Supreme Court of Ukraine)).

1505. CCU, Articles 13(4), 19(1), 26(4) and 228(3).

1506. Regulation of the Plenum of the Supreme Court of Ukraine 'On Resolution of Civil Disputes on Annulment of Transactions' No. 9 [Postanova plenumu Verzhovnoho Sudu Ukrayiny 'Pro sudovu praktyku rozgliadu tsyvilnykh sprav pro vyznannia pravochyniv nediysnymy'].

1507. For example, *see Prosecutor of Tysmenytsia local prosecutor's office v. Public JSC 'Concern Galnaftogaz', Judgment of 29 August 2017* Case No. 909/696/15 (Supreme Economic Court of Ukraine); *Public JSC 'Export-import bank of Ukraine' v. LLC 'Energia Plus', Judgment of 28 August 2017* Case No. 905/252/14 (Donetsk Apellate Economic Court).

1508. *Open JSC 'Brodyrembud' v. LLC 'Kom Invest', Judgment of 28 August 2017* Case No. 914/2316/16 (Supreme Economic Court of Ukraine).

1509. Hrytsak O, 'Moralni zasady suspilstva yak otsinochna kategoriya ukrayinskoho tsyvilnoho prava' (2010) Advokat 39, 43.

1510. Nowak R, 'Corporate Boards in the Netherlands' in Davies PL and others (eds), *Corporate Boards in Law and Practice: A Comparative Analysis in Europe* (1st edn, Oxford University Press 2013), 480.

required integrity and objectivity.[1511] In this definition, the notion of a conflict of interest is explained using other terms that are similarly subject to evaluation. While regarded as fairly efficient,[1512] this approach might prove difficult to understand. However, if moral grounds are interpreted by courts as also encompassing the rules for conflicts of interest, this definition could be used as an interpretative tool.

Besides the largely ineffective use of standards for annulling RPTs or approving resolutions, with occasional judgments of the Supreme Court and the newly adopted amendments of 20 September 2019, the JSC Law of Ukraine stipulates liability of a person with an interest in a transaction for harm caused to the company in connection with a breach of established procedure.[1513] This means that the company can claim damages from the interested person directly, based on this particular clause of the JSC Law of Ukraine, applied in conjunction with the general provisions of tort law under the CCU.[1514] Related parties in transactions with private companies are also liable for harm inflicted due to breaches of procedure, in so far as all the company's shareholders have agreed to include the procedural safeguards in the articles of association.[1515]

The application of this clause is subject to some significant hurdles. First, given that the related party might have a personal connection to the company's officers or major shareholder, it is doubtful that the company would pursue a claim against that related party, even though the possibility of derivative action was recently introduced, allowing minority shareholders with 10% or more of the company's share capital to sue its officers for damages.[1516] This right has only limited effect, with very few cases having been brought before the courts and minority shareholders being reluctant to pursue these claims. In addition, from the perspective of RPTs, the efficiency of these new amendments is reduced by the fact that related parties that can be held liable for harm in derivative suits are limited to the company's officers (while numerous other affiliated persons are omitted). Second, the burden of proof as it traditionally applies in cases involving damages,[1517] including the requirement to provide evidence of an illegal act or omission by a related party,[1518] the negative effect (harm) of an RPT and the causal link between the two, creates another significant obstacle to obtaining an award for damages against a related party. Taking into account the burden of proof, it becomes more unlikely that third parties (creditors) would have a chance of success in claiming damages directly from the related party. Such a claim would be based solely on the provisions of tort law from the CCU (Article 1166), since under the JSC Law of

1511. *Bruil/Kombex* 29 June 2007, JOR 2007/169 (Supreme Court of the Netherlands).
1512. Davies P and others, 'Boards in Law and Practice: A Cross-Country Analysis in Europe' in Davies PL and others (eds), *Corporate Boards in Law and Practice: A Comparative Analysis in Europe* (1st edn, Oxford University Press 2013), 51.
1513. JSC Law of Ukraine, Article 71(11).
1514. CCU, Article 1166.
1515. LLC Law of Ukraine, Article 45(3)(4).
1516. Economic Procedural Code of Ukraine [Hospodarskyi protsesualnyi kodeks Ukrayiny], Article 54.
1517. For example, *see*: *MPP 'Banistro Firm' v. Open JSC 'Krymenergo', Judgment of 20 March 2007* Case No. 2-3/91421-2006 (Supreme Economic Court of Ukraine).
1518. This would be especially difficult to demonstrate where the detrimental RPT was approved by a company body.

Ukraine and the LLC Law of Ukraine it is only the company that has the right to claim damages from the related party.

[C] General Notes on the Efficiency of the Standards Strategy

The standards strategy is beautiful in its flexibility. Its success depends largely on the enforcement actors, who must identify and police harmful transactions. The problem lies in how the enforcer should separate value-creating transactions from their harmful counterparts.[1519] Courts in Germany and the Netherlands have a long-standing history of path-dependent scrutiny of RPTs using culture-specific standards: group law (*Konzernrecht*) in Germany versus the legal principles of fairness and reasonableness (*redelijkheid en billijkheid*) in the Netherlands. Poland's approach, in contrast, is more casuistic, while in Ukraine the standards strategy is still in development.

Another problem with the standards strategy is that the wide discretionary powers that courts have to review RPTs are at odds with the principle of legal certainty that is so highly valued in civil law jurisdictions,[1520] although the importance of legal certainty in those jurisdictions should not be construed to imply that it carries no meaning in common law countries.[1521] Once the precedent has been established, nobody can contest its uncertainty.[1522] While in civil law jurisdictions the legislature seeks to initially predict all possible scenarios and cover them using statutory rules, in common law jurisdictions the role of filling any gaps rests primarily with the courts. As demonstrated in a recent study of the laws governing self-dealing in three Continental European countries (France, Germany and Italy), liability suits are still rare compared with the US.[1523] This study highlights the litigation culture that exists in the US, where the judiciary has the right to review conflicted transactions.[1524]

As far as the US state of Delaware is concerned, some suggestions clearly favour a more flexible and demanding approach to self-dealing, with less weight given to procedural safeguards.[1525] For Ukraine, the drawbacks to this degree of flexibility would largely outweigh its benefits, considering how ill-equipped the country's courts are.[1526] A substantive *ex post* review would require the courts to review the market price of the transaction and apply remedies if the contract price is different. The numerous economic issues associated with defining a market price, or rather, a fair

1519. Enriques L, 'Related Party Transactions: Policy Options and Real-World Challenges (with a Critique of the European Commission Proposal)', 8.
1520. Johnson S and others, 24.
1521. Hansen C, Johnston JF and Alexander FH, 'The Role of Disinterested Directors in "Conflict" Transactions: The ALI Corporate Governance Project and Existing Law' (1990) 45 The Business Lawyer 2083, 2089.
1522. Sørensen KE, 'Duty of Loyalty of Shareholders: A Possible Remedy for Conflicts in SMEs?', 155.
1523. Conac P-H, Enriques L and Gelter M, 528.
1524. Fan C, 62-63.
1525. Brown JR, 'Disloyalty Without Limits: "Independent" Directors and the Elimination of the Duty of Loyalty' (2012) 95 Kentucky Law Journal 53, 105; Hill CA and McDonnell B, 937-938.
1526. Pomelli A, 'Related-Party Transactions and the Intricacies of Ex Post Judicial Review: The Parmalat/Lactalis Case' (2016) 13 European Company and Financial Law Review 73, 105.

range for the price gap[1527] would then combine with one undeniable flaw of the standards strategy: it is impossible for the courts to verify the savings on transaction costs.[1528] This last drawback has in fact given some authors reason to argue the pointlessness of a fairness strategy.[1529]

Despite these drawbacks to a standards strategy, I am far from convinced that it is inappropriate. On the contrary: it would be desirable to have efficient institutions deciding cases, making the utmost of their intellectual resources, in order to ensure fairness in transactions between related parties. In the real world, unfortunately, this is not always practicable. Courts in some jurisdictions are not sufficiently developed to be entrusted with complex firm-specific corporate solutions, where insiders would perform better and more shrewdly. In Ukraine, the courts are more comfortable deciding cases where no deep substantial review is required. Still, this does not automatically mean that the standards strategy has no chance of succeeding in Ukraine. The Ukrainian jurisdiction, which relies heavily on trusteeship and the decision rights strategies for dealing with RPTs, is at a crossroad in its development. Regulation of RPTs in the US, for instance, has been described as having developed in three stages, in which decision rights occupied the second stage.[1530] This does not mean that the standards strategy is the future of RPT-related strategies in Ukraine. Rather, I would argue that the standards strategy, if it is implemented in Ukraine, should be introduced in combination with institutional development and must make allowance for the demands specific to the country, for instance proper allocation of the burden of proof in damage claims. An analysis of that institutional development would extend the boundaries of this research considerably, however. The factors that should be considered when designing the proper strategy for dealing with RPTs in Ukraine are discussed in more detail in Chapter 6.

§5.05 DEVELOPMENT OF STRATEGIES FOR RPTs IN THE EU

[A] The EU Framework for RPT-Related Strategies

[1] Overview of EU Law on RPT-Related Strategies

Until recently, regulation of RPTs under EU law could be characterized as modest, focusing mostly on accounting and transparency requirements. A landmark event occurred in 2017 when SRD II was adopted. This instrument has shaken up the European corporate realm and will be implemented in many of the EU's Member States. Before it is rolled out across the EU, scholars can analyse the process of its drafting and adoption, in order to facilitate its understanding and future application.

1527. Kang SY, 133, 137.
1528. Pacces AM, 'Procedural and Substantive Review of Related Party Transactions (RPTs): The Case for Non-controlling Shareholder-Dependent (NCS-Dependent) Directors' ECGI Law Working Paper N° 399/2018 (May 2018), available at: http://ssrn.com/abstract_id=3167519, accessed on 6 December 2018, 12.
1529. *Ibid.*, 14.
1530. Fan C, 57.

From the perspective of the present research, this analysis is of key importance, given the process of approximating Ukrainian company law to EU law. The drafting of SRD II and its eventual outcome are described in §5.05 [B]. The current section describes and discusses other sources of EU law besides SRD II where RPT-related strategies are introduced or recommended.

For the purposes of convenience, the next two subsections of this section deal with procedural and informational safeguards for RPTs, respectively. Two comments should be made about this structure. First, it does not diminish the fact that these strategies are reflected in SRD II. Second, the procedural and informational safeguards do not constitute an exhaustive list of possible safeguards for dealing with RPTs. EU law is sometimes phrased in vague terms, making it difficult to attribute its provisions to specific strategies. Article 65 of Directive 2017/1132 (formerly: Article 26 of the Second Council Directive) is an example of this type of provision. It requires Member States to implement sufficient safeguards to ensure that transactions concerning financial assistance to specific related parties (parent undertakings, officers of the parent or the company and their representatives) to acquire shares in a company do not conflict with the company's interests.[1531] This requirement from the Directive exists alongside special provisions on safeguards designed for third parties, under which transactions involving financial assistance to acquire shares must be conducted on fair terms, subject to prior approval from a company body, preparation of a special report and maintenance of corporate assets.[1532] In the Member States studied in this work (Germany, Poland and the Netherlands), the latter rule is reflected in statutory company law, specifically in the parts governing capital maintenance in public companies.[1533] While the substance of the statutory clauses in Poland and the Netherlands largely reiterates the relevant provisions of the Directive, in Germany these types of transactions are null and void, except in the case of contract-based corporate groups and the other exceptions listed in the text of the Directive.

[2] Procedural Safeguards

Besides the approval procedures set forth in SRD II, discussed below, RPT-related procedural safeguards can also be found in other sources of EU law. One such source is Article 52 of Directive 2017/1132 (formerly: Article 13 of the Second Council Directive), which establishes safeguards for post-formation acquisitions conducted within at least two years after the date of the company's incorporation and representing one-tenth of its share capital. Among other requirements, the agreement must be approved by the general meeting and a special expert's report must be prepared.[1534] As already shown, Germany, Poland and the Netherlands have all implemented this provision in their statutory laws for public companies.[1535] The manner in which it is

1531. Directive 2017/1132, Articles 64 and 65.
1532. *Ibid.*, Article 64(2-5).
1533. AktG, Article 71a; KSH, Article 345; BW, Article 2:98c.
1534. Directive 2017/1132, Article 52(1).
1535. AktG, Article 52; BW, Article 2:94c; KSH, Article 394.

implemented by the Member States varies: in Poland, the requirements include approval of RPTs by a majority of two-thirds of the votes in the general meeting and cover post-formation agreements benefitting dependent companies, while Germany has introduced an *ex post* fairness test of the acquisition price. The national approaches to regulation of post-formation acquisitions are covered in more detail in section §5.02.

Soft law also contains procedural safeguards for RPTs, to a degree. On 21 May 2003, following a flood of financial scandals across various continents, the European Commission defined an Action Plan to overcome the pressing issues.[1536] Among other notions, it recommended that non-executive and supervisory directors should decide on matters where executive directors have conflicting interests.[1537] Non-executive and supervisory directors were expected to fulfil this mission through specially formed audit committees.[1538] The European Commission followed this up in 2005 by recommending the creation of audit committees within supervisory boards of listed companies.[1539] In the same year, audit committees were made obligatory for public-interest entities under the Directive on statutory audits.[1540] These sources of EU law do not provide detailed rules for approving RPTs. Rather, they outline the internal ramifications of decision-making in listed companies, including decisions concerning RPTs. One of the tasks that companies may entrust to audit committees is overseeing RPTs.[1541] However, EU law does not recommend or require that supervisory boards of listed companies be eliminated and replaced by audit committees. The possibility was introduced to assign the functions of the audit committee to the supervisory board as a whole.[1542] In other words, nothing stands in the way of listed companies having their RPTs approved or blocked by the supervisory board, without involving any special committees. It is only advisable from the perspective of best practices, as expressed by the European Commission, to assign this task to an audit committee.

1536. Communication from the Commission to the Council and the European Parliament, Modernising Company Law and Enhancing Corporate Governance in the European Union – A Plan to Move Forward, COM (2003) 284 final, 21.5.2003.
1537. *Ibid.*, 15.
1538. *Ibid.*
1539. Commission Recommendation of 15 February 2005 on the role of non-executive or supervisory directors of listed companies and on the committees of the (supervisory) board [2005] OJ L 52/51, 25.2.2005, Article 5.
1540. Directive 2006/43/EC of the European Parliament and of the Council of 17 May 2006 on statutory audits of annual accounts and consolidated accounts, amending Council Directives 78/660/EEC and 83/349/EEC and repealing Council Directive 84/253/EEC [2006] OJ L157/87, 9.6.2006, Article 41.
1541. Mouthaan EH, 'The Audit Committee from a European Perspective' (2007) 4 European Company Law 10, 14.
1542. *Ibid.*, 12.

[3] Disclosure Requirements

Until recently, the EU legislature preferred disclosure techniques for dealing with RPTs and refrained from promoting the procedural or standards strategies at the EU level.[1543] The following disclosure tools have been employed.

The first large area of RPT disclosure is accounting. The Accounting Directive requires that companies use the IASs to prepare their financial statements.[1544] The IASs have been extensively employed by listed companies since the adoption of the IAS Regulation on a harmonized basis to achieve comparability and transparency of financial statements.[1545] One of them is IAS 24, which provides for complete information of the company's potentially related parties, and has been discussed in Chapter 3. The Accounting Directive also mandates disclosure of RPTs in the explanatory notes to financial statements of medium-sized and large undertakings and public-interest entities.[1546] Member States may provide an exemption from requiring disclosure of RPTs in the notes in the following cases: for RPTs concluded on normal market terms; for RPTs between members of a group with wholly owned subsidiaries; and for RPTs by medium-sized undertakings that do not fall under the specified types of RPTs subject to mandatory disclosure.[1547]

Further disclosure rules for RPTs are set forth in the Transparency Directive, obliging companies issuing shares to include major RPTs in their interim management reports (Article 5(4)).[1548] Admittedly, this requirement in the Transparency Directive is not confined to companies from the EU only, but also extends to foreign companies whose shares are traded on a regulated market in the EU.[1549] Another important requirement is that any company seeking to go public must disclose its RPTs in its prospectus.[1550] The duty to provide this information stems from the need to protect investors from acquiring shares in companies that have features carrying the risk of tunnelling: investors must be aware of what to expect.

It could also be argued that disclosure of information about RPTs is required under the MAR.[1551] This Regulation states that inside information concerning issuers of financial instruments admitted to trading on a regulated market in a Member State

1543. Van der Elst C, 'The Duties of Significant Shareholders in Transactions with the Company', 206.
1544. Accounting Directive, Articles 8(6), 23(8).
1545. IAS Regulation, Article 1.
1546. Accounting Directive, Article 17(1)(r).
1547. The definitions of small, medium-sized and large undertakings are given in Article 3 of the Accounting Directive and are based on three criteria: balance sheet, net turnover and number of employees. For medium-sized undertakings, the figures may not exceed two of three ranges: EUR 4-20 million, EUR 8-40 million and 50-250 employees, respectively.
1548. Transparency Directive, Article 5(4).
1549. Van der Elst C, 'The Duties of Significant Shareholders in Transactions with the Company', 206.
1550. Enriques L, 'Related Party Transactions: Policy Options and Real-World Challenges (with a Critique of the European Commission Proposal)', 21.
1551. Regulation (EU) No. 596/2014 of the European Parliament and of the Council of 16 April 2014 on market abuse (market abuse regulation) and repealing Directive 2003/6/EC of the European Parliament and of the Council and Commission Directives 2003/124/EC, 2003/125/EC and 2004/72/EC [2014] OJ L 173, 12.6.2014.

must be made public as soon as possible.[1552] This obligation includes an obligation for the issuer to post and maintain that information on its website for at least five years.[1553] Although the Regulation's text does not make any direct reference to RPTs, it would be negligent to disregard the possibility that information about RPTs would be qualified as inside information. For example, if a company conducts an RPT to sell a valuable business asset, it would be reasonable to expect that transaction to have a significant effect on the price of company's securities, and it falls under the definition of inside information.[1554]

[B] Recent Regulatory Developments in RPT-Related Strategies in the EU

[1] General Characteristics of SRD II

Adopted on 17 May 2017 and in force since 3 June 2017, the Shareholders' Rights Directive 2017/828 (or SRD II) is the result of several years of heated debate and discussion among its drafters, practitioners and scholars. It builds on the European Commission's stated goals under the 2012 Action Plan to make corporate relationships more transparent and to incentivize shareholders.[1555]

The new Directive substantially expands the provisions of the earlier Shareholders' Rights Directive 2007/36/EC (SRD I), increasing SRD I's scope by adding requirements incentivizing shareholders to act with a view to the long term.[1556] Besides the existing rules on shareholders' rights attached to voting shares at general meetings of listed companies having their registered offices in EU Member States, the new Directive also introduces new requirements for the identification of shareholders, transmission of information, transparency of institutional investors, asset managers and proxy advisors and remuneration of directors, as well as rules for RPTs.[1557] While some of the draft provisions, in particular the rules on remuneration, have received plenty of attention in literature,[1558] aspects of the Directive's development as it relates to RPTs require further examination. The rest of this section examines in detail how the parts of the draft Directive that are devoted to RPTs evolved, from the first draft proposal submitted by the European Commission in April 2014 to its final version.

1552. *Ibid.*, Article 17(1), subparagraph 1.
1553. *Ibid.*, Article 17(1), subparagraph 2.
1554. *Ibid.*, Article 7(1)(a).
1555. SRD II, recital 3.
1556. SRD II, Article 1(1)(a)(1).
1557. *Ibid.*, Article 1(1)(a)(1).
1558. For example, *see*: Dijkhuizen T, 'On the Remuneration of Directors of Listed Companies (Again)' (2014) 11 European Company Law 199; Asplund A, 'Who Should Say on Pay and for the Sake of Whom in a Listed Company?' (2015) 12 European Company Law 286; Van der Elst C, 'Shareholders Holding the Reins on Remuneration: The European Say on Pay' (2017) 14 European Company Law 114; Nijland J and Dijkhuizen T, 'Say on Pay and Focus on Sustainability of Companies: A Revised Shareholders' Rights Directive' (2017) 14 European Company Law 188.

[2] First Proposal for the Draft SRD II: Discussion about RPTs

The European Commission presented its first proposal for the draft SRD II to the public on 9 April 2014.[1559]

Essentially, one article in that draft was devoted to RPTs.[1560] It provided a number of protective mechanisms for transactions with related parties, depending on value: (a) transactions representing no more than 1% of the company's assets; (b) transactions representing more than 1%, but no more than 5% of the company's assets; (c) transactions representing more than 5% of the company's assets, or having a significant effect on profits or turnover. While the first category of transactions was not considered to pose any threat to the company's assets, the two other categories would trigger different protective mechanisms under the draft.

For transactions representing more than 1% of their assets, companies would be required to publicly announce the terms of transaction (its nature, the related party's name, the amount of the transaction and other vital information) and accompany the announcement with a report by an independent third party assessing whether the transaction was on market terms and confirming that it was fair and reasonable for the shareholders, including minority shareholders.[1561] The third category of transactions (representing more than 5% of the company's assets or a significant impact) would trigger the company's duty to have the transaction approved by the general meeting of shareholders, provided that any shareholders who were related parties were excluded from voting.[1562] For the purposes of this requirement, transactions with one and the same related party within a twelve-month period would be aggregated.[1563]

The draft proposal allowed the Member States to relax these requirements slightly for recurring transactions conducted with the same related party within a twelve-month period. For transactions representing between 1% and 5% of the company's assets, shareholders would have the option of providing an exemption from submitting the third-party report, while more significant transactions could be pre-approved by the shareholders, again provided that any shareholders who were related parties were excluded from voting.[1564] Last but not least, one more exemption was offered for intra-group transactions.[1565] The draft allowed Member States to exclude transactions with wholly owned subsidiaries from these requirements.[1566] This and

1559. Proposal for a Directive of the European Parliament and Council amending Directive 2007/36/EC as regards the encouragement of long-term shareholder engagement and Directive 2013/34/EU as regard certain elements of the corporate governance statement, COM (2014) 213 final 2014/0121 (COD), 9.4.2014.
1560. *Ibid.*, Article 9c.
1561. *Ibid.*, Article 9c(1), paragraph 1.
1562. *Ibid.*, Article 9c(2), paragraph 1.
1563. *Ibid.*, Article 9c(3).
1564. *Ibid.*, Article 9(1), paragraph 2; Article 9(2), paragraph 2.
1565. Dijkhuizen T, 'Report from Europe: The Proposal for a Directive Amending the Shareholders Rights Directive' (2015) 12 European Company Law 45, 49.
1566. Proposal for a Directive of the European Parliament and Council amending Directive 2007/36/EC as regards the encouragement of long-term shareholder engagement and Directive 2013/34/EU as regard certain elements of the corporate governance statement, COM (2014) 213 final 2014/0121 (COD), 9.4.2014, Article 9c(4).

other exemptions were added to the text based on the European Commission's desire to limit application of the requirements to potentially disadvantageous transactions with the potential to prejudice the rights of minority shareholders.[1567]

In general, the European Commission's purpose in drafting this proposal, as far as RPTs were concerned, was to improve the transparency of and shareholder oversight on RPTs.[1568] In order to achieve its purpose, the Commission decided to combine two policy options: additional transparency requirements and a shareholder vote for the most important transactions.[1569] These two options are preferred, as being considered to offer the most effective, efficient and coherent regulation, and balancing the interests of all the various stakeholder groups.[1570]

Despite the Commission's positive goal and full consideration of the European Corporate Governance Forum's statement on RPTs,[1571] its draft proposal met with strong criticism, especially in Germany.[1572] Some even saw it as a *frontal attack on German corporate law*.[1573] Primarily, opinions were divided on the need for action as posited by the European Commission: previously, the Reflection Group had seen no shortcomings in the transparency of corporate groups and had suggested no further steps for regulating RPTs.[1574] In addition, surveys showed that some stakeholders, in particular entrepreneurs and representatives of the financial markets, in contrast to retail investors, opposed the introduction of mechanisms for RPTs at the EU level.[1575]

From the perspective of the law in Germany and other jurisdictions that use the two-tier system of corporate governance, the requirement to subject transactions above the 5% threshold to a vote by the general meeting of shareholders was viewed as inappropriate.[1576] It not only was inherently at odds with the nature of the two-tier system but also entailed a shortcoming in terms of the adequacy of company bodies.[1577] Shareholders, especially absentee shareholders, do not always possess the knowledge and skills necessary to assess whether a transaction is on market terms. It was felt to make more sense, therefore, to grant either the supervisory board or a different body the authority to review and approve RPTs.

1567. European Commission, Staff Working Document Impact Assessment accompanying the document proposal for a Directive of the European Parliament and of the Council on amending Directive 2007/36/EC as regards the long-term shareholder engagement and Directive 2013/34/EU as regards certain elements of corporate governance statement and Commission Recommendation on the quality of corporate governance reporting ('comply or explain'), SWD (2014) of 9 April 2014, 31.
1568. *Ibid.*, 45.
1569. *Ibid.*, 61.
1570. *Ibid.*
1571. *Statement of the European Corporate Governance Forum on Related Party Transactions for Listed Companies – 10 March 2011* (2011).
1572. Bayer W and Selentin P, 'Related Party Transactions: Der neueste EU-Vorschlag im Kontext des deutschen Aktien-und Konzernrechts' (2015) Neue Zeitschrift für Gesellschaftsrecht 7, 8.
1573. Ungerer F, 288.
1574. Antunes JE and others, 80.
1575. Grabowski K, *Dyrektywa o prawach akcjonariuszy. Studium tworzenia prawa i przewodnik po dyrektywie* (Officyna Allerhanda 2014), 337.
1576. Vetter J, 'Regelungsbedarf für Related Party Transactions?' (2015) 179 ZHR: Zeitschrift für das gesamte handelsrecht und wirtschaftsrecht 273, 278.
1577. Bayer W and Selentin P, 9.

Besides the incompatibilities with corporate governance systems and the issue of adequacy of company bodies, subjecting every transaction representing more than 5 % of the company's assets to a vote by the general meeting of shareholders was simply seen as too onerous,[1578] as it would impose limitations on an unjustifiable number of transactions. Combined with the accumulation of transactions under the protective regulation, this rule would potentially create unnecessary obstacles for corporate groups, leading to delays in transactions and additional costs for convening extraordinary shareholders' meetings.[1579]

Lastly, further criticism was levelled at the definition of RPTs, which the draft SRD II did not formulate directly, instead referring to the IASs. In the opinion of the critics commenting on the draft, the definition given in IAS 24 was appropriate for accounting purposes, but too broad for corporate governance.[1580] For instance, as mentioned above, significant influence corresponding to a shareholding of at least 20 %[1581] is already sufficient to qualify as a related party under IAS 24. Coupled with the broad definition of close relatives as related parties and an adherence to substantive over formal criteria, this made the definition of a related party vague and detracted from the legal certainty.

Despite these negative messages, some authors refrained from criticizing the proposal's core ideas, focusing instead on the interpretative shortcomings and, in general, expressing a favourable view of the European Commission's work to establish a framework of strong corporate governance in Europe.[1582] Kristinn Reynisson raised the following justifiable questions: (a) what transactions are covered by *transactions having significant impact on profits and turnover*;[1583] (b) whether the provision on accumulation of transactions *with the same related party* was intended to mean that particular entity, or other related parties as well, e.g. a subsidiary;[1584] (c) whether the provision on vote exclusion when *transactions involve a shareholder* was intended to refer only to shareholders, or their related parties, such as family members.[1585] These are significant remarks. If the provisions are given a narrow interpretation, it places the whole objective of the Directive at risk, leaving strict requirements without actually achieving the desired effect; if they are given a broad interpretation, the Directive would have a detrimental effect on companies and render transactions excessively onerous. That is why these comments are just as important as the more conceptual problems highlighted above.

1578. Grabowski K, 355.
1579. Bayer W and Selentin P, 9.
1580. *Ibid.*, 14; Vetter J, 282.
1581. Where the 'one share, one vote' principle applies.
1582. Reynisson K, 'Related Party Transactions: Analysis of Proposed Article 9c of Shareholders' Rights Directive' (2016) 13 European Company Law 175, 182.
1583. *Ibid.*, 179.
1584. *Ibid.*, 181.
1585. *Ibid.*

[3] *Italian Presidency Compromise Text: Main Provisions and Differences with the First Proposal*

The critical comments on the draft SRD II did not go unnoticed.[1586] During the Italian Presidency of the Council of the European Union, the Council discussed the draft on a number of occasions and on 10 November 2014 presented the Italian Presidency compromise text.[1587] This new document took into account the criticism that had been expressed and significantly modified some key provisions of the first proposal.

The most obvious change in the text of 10 November 2014 was that the thresholds (1% and 5%) had been abolished, which under the draft proposal of 9 April 2014 had divided transactions into three categories and triggered specific protective mechanisms. Instead of thresholds, the new text introduced the concept of a 'material transaction' without, however, defining this concept. To identify material transactions, Member States would then suggest one or more quantitative ratios, based on market capitalization and assets or revenues of companies, with the option of including the nature of the transaction and the position of the related party. Member States were not obliged to establish a unified materiality threshold: they could introduce separate thresholds for the announcement obligation (accompanied by an obligation to submit a report from an independent third party) and the approval obligation, depending on company size.[1588] As such, the new text gave the Member States the responsibility to define their own materiality criteria in order, first, to establish what RPTs fell within the scope of the draft SRD II and, second, to suggest separate criteria for 'minor' and 'major' transactions that were covered by the requirements.

For the announcement, report and approval mechanisms triggered by the various categories of RPT, the text had also undergone some modifications. Additional requirements had been added for the information to be disclosed in the announcement, specifically the date of the transaction.[1589] The report of the independent third party had to explain, in addition to the information stipulated in the earlier version, what assumptions and methods served as its basis. The new version of the draft SRD II allowed Member States to authorize independent directors of the company or its administrative or supervisory body to produce these reports, on the condition that related parties were prohibited from playing a deciding role.[1590]

Changes to the approval mechanism adopted the criticism that had been expressed regarding the general meeting of shareholders as the only body with the authority to decide on RPTs. Under the new version of the draft SRD II, the company's administrative or supervisory bodies could also be given this authority, provided that the approval procedure prevented related parties from taking advantage of their

1586. Bayer W and Selentin P, 10.
1587. *Presidency compromise text 10.11.2014 of the Proposal for a Directive of the European Parliament and of the Council amending Directive 2007/36/EC as regards the encouragement of long-term shareholder engagement and Directive 2013/34/EU as regards certain elements of the corporate governance statement* (2014).
1588. *Ibid.*, Article 9c(6).
1589. *Ibid.*, Article 9c(1).
1590. *Ibid.*, Article 9c(1a).

position and provided sufficient protection for minority shareholders. Logically, vote exclusion was introduced not only for shareholders but also for directors, if the transaction was approved by an administrative or supervisory body composed of directors. In addition, to accommodate the criticism, vote exclusion became applicable to a broader list of persons, viz. related parties of shareholders or directors.[1591] These suggestions were, on the whole, welcomed by the German public.[1592]

Bearing in mind that the new compromise text assigned directors a role in the approval mechanism for RPTs, the definition of a director as given in Article 1 of the Directive[1593] acquired relevance for Article 9c. Compared with the first draft of SRD II, the notion of a director covered chief executive officers and deputy chief executive officers, in addition to the members of the administrative, management or supervisory body as it had in the previous version. Member States were also authorized to designate other persons as directors if they performed functions similar to those of the company's various bodies.

The compromise text extended the list of possible exemptions for RPTs. Intra-group transactions could be exempted either if no related party had an interest in a subsidiary or if adequate protection was given to the minority shareholders in the subsidiary.[1594] Surprisingly, no reference was made to intra-group transactions with wholly owned subsidiaries in the compromise text, although logically wholly owned subsidiaries do not have any minority shareholders or shareholders as related parties. At the same time, directors as a company's related parties might of course also be directors of subsidiaries too, although the control rights of a parent with full ownership of the share capital would reduce their influence.

The compromise text allowed Member States to exempt RPTs concluded on market terms and in the company's ordinary course of business from the requirements, provided that an assessment of the terms was safeguarded by internal procedures.[1595]

Instead of giving Member States the right to allow shareholders to grant specifically defined types of recurring RPTs with an identified related party within twelve months exemption from the reporting obligation or to pre-approve specific RPTs, the compromise text changed the wording of the provision. It now allowed Member States to define types of transactions that were not disadvantageous to minority shareholders, such as issuances of shares on a pre-emptive basis or dividend payments, provided that the related party was subject to terms that were not more favourable than those to which other shareholders were subject, and exclude those transactions from the announcement, report and approval obligations.[1596]

1591. *Ibid.*, Article 9c(2).
1592. Ungerer F, 294.
1593. *Presidency compromise text 10.11.2014 of the Proposal for a Directive of the European Parliament and of the Council amending Directive 2007/36/EC as regards the encouragement of long-term shareholder engagement and Directive 2013/34/EU as regards certain elements of the corporate governance statement* (2014), p. 14.
1594. *Ibid.*, Article 9c(4)(b).
1595. *Ibid.*, Article 9c(4)(a).
1596. *Ibid.*, Article 9c(4)(c).

The compromise text of 10 November 2014 preserved the accumulation of transactions concluded within a period of one year, though in slightly different wording, specifying the company's financial year rather than a twelve-month period.[1597]

Two new paragraphs had been added in the text of 10 November. First, in response to the earlier criticism, transactions with a company were given a broader interpretation for the purposes of Article 9c, also encompassing transactions with the company's subsidiaries and so making allowance for the enterprise theory of companies.[1598] Second, Member States were given the option of introducing a duty of directors and significant shareholders to inform the administrative, management or supervisory bodies of any direct or indirect material interest in a transaction.[1599]

The publication of the Italian Presidency compromise text was followed by a new round of discussions, which soon resulted in a new version of the Italian Presidency compromise text, dated 5 December 2014.[1600]

Overall, the new compromise text of 5 December 2014 preserved the new additions and concepts of the previous version. However, it also contained some seemingly minor changes.

Primarily, the new compromise text outlined detailed criteria for materiality of transactions. In addition to the factors that Member States were required to consider under the compromise text of 10 November 2014, including market capitalization, assets and revenues of companies, two new factors were introduced for Member States to take into account. For the purposes of materiality, it was now relevant, first, how the information about the transactions might affect the decisions of a company's shareholders and, second, what risk the transaction created for a company and its minority shareholders.[1601]

Another change, and one that was almost unnoticeable, occurred in the definition of materiality. Instead of allowing Member States to take into account the nature of the transaction and the position of the related party when establishing quantitative ratios for applying the various obligations (phrased as *and which may take into account* ...), the draft specified an ambiguous alternative duty (*or take into account* ...). The ambiguity here lies in the difficulty in understanding which alternative duty opposed the obligation to take into account the nature of the transaction and the position of the related party: the duty of Member States to use quantitative ratios, or merely the criteria on which those quantitative ratios may be based. This drafting technique seems to have a major drawback. A solution where the legislature must omit a quantitative criterion in favour of a qualitative criterion to define material transactions, or vice

1597. *Ibid.*, Article 9c(7).
1598. *Ibid.*, Article 9c(5).
1599. *Ibid.*, Article 9c(8).
1600. *Presidency compromise text 05.12.2014 of the Proposal for a Directive of the European Parliament and of the Council amending Directive 2007/36/EC as regards the encouragement of long-term shareholder engagement and Directive 2013/34/EU as regards certain elements of the corporate governance statement* (2014).
1601. *Ibid.*, Article 9c(6).

versa, can be characterized as one-sided. Interpreted literally, this provision forces the legislature to sacrifice one important criterion in order to apply another.

The other changes compared with the previous compromise text had less impact on the overall regulation of RPTs. Instead of the notion of the 'amount of the transaction', the new version referred to the 'value of the transaction' in connection with the requirements for the information to be announced.[1602] The duty of Member States to stipulate an obligation for companies to accompany their announcement regarding an RPT with a report from a third party became the right of Member States to do so.[1603] Similarly, the new requirements were relaxed for some of the exemptions; specifically, instead of only allowing Member States to exclude transactions on market terms that were concluded in the ordinary course of business, under the new compromise text the announcement, report and approval obligations no longer applied to such transactions.[1604] The only stipulation was that RPTs must be reviewed by the company's administrative or supervisory body, with related parties prohibited from playing a decisive role. Additionally, the right of Member States to stipulate a duty of directors and significant shareholders to inform the company of any material interest in an RPT no longer appeared in the draft version of 5 December 2014.

Lastly, despite the exemptions and derogations described above, the text of 5 December 2014 included a number of provisions aimed at safeguarding the interests of minority shareholders. For instance, it allowed Member States to grant shareholders the authority to vote on RPTs previously approved by an administrative or supervisory body of the company, i.e. a system of double approval for RPTs.[1605] The text also obliged Member States to ensure the protection of the interests of minority shareholders in connection with RPTs between a company's related party and a subsidiary.[1606]

[4] Latvian Presidency Compromise Text and Further Modified Version of 20 March 2015

Work on the draft SRD II did not stop with the Italian Presidency compromise text of 5 December 2014. Under the Latvian Presidency, the Council continued to improve the draft, working together with other EU bodies. The new Presidency compromise text was presented on 14 January 2015, during the Latvian Presidency.[1607]

The Latvian Presidency compromise text presents an interesting development in the draft SRD II: some elements that had earlier been abandoned (such as the

1602. *Ibid.*, Article 9c(1).
1603. *Ibid.*, Article 9c(1a).
1604. *Ibid.*, Article 9c(2a).
1605. *Ibid.*, Article 9c(2).
1606. *Ibid.*, Article 9c(5).
1607. *Presidency compromise text 14.01.2015 of the Proposal for a Directive of the European Parliament and of the Council amending Directive 2007/36/EC as regards the encouragement of long-term shareholder engagement and Directive 2013/34/EU as regards certain elements of the corporate governance statement* (2015).

exemption for intra-group transactions between parents and wholly owned subsidiaries) made a reappearance,[1608] while other recently introduced changes (e.g., the exemption for clearly defined types of RPTs) were removed.[1609] It seems that the Council's intention with this new compromise text was to balance the relaxed regime from earlier versions with more stringency.[1610] Instead of obliging Member States to ensure consideration of all shareholder interests during the announcement, reporting and approval procedures, the new compromise text obliged them to ensure only that the interests of shareholders who were not related parties would be taken into account.[1611] In addition, related parties were excluded from preparing the report accompanying the announcement[1612] and from the process of approving RPTs.[1613] Investor protection was improved by the requirement to announce material RPTs no later than when they were effected, rather than when they were approved, as the previous version of the draft had stipulated.[1614]

Despite the general investor-oriented spirit of the text, some changes in the Latvian Presidency compromise text contradict that spirit, making it difficult to explain. In particular, the sentence in Article 9c expanding the scope of RPTs to include transactions between a company's subsidiaries and its related parties was removed from the draft.[1615] This deleted provision had seemed a step forward in the regulation of RPTs, by eliminating an easy possibility for companies to circumvent the requirements. The only probable reason for the Council to remove this sentence lies in an adherence to legal entity doctrine, which does not allow parents and their subsidiaries to be treated as a single economic unit. However, this approach ignores the issues and challenges of corporate groups, as outlined above.

After the Council, under the Latvian Presidency, had issued its compromise text in January 2015, work continued to prepare a draft for discussion with the EP. That preparatory draft text was completed on 20 March 2015.[1616]

The new preparatory text preserved the major structural and principal ideas of the previous draft. The Council retained the criteria established previously for defining material transactions within the scope of the Directive and the key requirements (announcement, report and approval) for RPTs.[1617] The principal difference between the two texts issued during the Latvian Presidency lay in the new exemptions introduced in the latest draft. First, it provided for the right of Member States to allow shareholders/related parties to participate in votes on RPTs, provided that national law

1608. *Ibid.*, Article 9c(4)(b).
1609. *Ibid.*, Article 9c(4)(c) and 9c(5).
1610. *Ibid.*, p. 4.
1611. *Ibid.*, Article 9c(1a), 9c(2), 9c(4)(b) and 9c(5).
1612. *Ibid.*, Article 9c(1a).
1613. *Ibid.*, Article 9c(2).
1614. *Ibid.*, Article 9c(1).
1615. *Ibid.*, Article 9c(5).
1616. *Preparatory text for an informal trialogue 20.03.2015 of the Proposal for a Directive of the European Parliament and Council amending Directive 2007/36/EC as regards the encouragement of long-term shareholder engagement and Directive 2013/34/EU as regard certain elements of the corporate governance statement* (2015).
1617. *Ibid.*, Article 9c(6), 9c(1), 9c(1a) and 9c(2).

ensured appropriate safeguards to protect the interests of shareholders that were not related parties and granted those shareholders or independent directors the right to have deciding influence to oppose specific decisions.[1618] Second, the exemption for clearly defined types of RPTs that had previously been removed now returned, subject to adequate protection of the interests of shareholders who were not related parties.[1619] Third, three previously unseen exemptions had been added to the latest text, governing the remuneration of directors,[1620] transactions by credit institutions to safeguard their stability[1621] and transactions offered to all shareholders on the same terms to ensure equal treatment.[1622]

Despite the overall exemption-oriented modifications in the new text of 20 March 2015, some changes were aimed more at adding further requirements for companies in the Member States. Specifically, the Directive would now include the possibility for Member States to allow companies to opt for the announcement, report and approval requirements for transactions on normal market terms that were conducted in the ordinary course of business.[1623] The new text also included specific requirements for transactions between a company's subsidiaries and its related parties, in particular by making the announcement of an optional report on these transactions mandatory.[1624]

[5] Discussion in the EP and the Slovak Presidency Compromise Text

As noted above, under the Latvian Presidency the Council prepared a draft text for use in the negotiations with the EP. That draft was discussed in the EP during the proceedings from 6 to 9 July 2015. The outcome of those proceedings, as far as the draft SRD II is concerned, was a new text, which was made public on 22 July 2015.[1625]

The new draft ensuing from the parliamentary proceedings was different from the document prepared by the Council under the Latvian Presidency. It appears that the EP took account of some of the core ideas underlying the Italian and Latvian Presidency compromise texts, in particular the concept of material transactions[1626] and aggregation of RPTs.[1627] However, it offered amendments based primarily on the Italian Presidency compromise text of 10 November 2014, and consequently the structure and

1618. *Ibid.*, Article 9c(2).
1619. *Ibid.*, Article 9c(4)(c).
1620. *Ibid.*, Article 9c(4)(d).
1621. *Ibid.*, Article 9c(4)(e).
1622. *Ibid.*, Article 9c(4)(g).
1623. *Ibid.*, Article 9c(2a).
1624. *Ibid.*, Article 9c(5).
1625. *Amendments by the European Parliament 22.07.2015 to the Proposal for a Directive of the European Parliament and of the Council amending Directive 2007/36/EC as regards the encouragement of long-term shareholder engagement and Directive 2013/34/EU as regards certain elements of the corporate governance statement* (2015).
1626. The materiality criteria were used instead of unified thresholds, as suggested in the First Proposal for a Directive, despite opposition from the European Commission, which was concerned about the possible dilution of the initial proposal and a lack of harmonized regulation, given that '40 per cent of shareholders were cross-border based' (*Ibid.*, 3).
1627. *Amendments by the European Parliament 22.07.2015 to the Proposal for a Directive of the European Parliament and of the Council amending Directive 2007/36/EC as regards the*

ideas of that version are reflected in the structure of the EP text, which omits some key provisions from the Latvian Presidency compromise text, e.g. the rules on transactions between a company's subsidiaries and its related parties, and adds new provisions, such as the duty to consider the company's interest in the approval process.[1628]

The most obvious amendments in the EP text were the removal of exemptions for clearly defined types of transactions, the remuneration of directors, transactions by credit institutions to maintain their economic stability and transactions offered to all shareholders on the same terms. The exemptions for intra-group transactions and transactions in the ordinary course of business were also altered. Unlike in the preparatory text of 20 March 2015, intra-group transactions could now no longer be exempted as long as adequate protection was ensured for shareholders who were not related parties, which limited the exemption to transactions with wholly owned members of groups or joint ventures and to subsidiaries without any related party interest.[1629] The exemption for transactions in the ordinary course of business was also modified. In the preparatory text, these transactions had been subject to imperative exemption, while in the EP text they were again subject to optional exemption by Member States, as they had been in the Italian Presidency compromise text of 10 November 2014.[1630] The optional nature of the report requirement from the preparatory text was replaced by a mandatory requirement to add a report to announcements concerning RPTs.[1631]

Also removed in the EP draft text were the provisions obliging companies to announce transactions between their subsidiaries and related parties, which had appeared in the preparatory text of the Latvian Presidency of 20 March 2015. Those changes have a different effect that the new exemption provisions outlined above. While the removal of the exemptions might be considered to impose more onerous requirements on companies, the elimination of the regulation for subsidiary RPTs represented a step towards greater flexibility, and as such the EP text cannot be characterized from a one-sided perspective since its provisions vary from the previous drafts in a number of different ways.

The EP text largely reiterated the substance of the Italian Presidency compromise text of 10 November 2014, rather than the preparatory text. Specifically, those were the provisions about the information to be included in announcements of RPTs ('amount of the transaction' instead of 'date and value of the transaction') and in the accompanying reports (requiring an assessment of whether the transaction is 'on market terms')[1632] and about which body has the power to approve RPTs ('shareholders' instead of the 'general meeting').[1633] Surprisingly, when outlining the rule on vote exclusion in the approval mechanism, the EP only referred to shareholders as related

encouragement of long-term shareholder engagement and Directive 2013/34/EU as regards certain elements of the corporate governance statement (2015), Article 9c(2).

1628. *Ibid.*, Article 9c(3).
1629. *Ibid.*, Article 9c(4).
1630. *Ibid.*, Article 9c(4).
1631. *Ibid.*, Article 9c(1).
1632. *Ibid.*, Article 9c(1).
1633. *Ibid.*, Article 9c(2).

parties, as in the first proposal, and omits directors, as in the preparatory text.[1634] This must be a mistake in the drafting of the rule on vote exclusion, since in the EP text the list of bodies authorized to approve RPTs was not limited to shareholders only, as in the first proposal, but included other bodies of the company that might have directors.[1635] This contradiction cannot be explained as a narrower interpretation of the concept of a director in the EP text, disallowing Member States to regard other persons performing similar functions as directors, given that members of the administrative and supervisory bodies were still viewed as directors.[1636]

Part of the EP text was concerned with clarifying the earlier provisions on material transactions and the requirement of double approval for RPTs by shareholders. In particular, the EP text gave Member States more detailed criteria to consider when defining material transactions, namely the transaction's impact on the company's results, assets, capitalization or turnover and the position of the related party.[1637] For the double approval of RPTs by shareholders, the EP text contained a special clause explaining what the legislators had intended when drafting the provisions, including a desire to protect the company's interest.[1638] However, the need for this provision is debatable, given its lack of explicit regulatory effect.

After the EP had issued its version of the text, the Council continued its work on the draft SRD II under the Luxembourg Presidency in the second half of 2015 and under the Dutch Presidency in the first half of 2016. These periods featured a series of technical meetings and Working Party meetings,[1639] where it was decided that the key elements of the preparatory text of 20 March 2015 would not be changed as far as Article 9c was concerned.[1640] In other words, Article 9c, which was devoted entirely to RPTs, was left as it had been in the Latvian Presidency preparatory text of 20 March 2015, as a basis for negotiations with the EP.[1641] Though further versions of the draft SRD II emerged during this time, Article 9c underwent no more changes during the Dutch Presidency.[1642]

1634. *Ibid.*, Article 9c(2a).
1635. *Ibid.*, Article 9c(2).
1636. *Ibid.*, Article 1(l).
1637. *Ibid.*, Article 9c(4a)(b).
1638. *Ibid.*, Article 9c(2).
1639. *Preparatory text for an informal trialogue 20.05.2016 of the Proposal for a Directive of the European Parliament and Council amending Directive 2007/36/EC as regards the encouragement of long-term shareholder engagement and Directive 2013/34/EU as regard certain elements of the corporate governance statement* (2016), 2.
1640. *Ibid.*, 3.
1641. *Ibid.*, 4.
1642. *Preparatory text for an informal trialogue 22.06.2016 of the Proposal for a Directive of the European Parliament and Council amending Directive 2007/36/EC as regards the encouragement of long-term shareholder engagement and Directive 2013/34/EU as regard certain elements of the corporate governance statement* (2016), 49-52; *State of play 30.06.2016 of the Proposal for a Directive of the European Parliament and Council amending Directive 2007/36/EC as regards the encouragement of long-term shareholder engagement and Directive 2013/34/EU as regard certain elements of the corporate governance statement* (2016), 54-58.

The interim result of the negotiations between the Council and the EP regarding the draft SRD II was the Slovak Presidency compromise text of 22 November 2016.[1643] This draft text built extensively on the text that the Council had prepared and issued on 20 March 2015 under the Latvian Presidency. Unlike the EP text, the Slovak Presidency compromise text also contained exemptions for clearly defined types of transactions, remuneration of directors, transactions by credit institutions to safeguard their stability, transactions offered to all shareholders on the same terms and requirements for transactions between a company's related parties and its subsidiaries.[1644] Overall, the structure of the new compromise text followed that of the Latvian preparatory text, except for the paragraph outlining the materiality criteria, which moved from 9c(5) to 9c(1). The language of the Slovak Presidency compromise text also largely followed the text of 20 March 2015, except that the expression *related parties are excluded from the vote* was replaced by the wording *related parties shall not take part in the vote.*[1645]

The EP text had a modest reflection in the Slovak Presidency compromise text. First, the new draft Article 9c contained numerous references to the notion of a company's interest, which had been absent previously.[1646] Second, the body authorized to approve transactions was described as 'shareholders in the general meeting' instead of 'general meeting' as used in the Latvian Preparatory Text and 'shareholders' in the EP text.[1647] These few additions represent the total influence of the EP version on the Slovak Presidency compromise text and, by themselves, had no impact on the core ideas that the Council had previously introduced in the draft SRD II.

[6] Further Negotiations and the Final Version of SRD II

The draft SRD II was further negotiated based on the Slovak Presidency compromise text of 22 November 2016. The next interim result of the discussions was a new preparatory document that was issued on 2 December 2016.[1648]

As the substance of that document indicates, the issue of RPTs was not on the minds of the Council and the EP at that stage. Among the main outstanding issues were the identification of shareholders and the transparency of asset managers.[1649] This is where the various delegations had different approaches, whether ambitious or moderate. The issues of RPTs were now less contentious, and some of the changes to Article

1643. *Presidency compromise text 22.11.2016 of the Proposal for a Directive of the European Parliament and of the Council amending Directive 2007/36/EC as regards the encouragement of long-term shareholder engagement and Directive 2013/34/EU as regards certain elements of the corporate governance statement* (2016).
1644. *Ibid.*, Article 9c(2a), 9c(d), 9c(e), 9c(g) and 9c(5).
1645. *Ibid.*, Article 9c(1a) and 9c(2).
1646. *Ibid.*, Article 9c(1), 9c(1a), 9c(2), 9c(4)(b), 9c(4)(c), 9c(4)(g) and 9c(5).
1647. *Ibid.*, Article 9c(2).
1648. *Preparatory text for the trialogue 2.12.2016 of the Proposal for a Directive of the European Parliament and Council amending Directive 2007/36/EC as regards the encouragement of long-term shareholder engagement and Directive 2013/34/EU as regard certain elements of the corporate governance statement* (2016).
1649. *Ibid.*, 3.

9c were not major, instead concerning the language or added more nuance to mechanisms already stipulated.

The draft of 2 December 2016 suggested more detailed criteria for Member States to set quantitative ratios for material transactions, in particular the amount of equity to be considered when defining material transactions.[1650] In addition, the wording of the exemption for intra-group transactions was expanded by adding another condition for its application: the Member State's national law must properly protect the interests of the company's subsidiaries and their non-related party shareholders, as well as the interests of the company and its non-related party shareholders.[1651] This was the only reference in Article 9c to any requirement to consider the interests of subsidiaries; other paragraphs stated only that the interests of a particular company had to be considered, which is logical, given the special nature of intra-group transactions.

Although the negotiations did not end up with the preparatory text of 2 December 2016, the substance of Article 9c and the related provisions in Article 1 (the concepts of a director and a related party) remained unaltered in all further preparatory documents and compromise texts.[1652] The version of the Directive that was adopted by the EP on 14 March 2017 reflected the compromise text agreed previously, with only some changes in the numbering of paragraphs and subparagraphs.[1653] The final text of Article 9c and its related provisions that passed the vote of the Council of the EU on 3 April 2017[1654] contained no differences compared with the version approved by the EP, and its substance corresponded to the preparatory text of 2 December 2016.

[7] Summary of the Development of SRD II

As this comparison of the various versions of the draft SRD II produced by the EU institutions shows, the final version of SRD II differs significantly from the first proposal issued during the Greek Presidency of the Council in April 2014. Table 5.1 contains a summary of the stages of SRD II's development, as far as regulation of RPTs is concerned.

1650. *Ibid.*, Article 9c(1).
1651. *Ibid.*, Article 9c(4)(b).
1652. *Preparatory text for the trialogue 6.12.2016 of the Proposal for a Directive of the European Parliament and Council amending Directive 2007/36/EC as regards the encouragement of long-term shareholder engagement and Directive 2013/34/EU as regard certain elements of the corporate governance statement* (2016); *Analysis of the final compromise text with a view to agreement 13.12.2016 of the Proposal for a Directive of the European Parliament and Council amending Directive 2007/36/EC as regards the encouragement of long-term shareholder engagement and Directive 2013/34/EU as regard certain elements of the corporate governance statement* (2016).
1653. *Outcome of the European Parliament's first reading (Strasbourg, 13 to 16 March) 21.03.2017 of the Proposal for a Directive of the European Parliament and Council amending Directive 2007/36/EC as regards the encouragement of long-term shareholder engagement and Directive 2013/34/EU as regard certain elements of the corporate governance statement* (2017), 2.
1654. *Voting result during the 3529th meeting of the Council of the European Union 3.04.2017 of the Proposal for a Directive of the European Parliament and Council amending Directive 2007/36/EC as regards the encouragement of long-term shareholder engagement and Directive 2013/34/EU as regard certain elements of the corporate governance statement* (2017).

Table 5.1 Development of the Draft SRD II Regarding RPTs (Article 9c)

Version Date	*Version Name*	*Key Additions/Differences Compared with the Previous Version*
9/4/2014	First draft (Greek Presidency)	- RPTs representing more than 1% of a company's assets should be publicly announced, accompanied by an independent third-party report. - Announcements of RPTs should include information about the nature of the related party relationship, the amount of the transaction and any other information necessary to assess the transaction. - The independent third-party report should state whether the transaction is on market terms and whether it is fair and reasonable from the shareholders' perspective. - RPTs representing more than 5% of a company's assets should be subject to a shareholder vote. Shareholders that are related parties are excluded from this vote. - Member States may exclude intra-group transactions with wholly owned subsidiaries from these requirements. - Member States may allow companies to request shareholders to exempt clearly defined types of RPTs with a specific party during a period of no more than twelve months after the exemption is granted. - Non-approved RPTs concluded during the previous twelve months are aggregated for the purposes of these requirements.
10/11/2014	Italian Presidency compromise text	- Thresholds (1% and 5%) are removed, materiality criteria are determined by Member States depending on company size, among other factors. - RPTs are subject to requirements if they concern material transactions, to be identified by Member States using one or more quantitative ratios, based on company's market capitalization, assets or revenues, and possibly taking into account the nature of transactions. - Additional information to be included in the announcement: the date of the transaction. - Besides an independent third party, the report may be prepared by an administrative or supervisory body of the company, or independent directors, provided that interested parties and their related persons are prohibited from playing a deciding role in its preparation. - Additional information to be included in the report: explanation of the assumptions and methods used.

Version Date	*Version Name*	*Key Additions/Differences Compared with the Previous Version*
		- Besides shareholders, an administrative or supervisory body of the company may be authorized to approve RPTs, provided that procedures are in place to prevent related parties from taking advantage of their position, with adequate protection for minority shareholders. Shareholders and directors, if they are interested parties or their related persons, are excluded from the vote, or at least from playing a deciding role in the approval process. - Exemption for RPTs with wholly owned subsidiaries is removed. Instead, Member States may exclude RPTs with subsidiaries, provided that no related party of the company has an interest in the subsidiary, or if adequate protection is in place for minority shareholders in those subsidiaries. - Member States may exclude RPTs on market terms and concluded in the ordinary course of business, provided that safeguards ensure internal assessment of these transactions. - The wording of the exemption for clearly defined types of transactions is changed: Member States may exclude clearly defined types of transactions that are not disadvantageous to minority shareholders, such as issuances of shares on a pre-emptive basis or payments of dividends, provided that the related party is subject to terms that are not more favourable than those for shareholders. - New: transactions between a company's subsidiaries and its related parties are subject to the same requirements as RPTs between the company and its related parties. - Changed wording for aggregation of RPTs: RPTs are aggregated if they are concluded in the current financial year and were not subject to the requirements. - New: directors and significant shareholders have a duty to inform one of the company's bodies about direct or indirect material interests in transactions concluded by the company.
5/12/2014	Italian Presidency compromise text	- Criteria of materiality of RPTs expanded: material RPTs should be defined taking into account (a) what influence the information about the transaction might have on shareholders' decisions and (b) what risk the transaction creates for the company and its minority shareholders.

Version Date	*Version Name*	*Key Additions/Differences Compared with the Previous Version*
		- An ambiguous alternative is inserted in the obligation to define material transactions, obliging Member States 'to set one or more quantitative ratios based on the impact of the transaction on the revenues, assets, capitalisation or turnover of the company or take into account the nature of transaction and the position of the related party'. - Information required in the announcement changed: instead of the amount of the RPT, now the value of the RPT. - The duty of Member States to ensure that the announcement of an RPT is accompanied by a third-party report changed to the right of Member States to require that the announcement must be accompanied by a third-party report. - The requirements for the substance the report changed: it no longer needs to assess whether the RPT is on normal market terms (only whether it is fair and reasonable). - The list of bodies that may produce a report is expanded to include the audit committee or any committee with a majority consisting of independent directors. - New: Member States may provide for double approval of RPTs, by a company body and by shareholders. - The provision authorizing Member States to exclude transactions conducted in the ordinary course of business becomes imperative: this provision is excluded from the requirements as mandatory, provided that related parties are prohibited from playing a deciding role in the assessment. - Additional provisions for transactions between a company's subsidiaries and its related parties: minority shareholders must be given proper protection. - Changed wording for the aggregation of RPTs: RPTs are aggregated if they are concluded in any 12-month period or in the current financial year and were not subject to the requirements. - Duty of directors and significant shareholders to report material interest in transactions is removed.
14/1/2015	Latvian Presidency compromise text	- Changed criteria for the materiality of transactions: only the economic decisions of shareholders are considered when assessing the influence of information about RPTs. - Changed deadline for the announcement of RPTs: when the RPT is effected, instead of when it is approved.

Version Date	*Version Name*	*Key Additions/Differences Compared with the Previous Version*
		- Changed requirements for the independent third-party report: only the interests of non-related-party shareholders are considered when assessing whether the RPT is on market terms and whether the RPT is fair and reasonable. - Changed conditions for preparing the report: interested parties and persons related to them should be excluded from its preparation, rather than just prohibited from playing a deciding role. - Changed conditions for approving RPTs: adequate protection for non-related-party shareholders, rather than protection of the interests of minority shareholders only. - Changed wording for the vote exclusion for RPTs: shareholders and directors must be excluded from the vote on approval, instead of only from playing a deciding role in the RPT's approval. - Exemption for RPTs with wholly owned subsidiaries returned: Member States may exclude these RPTs from the requirements. - Changed exemption for transactions on market terms and conducted in the normal course of business: related parties are excluded from the assessment of these transactions, instead of only from playing a deciding role. - Exemption for clearly defined types of RPTs removed. - Provision subjecting transactions between a company's subsidiaries and its related parties to the same requirements as RPTs between the company and its related parties is removed. The general obligation of Member States to ensure protection of the interests of minority shareholders in connection with transactions between a company's related parties and its subsidiaries remains.
20/3/2015	Text in preparation for the informal trialogue	- Changed criteria for materiality of transactions: when assessing the risk posed by an RPT, the interests of non-related-party shareholders are considered, rather than the interests of minority shareholders only. - Additional provision authorizing Member States to allow shareholders that are related parties to take part in the vote, provided that their national laws ensure appropriate safeguards to protect non-related-party shareholders. - Member States are entitled not only to exclude intra-group transactions but also to allow companies to exclude RPTs. - Unconditional nature of the exemption for RPTs on market terms and conducted in the normal course of business becomes more detailed: Member States may state that companies must apply requirements for these RPTs.

Version Date	*Version Name*	*Key Additions/Differences Compared with the Previous Version*
		- Exemption for clearly defined types of RPTs returned: Member States may exclude or allow companies to exclude clearly defined types of RPTs for which their national laws require approval by the general meeting, provided that they ensure fair treatment of all shareholders and safeguard the interests of non-related-party shareholders, including minority shareholders, in such RPTs. - More exemptions for RPTs: Member States may exclude or allow companies to exclude: (i) transactions regarding remuneration of directors, or certain elements of remuneration of directors, awarded or due in accordance with the requirements of Article 9a; (ii) transactions conducted by credit institutions on the basis of measures to safeguard their stability, adopted by the competent authority exercising prudential supervision within the meaning of European legislation; (iii) transactions offered to all shareholders on the same terms, where equal treatment of all shareholders is ensured. - Provision ensuring that the interests of minority shareholders in transactions between a company's related parties and its subsidiaries changed: Member States must ensure that companies publicly announce material transactions between a company's related party and its subsidiaries, with the right of Member States to subject these transactions to the independent third-party report requirement.
22/7/2015	Outcome of the EP's proceedings	- Changed criteria for materiality of transactions: in addition to other criteria, the impact of the transaction on the company's results, assets, capitalization or turnover and the position of a related party must be considered. - Throughout the text, the requirement to consider the interests of a company (in addition to the interests of non-related-party shareholders) is expressed. - Changed requirements for the substance of the announcement: instead of the transaction value and date, the transaction amount is required (returning to the first Italian Presidency compromise text of 10/11/2014), and information must specifically assess the economic fairness of a transaction from the company's perspective.

Version Date	*Version Name*	*Key Additions/Differences Compared with the Previous Version*
		- The right of Member States to subject RPTs to a third-party report obligation in addition to announcement obligations changed into a duty of Member States to ensure that the announcement is accompanied by a third-party report (return to the first Italian Presidency compromise text of 10/11/2014). - The requirements for the substance of the report changed: among other information, it must state whether the RPT is on normal market terms (return to the first Italian Presidency compromise text of 10/11/2014). - Exemption for intra-group transactions changed: adequate protection of non-related-party shareholders is no longer considered. - Exemption for transactions on market terms and conducted in the normal course of business changed: instead of an imperative exemption, it is again left to the discretion of the individual Member State (return to the first Italian Presidency compromise text of 10/11/2014). - Exemptions for clearly defined types of transactions and exemptions introduced in the Text in preparation for the informal trialogue of 20/3/2015 removed. - Regulations for transactions between a company's related parties and its subsidiaries removed.
22/11/2016	Slovak Presidency compromise text	- Essentially a return to the Text in preparation of informal trialogue of 20.3.2015, including provisions on: (i) materiality conditions; (ii) announcement requirements; (iii) discretion of Member States to stipulate that the announcement must be accompanied by a report; (iv) the content of the report; (v) persons producing the report; (iv) exemption for intra-group transactions; (v) exemption for transactions in the normal course of business and on normal market terms; (vi) exemption for clearly defined types of transactions; (vii) exemptions introduced in the Text for preparation of informal trialogue of 20/03/2015; (viii) provisions on transactions between a company's related parties and its subsidiaries. - Only the wording of the provisions on double approval of RPTs is changed. - The requirement to consider the company's interests is preserved from the previous version.

Version Date	*Version Name*	*Key Additions/Differences Compared with the Previous Version*
2/12/2016	Text in preparation for the trialogue	- Additional details in the materiality criteria, obliging Member States to consider equity within capitalization when subjecting material transactions to the requirements. - Exemption for intra-group transactions changed: it may be applied if adequate protection is ensured for the company, the subsidiary and their shareholders; i.e., the interests of a company's subsidiary and its shareholders must be considered.
17/5/2017	Final text of SRD II	- No changes introduced compared with the previous version.

An analysis of the first proposal of 9 April 2014 and the Italian Presidency compromise text provides sufficient evidence to support the argument that the latter version of the draft demonstrated a shift towards more flexible regulation of RPTs in listed companies. Compared with the provisions of the first proposal of 9 April 2014, the later draft gave Member States freedom to define the materiality criteria for subjecting RPTs to the announcement, report and approval requirements, to authorize a specific company body to approve RPTs and to provide exemptions from the requirements.

In spite of the fact the Italian Presidency compromise text accommodated the criticism described above, regarding which body was authorized to approve transactions and the excessively onerous materiality criteria,[1655] apparently possibilities for improvement were still found. For instance, some of the criticism concerned the excessively broad definition of a related party, as mentioned above, and insufficient consideration for provisions regarding de facto groups in German law.[1656] However, an examination of the texts detailed by the EP (22 July 2015) and the Council under the Latvian Presidency (14 January and 20 March 2015) and under the Slovak Presidency (22 November 2016 and 2 December 2016) shows that the Member States decided not to limit the concept of a related party. One of the reasons behind this decision was a desire to simplify the implementation of the Directive in the Member States.[1657] As a result, SRD II uses the same definition of a related party as the Accounting Directive and the IASs. The legislators drafting the Directive might have wished to make the concept of a related party more uniform. At the same time, however, that uniformity is clearly lacking for the understanding of material transactions, as the various draft versions of the Directive following the Italian Presidency compromise text and the final version of SRD II did not return to the initial 1 % and 5 % thresholds of the first proposal. Given that RPTs often involve cross-border transactions, this regulation might present difficulties for the authorities enforcing the law, if individual Member States decide to

1655. Vetter J, 278.
1656. Bayer W and Selentin P, 14.
1657. Ungerer F, 296.

regulate these matters differently. Moreover, the criteria for materiality in SRD II do not match the definition of materiality under the IASs,[1658] which creates some ambiguity on how these notions should be reconciled.

Although the Italian Presidency compromise text laid the foundations for the understanding of where and how the announcement, report and approval mechanisms should be triggered, the input provided during the Latvian and Slovak Presidencies should not be underestimated. It was in the Council's text of 20 November 2015, under the Latvian Presidency, where most of the exemptions and specific provisions for transactions between a company's related parties and its subsidiaries made their first appearance. Those provisions were preserved in the Slovak Presidency compromise text and passed into the final Directive. The version of Article 9c in the text prepared and issued by the Council under the Slovak Presidency on 2 December 2016 is the final version and did not undergo any substantial change beyond that point. The merit of the Council's work under the Luxembourg, Dutch and Slovak Presidencies lay in striking a balance between the various versions of the draft SRD II. As a result, while some ideas from the EP text (22 July 2015) were considered by the Council, overall the version of Article 9c as it appeared in the preparatory text of 20 March 2015 (under the Latvian Presidency) largely remained the same until the end.

[8] RPT-Related Strategies in the EU Based on Recent Regulatory Developments

With the adoption of SRD II, disclosure through financial statements and management reports is no longer the only instrument for eliminating detrimental RPTs of listed companies. As can be inferred from the Directive's final version, the EU legislature undertook to combine several different strategies into a single act: the procedural rights strategy (entailing both the trusteeship and decision rights safeguards), mandatory disclosure in combination with a fairness opinion and, to a limited extent, the standards strategy.

Based on an examination of the German, Polish and Dutch company law regimes, the conclusion is justified that the existing approval procedures for RPTs of listed companies in these jurisdictions are more relaxed than the new EU rules. This has forced the Member States to take steps to be able to implement SRD II. For instance, on 6 November 2019, the Dutch government adopted a bill incorporating the Directive's provisions into the BW, by adding a new section devoted to RPTs of NVs in Title 4 of the Book 2 (Articles 167-170).[1659] These new provisions include three blocks of rules:

1658. *Ibid.*, 318.
1659. Wet van 6 november 2019 tot wijziging van Boek 2 van het Burgerlijk Wetboek, de Wet op het financieel toezicht en de Wet giraal effectenverkeer ter uitvoering van Richtlijn 2017/828/EU van het Europees Parlement en de Raad van 17 mei 2017 tot wijziging van Richtlijn 2007/36/EG wat het bevorderen van de langetermijnbetrokkenheid van aandeelhouders betreft (PbEU 2017, L 132), available at: https://zoek.officielebekendmakingen.nl/stb-2019-423.html?utm_medium=email.

(i) transactions governed by the new rules, (ii) disclosure obligations and (iii) approval obligations.

What is particularly notable in the new statute is how its legislators approach the concept of RPTs covered by the rules. As under SRD II, the notion of a related party is defined by reference to the IASs. The broad concept of a related party as posited by IAS 24 is limited by the ramifications of materiality of RPTs, as explained in Article 2:167(3) of the BW, implementing subparagraphs 1 and 2 of Article 9c(1) of SRD II.

Article 2:167(3) mainly concerns the implementation of subparagraph 2 of Article 9c(2). Here, the legislators have chosen to adhere to the strict literal interpretation of the provision, as originally formulated in the Italian Presidency compromise text of 5 December 2014, containing only the suggestion *to take into account the nature of the transaction and the position of a related party*. The duty to additionally impose quantitative ratios is held to be superfluous, due to the alternative wording used in subparagraph 2 of Article 9c(1).[1660] This literal interpretation of subparagraph 2 of Article 9c(1) is debatable, however, for the following reasons.

First, the recitals and Article 9c(2) of SRD II require companies to announce their material transactions, identifying any related parties, the nature of the RPT, its date and its value and any other information necessary to assess whether the transaction is fair and reasonable.[1661] Given the existence of these provisions and the scope of disclosure, it seems inappropriate to adopt a one-sided interpretation of materiality, omitting either the quantity or the quality criteria. Second, before the present definition of materiality was formulated in Article 9c, the first draft proposal of 9 April 2014 and the Italian Presidency compromise text of 10 November 2014 had focused on quantitative criteria for the disclosure and approval obligations. Therefore, the fact that the role of quantitative criteria was curtailed so drastically is not based on the legislators' initial efforts.

Several points are worth noting in connection with how the nature of the transaction and the position of the related party are accommodated in the statute. For taking the nature of the transaction into consideration, the legislators suggest applying Article 2:167(3)(a) of the BW, which refers to Article 7(1) of the European MAR to explain materiality in RPTs. A transaction is regarded as material if it falls under the definition of inside information as employed by the MAR. On the one hand, the idea of defining material transactions through the concept of inside information sounds reasonable. The obligation to disclose information with a significant effect on the price of securities already exists,[1662] and this approach by the legislature would simplify matters for companies, by combining the two announcement obligations. On the other hand, doubts have been expressed as to whether this is the best solution: first, the definition of inside information is not sufficiently specific and needs further explanation, and second the idea of materiality as given shape in accounting regulations is

1660. Groenland IC, 'Related Party Transactions in the Revised Shareholders' Rights Directive: The EU Perspective and Implementation in National Law' (2019) 16 European Company Law 44, 46.
1661. SRD II, recital 44, Article 9c(2).
1662. Pursuant to Article 17 of the MAR.

essentially different from inside information. Only material information is subject to disclosure under IFRS.[1663] While IAS 24 makes no direct mention of materiality in connection with disclosure of RPTs, the concept is in the very definition of an RPT as a *transfer of resources, services or obligations between a reporting entity and a related party, regardless of whether the price is charged.*[1664] In other words, for accounting purposes the concept of materiality concerns mainly the internal features of an RPT, i.e. its object, value, etc., rather than its external effect, as is the case with the inside information.[1665]

For considering the position of a related party, Article 2:167(3)(b) of the BW defines three categories of related parties: (i) one or more holders of shares that alone or jointly represent at least one-tenth of the issued capital; (ii) a director of the company; (iii) or a supervisory director of the company. This provision outlines the criteria for related parties in conjunction with the IASs, as described in Article 2:167(2). Moreover, by viewing shareholders with one-tenth of share capital as related parties, Article 2:167(3)(b)(i) in fact has an extensive scope as it goes beyond the requirements of the IASs, where the prerequisite for a shareholder to be viewed as a related party is one-fifth of the share capital.[1666] This step was explained by a desire to apply the best practices provisions,[1667] as contained in the Dutch CGC.[1668]

Therefore, it can be inferred from the substance of Article 2:167(3) of the BW that the Dutch legislators have decided to apply the qualitative concept of the materiality only, having abandoned the quantitative criteria. This approach might match the literal wording of Article 9c(1) of SRD II and could have similarly been used by the legislatures of other jurisdictions. In Germany, the legislature has also interpreted subparagraph 2 of Article 9c(1) of SRD II as an alternative obligation and has opted to apply the quantitative criteria instead. According to Article 111b(1) and 111c(1) of the AktG, rules on approval and disclosure apply if the transaction represents more than 1.5% of the company's assets according to its financial statements.[1669] Again, while this approach does not deviate from the literal wording of the provisions of the Directive, it has another major drawback: it defines materiality from a one-sided perspective, which is contrary to the stated flexible nature of SRD II.[1670]

1663. Enriques L, 'Related Party Transactions: Policy Options and Real-World Challenges (with a Critique of the European Commission Proposal)', 9; International Financial Reporting Standard 1, as adopted by Commission Regulation (EC) No. 1126/2008 of 3 November 2008 adopting certain international accounting standards in accordance with Regulation (EC) No. 1606/2002 of the European Parliament and of the Council [2008] OJ L 320/1, 29.11.2008, paragraph 31.
1664. IAS 24, paragraph 9.
1665. MAR, Article 7(1).
1666. *See* section §3.03 [A] [2].
1667. Kamerstuk 35058 nr. 3, available at: https://zoek.officielebekendmakingen.nl/dossier/35058/kst-35058-3?resultIndex=3&sorttype=1&sortorder=4.
1668. Dutch CGC, section 2.7.5.
1669. Gesetz zur Umsetzung der zweiten Aktionärsrechterichtlinie (ARUG II) Vom 12. Dezember 2019, available at: https://www.bmjv.de/SharedDocs/Gesetzgebungsverfahren/Dokumente/BGBL_ARUG_II.pdf;jsessionid=BFCA63204411788FDA338B992C3D4E43.1_cid289?__blob=publicationFile&v=1 (Federal Law Gazette I Nr. 50, issued in Bonn on 19 December 2019).
1670. Ungerer F, 319.

For the announcement and approval obligations, the Dutch government has followed the requirements of SRD II[1671] and requires companies to introduce internal mechanisms to monitor whether RPTs are conducted on normal market terms and in the ordinary course of business (Article 2:168 of the BW). Only RPTs that fail to satisfy those characteristics should be subject to the announcement and approval obligations (Article 2:169(1-3)). The provisions of SRD II regarding transactions between a company's subsidiary and its parties[1672] and aggregation of transactions[1673] are also reflected in the statute (Article 2:167(4) and 2:170). Furthermore, in its analysis of whether Dutch law already prohibits officers from participating in the approval of or votes on transactions in which they themselves are involved, as SRD II requires,[1674] the company law committee found that Article 2:129(6) and 2:140(5) of the BW do not conform sufficiently to SRD II.[1675] The scope of Article 2:129(6) and 2:140(5) is held to be limited by officers' personal interests, whereas in RPTs the interests of officers might not always be personal – for instance, if an officer only fulfils a function within a company that is a related party.[1676] The recent debate concerning the concept of a 'personal interest' has already been mentioned in sections §2.03 and §5.02, where it was noted, among other findings, that the very concept of a 'personal interest' might not stand in the way of the effect of reasonableness and fairness in preventing conflicts of officers' non-personal qualitative interests. Still, notwithstanding the role of Dutch legal principles, to ensure *ex ante* clarity[1677] it makes sense that Article 9c(4) subparagraph 3 of SRD II is implemented separately in Article 2:169(4).

On the subject of the optional provisions of SRD II, the Dutch government's company law committee decided not to impose an additional onus on companies, by not forcing them to add a report to the mandatory announcement,[1678] submit transactions to the general meeting of shareholders for approval[1679] or apply announcement and approval requirements to RPTs on normal market terms and concluded in the ordinary course of business.[1680] The preference for a flexible regime for companies is further evidenced by the fact that almost all exemptions for RPTs in SRD II have found their way into Article 2:169(5), except for the exemption for clearly defined RPTs.[1681] At the same time, the legislators have decided not to limit the requirements to public companies (NVs) only. It has been suggested that private companies (BVs) listed on a stock exchange should also fall under these rules (Article 2:187); this might reflect an exception to the relaxed regime chosen here.

1671. SRD II, Article 9c(5).
1672. *Ibid.*, Article 9c(7).
1673. *Ibid.*, Article 9c(8).
1674. *Ibid.*, Article 9c(4), subparagraph 3.
1675. Kamerstuk 35058 nr. 3, available at: https://zoek.officielebekendmakingen.nl/dossier/35058/kst-35058-3?resultIndex=3&sorttype=1&sortorder=4.
1676. *Ibid.*
1677. Bartman SM and Dorresteijn AF, 913, 918-919.
1678. SRD II, Article 9c(3).
1679. *Ibid.*, Article 9c(4).
1680. *Ibid.*, Article 9c(5), subparagraph 2.
1681. *Ibid.*, Article 9c(6).

This analysis of the new statute shows a flexible approach for companies and a high degree of alignment with the provisions of SRD II, except for the parts concerning the definition of a material transaction. In those parts, the legislators have decided to use unclear abstract wording and apply a literal, but arguably accurate, interpretation of the Directive's provisions. Ultimately, their practical application will show how efficient these new requirements are.[1682] Doubts remain as to whether these changes will significantly alter the situation, given that SRD II sets forth numerous exemptions from the procedural, disclosure and expert obligations.[1683] In addition, even if the changes fail to ensure efficient scrutiny of conflicted transactions in Germany and the Netherlands, the standards strategy, employing the duty of loyalty and the legal principles, will help prevent matters from going too far off course.

[9] Ukrainian Company Law Against the Background of Recent Regulatory Developments on RPTs in the EU

Ukraine is not an EU Member State, and even though SRD I is one of the Directives subject to implementation under the EU-Ukraine Association Agreement, this obligation does not extend to newly adopted EU instruments. As such, Ukraine only has a right, and not an obligation, to implement the new rules. Interestingly, however, the procedural safeguards for public companies and (optionally) for private companies that are already in place in Ukraine are similar to what SRD II seeks to achieve. For example, in both cases, RPTs must undergo a procedure of approval by a competent disinterested body of the company, be subjected to a third-party expert's fairness opinion and be publicly announced. Another point that the two regimes have in common is the use of materiality criteria in both the JSC Law of Ukraine and SRD II. The difference here lies in how abstract those criteria are: the materiality criteria in SRD II are no more than guidelines for Member States to consider and to interpret in their national laws, while in Ukraine the criteria are more specific. The JSC Law of Ukraine requires that the safeguards apply only to transactions with interest that represent a value in excess of 1 % of the company's assets, with approval from the general meeting of shareholders being mandatory for transactions representing 10% or more of the company's assets.

Despite the striking similarities between the two instruments, some significant differences remain. First, SRD II applies to listed companies only, while the JSC Law of Ukraine imposes its safeguards on all public companies, regardless of whether or not they are listed. Second, the JSC Law of Ukraine employs the concept of a transaction with interest, which is broader than the concept of an RPT. Besides RPTs, transactions with interest also include transactions where an interested person acts as a representative, broker, beneficiary or controller of a legal entity that is party to a transaction.

1682. Horak H, *The Newly Amended Shareholders Rights Directive: Lots of Rights, What about Implementation?* (22nd International Scientific Conference on Economic and Social Development – 'Legal Challenges of Modern World'), 548.

1683. Van der Elst C, 'The Duties of Significant Shareholders in Transactions with the Company', 219.

Third, they define a related party differently: the JSC Law of Ukraine provides for its own concept of an interested person, while SRD II defines related parties by referring to the IASs, specifically IAS 24, which contains a broader, though still comparable, definition.[1684] Fourth, SRD II employs the standards strategy to some extent, by exempting transactions that are on normal market terms and conducted in the ordinary course of business. For those transactions, the company must establish an internal procedure to periodically assess whether the conditions are fulfilled. The JSC Law of Ukraine does not contain any similar provisions. Fifth, SRD II provides for different exemptions than the JSC Law of Ukraine does and formulates them in vaguer terms. Sixth, SRD II provides for aggregation of RPTs for the purposes of the safeguards, which the JSC Law of Ukraine does not. Seventh, the list of persons permitted to prepare fairness reports on RPTs is longer in SRD II, while the JSC Law of Ukraine dictates that these reports must come from either the auditor or an appropriately qualified person. Last, unlike SRD II, the JSC Law of Ukraine does not place any constraints on transactions between a company's subsidiaries and its related parties.

It would be negligent to unconditionally favour SRD II over the JSC Law of Ukraine in all these differences, without a careful discussion of the factors that could influence the choice of an RPT strategy in Ukraine. Before discussing whether SRD II should be implemented in Ukraine in its entirety, it is vital to first analyse whether that would even be practical. That analysis is presented in the next chapter.

1684. The concept of a related party is covered in detail in Chapter 3.

CHAPTER 6
Choice of Strategy for RPTs in Ukraine

§6.01 FACTORS INFLUENCING THE CHOICE OF STRATEGY

[A] Introduction

The strategies described in Chapter 5 are capable of being applied in various jurisdictions. The effect of their use differs, however, depending on the specific circumstances. This section presents the factors that the legislature should take into account when choosing the best strategy or strategies for dealing with RPTs, based on empirical and legal evidence from the jurisdictions in focus.[1685]

[B] Implementation of RPT-Related Strategies in Germany, Poland and the Netherlands

According to a study published by the OECD based on the 2008 CFA Institute Report, from a sample of ninety-five German companies, 7% reported RPTs; from a sample of fourteen Polish companies, 14% reported RPTs; and from thirty Dutch companies 0% reported RPTs.[1686] These data should not be interpreted as meaning that companies in the Netherlands do not employ RPTs at all: the scope of the research was limited to the companies included in the major market index, and other companies that might conduct RPTs were omitted. Nor does it imply that the RPTs reported in Germany and Poland were disadvantageous to the reporting companies: to conclude that a particular RPT caused damages would require applying special cost/benefit measurements to evaluate both the costs and savings of the transaction.[1687] In other words, this information shows only that RPTs existed, without proving any specific details of what

1685. The empirical data from the relevant jurisdictions have already been discussed in Chapter 1.
1686. OECD, *Related Party Transactions and Minority Shareholder Rights* (OECD Publishing, 2012), 31.
1687. Pacces AM, 2.

they mean to the enterprises concerned. The only conclusion that can be drawn based on the figures presented in the OECD report, which is consistent with the view expressed in academic works,[1688] is that concentrated ownership systems show a higher frequency of RPTs.

Similarly to how information concerning the number of RPTs in a given jurisdiction does not reveal what is behind those RPTs, information about the ownership structures of companies does not automatically give evidence of RPTs in a certain jurisdiction, nor does it provide reliable information as to their nature (detrimental or not). Nevertheless, details of the stock market structure and the key shareholders in companies as established in a particular jurisdiction have value from the perspective of showing what transactions are most likely to be conducted in that jurisdiction.

The commonly heard observation that corporate ownership in Continental Europe is becoming increasingly concentrated[1689] might seem, to a certain extent, misleading, from a closer look at specific jurisdictions. As discussed in section §1.05, since the beginning of the 1990s, the development of the stock markets in Germany, Poland and the Netherlands has picked up pace. In Poland, the stock market emerged through the effectively organized privatization processes emerging from the ashes of Communist rule, when private property was recognized only for individuals and extended to private belongings only. The story was different in Germany and the Netherlands, where private property had existed for a long time, but where the capital markets, until the 1990s, were not as developed as in the US and UK. The data presented in section §1.05 show the new trends that emerged in the 1990s,[1690] e.g. that German banks retreated from ownership of companies, while in the Netherlands substantial blocks of shares came to be owned by foreign investors.

Although the stock markets in Germany and the Netherlands have become more dispersed in recent decades, the numbers quoted indicated that ownership concentration was still the rule.[1691] This is not necessarily a negative, however: concentration of capital is often viewed as a natural reaction to inadequate investor protection.[1692] Increased share capital allows investors to exert greater influence over their controlled companies and establish long-term relationships with their partners.[1693] This is not always feasible with dispersed ownership, where reconciling the interests of shareholders is a prominent and difficult issue.

At the same time, concentrated ownership is not without its drawbacks. It creates a risk of private benefits extraction.[1694] Controlling shareholders might be tempted to tunnel corporate assets, especially if investor protection is weak.[1695] Yet even if the

1688. Sáez MI and Riaño D, 362.
1689. Lannoo K, 'Corporate Governance, West and East: A Synthesis of the EU Framework in the Perspective of Enlargement' in Balling M (ed.), *Corporate Governance, Financial Markets and Global Convergence* (Springer 1998), 212.
1690. Bolt W and Peeters M, 95.
1691. Tamowicz P, 95.
1692. Becht M and Mayer C, 4.
1693. Mayer C, 'Corporate Governance, Competition and Performance' in Balling M (ed.), *Corporate Governance, Financial Markets and Global Convergence* (Springer 1998), 256.
1694. *Ibid.*
1695. Friedman E, Johnson S and Mitton T, 748.

controlling shareholder behaves fairly and reasonably, concentrated ownership does not prevent a firm from economic failure. For instance, in Germany a positive correlation was observed between corporate control and firm performance in the 1970s and 1980s, and this changed to a negative correlation in the 1990s.[1696] Even assuming that malicious intent was not the reason for the firm's performance failures and that the real cause lay in unintentional errors in business decisions initiated by blockholders, those blockholders would still have been more likely to succeed if their errors could have been properly monitored and constrained.

Germany previously had a reputation as a jurisdiction where financial institutions, notably banks, coordinated their efforts with shareholders in corporate policy efficiently.[1697] According to academic sources, those banks now lack the same strong oversight, although thoughts on its effect are mixed: while some scholars have expressed the opinion that the result will be disastrous without proper external oversight,[1698] others have highlighted the absence of reliable evidence confirming the banks' positive monitoring role.[1699] Whatever the real effect of that monitoring is, the argument posited by Zohar Goshen cannot be ignored: sophisticated investors are capable of designing effective counteractive measures.[1700] So, if the banks' participation in the corporate governance of German companies was successful in preventing any looting of corporate assets, its disappearance could have created an apparent gap.

Despite the arguable lack of a pre-existing element of German corporate governance, as represented by financial institutions, I am far from convinced that the reduction of the banks' influence is catastrophic. The German jurisdiction possesses sufficient and flexible means to address the issues of abusive actions by shareholders, in particular through claims to compensate loss or damage caused by breaches of the shareholder's duty of loyalty.[1701] In the Netherlands, the provisions of tort law in combination with the principles of reasonableness and fairness, which also play a key role in Dutch enquiry proceedings, have been used to successfully penalize shareholder misconduct. In addition, Germany, Poland and the Netherlands have capital maintenance regulations that can be used against shareholders seeking to extract corporate wealth. These *ex post* mechanisms may all be helpful in combatting

1696. Goergen M, Manjon MC and Renneboog L, 'Recent Developments in German Corporate Governance' (2008) 28 International Review of Law and Economics 175, 190.
1697. Goshen Z, 'The Efficiency of Controlling Corporate Self-Dealing: Theory Meets Reality', 434.
1698. Tröger T, 'Germany's Reluctance to Regulate Related Party Transactions: An Industrial Organization Perspective', 22-23.
1699. Goergen M, Manjon MC and Renneboog L, 190.
1700. Goshen Z, 'The Efficiency of Controlling Corporate Self-Dealing: Theory Meets Reality', 424.
1701. Some authors have argued that the mechanisms to protect against self-dealing by controlling shareholders in Belgium, France and the Netherlands are insufficient (Hallemeesch N, 'Self-Dealing by Controlling Shareholders: Improving Minority Protection in Light of Article 9 c SRD' (2018) 15 European Company and Financial Law Review 197, 235). Nonetheless, these countries are all developed economies where the legal principles are enforced to a high level, and the courts provide a highly satisfactory standard of protection compared with developing legal systems.

inappropriate extractions of corporate benefits, in accordance with the idea of remedying distributions to shareholders that are not pro rata.[1702]

While *ex post* remedies for RPTs carry much weight in Germany, Poland and the Netherlands, it would be a mistake to underestimate the effect of *ex ante* tools in these jurisdictions. This is another argument for overcoming any concerns about the banks' retreat from corporate governance. The value of *ex ante* procedural scrutiny lies not only in its preventive effect[1703] but also in the presence of various different types of stakeholders whose interests must be taken into account in these countries: employees, who enjoy representation in company bodies based on co-determination provisions in the relevant jurisdictions (Germany and the Netherlands), and institutional investors, whose monitoring function is supported in literature.[1704] Their input might be crucial in preventing detrimental transactions by controlling shareholders. In other words, even without banks as a major influence, companies in these jurisdictions apparently have other stakeholders that can effectively monitor RPTs.

For RPTs with shareholders and their related parties, one major obstacle stands in the way of effective monitoring: statutory law in Germany, Poland and the Netherlands is not much concerned with procedural and informational scrutiny of transactions with shareholders or their related parties.[1705] The focus is primarily on misconduct by managers, supervisory board members and their related parties. This is surprising: while the main issue with dispersed ownership is the agency conflict between shareholders and managers, with the concentrated ownership that is said to be so intrinsic in Germany, Poland and the Netherlands, the need to limit controlling shareholder's behaviour is apparent.[1706] This does not mean that controlling shareholders should be treated as suspects in the company and be deprived of its benefits; nor does it mean, however, that any liability of officers is always groundless. In fact, even in controlled closed corporations, officers can deviate from their shareholders' instructions and cause harm. What I am saying here is that, given the need to balance the interests of various stakeholder groups in a society with concentrated corporate ownership, *ex ante* safeguards for RPTs with shareholders and their related parties would be too important to neglect.

Lastly, ownership structure, while being undeniably important for the design of RPT-related strategies in a given jurisdiction, is not the only influencing factor that should be taken into account. Other significant aspects must also be considered. For

1702. Rock E and Wachter ML, 'Waiting for the Omelet to Set: Match-Specific Assets and Minority Oppression' in McCahery J and Vermeulen EM (eds), *The Governance of Close Corporations and Partnerships: US and European Perspectives* (Oxford University Press on Demand 2004), 130.
1703. Chugh D, Bazerman MH and Banaji MR, 'Bounded Ethicality as Psychological Barrier to Recognizing Conflicts of Interest' in Moore DA and others (eds), *Conflicts of Interest: Challenges and Solutions in Business, Law, Medicine, and Public Policy* (Cambridge University Press 2005), 91; Issacharoff S, 201.
1704. Mezzanotte FE and Fung S, 'Do Institutional Owners Monitor? Evidence from Voting on Connected Transaction Proposals in Hong Kong-Listed Companies' (2018) 7 Michigan Business & Entrepreneurial Law Review 221, 240.
1705. So far as the SRD II is not implemented therein.
1706. Davies P and others, 91.

instance, company law itself shapes investors' decisions to buy shares or exit companies.[1707] Where the legal requirements for entering a market are excessively onerous, potential investors might be deterred from establishing companies or acquiring equity. In terms of their appeal to investors, Germany, Poland and the Netherlands are all positioned higher in the 2019 Doing Business ranking of jurisdictions than Ukraine.[1708] This and other factors are discussed in the next section.

[C] Factors to Consider in the Design of RPT-Related Strategies

In order to provide for efficient regulation of RPTs in a country, it is vital to take account of the existing situation in that country. The ownership structure of companies, demonstrating who the key participants in corporate relationships are, is a crucial factor for designing rules to deal with conflicted behaviour. Information about the key owners of companies provides powerful insight into the principal stakeholders and their interests. This does not diminish the need to draft laws and regulations in order to attract new stakeholders, particularly investors, to the country; instead, it presents an argument for considering the interests of the existing players. As has been seen above, concentrated ownership is common in Continental Europe, meaning that large blockholders provide the context of corporate governance in Europe.

Their influence is twofold. On the one hand, blockholders are positioned strongly to monitor the company's management.[1709] A majority stake in the company's capital is usually sufficient to dismiss managers who breach their duties; this allows controlling shareholders an effective way to curb self-dealing.[1710] The fear of dismissal is expected to cause managers to act with greater loyalty towards the company and with due care. However, this is contingent on large shareholders being interested in improving the firm's performance. On the other hand, blockholders can become tempted to extract private benefits of their control.[1711] These value-destructive extractions often take the form of RPTs and as such are viewed as the major cost of concentrated ownership.[1712] For instance, empirical evidence from China in the 2001-2008 period showed that the most severe instances of tunnelling occurred in companies with ownership concentration varying between 34.46% and 39.01%.[1713] The equilibrium of negative consequences produced by concentrated ownership is embodied in control premium, showing the difference between the market price of

1707. Cheffins BR, 33.
1708. *Doing Business 2019: Training for Reform*, 5.
1709. Sulaiman ANM, 'Responding to Concentrated Ownership: The Related-Party Transaction Provisions of Some Asian Countries' (2007) 3 Corporate Governance Law Review 70, 71.
1710. Enriques L, Hertig G and Kanda H, 'Related-Party Transactions' in Kraakman R and others (eds), *The Anatomy of Corporate Law A Comparative and Functional Approach* (2nd edn, Oxford University Press 2009), 178.
1711. Dyck A and Zingales L, 'Private Benefits of Control: An International Comparison' (2004) 59 The Journal of Finance 537, 589.
1712. Hopt KJ and Pistor K, 'Company Groups in Transition Economies: A Case for Regulatory Intervention?' (2001) 2 European Business Organization Law Review 1, 11.
1713. Chen W, Li S and Chen CX, 2.

shares and how much the controlling shareholders are willing to pay to maintain their control.[1714]

Acknowledging the potential negative effect of concentrated ownership does not mean that large shareholders bring destruction only, however. This point, which has been stressed before and deserves emphasizing again, is confirmed by empirical data.[1715] Where regulation makes blockholdings excessively onerous, this move may turn strongly performing firms owned by large shareholders into market failures. Still, allowing blockholders to have too much power can result in expropriation.[1716] Shareholder conduct must be managed carefully, to balance the interests of other stakeholders, including minority shareholders and employees.

Although it is one of the key defining factors in shaping corporate governance practices, including practices regarding conflicts of interest, ownership structure is far from the only factor available.[1717] Drafting rules for RPTs based exclusively on ownership structure reflects a one-sided approach. Information about ownership structures, taken out of its economic and legal context, has little practical effect. Some economies with ownership concentration prosper while others fail: Continental Europe, which is known for concentrated ownership, has examples of both. That is why this analysis would be incomplete if it did not consider other circumstances as well.

In order to design RPT-related strategies properly, it is important to take account of the general state of a country's economy. The success of the economy in developed countries correlates to how the legal system is protected there.[1718] Developed countries have invested vast sums of money in their legal systems, by supporting institutions and relevant enforcement mechanisms. In these jurisdictions, the judiciary possesses sufficient knowledge, skills and resources to properly resolve complex cases, by simply drawing on the available guidelines and principles. Any self-dealing will therefore encounter strong control by institutions.[1719] The same does not hold true for weak institutions in transitional countries, which are prone to using rules rather than standards.[1720] This does not automatically mean that standards should be neglected in the latter jurisdictions, however. On the contrary, application of standards should be encouraged and improved by supporting institutions to allow them to respond to real challenges with more sophisticated court decisions,[1721] e.g. by being able to assess a company's corporate policy or to identify instances of mismanagement, as the case is in the Netherlands.

1714. McCahery JA and Vermeulen EP, *Corporate Governance of Non-listed Companies*, 224.
1715. Hopt KJ and Pistor K, 12.
1716. Morck RK and Steier L, 50.
1717. Hopt KJ and Pistor K, 39.
1718. Berglöf E and Claessens S, 'Enforcement and Corporate Governance' World Bank policy research Working Paper 3409, September 2004, available at: http://documents.worldbank.org/curated/en/516141468765315959/pdf/wps3409.pdf, accessed on 18 November 2018, 2.
1719. McCahery JA and Vermeulen EP, *Corporate Governance of Non-listed Companies*, 225.
1720. Schaefer H-B, 'Rule Based Legal Systems as a Substitute for Human Capital: Should Poor Countries Have a More Rule Based Legal System?' (2002) 2001 German Working Papers in Law and Economics 2, 27.
1721. Schäfer H-B and Cooter RD, 'Growth-Oriented Legal Reforms' in Parisi F (ed.), *Production of Legal Rules* (Edward Elgar Publishing 2012), 415.

Historically, rules have come first to developed economies.[1722] Those countries had to undergo centuries of wins and losses to achieve their high level of judicial enforcement. Introducing well-developed standards or replacing rules by vague standards, including the duty of loyalty for shareholders in Germany or the Rozenblum doctrine in France, or extrapolating the use of the principles of reasonableness and fairness from the Netherlands to transitional economies would not match the stage of those economies' development. These elaborate solutions might be used in ways that do not match their initial goals.[1723] This is different with rules. Their advantages, including fewer court delays, less corruption and substitution of human capital, have been amply described by Hans-Bernd Schaefer.[1724] It is easier for courts to deal with breaches of clearly defined rules than to draw on sophisticated expertise or analyse capital markets.[1725]

At the same time, transitional economies should not be barred from moving towards developing standards. The great advantage of standards is that they can fill gaps, which is a role that rules cannot fulfil. That is why the most desirable solution in transitional economies is to implement standards for RPTs gradually, starting with detailed rules and gradually increasing their flexibility and discretionary application.

It is of course more likely for developing legal systems to wish to learn from their developed counterparts, meaning that legal transplants are more probable to flow into developing regimes than the other way around. For standards, it is doubtful that wholesale transplants from developed to developing regimes would prove beneficial,[1726] at least at some stages in the country's development. Nevertheless, dismissing the possibility of legal transplants out of hand is not the solution either. Successful cases of such transplants do exist, as illustrated by Japan's effective incorporation of German law.[1727] Still, legal vehicles for RPTs or other aspects of corporate life should be implemented judiciously, with due consideration of some key factors.

The first of these is path dependency. This characteristic refers to both domestic peculiarities and, more generally, how a country relates to a specific family of legal systems. It is conceivable for a country to borrow rules from another country in the same legal family,[1728] which would match its legacy.[1729] However, altering a country's affiliation from the Continental legal system to the common law system would require too a high price. The change is a matter not only of laws and their enforcement but also of people's minds, which is a very delicate issue.

Path dependency has one notable exception: rules that are universally applicable. While these rules are not many,[1730] with the development of law and enforcement

1722. Schaefer H-B, 21-23.
1723. Hopt KJ and Pistor K, 30.
1724. Schaefer H-B, 5-8.
1725. Tajti T, 'Corporate Governance: An Oversold Elitist Idea of No Interest to or for the Central European Transitory Economies' (2005) 1 Corporate Governance Law Review 21, 60.
1726. Berglöf E and Claessens S, 29.
1727. Morck RK and Steier L, 59.
1728. Mäntysaari P, *Organising the Firm: Theories of Commercial Law, Corporate Governance and Corporate Law* (Springer Science & Business Media 2011), 31.
1729. Hopt KJ and Pistor K, 15.
1730. Their existence is even denied by some authors (*see* Tajti T, 26).

mechanisms they have become either self-explanatory or else have risen to the level of best practices. An example of a self-explanatory provision is the limited liability of companies, which, while not without exceptions (piercing of the corporate veil), has become widely accepted as a necessary feature of modern companies.[1731] Best practices in turn originate in certain jurisdictions and are recommended for introduction based on empirical evidence, extensive research and discussion. The following techniques may be viewed as the best practices for dealing with RPTs: introduction of audit committees and disclosure through accounting standards.[1732]

The second factor is the balance between freedom and coercion. The regulation to be introduced should not be so prohibitive as to exclude routine or beneficial agreements. Conflicts of interest are one of the major constraints limiting the choice of business form by market participants.[1733] Overly restrictive rules governing conflicts of interest are more likely to cause business owners to abandon the idea of establishing a company in that jurisdiction, and instead move to a more favourable jurisdiction that has no rules on conflicts of interest. This is especially true for large enterprises, which can afford to cherry-pick their jurisdictions. However, this analysis has its limitations. Moving to a different jurisdiction is not beneficial in every case, as the cost of a particular business form in another country might outweigh the cost of doing business in compliance with the conflict of interest rules.

The issue of balancing rights and prohibitions is especially critical in the regulation of listed and non-listed companies. Listed companies have traditionally been more strictly regulated, due to the existence of outside shareholders. This is evidenced by the volume of EU company law regulating listed companies, compared with how non-listed companies are handled. The instruments of EU law governing non-listed companies are confined to a few Directives, while listed companies are subject to a much broader set of documents, including Regulations, Directives and Recommendations. Even the Commission Recommendations for dealing with non-executive and supervisory directors,[1734] despite being soft law, are directed exclusively at listed companies. Similarly, non-listed companies are not covered by the scope of national CGCs. To a certain extent, this leaves a gap in the regulation of non-listed companies.[1735] To close it, McCahery and Vermeulen have put forward optional guidelines for non-listed companies, in support of a one-size-fits-all approach.[1736] Among other possibilities, they suggest establishing audit committees.[1737] Still, this suggestion might

1731. Kraakman R and others, *The Anatomy of Corporate Law: A Comparative and Functional Approach* (3rd edn, Oxford University Press 2017), 8.
1732. Berglöf E and Claessens S, 10; Hopt KJ and Pistor K, 15; Djankov S and others, 463.
1733. Vermeulen EM, *The Evolution of Legal Business Forms in Europe and the United States: Venture Capital, Joint Venture and Partnership Structures* (Kluwer Law International 2003), 183.
1734. Commission Recommendation of 14 December 2004 fostering an appropriate regime for the remuneration of directors of listed companies [2004] OJ L 385/55, 29.12.2004; Commission Recommendation of 15 February 2005 on the role of non-executive or supervisory directors of listed companies and on the committees of the (supervisory) board [2005] OJ L 52/51, 25.2.2005.
1735. Sulaiman ANM, 92.
1736. McCahery JA and Vermeulen EP, *Corporate Governance of Non-listed Companies*, 203.
1737. *Ibid.*

not be appropriate for all non-listed companies, especially those with little capital and small workforces. Considering that every company is a separate mechanism of inner operations governed by conflicting interests and complicated rules, which become even more sophisticated in corporate groups, it is unlikely that legislatures will be capable of producing a single solution for this issue that fits all companies.[1738] For this reason, flexibility is indispensable in the regulation of non-listed companies.

This is also where the dilemma lies between the top-down and bottom-up approaches. For instance, it has been claimed that the key to improving board performances is not government action, but rather board action. This view was based on interviews with board members, many of whom opposed additional regulatory interference, arguing that is was unnecessary and inefficient. The board members interviewed rejected the one-size-fits-all approach and instead preferred individual policies that could be adopted by different companies.[1739] While the results of these interviews should not be treated as irrefutable truth, given that they are likely to reflect the interests of specific companies or their beneficiaries, these statements are nevertheless laudable. Success stories of firms adopting sufficiently specific business practices to efficiently deal with detrimental RPTs carry more weight than top-down recommendations or mandatory requirements.[1740] A bottom-up approach of introducing best practices based on firm-specific considerations deserves to be incentivized and promoted by governments.

The third factor is the issue of *ex ante* safeguards versus *ex post* remedies. The choice between these two options relates to the issue of enforcement and how well developed institutions are. If institutions, i.e. primarily courts, are capable of employing expertise at a high level, by reaching findings on mismanagement or determining a fair price for an RPT, then *ex post* remedies are reliable. Conversely, if those institutions are weak, it is more efficient to rely on *ex ante* disclosure and approval procedures, reserving a limited role for court interference and granting shareholders appraisal and buyout rights.

Although countries sometimes emphasize one type of protection (either *ex ante* or *ex post*),[1741] it is possible for these safeguards to exist side by side. Their ultimate effectiveness depends on factors beyond institutional development. The wording of these remedies in statutory law and their subsequent interpretation is also important. Concerning *ex post* remedies for RPTs, two main remedies are identified: nullification and damages.[1742] Commenting on the regulation of RPTs in Russia, Bernard Black criticized them both. He argued that nullification had an excessive scope, by penalizing every procedural breach, even if an RPT was fair.[1743] With damages, Black criticized

1738. Davies P and Hopt K, 371.
1739. Lorsch JW, 'Board Challenges 2009' in Sun W, Stewart J and Pollard D (eds), *Corporate Governance and the Global Financial Crisis: International Perspectives* (Cambridge University Press 2011), 167.
1740. Berglöf E and Claessens S, 41.
1741. *Ibid.*, 8.
1742. Sulaiman ANM, 86.
1743. Black BS, Kraakman RH and Tarassova AS, *Guide to the Russian Law on Joint Stock Companies* (Kluwer Law International 1998), 460.

the limited standing of parties to claim damages, suggesting that minority shareholders, as key victims of tunnelling, and not the company alone should have the right to claim damages.[1744] This criticism demonstrates how minor details of statutory regulation, worded in abstract terms,[1745] can undermine the whole idea of regulation. The situation is similar for *ex ante* safeguards. Djankov and others advocate using the following safeguards: disclosure, approval by disinterested members and a limited degree of criminal liability.[1746] The role of disclosure is also prized by the World Bank in its Doing Business rating.[1747] However, these safeguards are susceptible to failure if the disclosure rules are not inclusive or if the notion of a related party is too narrow to apply to conflicted members. These strategy-related issues have been discussed in greater detail in Chapters 3 and 5.

Fourth, and most importantly, laws for RPTs should not be paper laws only. If access to courts is impeded, and it is impossible to enforce the written rules and standards, this manner of regulation is no different from a non-intervention approach to RPTs.[1748] It is not enough to lay down best practice provisions in statute without ensuring their actual implementation. It takes time and resources for statutory provisions to reach the point of successful implementation. Implementation of RPT-related strategies can also be precluded by non-legal obstacles, such as cultural or attitude issues, or by influential players with rights of veto.[1749] Overall, implementation and enforcement require a more in-depth discussion of process characteristics and the related issues that would extend the scope of this work significantly.

Lastly, despite the existence of specifically designed strategies for dealing with RPTs, which have been the subject of many heated discussions among scholars, one further important factor must be mentioned. Some countries have applied unusual measures to successfully combat tunnelling. China reduced tunnelling through an unprecedented anti-corruption campaign.[1750] This and other measures have improved the population's welfare and helped to create a more pleasant business environment.[1751] In other words, the reduction of tunnelling was only one of the results of a complex state policy. This was an extraordinary case. While it is possible to conceive all manner of sophisticated and reasonable solutions for dealing with RPTs, if the overall environment promotes fraudulent conduct, this will undermine the effect of the most meticulously designed anti-tunnelling measures. That is why tunnelling in companies should not be considered without also considering the environment where it occurs. To efficiently combat tunnelling, it is vital to create conditions that make it excessively dangerous and largely superfluous to perpetrate tunnelling (and of course other wrongful conduct).

1744. *Ibid.*, 462.
1745. Tajti T, 78.
1746. Djankov S and others, 463.
1747. *Doing Business 2019: Training for Reform*, 4.
1748. Goshen Z, 'The Efficiency of Controlling Corporate Self-Dealing: Theory Meets Reality', 408.
1749. Schäfer H-B and Cooter RD, 401.
1750. Xu G and others, 27.
1751. Schäfer H-B and Cooter RD, 411.

§6.02 IMPLEMENTATION OF RPT-RELATED STRATEGIES IN UKRAINE

As discussed in section §6.01, company ownership is one of the most principal factors to be considered in the design of a jurisdiction's RPT strategy. As it is in other countries in Continental Europe, company ownership in Ukraine is concentrated. However, in contrast to how concentrated this ownership came about in Germany and in the Netherlands, in Ukraine it resulted primarily from slow, non-transparent and destructive privatization processes that led to the formation of many JSCs. As explained in section §1.02, privatized plants and factories in the form of JSCs exist in which small numbers of ultimate beneficiaries exert dominant influence, while thousands of shares are distributed among minority shareholders with small percentages of the share capital, if even that.

Although public companies that mostly emerged from the privatization process in Ukraine are important, they do not actually play an overwhelming role in the country's economy. Of the 200 companies with the largest profits in 2016, more than 100 were private companies and other similar business forms.[1752] According to some valuations, private companies represent more than 75% of Ukraine's GDP.[1753] Ownership in these companies is also concentrated, and in 53% of all companies, one of the shareholders is a director.[1754] Some lawyers have commented on these figures that owners of Ukrainian companies do not trust their executives and are not ready to relinquish control.[1755]

Corporate groups are also a prominent feature of Ukraine's corporate landscape. Most of the respondents in the Google Forms survey gave positive answers regarding the existence of corporate groups in Ukraine. However, they are less regulated in Ukraine than in Germany, Poland and the Netherlands. The legal entity doctrine dominates, although the enterprise theory emerges from time to time in legislative measures.[1756] This dominance of the legal entity doctrine means that intra-group transactions, including intra-group loans, are usually treated in the same manner as similar transactions between separate market participants. This is also true for the regulation of RPTs under the JSC Law of Ukraine, unless a subsidiary that enters into an intra-group transaction with its parent is wholly owned by the parent.[1757]

The configuration of market players described above places demands on the legislature. The key challenge is to offer better protection to investors, without disincentivizing large shareholders.[1758] This is impossible to achieve properly without allowing for the characteristics of Ukraine's legal system. Ukraine's system is part of

1752. Holovniov S and Vinnichuk Yu.
1753. Antonenko L, 21.
1754. 'Marker nezrilosti: V 53% zasnovnyk ye dyrektorom kompanii' (2017), available at: https://opendatabot.ua/blog/75-founders-ceo, accessed on 30 September 2018.
1755. *Ibid.*
1756. For instance, consolidated financial statements have long been recognized in Ukraine, under the Law of Ukraine 'On Accounting and Financial Reporting'.
1757. JSC Law of Ukraine, Article 71(2)(2).
1758. Berglöf E and Claessens S, 10.

the Romano-Germanic Continental legal tradition.[1759] By and large, the legislators drafting company laws have drawn inspiration from German law, having introduced LLCs and the two-tier board structure (which is mandatory for public companies with ten or more shareholders).[1760] Other aspects have been borrowed from Dutch law, including rules governing liability.[1761] The accommodation of legal transplants from those said jurisdictions has been satisfactory.[1762]

At present, Ukraine is in the process of implementing European company law, in accordance with its obligations under the EU-Ukraine Association Agreement. Ukraine's company law has already been matched to various EU Directives to a considerable extent[1763] and had been even before the Association Agreement entered into force.[1764] This development has a downside, however: the legislature has demonstrated a clear habit of cherry-picking and oversimplification when implementing provisions of EU law.[1765] One example of cherry-picking that might concern RPTs is the area of capital maintenance rules. As described in section §5.01, Ukraine's legislature has partly implemented the rules from the Second Council Directive while omitting some of their key details.

This cherry-picking approach to implementing the capital maintenance rules clearly does nothing to benefit the rights of creditors. Moreover, the assets and net profits tests for public companies and the liquidity test for private companies cover payments of dividends in Ukraine only, as opposed to Germany, for instance, and to a lesser extent Poland, where the doctrine of hidden (i.e., concealed) distributions has its roots.[1766] In Ukraine, shareholders, and especially those who control their companies, can use a variety of methods to siphon off funds, including RPTs, without any thought for complying with capital requirements. This is especially true for non-listed companies. Creditors, having no say in the approval of RPTs, are unable to influence the approval process. The approval regulations for substantial transactions also offer creditors little succour.[1767] As a result, procedural safeguards for RPTs have little value for creditors. Similarly, the amount of a company's equity does not provide creditors with sufficient guarantees, especially in private companies, where the minimum share capital is UAH 1.[1768] Generally, creditors of both public and private companies have insufficient protection against RPTs. To better protect creditors of public companies,

1759. Bondaryev T and Zorya A, 'Ukraine' in Kawamura A (ed.), *Corporate Governance* (Thomson Reuters 2015), 469.
1760. Radwan A, Nadzon A and Zdiruk V, 24.
1761. *Ibid.*, 21.
1762. *Ibid.*, 25.
1763. Romashchenko I, 'Corporate Law Development in Ukraine: From Post-Soviet Past to European Future' (2015) 12 European Company Law 217, 222.
1764. One illustrative example is the implementation of the Twelfth Company Law Directive in the CCU. However, whether by intent or through negligence, some previously adopted rules prohibiting the formation of companies by one-person entities were removed from the CCU under the 2018 version of the LLC Law of Ukraine.
1765. Antonenko L, 28.
1766. This has already been covered at length in previous chapters.
1767. JSC Law of Ukraine, Articles 70, 72.
1768. 'Pro scho hovoryt statutnyi kapital?' (2017), available at: https://opendatabot.ua/blog/73-fake-capital, accessed on 30 September 2018.

the asset-based test and the net profits test must be improved, and the liquidity test introduced. The assets and net profits tests should also be introduced for private companies. Similarly, from the perspective of creditor protection, it is not enough for those tests to apply to dividends only: other distributions under loan agreements and excessive purchases should also be covered.

One of the problems with disguised (i.e., concealed) distributions is how they should be reviewed. While dividends, by their very nature, are always distributions to shareholders, to understand whether the distribution under a particular agreement is excessive, it must be established as not being on market terms. Moreover, an agreement might not be on market terms, while nevertheless ultimately benefitting the company. For instance, a company might conclude a high-interest loan agreement with a shareholder, if it urgently needs the funds that the shareholder can provide. Other examples exist of agreements on non-market terms that nonetheless work in the company's favour, such as transactions to sell perishable goods. As such, if the doctrine of disguised distributions is introduced in Ukraine, the courts will be responsible for reviewing every transaction on a case-by-case basis.

Another issue that would follow if the doctrine of disguised distributions is introduced is the need for exemptions. For example, corporate groups create an obvious need to allow disguised distributions between group members. Without such an exemption, it is possible that transactions between group members would simply stop if they are on non-market terms; this is not in the group's interests. The concept of disguised distributions should therefore certainly not be adopted if it is not accompanied by exemptions.

Besides the Second Council Directive, SRD I must also be implemented under the EU-Ukraine Association Agreement. However, Ukraine is not obliged to implement SRD II, yet SRD II might give Ukrainian law broader coverage for RPTs, and more efficient regulation, due to its rules for considering whether RPTs are on market terms. In other words, SRD II combines stricter requirements for preventing circumvention with relaxed rules for some RPTs in the form of exemptions. Moreover, SRD II's implementation in Ukraine is unlikely to meet with strong opposition, given the path-dependent history of the procedural safeguards that the JSC Law of Ukraine has imposed since its adoption in 2008.

The need for further changes in the regulation of RPTs stems not only from the need to implement the EU-Ukraine Association Agreement but also from public demands. Most of the respondents answering the Google Forms survey were unhappy with the current state of regulation of RPTs. The evaluation of RPT-related strategies leads to the conclusion that Ukraine's legislature has already examined the procedural strategy and the information rights strategy at length. As far as procedural safeguards are concerned, the regulation of approval requirements for public companies is sufficiently detailed, yet the same is not true for private companies, even large ones. It would therefore be reasonable to improve corporate governance regulations for private companies that resemble public companies in terms of shareholder numbers and share capital, and to make it mandatory for those private companies to have a supervisory board and implement the approval procedure for their RPTs.

Another obstacle to the development of Ukrainian company law and corporate governance, and one that sets Ukraine apart from countries with more developed legal systems, is that its institutions are weak. Courts are overloaded with cases and are often unable or reluctant to identify effective solutions to complex issues. Standards, including the concept of a fiduciary duty and legal principles, remain underdeveloped.[1769] For RPTs, neither minority shareholders nor creditors have an efficient way to claim damages from related parties. Statutory law does not grant those parties the right to bring direct claims; arguably, shareholders and creditors can rely only on abstract rules for civil liability.[1770]

Nevertheless, taking the opposite approach to regulation, by granting minority shareholders the right to claim damages from related parties, might not prove beneficial either. First, if minority shareholders have this right 'on paper', judges will need to learn how to calculate the damages: they will have to compare the market value of shares before and after each RPT. This would be a difficult exercise, due to the influence of other factors besides the RPT on the market value, however detrimental to the company the RPT might be. Second, if both the company and minority shareholders are entitled under statute to claim damages, then the related party would be held liable twice for the same act (and the same argument applies to creditors), and it is incompatible with Article 61 of the Constitution of Ukraine to claim the same form of liability of a person twice for the same offence.[1771] As such, it makes more sense from the perspective of fairness to enable shareholders to bring these proceedings on behalf of the company under derivative suits. It is easier for courts to calculate loss or damage caused to a company than indirect loss or damage caused to its shareholders and creditors.

Minority shareholders can be given more extensive rights in the following areas. First, under the current rules shareholders with 10% or more of a company's share capital have access to one type of derivative suits only: they may seek compensation for loss or damage caused by company officers. However, they do not have standing, at least in statute, to claim damages from related parties other than company officers, or to challenge transactions with interest conducted in breach of procedure. Second, shareholders in public companies have appraisal rights regarding RPTs only if they vote against approving the transactions with interest at the general meeting of shareholders. For situations where a supervisory board member, as the shareholders' representative, votes against the transaction, the appraisal right does not exist. Third, the right of exit from private companies should be restricted; at present, it is unconditional for shareholders with less than 50% of the company's share capital. This might be changed by extending the meaning to include both direct and indirect owners of share capital in companies. Lastly, statutory law does not properly regulate what the role of special audit reports is in public and private companies.

1769. Bondaryev T and Zorya A, 469; Boyarchuk K, 172.
1770. Similarly, subsidiaries are unlikely to succeed in damage claims against their parent companies.
1771. Constitution of Ukraine [Konstytutsiya Ukrayiny] of 28 June 1996, published in Vidomosti Verkhovnoyi Rady Ukrayiny, 1996, No. 30, St. 141.

For the enforcement of regulations regarding RPTs and the use of standards, Ukrainian courts have adhered to a formal, rather than a functional, interpretation of the facts, except for the stance that the Supreme Court is now starting to display.[1772] With RPTs, the courts have developed judicial approaches that penalize breaches relating to RPT approval, without considering whether the RPT was detrimental to the company: identifying possible breaches of the approval procedure has been more important. From the perspective of fairness, this approach is not universally appropriate. Invalidating an RPT is a severe remedy[1773] and is not justified in situations where the RPT creates value. According to the 20 September 2019 amendments to the JSC Law of Ukraine, courts now in fact have the power to invalidate approved transactions if they are not on market terms. These changes represent an attempt by the Parliament of Ukraine to introduce a substance-based evaluation of RPTs, rather than a formal review only. However, the problem with these amendments is that the formal approach will not disappear: even after 20 September 2019, transactions with interest may still be invalidated by reason of a procedural breach. As a result, two separate grounds are available for annulling transactions with interest: (i) breach of procedural requirements and (ii) inconsistency with market prices. Nor does the solution lie in abolishing the invalidation remedy, for being deficient. Its great advantage lies in its clear-cut and understandable rules. Rather, instead of introducing two separate grounds for invalidating transactions with interest, it would be wiser to suggest a single ground. Transactions should be invalidated if they are both contrary to procedural requirements and based on a transaction price that is less favourable than the market price. This approach could be combined with more rights for shareholders to access additional remedies, including invalidation of transactions with interest and compensation for loss or damage inflicted by interested persons, as part of derivative suits.

§6.03 DEVELOPMENT OF UKRAINIAN LAW ON RPTs: PROSPECTS AND SOLUTIONS

[A] Implementation of EU Law on RPTs

[1] Implementation of SRD II

Ukrainian company law has been in a state of flux for some time. One of the engines driving these changes is the implementation of the EU Directives in accordance with the EU-Ukraine Association Agreement. When the Agreement was drafted, signed and ratified, the current version of EU company law, with its most recent codifications and amendments, was not yet in place, including SRD II. However, as long as the new elements inspired by EU law will help to improve investor protection and corporate governance, it makes sense to implement them.

1772. Radwan A, Nadzon A and Zdiruk V, 83; Khort YV, 189.
1773. Black BS, Kraakman RH and Tarassova AS, 460.

The first notable difference between the current provisions of the JSC Law of Ukraine and SRD II is the definition of a related party. In general, the concept of a related party is broader under SRD II, being based on IAS 24. Interested persons according to the JSC Law of Ukraine (Article 71(1)) primarily consist of shareholders with 25% or more of the company's share capital and company officers. Under IAS 24, applied in conjunction with IAS 28, related parties include persons possessing 20% or more of the voting rights. While the difference between 20% and 25% is minor, it has no proper economic or legal justification, and besides the IASs, the LLC Law of Ukraine (Article 45(1)), the CCU (Article 118(1)) and the Tax Code of Ukraine (Article 14) also stipulate the figure of 20%. Therefore, for the purposes of uniformity it seems reasonable to regard shareholders with 20% or more of a company's share capital (and where applicable the voting rights) as interested persons for the purposes of the JSC Law of Ukraine.

IAS 24 also makes extensive use of the notions of 'control' and 'significant influence'. Under IAS 24, the meaning of these terms is not confined to share ownership or official duties only. Other types of 'control' and 'significant influence' can also cause persons to be viewed as related parties, e.g. special agreements. In other words, IAS 24 applies substantive criteria, rather than formal ones, to explain control and significant influence. Using substantive criteria would pose major difficulties for any efforts to compose predefined lists of related parties, as those related parties would be subject to interpretation on a case-by-case basis. Additionally, different interpretations might be given by different actors, including courts that are ill-equipped for the task. As a result, if a company enters into an RPT without approval from the appropriate body, and the court recognizes one party as being related based on substantive criteria, this interpretation may then serve as grounds for invalidating the transaction (Article 72). Therefore, for the purposes of legal certainty and the predictability of procedural safeguards, it is preferable not to apply broad categories of 'control' and 'significant influence' to define the concept of an interested person as employed by the JSC Law of Ukraine. The same reasons serve as justification for not introducing the notions of a domestic partner, his/her children and dependents in the definition of an interested person in the JSC Law of Ukraine.

The next difference where it would be worthwhile to align the JSC Law of Ukraine more closely with SRD II is that the Directive's requirements cover transactions between a company's related parties and its subsidiaries. It makes sense to include this provision in Ukrainian law: a transaction that a company's subsidiary conducts with a related party of the company, on the company's instructions, has the effect as if the parent company were involved. Excluding transactions between subsidiaries and related parties from the scope of the procedural safeguards as contained in the JSC Law of Ukraine would create a large and unacceptable gap in the RPT-related strategies. To overcome this gap, a new paragraph could be added to Article 71 of the JSC Law of Ukraine, obliging companies to publicly announce transactions between their subsidiaries and their interested persons, while simultaneously presenting a third-party report assessing whether the transaction is fair and reasonable from the perspective of the company and its shareholders who are not interested persons, and explaining the assumptions and methods applied. This new requirement should then be subject to the same exemptions and thresholds as transactions with interest are.

SRD II furthermore provides for aggregation of transactions with the same related party that are conducted within a single financial year. The JSC Law of Ukraine contains a similar provision for fundamental transactions, prohibiting these transactions from being broken into separate parts (Article 70). While this rule does not apply to transactions with interest, it would be reasonable to implement the SRD II provision, given that companies might try to avoid the rules governing transactions with interest by conducting multiple transactions that remain below the established threshold. As a suggestion for implementing these requirements, a rule might be added to Article 71 of the JSC Law of Ukraine, governing aggregation of transactions with the same interested person within any twelve-month period or within a single financial year that are not otherwise subject to disclosure and other procedural requirements.

A further provision of SRD II that would be logical to carry over to the JSC Law of Ukraine is the exemption for transactions concluded in the ordinary course of business and on normal market terms. As noted above, invalidation of RPTs conducted in breach of the procedural requirements, even those that create value, is overinclusive. Invalidation is a serious remedy that should be available only where an RPT destroys value. It would be advisable, therefore, to make invalidation of transactions with interest available in connection with transactions that are not only in breach of procedure but also not conducted on normal market terms. The courts would then have the ability to verify whether an RPT is on normal market terms based on information from a third party's report, e.g.. The other element of this exemption ('in the ordinary course of business') might only add ambiguity to the enforcement mechanism, however, if it is applied in combination with the 'normal market terms' rule. For the courts, this might create further complexities. The approach introduced with the amendments of 20 September 2019 would be overly restrictive, as it does not eliminate the problem of formality-based jurisprudence. Instead of two separate grounds for annulling transactions with interests, it makes more sense to introduce a single ground: breach of the procedural requirements and inconsistency with market prices.

[2] Implementation of the Second Council Directive and Improvement of Other Capital Maintenance Rules

While no provision is made for SRD II in the EU-Ukraine Association Agreement, the same does not apply to the Second Council Directive. The rules on distributions under that Directive, if interpreted in a broad sense, as they are in Germany, e.g., have bearing on the protection of the assets and stakeholders (minority shareholders, creditors and employees) of companies. This would be amplified if Ukraine adopted the doctrine of hidden distributions, in the same manner as Germany and Poland already have. At present, the limitations on distributions under the JSC Law of Ukraine and the LLC Law of Ukraine apply only to dividends. The doctrine of hidden distributions, conversely, assumes that distributions may also take the form of loans, purchase contracts, remuneration, etc. This doctrine would afford additional protection to creditors, who currently have no say in the approval of RPTs and enjoy limited standing to claim damages caused by detrimental RPTs. The main remedy available to creditors is debt collection, which can be exercised to effect only if the debtor has sufficient funds remaining after its assets have been tunnelled by related parties. As such, further capital maintenance restrictions would provide additional guarantees in terms of the amount of capital that debtors must have. However, if it is adopted without proper exemptions for corporate groups, the doctrine of disguised distributions could lead to rigid and elaborate legal regulation. Another risk is that institutions might misinterpret this doctrine. Its adoption should therefore depend on whether it can be balanced by a list of necessary exemptions and be made conditional on proper enforcement by the courts.

Even if the doctrine of hidden distributions is not implemented, possibilities exist to improve the current regulation of distributions, in accordance with the Second Council Directive. Neither the asset-based test (the balance sheet test) nor the net profits test as set forth in the JSC Law of Ukraine matches the Directive's wording, having suffered from a cherry-picking exercise by the legislature.[1774] Proper implementation of the Second Council Directive's provisions could be ensured by the following changes: (1) amend Article 30(2) of the JSC Law of Ukraine to include carry-forward losses and additions to reserves for the purpose of calculating the dividends payable to shareholders (net profits test); and (2) amend Article 31(1) of the JSC Law of Ukraine, containing the restrictions on dividend payments, to include another condition that will prevent payment of dividends: if payment of the dividend *would cause* the net assets as presented in the company's financial statements to drop below the amount of the subscribed capital plus non-distributable reserves (asset-based or balance sheet test).

For public companies, similarly, the liquidity test as posited by the self-enforcing theory is not applied. The situation is the opposite for private companies: no provision is made for the asset-based and net profits, yet the liquidity test does in fact apply. As a suggestion for increased creditor protection, the asset-based and net profits tests should be introduced for private companies, in addition to the liquidity test, and the capital maintenance requirements for public companies should be expanded by including the liquidity test. The following changes are proposed: (1) introduce the liquidity test for public companies, add a further condition to Article 31(1) of the JSC Law of Ukraine that will prevent dividend payments: *if a company's assets are insufficient, or will become insufficient as a result of payment of any dividends, to satisfy all due and payable claims of creditors*; and (2) introduce the assets (or balance sheet) test for private companies, add a further condition to Article 27(1) of the LLC Law of Ukraine that will prevent dividend payments: *if on the closing date of the previous financial year, the net assets as presented in the company's financial statement accounts are less than, or as a result of the dividend distribution would drop below, the amount of the subscribed capital.*

1774. Antonenko L, 28.

[B] Special Regulation of Corporate Groups

[1] Recognition of the Notion of a Group Interest

As explained above, if the doctrine of hidden (or concealed or disguised) distributions is implemented in Ukraine, it will also require the introduction of exemptions for groups. The possible measures for tackling corporate groups in Ukraine should be examined more closely in this context.

It is important to stress that corporate groups do in fact exist in Ukraine. Turning a blind eye to their existence is a poor way of regulating corporate relationships. The legislature has already introduced measures in this area, e.g. by exempting public companies owned by a single shareholder from the need to comply with the procedural and announcement requirements governing RPTs (Article 71). Nevertheless, group-related issues are still topical.

As discussed above, it is unclear whether company law in Ukraine grants parent companies the right to issue instructions to their subsidiaries to act in the best interests of the group as a whole. A form of regulation similar to how it is done in the Netherlands[1775] is therefore recommended: establish that a company's articles of association may stipulate that management must conduct itself in accordance with the directions of a company body in respect of the general policy to be pursued in the areas specified in the articles. A provision to this effect obliges a company's management to respect the group's interests, as well as the separate interests of the subsidiary. It also indemnifies management against liability for acting in the group's interest and contrary to the subsidiary's interests.

This rule would be practicable for both public companies (whether listed or non-listed) and private companies. The problem associated with recognizing the notion of a group's interest, at least in part, is that it is subject to interpretation. If the rule described above were to be added to statutory law, courts deciding cases involving the liability of management would be forced to interpret the notion of group interest. In the absence of earlier case law and proper knowledge of group law, this might present a serious challenge. However, these circumstances should not stand in the way of developing jurisprudence and can be overcome by introducing the concept gradually.

In addition, no specific rules regulate a parent's liability for loss or damage that its detrimental instructions cause to its subsidiary. In the present situation, these relationships are governed by the general provisions of tort law.[1776] To change this state of affairs, a clause on parental liability should be added to the CCU, by expanding Article 118 to include new paragraphs that allow for the possibility of instructions from company bodies of parent companies and parental liability for detrimental instructions:

(a) The articles of association of the dependent company may provide that management of the dependent company must conduct itself in accordance with the directions of another company body of the parent company and/or the dependent company.

1775. BW, Article 2:129(4) and 2:239(4).
1776. CCU, Article 1166.

(b) Loss or damage caused to the dependent company as a result of carrying out the instructions of a company body of the parent company must be compensated.

[2] Intra-group Loans

Intra-group loans are a popular instrument for cash pooling. Despite the increasing possibility of harmful loans, their use is widespread and often a matter of regular practice.

In Ukraine, intra-group loans of public and private companies do not face serious scrutiny from the perspective of capital maintenance rules, as the associated tests (asset-based, net profits and liquidity) are used only for dividends. To some extent, this shortcoming is compensated by the procedural and announcement obligations for fundamental transactions[1777] and RPTs.[1778] However, those requirements do not always give full consideration to the rights of creditors, who have no power to influence the approval procedure. As such, extending the doctrine of hidden distributions to various other transactions, by extrapolating the use of relevant tests that in the current regime apply only to dividends, would benefit creditor protection.

At the same time, the doctrine of hidden distributions can only be implemented in combination with recognition of the notion of a group interest. Distributions made in the group's interests, including intra-group loans, should be excluded from the strict capital maintenance rules, to avoid undermining the balance of interests. Again, the problem is that the notion of group interest is almost unknown in Ukraine's company law jurisprudence and would present the courts with an interpretation challenge. Before they can be implemented in Ukraine, and even once they have been implemented, the doctrine of hidden distributions and recognition of the group interest notion must be discussed and reviewed at length by scholars and practitioners. If the Parliament of Ukraine introduces the hidden distributions doctrine for public and private companies, that doctrine should have associated exemptions for groups of companies. The doctrine and the exemptions could be introduced by adding a new Article 31-1 to the JSC Law of Ukraine and an Article 27-1 to the LLC Law of Ukraine, reading as follows:

(a) Distributions from a company's capital that are not dividends, including but not limited to excessive remuneration, excessive payments under agreements for the provision of services, purchase of goods and/or performance of works and other agreements that are not on normal market terms, are subject to the same restrictions that apply to dividend distributions.
(b) Distributions made in breach of paragraph 1 of this Article must be refunded to the company.
(c) Paragraphs (a) and (b) of this Article do not apply to distributions made between separate members of the same group.

1777. JSC Law of Ukraine, Article 70; LLC Law of Ukraine, Article 44.
1778. JSC Law of Ukraine, Article 71; LLC Law of Ukraine, Article 45.

If the concept of hidden distributions is introduced in the manner described above, the regulation would be incomplete if no explanation of the group concept was set out in the JSC Law of Ukraine and in the LLC Law of Ukraine. This can be done by using the control-based group concept as used in the Accounting Directive: *a parent undertaking and all its subsidiary undertakings.*[1779]

[C] Derivative Suits and Additional Minority Shareholder Rights

[1] Derivative Suits

One of the areas not regulated by EU law is the area of derivative suits. In Ukraine, shareholders with 10% or more of a company's share capital may currently file only one type of derivative suit on the company's behalf: claims for compensation of loss or damage caused by company officers. In addition, if their own rights are infringed, they may apply for resolutions passed by company bodies to be annulled.[1780] However, shareholders do not have standing under the law in derivative suits to claim annulment of transactions with interest or fundamental transactions, nor to claim compensation for loss or damage caused to the company by related parties, including controlling shareholders. The 20 September 2019 amendments grant shareholders standing to claim invalidation of transactions with interest only where the transaction was not conducted on market terms.

As a suggestion for improving the current regulation, shareholders owning 10% or more of a company's share capital could be granted standing to bring claims on the company's behalf to seek invalidation of transactions with interest and fundamental transactions that have been concluded in breach of proper procedure and that are not on normal market terms and to seek compensation for loss or damage caused by interested persons. Given the prevalence of abusive practices and corporate raiding in Ukraine, these changes could be introduced in combination with some or all of the additional preventive safeguards already described in literature, such as a minimum shareholding duration as a prerequisite for filing these claims.[1781] These changes could be introduced by adding an Article 54-1 to the Economic Procedural Code of Ukraine, granting shareholders with 10% or more of a company's share capital the right to claim invalidation of fundamental transactions and transactions with interest, and to claim compensation for loss or damage inflicted by detrimental transactions with interested persons, and combining this amendment with safeguards under which the right to file derivative suits vests only with shareholders that had owned their shares for five years or longer before the transaction was concluded.

1779. Accounting Directive, Article 2(11).
1780. Regulation of the Plenum of the Supreme Economic Court of Ukraine 'On Certain Aspects of Resolution of Disputes arising from Corporate Legal Relationships' No. 4 [Postanova plenumu Vyschoho hospodarskoho sudu Ukrayiny 'Pro deyaki pytannia praktyky vyrishennia sporiv, scho vynykayut z korporatyvnykh pravovidnosyn'] of 25 February 2016, published in Visnyk hospodarskoho sudochynstva, 2016, No. 1, Stor. 72, 1.7.
1781. Shtym T, 189; Khort YV, 181.

[2] Other Methods of Protecting Minority Shareholders

Shareholders in public companies have the right to demand that the company repurchase their shares if they vote against transactions with interest at the general meeting of shareholders.[1782] This appraisal right of shareholders could be improved by granting minority shareholders the right to demand a repurchase of their shares if a supervisory board member appointed by the shareholder's quota or an independent director votes against approval of a transaction with interest. This amendment would expand the scope of the appraisal right of minority shareholders seeking to exit the company.

Shareholders in private companies who own less than 50% of the company's share capital have an unconditional right to exit the company.[1783] The exit triggers an obligation for the company to pay the value of the shares within one year after the shareholder's exit.[1784] However, this arrangement does not take into account situations where a shareholder indirectly owns more than 50% of the share capital, i.e. through other entities that the shareholder controls. Given the high risk of abuse of shareholder rights in these situations, the concept of 'indirect ownership' within the meaning of the JSC Law of Ukraine (Article 1(11-1)) should also apply to private companies. To introduce this concept, Article 24(1) of the LLC Law of Ukraine could be amended to state that an exit by one or more persons who directly or indirectly own 50% or more of a company's share capital requires the other shareholders' consent, for which purposes 'indirect' ownership has the same meaning as given in Article 1(11-1) of the JSC Law of Ukraine.

Shareholders in public companies that own more than 10% of shares (for private companies: 10% or more) have the right to appoint a special auditor.[1785] By law, companies are obliged to provide these auditors with access to and copies of any requested documents.[1786] At the same time, the law provides no rules to regulate how the auditor's findings should be considered, or what should be done if the company refuses to give access. Instead, these matters are left entirely to internal regulation and to the courts, in their role of filling in gaps in the law. Compared with the rules on appointments of auditors in Germany[1787] and Poland,[1788] and compared with the sophisticated enquiry proceedings in the Netherlands,[1789] Ukraine provides for little statutory regulation of these independent audits. The suggestion is therefore to amend the regulation by providing more detailed rules for how these reports should be considered and what the procedure and terms of these audits should be if they are not defined in the articles of association, and what the consequences are of a company's

1782. JSC Law of Ukraine, Article 68(1).
1783. LLC Law of Ukraine, Article 24(1).
1784. *Ibid.*, Article 24(7).
1785. JSC Law of Ukraine, Article 75(5); LLC Law of Ukraine, Article 41(1).
1786. JSC Law of Ukraine, Article 75(6); LLC Law of Ukraine, Article 41(3, 4).
1787. AktG, Articles 142-146.
1788. KSH, Articles 223-226.
1789. BW, Articles 344-359.

breach of its duty to provide access to and copies of requested documents. Furthermore, institutional improvement is crucial to ensure proper protection of these rights, together with the respective material safeguards. However, this largely goes beyond the scope of this study.

[D] RPT-Related Strategies

[1] Procedural Safeguards

The optional nature of supervisory boards and procedural safeguards for RPTs of private companies seems unfair in some situations. In Poland, for instance, private companies with a share capital of more than PLN 500,000 and more than twenty-five shareholders are required to have either a supervisory board or an audit committee.[1790] In Ukraine, before the LLC Law of Ukraine came into effect, the number of shareholders that private companies could have was capped at 100.[1791] In addition, to encourage share transferability, if a public company has more than 100 shareholders, it is automatically prohibited from granting its shareholders a pre-emptive right to purchase the shares of other shareholders.

These arrangements show that 100 is already a familiar threshold in Ukrainian company law, in terms of numbers of shareholders. If a company has more than 100 shareholders, this points towards the presence of minority shareholders and requires improved shareholder oversight. The suggestion is therefore to adopt a system similar to that in Poland, making supervisory boards mandatory for private companies with more than 100 shareholders and a share capital representing 1,250 times the minimum wage or more (i.e., the same as for public companies[1792]). Similarly, for private companies that reach these thresholds, it would be fair to dictate a mandatory approval procedure for transactions with interest: Articles 38 and 45 of the LLC Law of Ukraine would of course need to be amended accordingly.

[2] Disclosure

On 1 May 2016, a rule came into effect requiring public companies to disclose approved transactions with interest to the NSSMC and announce them on the public website www.smida.gov.ua. It would be preferable if transactions with interest were instead disclosed *ex ante*, i.e. before they are approved, to give stakeholders more opportunity to take measures. However, the current regulation is a positive achievement, as it offers a user-friendly method of sharing key information on approved transactions.

1790. KSH, Article 213(2).
1791. Law of Ukraine 'On Economic Companies' [Zakon Ukrayiny 'Pro hospodarski tovarystva'], Article 50.
1792. JSC Law of Ukraine, Article 14(1).

[3] Standards

The standards strategy remains underdeveloped in Ukraine. Compared with the German regime, Ukrainian company law does not explicitly recognize a duty of loyalty for shareholders, and unlike Dutch law it does not place the same value on legal principles. Except for the Supreme Court, Ukrainian courts tend to apply statutory rules only and largely ignore abstract legislative provisions. Even though it is possible under the CCU to draw on legal principles and moral grounds to assess the issues of a claim for invalidation of a transaction,[1793] it is very difficult to find any cases where these provisions have been applied in a systematic and consistent manner. The formal interpretation therefore prevails over the functional interpretation, as can be seen in how disputes concerning RPTs are resolved. Courts primarily consider whether the approval procedure was followed, and if it was not, the consequence is invalidation of the RPT.[1794]

The amendments of 20 September 2019 might lead to a more widespread use of standards in disputes regarding RPTs. However, the legislature's suggestions do not possess the power to override formality-based approach preferred by the courts. As such, and as has already been recommended in the present section, the legal grounds for the overly broad remedy of invalidation should be redressed, to allow invalidation only where an RPT is both in breach of procedural requirements and not concluded on normal market terms. This would also match the provisions of SRD II. Although Ukraine's courts might find it difficult to interpret normal market terms when resolving cases on the invalidation of RPTs, this regulation nonetheless seems preferable. The courts will need to gradually develop jurisprudence by interpreting nebulous and evaluative concepts. Of course, in a country with a developing legal system, immediately replacing rules and procedures by standards would have a destructive outcome. Ukraine's courts are currently weak institutions, and hardly capable of coping with sophisticated tasks. However, if standards are developed gradually, including legal principles and moral grounds, in the long term the outcome will be positive. From the perspective of RPTs, it should lead to more efficient and fewer detrimental and abusive transactions.

[E] Conflicts of Interest

If a related party enters into an RPT in order to extract wealth from the company, this gives rise to a conflict of interest. However, conflicts of interest take other forms besides abusive and harmful self-dealing only. Misappropriation of business opportunities and competition with the company are other detrimental events that companies face. In these situations, the company might not feel an immediate reduction in its material assets. Ultimately, however, the indirect impact can be even worse, potentially leaving the company without business partners or prospects for success. It is

1793. CCU, Articles 3, 509, 203.
1794. JSC Law of Ukraine, Article 72.

therefore reasonable to prohibit company officers from misappropriating business opportunities and competing with the company.

In Ukraine, abstract rules for the business opportunities doctrine and the non-compete obligation are set out in the Principles of Corporate Governance.[1795] The non-compete obligation also supplements the general duty of loyalty under the LLC Law of Ukraine.[1796] Conversely, neither the CCU[1797] nor the JSC Law of Ukraine[1798] provides any specific details in their clauses on the duty of loyalty of company officers. As such, it is recommended that provisions to redress this lack should be added directly in those two laws (in Article 92(3) of the CCU and Article 63(1) of the JSC Law of Ukraine), to help improve the understanding of the duty of loyalty.

For the concept of conflicts of interest, the recently adopted LLC Law of Ukraine defines what constitutes a company officer's conflict of interest;[1799] its effect covers even situations where the officer's affiliated persons are enriched by third parties in connection with the officer's performance of his or her duties.[1800] This broad understanding of the concept could place an unnecessary burden on company officers, who might be unaware of gains received by affiliated persons. Moreover, the fact that an affiliated person enjoys this manner of income is not necessarily harmful to the company. As such, the broad interpretation of the concept of a conflict of interest under the LLC Law of Ukraine should be narrowed, by expanding the definition contained in Article 42(3) of the LLC Law of Ukraine to include a reference to a detrimental effect of the gain received by the affiliated person.

Under the JSC Law of Ukraine, indirect conflicts of interest should be regarded through the lens of the procedural and disclosure safeguards for RPTs.[1801] It would be unrealistic to neglect the risk of tunnelling by persons close to or controlled by shareholders or company officers, and indirect conflicts should be covered by the legal regulation. However, the problem with this concept lies in the degree of clarity. A non-exhaustive list of related parties could produce unfair results, bearing in mind the risks of judicial errors and abuse. The more specific the definition of a related party (or interested person) is under the JSC Law of Ukraine, the more easily the rules can be enforced. However, once Ukraine's courts reach the proper level of development, it would be reasonable to start applying (as a tool for interpretation) the features of indirect conflicts of interest used by the courts in the Netherlands (as expressed in the celebrated *Bruil/Kombex* case[1802]).

1795. Principles of Corporate Governance, approved by the Decision of the National Securities and Stock Market Commission of Ukraine of 22 July 2014, No. 955 [Pryntsypy korporatyvnoho upravlinnia, zatverdzheni rishenniam Natsionalnoyi komisii z tsinnykh paperiv ta fondovoho rynku vid 22 lypnia 2014 roku No. 955], sections II, 3.3.
1796. LLC Law of Ukraine, Article 40.
1797. CCU, Article 92(3).
1798. JSC Law of Ukraine, Article 63(1).
1799. LLC Law of Ukraine, Article 42(3).
1800. *Ibid.*, Article 42(5).
1801. JSC Law of Ukraine, Article 71.
1802. *Bruil/Kombex* 29 June 2007, JOR 2007/169 (Supreme Court of the Netherlands).

[F] RPTs in CGCs

A special feature of corporate governance in Ukraine is that the Principles of Corporate Governance, the national analogue to a CGC, were designed and adopted by a governmental authority, the NSSMC. This peculiarity does not mean that the Principles constitute hard law, however. Listed public companies must apply the comply-or-explain principle when they choose a compliance strategy. Given Ukraine's weak institutional development, this reduces the effect of the Principles of Corporate Governance. Research shows that courts are reluctant to draw on the Principles as a source of law, as is natural for a country with a developing legal system and underdeveloped institutions.[1803] Considering the soft nature of the Principles of Corporate Governance and their limited practical impact, the possibility of abusive application by enforcement actors is of little concern. With this in mind, their phrasing could be more abstract and restrictive, without creating much fear of misinterpretation.

First, RPTs should be governed more according to their substance, similarly to the approach adopted in the Dutch CGC.[1804] The following clause is suggested for inclusion in the Principles of Corporate Governance: *Loans and fundamental transactions with related parties should be conducted in the normal course of business only, on terms that apply to the whole workforce, and with no possibility for remission.*

Second, the concept of a related party should be broadened. Unlike the Dutch CGC and the WSE Best Practice in Poland, Ukraine's Principles of Corporate Governance do not treat shareholders as related parties. Only company officers and their affiliated persons have a duty of loyalty.[1805] However, given the extent of ownership concentration in Ukrainian companies and the associated risk of abuse, it would be reasonable to impose restrictive regulations on transactions between companies and their shareholders. It is also justifiable to look beyond shareholders as related parties since control and significant influence can be exercised through other vehicles too. It is therefore suggested that the definition of related parties under the Principles of Corporate Governance should match the meaning under IAS 24.

[G] Final Notes

In Ukraine, and under the conditions that prevail there, minority shareholders as a class remain underrepresented. Amendments to company law and corporate governance can therefore not be justified by the need to protect minority shareholders only. Given this situation in Ukraine, the need to reinforce the capital maintenance rules

1803. Cuomo F, Mallin C and Zattoni A, 234; Du Plessis JJ and Low CK (eds), *Corporate Governance Codes for the 21st Century* (Springer 2017), 111; Aguilera RV, Cuervo-Cazurra A and Kim S, *Taking Stock of Research on Codes of Good Governance*, available at SSRN: https://ssrn.com/abstract=1773087 Go to ISI://WOS:000271128400001, accessed on 18 November 2018, 18.
1804. Dutch CGC, section 2.7.6.
1805. Principles of Corporate Governance, approved by the Decision of the National Securities and Stock Market Commission of Ukraine of 22 July 2014, No. 955 [Pryntsypy korporatyvnoho upravlinnia, zatverdzheni rishenniam Natsionalnoyi komisii z tsinnykh paperiv ta fondovoho rynku vid 22 lypnia 2014 roku No. 955], sections II, 3.3.1.

derives more from respect for other stakeholders, including creditors. The prevalence of corporate groups also necessitates the implementation of the notion of a group interest, and greater focus on the corporate opportunities doctrine, to expand the scope of conflicts of interest and the duty of loyalty. While the procedural requirements for RPTs under Ukraine's company law regime are already detailed, the country's poorly functioning court system means that the standards strategy remains underdeveloped.

CHAPTER 7
Conclusions and Recommendations

The main goal of the present research, as envisaged in Chapter 1, was to understand what solutions the legal systems of Germany, Poland, the Netherlands and the EU can offer to help overcome the problems of RPTs within and outside corporate groups in Ukraine and improve the efficiency of regulation in Ukraine. The emphasis was on the need for a meticulous study of Ukrainian company law, its statutes and their implementation, compared with the Polish, German and Dutch company law regimes, against the background of their implementation of relevant instruments of EU law. An inter-jurisdictional comparison of existing doctrines, strategies and statutory and judicial approaches, as well as the economic and legal situations in the countries studied, would allow for a better understanding of Ukraine's laws and create the possibility to suggest solutions that, if implemented properly, might help to balance the interests of the various groups of stakeholders in RPTs and improve the efficiency of regulation from the perspective of its costs and benefits for Ukraine. These solutions are described in section §6.03 and can be summarized as follows.

1 – Implementation of SRD II

Shareholders with 20% or more of a company's share capital, rather than 25% or more, should be viewed as interested persons under the JSC Law of Ukraine.

For the purposes of legal certainty and predictability of procedural safeguards, it is important to avoid broad interpretations of 'control' and 'significant influence' for defining what constitutes an interested person under the JSC Law of Ukraine. For the same reason, domestic partners, their children and dependents should also be left out of the concept of an interested person under the JSC Law of Ukraine.

To close the gap in RPT-related strategies, a new paragraph should be introduced in Article 71 of the JSC Law of Ukraine, obliging companies to publicly announce transactions between their subsidiaries and their interested persons, accompanied by a third-party report assessing whether the transaction is fair and reasonable from the perspective of the company and its shareholders who are not interested persons, and explaining the assumptions and methods applied. This new requirement should be subject to the same exemptions and thresholds as transactions with interest.

Another suggestion is to introduce a rule in Article 71 of the JSC Law of Ukraine governing aggregation of transactions concluded with the same interested person within a given twelve-month period or during a single financial year but were not subject to the disclosure and procedural requirements.

It is also advisable to make invalidation of transactions with interest available if, besides being in breach of procedure, the transactions were not conducted on normal market terms. The approach introduced by the amendments of 20 September 2019 should be tweaked, by introducing a single ground for invalidating transactions: a breach of procedural requirements coupled with inconsistency with market price.

2 - Implementation of the Second Council Directive and improvement of other capital maintenance rules

The German doctrine of hidden (or concealed, or disguised) distributions is capable of implementation in Ukraine, as long as it is balanced by a range of necessary exemptions and is made conditional on proper enforcement by the courts.

The net profits test should be improved for public companies, by amending Article 30(2) of the JSC Law of Ukraine to require that carry-forward losses and additions to reserves be taken into account for the purposes of calculating the dividends that can be paid to shareholders. The asset-based (or balance sheet) test for public companies should also be improved, by modifying Article 31(1) of the JSC Law of Ukraine, which sets out the restrictions on dividend payments, to include another condition that will prevent dividend payments: if the dividend *would cause* the net assets as presented in the company's financial statements to drop below the company's subscribed capital plus non-distributable reserves.

Looking beyond the Second Council Directive, the liquidity test should be introduced for public companies, by adding further conditions that will prevent dividend payments to Article 31(1) of the JSC Law of Ukraine: *if a company's assets are insufficient, or will become insufficient as a result of payment of any dividends, to satisfy all due and payable claims of creditors*. For private companies, the asset-based (or balance sheet) test should be introduced, by adding a further condition that will prevent dividend payments to Article 27(1) of the LLC Law of Ukraine: *if on the closing date of the previous financial year, the net assets as presented in the company's financial statements are less than, or as a result of the dividend distribution would drop below, the amount of the subscribed capital.*

3 - Recognition of the notion of a group interest

A further recommendation is to establish a system, similar to the arrangement in the Netherlands, for both public and private companies that the company's articles of association may state that management must conduct itself in accordance with the instructions of a company body in respect of the general policy to be pursued in the areas specified in the articles. That provision may be introduced in combination with the possibility of parental liability for loss or damage caused to the subsidiary as a result of detrimental instructions, by expanding Article 118 to include new paragraphs:

(a) The articles of association of the dependent company may provide that management of the dependent company must conduct itself in accordance with the directions of another company body of the parent company and/or the dependent company.
(b) Loss or damage caused to the dependent company as a result of carrying out the instructions of a company body of the parent company must be compensated.

4 - Intra-group loans

A suggestion for protecting the interests of creditors is to implement the doctrine of hidden distributions, by extrapolating the use of the asset-based, net profits and liquidity tests, which at present apply only to dividends, to various other transactions. However, distributions that are made in the group's interests should be excluded from the strict capital maintenance rules. The doctrine of hidden distributions and the associated exemption can be introduced by adding an Article 31-1 to the JSC Law of Ukraine and an Article 27-1 to the LLC Law of Ukraine, stipulating the following:

(a) Distributions from a company's capital that are not dividends, including but not limited to excessive remuneration, excessive payments under agreements for the provision of services, purchase of goods and/or performance of works and other agreements that are not on normal market terms, are subject to the same restrictions that apply to dividend distributions.
(b) Distributions made in breach of paragraph 1 of this Article must be refunded to the company.
(c) Paragraphs (a) and (b) of this Article do not apply to distributions made between separate members of the same group.

Besides the introduction of the hidden distributions doctrine, the notion of a control-based group as used in the Accounting Directive (*a parent undertaking and all its subsidiary undertakings*) can also be added to the JSC Law of Ukraine and the LLC Law of Ukraine.

5 - Derivative suits

A further recommendation is to provide shareholders owning 10% or more of a company's share capital with standing to file claims on the company's behalf to seek invalidation of transactions with interest and fundamental transactions concluded in violation of the procedure and not on normal market terms and compensation for loss or damage caused by interested persons. These changes can be introduced by amending Article 54-1 of the Economic Procedural Code of Ukraine and can be combined with safeguards to ensure that the right to file these derivative suits vests only with shareholders that hold their shares for five years or longer before the transaction was concluded.

6 – Other methods of protecting minority shareholders

The appraisal right of shareholders in public companies can be improved by granting minority shareholders the right to demand that the company repurchase their shares if a supervisory board member appointed by the shareholder's quota or an independent director votes against approval of a transaction with interest.

For private companies, one recommendation is to introduce the concept of 'indirect ownership' within the meaning of the JSC Law of Ukraine (Article 1(11-1)), by amending Article 24(1) of the LLC Law of Ukraine to state that an exit by one or more persons who directly or indirectly own 50% or more of a company's share capital requires the other shareholders' consent.

Another suggestion is to amend the regulation governing the appointment of special auditors, by providing more detailed rules on how the auditor's report should be considered and what the procedure and terms of these audits should be, if they are not defined in the company's articles of association, and what the consequences are of a company's breach of its duty to provide access to and copies of requested documents. Institutional improvement is crucial to ensure proper protection of these rights, together with the respective material safeguards.

7 – Procedural safeguards

The suggestion here is to adopt a system similar to the arrangements under Polish law, making supervisory boards mandatory for private companies with more than 100 shareholders and a share capital representing 1,250 times the minimum wage or more. Similarly, for private companies that reach these thresholds, it would be fair to dictate a mandatory approval procedure for transactions with interest: Articles 38 and 45 of the LLC Law of Ukraine would need to be amended accordingly.

8 – Standards

As recommended above, the legal grounds for the overly broad remedy of invalidation should be redressed, to match SRD II, to allow invalidation only where an RPT is both in breach of procedural requirements and not concluded on normal market terms. The amendments of 20 September 2019, under which breach of procedural requirements and non-market prices could be adopted as separate grounds for invalidating an RPT, do not possess the power to override the formality-based approach preferred by the courts. In general terms, standards should be developed gradually, including legal principles and moral grounds, to achieve a positive outcome in the long term.

9 – Conflicts of interest

The recommendation here is that prohibition on misappropriating business opportunities and competing with the company should be added directly to Article 92(3) of the CCU and Article 63(1) of the JSC Law of Ukraine, to help improve the understanding of the duty of loyalty.

The broad interpretation of the concept of a conflict of interest under Article 42(3) of the LLC Law of Ukraine should be narrowed, by expanding the definition contained there to include a reference to a detrimental effect of the gain received by the affiliated person.

The issue of indirect conflict of interest needs to be addressed. Once Ukraine's courts reach the proper level of development, it would be reasonable to start applying (as a tool for interpretation) the features of indirect conflicts of interest as articulated in the celebrated *Bruil/Kombex* case that was decided by the Supreme Court of the Netherlands.

10 – RPTs in CGCs

RPTs should be addressed more substantially in the Ukrainian Principles of Corporate Governance, similar to how the Dutch CGC approaches this issue, by inserting the following clause: *Loans and fundamental transactions with related parties should be conducted in the normal course of business only, on terms that apply to the whole workforce, and with no possibility for remission.*

The concept of a related party should also be given a broader interpretation in the Ukrainian Principles of Corporate Governance. It is therefore suggested that the definition of related parties under the Principles of Corporate Governance should match the meaning under IAS 24.

These said recommendations are based on and inspired by the study of RPT-related strategies and other safeguards that are in place in Germany, Poland, the Netherlands and the EU. How successful these changes will be in practice depends on numerous factors, as discussed in section §6.01. Factors that will benefit the chances of these legal transplants from their jurisdictions to Ukraine succeeding include the fact they belong to the same legal family (the Continental (i.e., civil) law), the concentrated ownership of companies and their successful implementation under EU law, which is also relevant for Ukraine. Factors that could hinder the success of legal transplants from their jurisdictions to Ukraine are that the economies, capital markets and standards in those jurisdictions are more developed. Still, each of those objections can be countered with other arguments. First, the changes suggested here have largely been modified to reflect Ukraine's legal system, rather than simply carrying over foreign provisions in their original and unchanged form. Second, although the standards strategy is poorly developed in Ukraine, this does not mean that the situation will remain the same forever. Ukraine's economy and legal system are gradually developing, giving hope that the use of standards will become more widespread in the future. It would be pointless to deny the present weakness of Ukraine's courts and enforcement institutions, and the nebulous concepts described above, including hidden distributions, normal market terms, the group concept and loss or damage caused by a parent's instructions, will need to be discussed among scholars and practitioners before they are introduced. Additionally, if these suggestions become hard law, courts and practitioners should be afforded time to adjust their mindsets. The application of legal principles in corporate relationships and moral grounds as a basis for invalidating transactions will also need to be discussed in greater detail. This is where the concept of the indirect conflicts of interest, as described in Dutch jurisprudence, can be useful, although again it will need to be subjected to careful study and analysis.

Even though this research has focused on the German, Polish and Dutch jurisdictions as a means to understand how Ukrainian company law could be improved, it nevertheless shows that, at least as far as RPTs are concerned, Ukraine has the more detailed and nuanced procedural strategies. This might be connected to the relatively underdeveloped nature of the standards strategy in Ukraine, and the use of other means instead. Still, even if considered separately from Ukrainian company law, the laws of the EU Member States analysed here seem to be lacking in terms of procedural and disclosure instruments for tackling RPT-related issues. It appears that this gap will be filled by SRD II, whose development is described in section §5.05, by requiring Member States to implement the announcement, report and approval obligations for listed companies. Moreover, despite the argument that approval and disclosure strategies for RPTs are more developed in Ukraine, it would be far from accurate to conclude that Ukraine's RPT-related strategies reflect the pinnacle of regulation. Although these obligations have been in place for RPTs by Ukrainian public companies since 2009, much room for improvement remains in the current regime of safeguards under the JSC Law of Ukraine – as evidenced by the recommendations suggested above, including implementing SRD II.

Appendix: Results of the Google Forms Survey among Legal Experts and Practitioners

Part I: Related Party Transactions

1. Are you satisfied with the current state of regulation of RPTs in joint-stock companies?

Answer Options	Response Count
Yes	3
No	14
Other answers	2
Answered question	*19*
Skipped question	*0*

Other answers:

The regulation is not needed.
There is a positive tendency, but changes to the JSC Law of Ukraine that were made with the Law of Ukraine No. 1983 give possibility to the management to enter into these transactions easier.

2. In your practice did you have the need to go through the approval procedure as provided by Article 71 of the Law of Ukraine 'On Joint Stock Companies'?

Answer Options	Response Count
Yes	16
No	3
Answered question	*19*

Answer Options	Response Count
Skipped question	*0*

3. If you answered 'yes' to question 2, which body of the company gave the approval to the RPT?

Answer Options	Response Count
Supervisory board	5
General meeting of shareholders	11
Answered question	*19*
Skipped question	*3*

4. Which remedy should be used in case the procedure as indicated in Article 71 of the Law of Ukraine 'On Joint Stock Companies' is not followed?

Answer Options	Response Count
Invalidation of a transaction and damages (if any)	11
Unjust enrichment	6
Other answers	2
Answered question	*19*
Skipped question	*0*

Other answers:

Making the company officers liable (compensation of damages caused to the company). A derivative action has to work, so that a person is able to have its damages compensated!

5. Part 11 of Article 71 of the Law of Ukraine 'On Joint Stock Companies' provides: 'Liability for harm caused to a joint stock company by a transaction with interest entered into with the violation of requirements of this article should be borne by a person interested in a transaction'. Based on this article only the joint-stock company is entitled to claim damages for the harm caused by a transaction. Do you think other stakeholders should also be entitled to claim damages from the interested person?

Answer Options	Response Count
Yes, all kinds of stakeholders (shareholders, creditors, employees) should be entitled to claim damages directly from the interested person	3
Yes, but only shareholders should be entitled to claim damages directly from the interested person	7
Yes, but only those shareholders having a certain percentage of shares (e.g., more than 50%) should be entitled to claim damages directly from the interested person	3
No, only the joint-stock company should be entitled to claim damages from the interested person	5
Other answers	1
Answered question	*19*
Skipped question	*0*

Other answers:

The company and shareholders with 10 % of shares.

6. Part 11 of Article 71 of the Law of Ukraine 'On Joint Stock Companies' provides: 'Liability for harm caused to a joint stock company by a transaction with interest entered into with the violation of requirements of this article should be borne by a person interested in a transaction'. Based on the content of Article 71 of the Law of Ukraine 'On Joint Stock Companies' only those interested persons that are indicated in this Article may be held liable for the harm caused to a joint-stock company. Should the court be able to interpret the meaning of an interested person more extensively and hold liable also those interested persons that are not directly indicated in this Article, but by all features have a sufficient link to the company?

Answer Options	Response Count
Yes	13
No	5
Other answers	1
Answered question	*19*
Skipped question	*0*

Other answers:

In order to determine other persons it is necessary to develop clear features of these persons.

7. If a RPT has been approved in full accordance with Article 71, should the joint-stock company be entitled to claim damages when harm is in place?

Answer Options	Response Count
Yes	10
No	9
Answered question	*19*
Skipped question	*0*

8. Is there a need to have rules on RPTs for limited liability companies similar to the ones for joint-stock companies?

Answer Options	Response Count
Yes	16
No	2
Other questions	1
Answered question	*19*
Skipped question	*0*

Other answers:

LLCs should decide themselves.

9. Please, give your comments on the strengths of the current state of regulation of RPTs in joint-stock companies.

Answered question	*3*
Skipped question	*16*

Answers:

The algorithm of actions would be helpful.
The mere fact of existence of this construct is by itself a strength. One can also mention parts 4, 7 and 8 of Article 71 of the JSC Law of Ukraine.
The participant, thresholds.

10. Please, give your comments on the weaknesses of the current state of regulation of RPTs in joint-stock companies.

Answered question	*3*
Skipped question	*16*

Answers:

The concept of interest is not clear, there is no right of mandatory buy-out in case of preliminary provision of consent.
There is no unified approach in court practice. Besides, the legislative provisions are sometimes very general, giving more room for corruption in courts.
There is no definition of negative consequences of a transaction with interest. If a transaction does not lead to negative consequences, then ...

11. Here you may indicate any other suggestions for improvement of the regulation of RPTs.

Answered question	*2*
Skipped question	*17*

Answers:

It is difficult to suggest something, because, on the one hand, it is desirable not to have an overloaded law with more or less adequate court practice, and, on the other hand, taking into account some 'strange' judgments, the provisions of Article 71 should be more detailed.
There should be more practice and court practice, which will reveal non-obvious problems.

Part II: Groups of Companies

1. Are there groups of companies in Ukraine?

Answer Options	Response Count
Yes	16
No	3
Answered question	*19*
Skipped question	*0*

2. In some European states, the interest of the group is recognized by law. The core objective of such concept is to clarify and establish a minimum level of protection for the directors of both the parent company and the subsidiary, by officially recognizing their right to take into account the interest of the group in making management decisions. Do you think the interest of the group should also be recognized in Ukrainian

company law?

Answer Options	Response Count
Yes, for all kinds of companies (private and public ones)	12
Yes, but only for public ones	3
Yes, but only for financial institutions	1
No	2
Other answers	1
Answered question	*19*
Skipped question	*0*

Other answers:

For banks and public companies.

3. If you answered 'yes' to question 2, please explain how the group interest should be implemented in Ukraine:

Answer Options	Response Count
Through legislative amendments and subsequent case law	17
Without legislative amendments, but through case law based on the legal principles	0
Answered question	*19*
Skipped question	*2*

4. Should the regulation of RPTs in corporate groups be different from the regulation of RPTs outside corporate groups?

Answer Options	Response Count
Yes	7
No	11
Answered question	*19*
Skipped question	*0*

5. If you answered 'yes' to question 4, please explain how the regulation of RPT should differ for corporate groups.

Answered question	*0*
Skipped question	*19*

6. Please, give your comments on the strengths of the current state of regulation of corporate groups in Ukraine.

Answered question	*1*
Skipped question	*18*

Answers:

I do not see any particular strengths.

7. Please, give your comments on the weaknesses of the current state of regulation of corporate groups in Ukraine.

Answered question	*1*
Skipped question	*18*

Answers:

Tendentiousness, legislative provisions are often changed to satisfy the interests of a certain group in Ukraine.

8. Here you may indicate any other suggestions for improvement of the regulation of corporate groups in Ukraine.

Answered question	*1*
Skipped question	*18*

Answers:

Law-enforcement and court practice.

Bibliography

Adinolfi A, 'The Legal Notion of the Group Enterprise: The EEC Approach' in Sugarman D and Teubner G (eds), *Regulating Corporate Groups in Europe* (Nomos 1990).

Aguilera RV, Cuervo-Cazurra A and Kim S, *Taking Stock of Research on Codes of Good Governance*, available at SSRN: https://ssrn.com/abstract=1773087 Go to ISI://WOS:000271128400001, accessed on 18 November 2018.

Aharony J, Wang JW and Yuan HQ, 'Tunneling as an Incentive for Earnings Management During the IPO Process in China' (2010) 29 Journal of Accounting and Public Policy 1.

Ahmad E, *Dilemma of Subsidiary Directors* (Master thesis, University of Groningen 2015).

Ajani G, 'By Chance and Prestige: Legal Transplants in Russia and Eastern Europe' (1995) 43 The American Journal of Comparative Law 93.

Akinbami F, 'The Fiduciary Duties of Institutional Investors' in Tomasic R (ed.), *Routledge Handbook of Corporate Law* (Taylor & Francis 2017).

Alting C, 'Piercing the Corporate Veil in American and German Law-Liability of Individuals and Entities: A Comparative View' (1995) 2 Tulsa Journal of Comparative and International Law 187.

Andenæs MT and Wooldridge F, *European Comparative Company Law* (Cambridge University Press 2009).

Andersen PK and Balshøj DK, 'Directors' Conflicts of Interest: A Contribution to European Convergence' in Birkmose HS, Neville M and Sørensen KE (eds), *Boards of Directors in European Companies: Reshaping and Harmonising Their Organisation and Duties* (Wolters Kluwer Law & Business 2013).

Andersen PK, 'Directors' Duties – and the European Model Company Act' in Neville M and Sørensen KE (eds), *Company Law and SMEs* (Thomson Reuters 2010).

Andersen PK and others, 'European Model Company Act (EMCA) (September 1, 2017)' (Nordic & European Company Law Working Paper Nos 16-26, available at SSRN: https://ssrn.com/abstract=2929348, 2017).

Andres C, 'Large Shareholders and Firm Performance: An Empirical Examination of Founding-Family Ownership' (2008) 14 Journal of Corporate Finance 431.

Antonenko L, *The Myth of Transformation Through EU Law: A Case-Study of the Company Law Reform in Ukraine*, available at SSRN: https://ssrn.com/abstract =1485607, accessed on 18 November 2018.

Antunes JE, *Liability of Corporate Groups: Autonomy and Control in Parent-Subsidiary Relationships in US, German and EU Law: An International and Comparative Perspective* (Kluwer Law and Taxation Publisher 1994).

Antunes JE and others, *Report of the Reflection Group on the Future of EU Company Law* (European Commission Internal Market and Services 2011).

Armour J and others, *Report on the Recognition of the Interest of the Group (October 30, 2016)*, available at: https://ssrn.com/abstract=2888863, 2016.

Asplund A, 'Who Should Say on Pay and for the Sake of Whom in a Listed Company?' (2015) 12 European Company Law 286.

Atanasov VA, Black BS and Ciccotello CS, 'Unbundling and Measuring Tunneling' (2014) 2014 University of Illinois Law Review 1697.

Avgitidis DK, *Groups of Companies: The Liability of the Parent Company for the Debts of Its Subsidiary* (Ant. N. Sakkoulas Publishers 1996).

Bachmann G and others, *Regulating the Closed Corporation*, vol 4 (Walter de Gruyter 2013).

Barlowski M, 'Poland' in Baer G and Karen OF (eds), *Financing Company Group Restructurings* (Oxford University Press 2015).

Bartman SM, *Concernbeleid en aansprakelijkheid: over (oa) convergentie in rechtsdenken op het gebied van concernverhoudingen tussen Nederland en de Bondsrepubliek Duitsland* (Kluwer 1989).

Bartman SM, 'Dutch Supreme Court at a Loss over Groups' (2016) 13 European Company Law 123.

Bartman SM, 'From Autonomy of Interests to Concurrence of Interest in Dutch Group Company Law' (2007) 4 European Company Law 207.

Bartman SM, 'Of Groups and Ostriches' (2007) 4 European Company Law 190.

Bartman SM, 'Piercing the Corporate Veil in Haitian Poisoning Affair Rejected in First Instance: German HELM AG Not Found Liable under Dutch Corporate Law' (2016) 13 European Company Law 105.

Bartman SM, 'Report from the Netherlands' (2006) 3 European Company Law 33.

Bartman SM, 'The Impact of Optional EU Law Making on National Company Law' (2008) 5 European Company Law 271.

Bartman SM, 'The Obligation to Contribute in the Case of Group Financing under Dutch Law: How to Allocate the Pain among Group Members?' (2013) 10 European Company Law 15.

Bartman SM, Dorresteijn AFM and Olaerts M, *Van Het Concern* (Wolters Kluwer 2016).

Bartman SM and Dorresteijn AFM, 'Commissaris en Tegenstrijdig Belang: Handelt de Ondernemingskamer contra Legem?' (2018) Ars Aequi 913.

Baudry B and Chassagnon V, 'The Vertical Network Organization as a Specific Governance Structure: What Are the Challenges for Incomplete Contracts Theories and What Are the Theoretical Implications for the Boundaries of the (Hub-) Firm?' (2012) 16 Journal of Management & Governance 285.

Baums T and Scott KE, 'Taking Shareholder Protection Seriously? Corporate Governance in the United States and Germany' (2005) 53 The American Journal of Comparative Law 31.

Bava F and Gromis di Trana M, 'Disclosure on Related Party Transactions: Evidence from Italian Listed Companies' (2016) 6 Accounting, Economics and Law-A Convivium 119.

Bayer W, 'Horizontal Groups and Joint Ventures in Europe: Concepts and Reality' in Hopt KJ (ed.), *Groups of Companies in European Laws*, vol 2 (de Gruyter 1982).

Bayer W and Selentin P, 'Related Party Transactions: Der neueste EU-Vorschlag im Kontext des deutschen Aktien-und Konzernrechts' (2015) Neue Zeitschrift für Gesellschaftsrecht 7.

Bebchuk LA and Hamdani A, 'Independent Directors and Controlling Shareholders' (2017) 165 University of Pennsylvania Law Review 1271.

Bebchuk LA and Jolls C, 'Managerial Value Diversion and Shareholder Wealth' (1999) 15 Journal of Law, Economics, and Organization 487.

Becht M, 'European Corporate Governance: Trading off Liquidity Against Control' (1999) 43 European Economic Review 1071.

Becht M and Böhmer E, 'Ownership and Voting Power in Germany' in Barca F and Becht M (eds), *The Control of Corporate Europe* (Oxford University Press 2001).

Becht M and Böhmer E, 'Voting Control in German Corporations' (2003) 23 International Review of Law and Economics 1.

Becht M and Mayer C, 'Introduction' in Barca F and Becht M (eds), *The Control of Corporate Europe* (Oxford University Press 2001).

Becht M and Röell A, 'Blockholdings in Europe: An International Comparison' (1999) 43 European Economic Review 1049.

Beinert D, Burmeister F and Tries H-J, *Mergers and Acquisitions in Germany* (Verlag C.H. Beck München 2009).

Belcher A, 'The Boundaries of the Firm: The Theories of Coase, Knight and Weitzman' (1997) 17 Legal Studies 22.

Belcredi M and Ferrarini G, 'Corporate Boards, Incentive Pay and Shareholder Activism in Europe: Main Issues and Policy' in Belcredi M and Ferrarini G (eds), *Boards and Shareholders in European Listed Companies: Facts, Context and Post-Crisis Reforms* (Cambridge University Press 2013).

Beny LN, 'Do Insider Trading Laws Matter? Some Preliminary Comparative Evidence' (2005) 7 American Law and Economics Review 144.

Bergkamp L, 'The Environmental Liability Directive and Liability of Parent Companies for Damage Caused by Their Subsidiaries ("Enterprise Liability")' (2016) 13 European Company Law 183.

Bergkamp PA, 'Parent Company Liability after Okpabi v. Shell' (2018) 15 European Company Law 112.

Berglöf E and Claessens S, 'Enforcement and Corporate Governance' World Bank policy research Working Paper 3409, September 2004, available at: http://documents.worldbank.org/curated/en/516141468765315959/pdf/wps3409.pdf, accessed on 18 November 2018.

Berkowitz D, Pistor K and Richard J-F, 'The Transplant Effect' (2003) 51 The American Journal of Comparative Law 163.

Berle AA, 'Corporate Powers as Powers in Trust' (1931) 44 Harvard Law Review 1049.

Berle Jr AA, 'For Whom Corporate Managers Are Trustees: A Note' (1931) 45 Harvard Law Review 1365.

Berle A and Means G, *The Modern Corporation and Private Property* (McMillian 1932).

Bertrand M, Mehta P and Mullainathan S, 'Ferreting out Tunneling: An Application to Indian Business Groups' NBER Working Paper No. 7952, available at: https://www.nber.org/papers/w7952, accessed on 18 November 2018.

Beyer J and Hassel A, 'The Effects of Convergence: Internationalization and the Changing Distribution of Net Value Added in Large German Firms' in Clarke T (ed.), *Corporate Governance: Critical Perspectives on Business and Management* (Routledge 2005).

Black B and Kraakman R, 'A Self-Enforcing Model of Corporate Law' (1996) 109 Harvard Law Review 1911.

Black BS, Kraakman RH and Tarassova AS, *Guide to the Russian Law on Joint Stock Companies* (Kluwer Law International 1998).

Blumberg PI, 'Limited Liability and Corporate Groups' (1985) 11 Journal of Corporation Law 573.

Böckli P and others, 'A Proposal for the Reform of Group Law in Europe' (2017) 18 European Business Organization Law Review 1.

Bodnar T, 'Pravochyny aktsionernykh tovarystv, schodo vchynennia yakykh ye zainteresovannist' (2009) Yurydychna Ukrayina 36.

Boeri T and Perasso G, 'Privatization and Corporate Governance: Some Lessons for the Experience of Transitional Economies' in Balling M (ed.), *Corporate Governance, Financial Markets and Global Convergence* (Springer 1998).

Bohdanowicz L, 'Corporate Governance in Poland' in Kostyuk AN, Braendle U and Capizzi V (eds), *Corporate Governance: New Challenges and Opportunities* (Virtus Interpress 2017).

Bolt W and Peeters M, 'Corporate Governance in the Netherlands' in Balling M, Hennessy E and O'Brien R (eds), *Corporate Governance, Financial Markets and Global Convergence* (Springer 1998).

Bondaryev T and Zorya A, 'Ukraine' in Kawamura A (ed.), *Corporate Governance* (Thomson Reuters 2015).

Borrius Y, 'Directors' Liability: The Netherlands' (2011) 8 European Company Law 246.

Bortsevych P, 'Problemy ukladannia znachnykh pravochyniv ta pravochyniv, schodo yakykh ye zainteresovannist' (2014) Derzhava i pravo 159.

Borysova V and Zhylinkova I (eds), *Simeyne pravo Ukrayiny: pidruchnyk* (2nd edn, Yurinkom Inter 2009).

Boyarchuk K, 'Pravovi naslidky porushennia poriadku vchynennia pravochyniv iz zatsikavlenistiu' (2014) Nashe pravo 168.

Bratton WW and Wachter ML, 'Shareholder Primacy's Corporatist Origins: Adolf Berle and the Modern Corporation' (2008) 34 Journal of Corporation Law 99.

Bröhmer J, 'Germany' in Omar PJ (ed.), *Directors' Duties and Liabilities* (Ashgate/Dartmouth 2000).

Brown JR, 'Disloyalty Without Limits: "Independent" Directors and the Elimination of the Duty of Loyalty' (2012) 95 Kentucky Law Journal 53.

Brudney V, 'Contract and Fiduciary Duty in Corporate Law' (1997) 38 Boston College Law Review 595.

Bruner CM, 'Is the Corporate Director's Duty of Care a Fiduciary Duty: Does It Matter' (2013) 48 Wake Forest Law Review 1027.

Buxbaum RM and others, *European Economic and Business Law: Legal and Economic Analyses on Integration and Harmonization* (Walter de Gruyter 1996).

Cahn A, 'Capital Maintenance' in Fleischer H and others (eds), *German and Asian Perspectives on Company Law* (Mohr Siebeck 2016).

Cahn A, 'Intra-group Loans under German Law' (2010) 7 European Company Law 44.

Cahn A, 'The Shareholders' Fiduciary Duty in German Company Law' in Birkmose HS (ed.), *Shareholders' Duties* (Wolters Kluwer 2017).

Cahn A and Donald DC, *Comparative Company Law: Text and Cases on the Laws Governing Corporations in Germany, the UK and the USA* (Cambridge University Press 2010).

Cain DM, Loewenstein G and Moore DA, 'Coming Clean but Playing Dirtier: The Shortcomings of Disclosure as a Solution to Conflicts of Interest' in Moore DA and others (eds), *Conflicts of Interest: Challenges and Solutions in Business, Law, Medicine, and Public Policy* (Cambridge University Press 2005).

Cairns JW, 'Watson, Walton, and the History of Legal Transplants' (2012) 41 Georgia Journal of International and Comparative Law 637.

Carlton DW and Fischel DR, 'The Regulation of Insider Trading' (1983) 35 Stanford Law Review 857.

Cartwright J, 'Redelijkheid en billijkheid: a view from English law' (2016) 30 BW-krant Jaarboek 39.

Cheffins BR, *Corporate Ownership and Control: British Business Transformed* (Oxford University Press 2008).

Chen W, Li S and Chen CX, 'How Much Control Causes Tunneling? Evidence from China' (2016) China Journal of Accounting Research, available at: http://dx.doi .org/101016/jcjar201610001.

Cheung Y-L, 'Buy High, Sell Low: How Listed Firms Price Asset Transfers in Related Party Transactions' (2009) 33 Journal of Banking & Finance (Netherlands) 914.

Cheung YL and others, 'Tunneling and Propping Up: An Analysis of Related Party Transactions by Chinese Listed Companies' (2009) 17 Pacific-Basin Financ Journal 372.

Chong S and Dean G, 'Related Party Transactions: A Preliminary Evaluation of Sfas-57 and Ias-24 Using 4 Case Studies' (1985) 21 Abacus-A Journal of Accounting Finance and Business Studies 84.

Chugh D, Bazerman MH and Banaji MR, 'Bounded Ethicality as Psychological Barrier to Recognizing Conflicts of Interest' in Moore DA and others (eds), *Conflicts of Interest: Challenges and Solutions in Business, Law, Medicine, and Public Policy* (Cambridge University Press 2005).

Chyzhyk H, 'Pravochyny iz zainteresovannistiu ta znachni pravochyny v aktsionernykh tovarystvakh Ukrayiny' (2013) Studentskyi yurydychnyi zhurnal: dodatok do zhurnalu 'Pravo Ukrayiny' 45.

Coase RH, 'The Nature of the Firm' (1937) 4 Economica 386.

Coffee Jr JC, 'Understanding Enron: "It's About the Gatekeepers, Stupid"' (2002) 57 The Business Lawyer 1403.

Conac P-H, 'Director's Duties in Groups of Companies: Legalizing the Interest of the Group at the European Level' (2013) 10 European Company and Financial Law Review 194.

Conac P-H, 'Director's Duties in Groups of Companies: Legalising the Interest of the Group at the European Level' in Birkmose HS, Neville M and Sørensen KE (eds), *Boards of Directors in European Companies: Reshaping and Harmonising Their Organisation and Duties* (Wolters Kluwer Law & Business 2013).

Conac P-H, Enriques L and Gelter M, 'Constraining Dominant Shareholders' Self-Dealing: The Legal Framework in France, Germany, and Italy' (2007) 4 European Company and Financial Law Review 491.

Conac P-H, 'Proposal to Facilitate the Management of Cross-Border Company Groups in Europe' (2015) 12 European Company and Financial Law Review 299.

Cooter R and Freedman BJ, 'The Fiduciary Relationship: Its Economic Character and Legal Consequences' (1991) 66 New York University Law Review 1045.

Du Plessis JJ and Low CK (eds), *Corporate Governance Codes for the 21st Century* (Springer 2017).

'Corporate Group Law for Europe by Forum Europaeum' (2000) 1 European Business Organisation Law Review 165.

Corporate Groups Final Report, Prepared by Australian Companies & Securities Advisory Committee (The Committee 2000).

Cuomo F, Mallin C and Zattoni A, 'Corporate Governance Codes: A Review and Research Agenda' (2016) 24 Corporate Governance – An International Review 222.

Dabrowski M, Gomulka S and Rostowski J, 'Whence Reform? A Critique of the Stiglitz Perspective' (2001) 4 The Journal of Policy Reform 291.

Davies P and Hopt K, 'Corporate Boards in Europe: Accountability and Convergence' (2013) 61 American Journal of Comparative Law 301.

Davies P and others, 'Boards in Law and Practice: A Cross-Country Analysis in Europe' in Davies PL and others (eds), *Corporate Boards in Law and Practice: A Comparative Analysis in Europe* (1st edn, Oxford University Press 2013).

Davis EP and Steil B, *Institutional Investors* (MIT Press 2001).

De Brauw C, Groothuis L and Stevens R, *The Netherland Takeover Guide,* available at: https://www.ibanet.org/Document/Default.aspx?DocumentUid = 8E6BF591-D567-4594-BC81-00E0BA83AF39 (2014).

De Groot C, *Corporate Governance as a Limited Legal Concept*, vol 4 (Kluwer Law International 2009).

De Groot C, 'The Duty of Directors to Be Guided by the Best Interests of the Company' in Breedveld C and others (eds), *Core Concepts in the Dutch Civil Code: Continuously in Motion* (BW-krant Jaarboek 2016).

De Groot C, Van Nood A and Lambert F, 'The ABN AMRO Ruling: Some Commentaries' (2007) 4 European Company Law 168.

De Jong A and others, 'Ownership and Control in the Netherlands' in Barca F and Becht M (eds), *The Control of Corporate Europe* (Oxford University Press 2001).

De Jong A and Roell A, 'Financing and Control in the Netherlands: A Historical Perspective' in Morck RK (ed.), *A History of Corporate Governance Around the World: Family Business Groups to Professional Managers* (University of Chicago Press 2007).

De Savornin Lohman HA, *Duties and Liability of Directors and Shareholders under Netherlands Law: Piercing the Corporate Veil* (Kluwer Law International 1996).

De Vries PP, 'Exit Rights of Minority Shareholders in a Private Limited Company' (Dphil thesis, University of Groningen 2010).

Dearborn M, 'Enterprise Liability: Reviewing and Revitalizing Liability for Corporate Groups' (2009) 97 California Law Review 195.

Dijkhuizen T, 'On the Remuneration of Directors of Listed Companies (Again)' (2014) 11 European Company Law 199.

Dijkhuizen T, 'Report from Europe: The Proposal for a Directive Amending the Shareholders Rights Directive' (2015) 12 European Company Law 45.

Djankov S and others, 'The Law and Economics of Self-Dealing' (2008) 88 Journal of Financial Economics 430.

Dodd EM, 'For Whom Are Corporate Managers Trustees?' (1932) 45 Harvard Law Review 1145.

Doing Business 2019: Training for Reform (International Bank for Reconstruction and Development/The World Bank 2019).

Dorresteijn AFM, *Tegenstrijdig Belang van Bestuurders en Commissarissen: een Rechtsvergelijkende Studie* (Kluwer 1989).

Dorresteijn AF and others, *European Corporate Law* (2nd edn, Kluwer Law International 2009).

Dotevall R, 'Is a Common Structure of Company Directors' Duties Evolving in EU?' (2016) 27 European Business Law Review 285.

Dozhdiev D, *Rimskoye chastnoye pravo* (Nersesiants V ed., 3rd edn, M.: Norma 2008).

Drygala T, 'Directors Liability in the Member States of the European Union' in Lutter M (ed.), *Legal Capital in Europe* (Walter de Gruyter 2006).

Du Plessis JJ and others, *German Corporate Governance in International and European Context* (Springer Science & Business Media 2012).

Du Plessis JJ and others, *Principles of Contemporary Corporate Governance* (Cambridge University Press 2014).

Dyck A and Zingales L, 'Private Benefits of Control: An International Comparison' (2004) 59 The Journal of Finance 537.

Dzierzanowski M and Tamowicz P, 'The Corporate Governance Code for Polish Listed Companies (The Gdańsk Code)' (The Polish Corporate Governance Forum and The Gdansk Institute for Market Economics, 15 June 2002).

Easterbrook FH and Fischel DR, 'Contract and Fiduciary Duty' (1993) 36 The Journal of Law & Economics 425.

Easterbrook FH and Fischel DR, 'Voting in Corporate Law' (1983) 26 The Journal of Law & Economics 395.

Edesiri Okoro G and Jeroh E, 'Does Related-Party Transactions Affect Financial Performance of Firms in Nigeria' (2016) 6 Business Trends 47.

Eisenberg MA, 'Self-Interested Transactions in Corporate Law' (1987) 13 Journal of Corporation Law 997.

Enriques L, 'Bad Apples, Bad Oranges: A Comment from Old Europe on Post-Enron Corporate Governance Reforms' (2003) 38 Wake Forest Law Review 911.

Enriques L, 'Related Party Transactions: Policy Options and Real-World Challenges (with a Critique of the European Commission Proposal)' (2015) 16 European Business Organisation Law Review 1.

Enriques L, 'The Law on Company Directors' Self-Dealing: A Comparative Analysis' (2000) 2 International and Comparative Corporate Law Journal 297.

Enriques L, Hertig G and Kanda H, 'Related-Party Transactions' in Kraakman R and others (eds), *The Anatomy of Corporate Law A Comparative and Functional Approach* (2nd edn, Oxford University Press 2009).

Enriques L and others, 'Related-Party Transactions' in Kraakman R and others (eds), *The Anatomy of Corporate Law: A Comparative and Functional Approach* (3rd edn, Oxford University Press 2017).

Faccio M and Lang LH, 'The Ultimate Ownership of Western European Corporations' (2002) 65 Journal of Financial Economics 365.

Fama EF, 'Agency Problems and the Theory of the Firm' (1980) 88 The Journal of Political Economy 288.

Fan C, *Bringing Controlling Shareholders to Court: Standard-Based Strategies and Controlling Shareholder Opportunism* (Eleven International Publishing 2013).

Farrar JH, 'A Note on Dealing with Self Interested Transactions by Directors' (2000) 12 Bond Law Review 106.

Feleaga L and Neacsu I, 'Disclosure of Related Party Transactions and Information Regarding Transfer Pricing by the Companies Listed on Bucharest Stock Exchange' (2016) 15 Journal of Accounting and Management Information Systems 785.

Ferrarini G, 'Shareholder Value and the Modernization of European Corporate Law' in Hopt KJ and Wymeersch E (eds), *Capital Markets and Company Law* (Oxford University Press 2003).

Fleischer H, 'A Guide to German Company Law for International Lawyers: Distinctive Features, Particularities, Idiosyncracies' in Fleischer H, Hansen JL and Ringe W-G (eds), *German and Nordic Perspectives on Company Law and Capital Markets Law* (Mohr Siebeck 2015).

Fleischer H, 'Disguised Distributions and Capital Maintenance in European Company Law' in Lutter M (ed.), *Legal Capital in Europe* (Walter de Gruyter 2006).

Fleischer H, 'The Responsibility of the Management and Its Enforcement' in Ferrarini G and others (eds), *Reforming Company and Takeover Law in Europe* (Oxford University Press 2004).

Fohlin C, 'The History of Corporate Ownership and Control in Germany' in Morck RK (ed.), *A History of Corporate Governance Around the World: Family Business Groups to Professional Managers* (University of Chicago Press 2007).

Fox MB, 'Required Disclosure and Corporate Governance' in Hopt KJ and others (eds), *Comparative Corporate Governance: The State of the Art and Emerging Research* (Oxford University Press 1998).

Freedland M, 'Otto Kahn-Freund (1900-1979)' in Beatson J and Zimmermann R (eds), *Jurists Uprooted German-Speaking Émigré Lawyers in Twentieth-Century Britain* (Oxford University Press 2004).

Friedberg E, 'Conflict of Interest from the Perspective of the Sociology of Organised Action' in Peters A and Handschin L (eds), *Conflict of Interest in Global, Public and Corporate Governance* (Cambridge University Press 2012).

Friedman E, Johnson S and Mitton T, 'Propping and Tunneling' (2003) 31 Journal of Comparative Economics 732.

Frolov P, 'Pryvatyzatsiya v Ukrayini: retrospektyvy ta perspektyvy' *Dzerkalo tyzhnia* (No. 10 (17 March-23 March)), available at: https://dt.ua/macrolevel/privatizaciya-v-ukrayini-retrospektivi-ta-perspektivi-272273_.html, accessed on 7 December 2018.

Frommel SN and Bonn A, *Company Law in Europe* (Kluwer Academic Publishers 1975).

Galle JGCM, *Consensus on the Comply or Explain Principle Within the EU Corporate Governance Framework: Legal and Empirical Research* (Kluwer 2012).

Gan V, 'The Impact of Related Party Transactions on Performance and Valuation of Malaysian Listed Firms: Testing the Influence of Corporate Governance' (Thesis for the Degree of Master of Commerce, Swinburne University of Technology 2017).

Gelter M, 'Taming or Protecting the Modern Corporation? Shareholder-Stakeholder Debates in a Comparative Light' (2011) 7 New York University Journal of Law and Business 641.

Gerner-Beuerle C, Paech P and Schuster EP, *Study on Directors' Duties and Liability* (European Commission DG Markt 2013).

Gerner-Beuerle C and Schuster EP, 'Mapping Directors' Duties: Strategies and Trends in the EU' in Birkmose HS, Neville M and Sørensen KE (eds), *Boards of Directors in European Companies: Reshaping and Harmonising Their Organisation and Duties* (Wolters Kluwer Law & Business 2013).

Gispen G and Van Gangelen B, *Insolvency and Directors' Duties in the Netherlands: Overview* (Thomson Reuters Practical Law 2018), available at: https://uk.practicallaw.thomsonreuters.com/1-635-9172?transitionType = Default&context Data = (sc.Default)&firstPage = true&bhcp = 1, accessed on 17 May 2018.

Gleichmann K, 'The Law of Corporate Groups in the European Community' in Sugarman D and Teubner G (eds), *Regulating Corporate Groups in Europe* (European Institute, Florence 1990).

Goldsmith J, 'Lawyers' Responsibility for Advising on Corporate Social Responsibility' in Mullerat R (ed.), *Corporate Social Responsibility: The Corporate Governance of the 21st Century* (Kluwer Law International 2005).

Gordon EA and Henry E, *Related Party Transactions and Earnings Management*, available at SSRN: https://ssrn.com/abstract=612234 or http://dx.doi.org/102 139/ssrn612234, accessed on 27 November 2018.

Goshen Z, 'Controlling Corporate Self-Dealing: Convergence of Path Dependency?' in Milhaupt CJ (ed.), *Global Markets, Domestic Institutions: Corporate Law and Governance in a New Era of Cross-Border Deals* (Columbia University Press 2012).

Goshen Z, 'The Efficiency of Controlling Corporate Self-Dealing: Theory Meets Reality' (2003) 91 California Law Review 393.

Grabowski K, *Dyrektywa o prawach akcjonariuszy. Studium tworzenia prawa i przewodnik po dyrektywie* (Officyna Allerhanda 2014).

Grigoleit HC, 'Directors' Liability and Enforcement Mechanisms from the German Perspective: General Structure and Key Issues' in Fleischer H and others (eds), *German and Asian Perspectives on Company Law* (Mohr Siebeck 2016).

Goergen M, Manjon MC and Renneboog L, 'Recent Developments in German Corporate Governance' (2008) 28 International Review of Law and Economics 175.

Groenland IC, 'Related Party Transactions in the Revised Shareholders' Rights Directive: The EU Perspective and Implementation in National Law' (2019) 16 European Company Law 44.

Hopt KJ (ed.), *Groups of Companies in European Laws*, vol 2 (de Gruyter 1982).

Grundmann S and Glasow F, *European Company Law: Organization, Finance and Capital Markets* (2nd edn, Intersentia 2012).

Gupta P, *Tunneling and Propping: Indian Evidence* (Thesis within Fellowship Programme in Management, Indian Institute of Management Indore 2017).

Hadden T, *The Control of Corporate Groups* (Institute of Advanced Legal Studies, University of London 1983).

Haisler P, 'Codes of Conduct as a Means of Regulation: With Point of Departure in Corporate Governance Debate' in Neville M and Sørensen KE (eds), *The Regulation of Companies* (Forlaget Thompson 2003).

Hallemeesch N, 'Self-Dealing by Controlling Shareholders: Improving Minority Protection in Light of Article 9 c SRD' (2018) 15 European Company and Financial Law Review 197.

Hansen C, Johnston JF and Alexander FH, 'The Role of Disinterested Directors in "Conflict" Transactions: The ALI Corporate Governance Project and Existing Law' (1990) 45 The Business Lawyer 2083.

Harbarth S and Kienle F, 'Director Compensation under German Law and the Mannesmann Effect' (2006) 3 European Company Law 90.

Harper Ho VE, 'Theories of Corporate Groups: Corporate Identity Reconceived' (2012) 42 Seton Hall Law Review 879.

Harris R, 'The Private Origins of the Private Company: Britain 1862-1907' (2013) 33 Oxford Journal of Legal Studies 339.

Hasselbach K and Spengler M, 'Report from Germany' (2005) 4 European Company Law 113.

Heerstraßen F and Nebe F, *Cash Pooling after the Reform of the German Act on Limited Liability Companies (GmbHG)*, Loschelder Rechtsanwälte, available at: https://

loschelder.de/fileadmin/user_upload/downloads/pdf/aktuelles/2009/2009-01_DetailsAktuell.pdf, accessed on 5 December 2018.

Helm R and others, *Practitioner's Guide to Conflicts of Interest in the Financial Services Industry* (Sweet & Maxwell 2012).

Hermes N and Van Veen K, 'Corporate Governance in the Netherlands: Trends, Challenges and Opportunities (2008-2016)' in Kostyuk AN, Braendle U and Capizzi V (eds), *Corporate Governance: New Challenges and Opportunities* (Virtus Interpress 2017).

Hill CA and McDonnell B, 'Sanitizing Interested Transactions' (2011) 36 Delaware Journal of Corporate Law 12.

Hill J, 'Corporate Groups, Creditor Protection and Cross Guarantees: Australian Perspectives' (1994) 24 Canadian Business Law Journal 321.

Hill JG, 'Regulating Executive Remuneration: International Developments in the Post-Scandal Era' (2006) 3 European Company Law 64.

Hirte H, *Kapitalgesellschaftsrecht* (RWS-Verlag 2016).

Ho VH, 'Enlightened Shareholder Value: Corporate Governance Beyond the Shareholder-Stakeholder Divide' (2010) 36 Journal of Corporation Law 59.

Hollander C and Salzedo S, *Conflicts of Interest* (5th edn, Thomson Reuters 2016).

Holovniov S and Vinnichuk Yu, '200 naybilshykh kompaniy Ukrayiny 2016 roku' (*Business Censor (10 October 2017)* 2017), available at: https://biz.censor.net.ua/resonance/3033764/200_nayiblshih_kompanyi_ukrani_2016_roku, accessed on 31 December 2018.

Hommelhoff P, 'Protection of Minority Shareholders, Investors and Creditors in Corporate Groups: The Strengths and Weaknesses of German Corporate Group Law' (2001) 2 European Business Organization Law Review 61.

Hopt KJ, 'Comparative Corporate Governance: The State of Art and International Regulation' in Fleckner AM and Hopt KJ (eds), *Comparative Corporate Governance: A Functional and International Analysis* (Cambridge University Press 2013).

Hopt KJ, 'Conflict of Interest, Secrecy and Insider Information of Directors, a Comparative Analysis' (2013) 10 European Company and Financial Law Review 167.

Hopt KJ, 'Corporate Governance in Europe: A Critical Review of the European Commission's Initiatives on Corporate Law and Corporate Governance' European Corporate Governance Institute (ECGI) - Law Working Paper No. 296/2015, available at SSRN: https://ssrn.com/abstract=2644156 or http://dx.doi.org/10 2139/ssrn2644156, accessed on 5 December 2018.

Hopt KJ, 'Groups of Companies: A Comparative Study on the Economics, Law and Regulation of Corporate Groups' Law Working Paper N° 286/2015, available at: http://ssrn.com/abstract=2560935, accessed on 5 December 2018.

Hopt KJ, 'Rights of Minority Shareholders under German Law' in Perakēs E (ed.), *Rights of Minority Shareholders: XVIth Congress of the International Academy of Comparative Law* (Brisbane (Australia) 2002); General and National Reports (Bruylant 2004).

Hopt KJ, 'Self-Dealing and Use of Corporate Opportunity and Information: Regulating Directors' Conflicts of Interest' in Hopt K and Teubner G (eds), *Corporate Governance and Directors' Liabilities* (Walter de Gruyter 1985).

Hopt KJ, 'Trusteeship and Conflicts of Interest in Corporate, Banking, and Agency Law: Toward Common Legal Principles for Intermediaries in the Modern Service-Oriented Society' in Ferrarini G and others (eds), *Reforming Company and Takeover Law in Europe*, vol 4 (2004).

Hopt KJ and Leyens PC, 'Board Models in Europe: Recent Developments of Internal Corporate Governance Structures in Germany, the United Kingdom, France, and Italy' (2004) 1 European Company and Financial Law Review 135.

Hopt KJ and Pistor K, 'Company Groups in Transition Economies: A Case for Regulatory Intervention?' (2001) 2 European Business Organization Law Review 1.

Horak H, *The Newly Amended Shareholders Rights Directive: Lots of Rights, What about Implementation?* (22nd International Scientific Conference on Economic and Social Development – 'Legal Challenges of Modern World').

Hrytsak O, 'Moralni zasady suspilstva yak otsinochna kategoriya ukrayinskoho tsyvilnoho prava' (2010) Advokat 39.

Immenga U, 'Company Systems and Affiliations' in Frankel T (ed.), International Encyclopedia of Comparative Law, vol 13 (Amer Soc Comparative Law 1988).

Immenga U, 'The Law of Groups in the Federal Republic of Germany' in Wymeersch E and Fitchew MG (eds), *Groups of Companies in the EEC* (Walter de Gruyter 1993).

Issacharoff S, 'Legal Responses to Conflicts of Interest' in Moore DA and others (eds), *Conflicts of Interest: Challenges and Solutions in Business, Law, Medicine, and Public Policy* (Cambridge University Press 2005).

Iwanicki J and Nowacki A, 'Report from Poland' (2007) 4 European Company Law 90.

Jacobson MA, 'Interested Director Transactions and the (Equivocal) Effects of Shareholder Ratification' (1996) 21 Delawer Journal of Corporate Law 981.

Jensen MC and Meckling WH, 'Rights and Production Functions: An Application to Labor-Managed Firms and Codetermination' (1979) 52 The Journal of Business 469.

Jian M and Wong TJ, 'Propping Through Related Party Transactions' (2010) 15 Review of Accounting Studies 70.

Johnson S and others, 'Tunnelling' (2000) 90 AEA Papers and Proceedings 22.

Jong BJD, 'The Distinction Between Public and Private Companies and Its Relevance for Company Law: Observations from the United Kingdom and the Netherlands' (2016) 27 European Business Law Review 1.

Jurgens U, Naumann K and Rupp J, 'Shareholder Value in an Adverse Environment: The German Case' in Clarke T (ed.), *Corporate Governance: Critical Perspectives on Business and Management* (Routledge 2005).

Kahn-Freund O, 'On Uses and Misuses of Comparative Law' (1974) 37 The Modern Law Review 1.

Kang SY, 'Rethinking Self-Dealing and the Fairness Standard: A Law and Economics Framework for Internal Transactions in Corporate Groups' (2016) 11 Virginia Law and Business Review 95.

Karchevskyi K, '"Krupnyi aktsioner" yak storona pravochynu iz zainteresovanistiu' (2011) Aktualni pytannia tsyvilnoho ta hospodarskoho prava 18.

Karchevskyi K, 'Naslidky nedotrymannia poriadku vchynennia pravochynu aktsionernoho tovarystva, schodo vchynennia yakoho isnuye zainteresovannist (porivnialno-pravovyi analiz)' (2012) Pravo i Bezpeka 281.

Karchevskyi K, 'Porivnialno-pravova kharakterystyka poniattia "afiliyovana osoba"' (2013) Visnyk Kharkivskoho natsionalnoho universytetu vnutrishnikh sprav 217.

Karchevskyi K, 'Problemy vyznachennia kola posadovykh osib aktsionernoho tovarystva, zainteresovannist yakykh u pravochyni tiagne za soboyu neobkhidnist zastosuvannia spetsialnoho poriadku yoho vchynennia' (2010) Aktualni pytannia tsyvilnoho ta hospodarskoho prava 91.

Karchevskyi K, 'Rodynnyi kryterii poniattia afiliyovana osoba (v konteksti pravovoho rezhymu pravochyniv iz zainteresovannistiu)' (2014) Visnyk Kharkivskoho natsionalnoho universytetu vnutrishnikh sprav 160.

Kemp B, 'Aandeelhoudersverantwoordelijkheid: de Positieve Rol van de Aandeelhouder en Aandeelhoudersvergadering = Shareholder Responsibility: the Position and Role of the Shareholder and the Shareholders Meeting' (Dphil thesis, Wolters Kluwer 2015).

Keong LC, 'The Corporate Governance Debate' in Low CK (ed.), *Corporate Governance: an Asia-Pacific Critique* (Sweet & Maxwell Asia 2002).

Kespohl A, 'Germany' in Campbell D (ed.), *Shareholders' Liability (The Comparative Law Yearbook of International Business)*, vol Special Issue (Graham & Trotman/Martinus Nijhoff 2017).

Khort YV, 'Company Law in Ukraine: Recent Regulatory Developments' (2018) 80 Актуальні проблеми держави і права 179.

Kibenko O and Zaleska A, 'Vykhid uchasnyka iz tovarystva z obmezhenoyu vidpovidalnistiu: problemni pytannia ta praktychni rekomendatsii' (2012) Ukrayinske komertsiyne pravo 20.

Kluver J, 'European and Australian Proposals for Corporate Group Law: A Comparative Analysis' (2000) 1 European Business Organization Law Review 287.

Klymenko Ya, 'Afiliyovani osoby: Pokhodzhennia terminu, kryterii vyznachennia i zastosuvannia u vitchyznianiy ta mizhnarodniy praktykakh' (2014) Naukovi pratsi Kirovohradskoho natsionalnoho technichnoho universytetu Ekonomichni nauky 215.

Kolla P, 'The Mannesmann Trial and the Role of the Courts' (2004) 5 German Law Journal 829.

KPMG, *'First Impressions: Amendments to IAS 24 Related Party Disclosures', International Financial Reporting Standards, November 2009*, available at: https://home.kpmg.com/content/dam/kpmg/pdf/2010/01/First-Impressions-O-0911.pdf, 2009.

Kraakman R, 'Disclosure of Corporate Governance: An Overview Essay' in Ferrarini G and others (eds), *Reforming Company and Takeover Law in Europe* (Oxford University Press 2004).

Kraakman R and others, *The Anatomy of Corporate Law: A Comparative and Functional Approach* (2nd edn, Oxford University Press 2009).

Kraakman R and others, *The Anatomy of Corporate Law: A Comparative and Functional Approach* (3rd edn, Oxford University Press 2017).

La Porta R and others, 'Investor Protection and Corporate Governance' (2000) 58 Journal of Financial Economics 3.

La Porta R, Lopez-de-Silanes F and Shleifer A, 'Corporate Ownership Around the World' (1999) 54 The Journal of Finance 471.

Lafarre A and Van der Elst C, 'Executive Pay and Say-on-Pay in the Netherlands' in Van der Elst C (ed.), *Executive Directors' Remuneration in Comparative Corporate Perspective*, vol 11 (Kluwer Law International 2015).

Landers JM, 'A Unified Approach to Parent, Subsidiary, and Affiliate Questions in Bankruptcy' (1975) 42 The University of Chicago Law Review 589.

Langenbucher K, 'Do We Need a Law of Corporate Groups?' in Fleischer H and others (eds), *German and Asian Perspectives on Company Law* (Mohr Siebeck 2016).

Lannoo K, 'Corporate Governance, West and East: A Synthesis of the EU Framework in the Perspective of Enlargement' in Balling M (ed.), *Corporate Governance, Financial Markets and Global Convergence* (Springer 1998).

Lepel L, 'Poniattia afiliyovanykh osib u konkurentnomu zakonodavstvi Ukrayiny' (2007) Yurysprudentsiya: teoriya i praktyka 11.

Lipton P, 'The Mythology of Salomon's Case and the Law Dealing with the Tort Liabilities of Corporate Groups: An Historical Perspective' (2014) 40 Monash University Law Review 452.

Lorsch JW, 'Board Challenges 2009' in Sun W, Stewart J and Pollard D (eds), *Corporate Governance and the Global Financial Crisis: International Perspectives* (Cambridge University Press 2011).

Lukach I, *Teoretychni problemy pravovoho reguliuvannia korporatyvnykh vidnosyn v Ukrayini: [monographiya]* (K.: Lira-K 2015).

Lux J, Skadegard Thorsen S and Meisling A, 'The European Initiatives' in Mullerat R (ed.), *Corporate Social Responsibility: The Corporate Governance of the 21st Century* (Kluwer Law International 2005).

Maassen G and Van Den Bosch F, 'On the Supposed Independence of Two-Tier Boards: Formal Structure and Reality in the Netherlands' (1999) 7 Corporate Governance: An International Review 31.

Mader D and Schümann-Kleber K, 'Germany' in Willems M (ed.), *Cash Pooling and Insolvency: A Practical Global Handbook* (Globe Business Publishing Ltd 2012).

Mahtani U, 'An Analysis of Related-Party Transactions in India' Working Paper Series Wp No: 2017/01/FN (Goa Institute Of Management, Poriem, Sattari, Goa 403505), available at: https://www.gim.ac.in/newpdfs/Related-party-transactions-Group-and-Non-Group-Company-Perspective-Jan2017pdf and http://www.iimb.ernet.in/sites/default/files/WP%20No.%20402_0.pdf, accessed on 6 December 2018.

Maigoshi ZS, Latif RA and Kamardin H, 'Earnings Management: A Case of Related Party Transactions' (2016) 6 International Journal of Economics and Financial Issues 51.

Makhinchuk V, *Zniattia korporatyvnoyi vuali: monographia* (Ivano-Frankivsk: 'Foliant' 2017).

Marenych T, 'Zaprovadzhennia mizhnarodnykh standartiv bukhgalterskoho obliku ta finansovoyi zvitnosti u vitchyznianu praktyku' (2012) Ekonomika ahropromyslovoho kompleksu 44.

Mäntysaari P, *Comparative Corporate Governance: Shareholders as a Rule-Maker* (Springer Science & Business Media 2005).

Mäntysaari P, *Organising the Firm: Theories of Commercial Law, Corporate Governance and Corporate Law* (Springer Science & Business Media 2011).

'Marker nezrilosti: V 53% zasnovnyk ye dyrektorom kompanii' (2017), available at: https://opendatabot.ua/blog/75-founders-ceo, accessed on 30 September 2018.

Marks SG, 'The Separation of Ownership and Control' (1999) Encyclopedia of Law and Economics 692.

Martin MR, 'Report from the Netherlands' (2008) 5 European Company Law 195.

Masouros PE, *Corporate Law and Economic Stagnation: How Shareholder Value and Short-Termism Contribute to the Decline of the Western Economies* (Eleven International Publishing 2013).

Masouros PE, 'Is the EU Taking Shareholder Rights Seriously?: An Essay on the Impotence of Shareholdership in Corporate Europe' (2010) 7 European Company Law 195.

Mayer C, 'Corporate Governance, Competition and Performance' in Balling M (ed.), *Corporate Governance, Financial Markets and Global Convergence* (Springer 1998).

McCahery J and Vermeulen EM, 'Conflict Resolution and the Role of Courts: Empirical Study' in Neville M and Sørensen KE (eds), *Company Law and SMEs* (Thomson Reuters 2010).

McCahery JA and Vermeulen EPM, 'Corporate Governance Crises and Related Party Transactions: A Post-Parmalat Agenda' in Hopt K and others (eds), *Corporate Governance in Context: Corporations, States, and Markets in Europe, Japan, and the US* (Oxford University Press 2005).

McCahery JA and Vermeulen EP, *Corporate Governance of Non-listed Companies* (Oxford University Press 2010).

McCarthy KJ, Fiolet M and Dolfsma W, *The Nature of the New Firm: Beyond the Boundaries of Organisations and Institutions* (Edward Elgar Publishing 2011).

McCormack G, 'Fiduciary Obligations in a Changing Commercial Climate' in Rider B and Andenas M (eds), *Developments in European Company Law*, vol 1/1996 (Kluwer Law International 1997).

Melis G and Melis A, 'Financial Reporting, Corporate Governance and Parmalat: Was It a Financial Reporting Failure?' in O'Brien J (ed.), *Governing the Corporation: Regulation and Corporate Governance in an Age of Scandal and Global Markets* (John Wiley & Sons 2005).

Merkt H, 'Germany: Internal and External Corporate Governance' in Fleckner AM and Hopt KJ (eds), *Comparative Corporate Governance: A Functional and International Analysis* (Cambridge University Press 2013).

Mevorach I, 'Transaction Avoidance in Bankruptcy of Corporate Groups' (2011) 8 European Company and Financial Law Review 235.

Mezzanotte FE and Fung S, 'Do Institutional Owners Monitor? Evidence from Voting on Connected Transaction Proposals in Hong Kong-Listed Companies' (2018) 7 Michigan Business & Entrepreneurial Law Review 221.

Miller PB, 'Justifying Fiduciary Duties' (2013) 58 McGill Law Journal/Revue de droit de McGill 969.

Mita AF and Utama S, 'The Influence of Corporate Governance Mechanism on the Relationship Between Related Party Transactions and Earnings Management' (2015) 7 International Research Journal of Business Studies 1.

Mitręga E, *Contemporary Enforceable Directors' Duties in Switzerland and in Poland: The Path of (GRC) Corporate Governance, Compliance and Risk Management from Soft Law to Hard Law?* (Schulthess 2016).

Morck RK and Steier L, 'The Global History of Corporate Governance: An Introduction' in Morck RK (ed.), *A History of Corporate Governance around the World: Family Business Groups to Professional Managers* (University of Chicago Press 2007).

Moscariello N, 'Related Party Transactions in Continental European Countries: Evidence from Italy' (2012) 9 International Journal of Disclosure and Governance 126.

Mouthaan EH, 'The Audit Committee from a European Perspective' (2007) 4 European Company Law 10.

Mucha A, 'Dobre Praktyki Spółek Notowanych na GPW 2016 – kontynuacja czy rewolucja? (Best Practice for Warsaw Stock Exchange Listed Companies 2016–Continuation or Revolution?)' Allerhand Working Papers, 3 March 2016, available at SSRN: https://papers.ssrn.com/sol3/paperscfm?abstract_id=2741 585, accessed on 6 December 2018.

Müller KJ, *The GmbH: A Guide to the German Limited Liability Company* (CH Beck 2016).

Muller MH (ed.), *Corporate Law in the Netherlands* (3rd edn, Wolters Kluwer Law & Business 2013).

Muller W, 'Group Accounts under the Proposed Seventh EEC Directive: A Practitioner's View' in Hopt KJ (ed.), *Groups of Companies in European Laws*, vol 2 (de Gruyter 1982).

Murashko N, 'Some Aspects of Shareholders' Rights Protection: Legal Practice Review' (2013) Studentskyi yurydychnyi zhurnal: dodatok do zhurnalu 'Pravo Ukrayiny' 69.

Mwaura K, 'Internalization of Costs to Corporate Groups: Part-Whole Relationships, Human Rights Norms and the Futility of the Corporate Veil' (2012) 11 Journal of International Business & Law 85.

'Natsionalnyi bank vitaye posylennia roboty pravookhoronnykh organiv schodo prytiagnennia do vidpovidalnosti vlasnykiv ta top-menedzheriv bankiv' Web-site of the National Bank of Ukraine (12 December 2016), available at: https://bank.gov.ua/control/uk/publish/article?art_id=40777652&cat_id=55838, accessed on 14 September 2019.

'Natsionalnyi bank vyznachyv 14 bankiv systemno vazhlyvymy' web-site of the National Bank of Ukraine, available at: https://bank.gov.ua/news/all/natsionalniy-bank-viznachiv-14-bankiv-sistemno-vajlivimi, accessed on 4 September 2019.

Nijland J and Dijkhuizen T, 'Say on Pay and Focus on Sustainability of Companies: A Revised Shareholders' Rights Directive' (2017) 14 European Company Law 188.

Nix P and Chen J, *The Role of Institutional Investors in Corporate Governance: An Empirical Study* (Springer 2013).

Nolan RC, 'The Legal Control of Directors' Conflicts of Interest in the United Kingdom: Non-executive Directors Following the Higgs Report' in Armour J and McCahery JA (eds), *After Enron: Improving Corporate Law and Modernising Securities Regulation in Europe and the US* (Bloomsbury Publishing 2006).

Nowak R, 'Corporate Boards in the Netherlands' in Davies PL and others (eds), *Corporate Boards in Law and Practice: A Comparative Analysis in Europe* (1st edn, Oxford University Press 2013).

Nzafashwanayo D, 'Corporate Groups under the Laws of Rwanda: An Economic Reality Without Legal Identity' (2016) 7 Beijing Law Review 95.

O'Connor MA, 'How Should We Talk about Fiduciary Duty-Directors' Conflict-of-Interest Transactions and the ALI's Principles of Corporate Governance' (1992) 61 The George Washington Law Review 954.

OECD, *G20/OECD Principles of Corporate Governance* (OECD Publishing 2015).

OECD, *Improving Corporate Governance in India: Related Party Transactions and Minority Shareholder Protection* (OECD Publishing 2014).

OECD, *Legal Issues with Regard to Business Operations and Investment in Ukraine* (OECD Publishing 2004).

OECD, *Related Party Transactions and Minority Shareholder Rights* (OECD Publishing 2012).

Oostrum CHAv, 'Regres bij concernfinanciering' (Dphil thesis, Wolters Kluwer 2019).

Oostwouder W, 'Can You Trust the Dutch (Company Law System)?' (2007) 4 European Company Law 211.

Opalski A, 'Transakcje między podmiotami powiązanymi w prawie spółek' (2012) Przegląd Prawa Handlowego 4.

Oplustil K, 'Regulaminy (kodeksy) grup spółek jako instrument realizacji interesu koncernowego' in Olejniczak A, Orlicki M and Pokrzywniak J (eds), *Z badań nad prawem prywatnym: księga pamiątkowa dedykowana Profesorowi Andrzejowi Kochowi* (Poznań: Wydawnictwo Naukowe UAM 2017).

Oplustil K and Radwan A, 'Company Law in Poland: Between Autonomous Development and Legal Transplants' in Jessel-Holst C, Kulms R and Trunk A (eds), *Private Law in Eastern Europe* (2010), available at: https://ssrn.com/abstract=3079494, accessed on 6 December 2018.

Pacces AM, 'Procedural and Substantive Review of Related Party Transactions (RPTs): The Case for Non-controlling Shareholder-Dependent (NCS-Dependent) Directors' ECGI Law Working Paper N° 399/2018 (May 2018), available at: http://ssrn.com/abstract_id=3167519, accessed on 6 December 2018.

Parkinson JE, *Corporate Power and Responsibility: Issues in the Theory of Company Law* (Oxford University Press Catalogue 1995).

Peck S and Ruigrok W, 'Hiding Behind the Flag? Prospects for Change in German Corporate Governance' (2000) 18 European Management Journal 420.

Pendse SJ, 'International Transfer Pricing: A Review of Non-tax Outlook' (2012) 37 Procedia-Social and Behavioral Sciences 337.

Perakēs E, 'Rights of Minority Shareholders General Report' in Perakēs E (ed.), *Rights of Minority Shareholders: XVIth Congress of the International Academy of Comparative Law,* (Brisbane (Australia) 2002); General and National Reports (Bruylant 2004).

'Pered natsionalizatsiyeyu z 'Privatbanku' vyvely desiatky milyardiv hryven, – 'Schemy'. VIDEO' CensorNET (12 May 2017), available at: https://censor.net.ua/ua/video_news/439605/pered_natsionalizatsiyeyu_z_pryvatbanku_vyvely_desyatky_milyardiv_gryven_shemy_video, accessed on 4 September 2019.

Peters A, 'Conflict of Interest as a Cross-Cutting Problem of Governance' in Peters A and Handschin L (eds), *Conflict of Interest in Global, Public and Corporate Governance* (Cambridge University Press 2012).

Picciotto S, *Regulating Global Corporate Capitalism* (Cambridge University Press 2011).

Pistor K and Xu C, 'Fiduciary Duty in Transitional Civil Law Jurisdictions' in Milhaupt CJ (ed.), *Global Markets, Domestic Institutions: Corporate Law and Governance in a New Era of Cross-Border Deals* (Columbia University Press 2012).

Pizzo M, 'Related Party Transactions under a Contingency Perspective' (2013) 17 Journal of Management & Governance 309.

Poizner A and Mykhalchuk I, 'Pravochyny, v yakykh prysutnia zainteresovannist' Yurydychna hazeta (17 August 2010).

Pomelli A, 'Related-Party Transactions and the Intricacies of Ex Post Judicial Review: The Parmalat/Lactalis Case' (2016) 13 European Company and Financial Law Review 73.

Potjewijd G and Van der Kroon J, 'Report from the Netherlands' (2007) 4 European Company Law 235.

Poyedynok V, 'Novely korporatyvnoho upravlinnia v derzhavnykh pidpryyemstvakh' (Adaptatsiya korporatyvnoho zakonodavstva Ukrayiny do prava Yevropeyskoho Soyuzu: Zbirnyk naukovykh prats za materialamy Mizhnarodnoyi naukovo-praktychnoyi konferentsii (30 veresnia – 1 zhovtnia 2016, Ivano-Frankivsk)).

Prigge S, 'A Survey of German Corporate Governance' in Hopt K (ed.), *Comparative Corporate Governance: The State of the Art and Emerging Research* (Oxford University Press 1998).

'Pro scho hovoryt statutnyi kapital?' (2017), available at: https://opendatabot.ua/blog/73-fake-capital, accessed on 30 September 2018.

Putra LD, 'Related Party Transaction Disclosures [IAS 24]' (*Accounting, financial and tax,* available at: http://accounting-financial-tax.com/, accessed on April 2009) http://accounting-financial-tax.com/2009/04/related-party-transaction-disclosures-ias-24/, accessed on 25 July 2016.

PwC, *International Transfer Pricing 2015/16,* available at: https://www.pwc.com/gx/en/international-transfer-pricing/assets/itp-2015-2016-final.pdf, 2015.

Radwan A and Regucki T, 'Legal Aspects of Executive Remuneration in Polish Listed Companies' in Van der Elst C (ed.), *Executive Directors' Remuneration in Comparative Corporate Perspective*, vol 11 (Kluwer Law International 2015).

Radwan A and Regucki T, 'The Possibilities For and Barriers to Sustainable Companies in Polish Company Law' 11 International and Comparative Corporate Law Journal, Forthcoming; University of Oslo Faculty of Law Research Paper No. 2012-32, available at: http://ssrn.com/abstract=2159217, https://ssrn.com/abstract=2159217, accessed on 6 December 2018.

Radwan A, Nadzon A and Zdiruk V, *Assessment of Approximation Level of the Present Company, Corporate Governance, Accounting and Auditing Legislation and Existing Practices in Ukraine to EU Standards and Practices* (Contract N°2013/328606/2, available at SSRN: https://ssrn.com/abstract=3090335 or http://dx.doi.org/102139/ssrn3090335, 2014).

Rajak H, 'Corporate Groups and Cross-Border Bankruptcy' (2008) 44 Texas International Law Journal 521.

Reynisson K, 'Related Party Transactions: Analysis of Proposed Article 9c of Shareholders' Rights Directive' (2016) 13 European Company Law 175.

Ringe W-G, 'Changing Law and Ownership Patterns in Germany: Corporate Governance and the Erosion of Deutschland AG' in Hill JG and Thomas RS (eds), *Research Handbook on Shareholder Power* (Edward Elgar Publishing 2015).

Rock E and Wachter ML, 'Waiting for the Omelet to Set: Match-Specific Assets and Minority Oppression' in McCahery J and Vermeulen EM (eds), *The Governance of Close Corporations and Partnerships: US and European Perspectives* (Oxford University Press on Demand 2004).

Romashchenko I, 'Corporate Law Development in Ukraine: From Post-Soviet Past to European Future' (2015) 12 European Company Law 217.

Rosengarten J, Burmeister F and Klein M, *The German Limited Liability Company: An Introduction to the Act on Limited Liability Companies with German/English Text, Synoptically Arranged, of the Act, a Sample of Articles of Association, Samples of the Other Formation Documents of the Company, the Classification of the Balance Sheet and the Profit and Loss Statement of a Company and an Extract from the Commercial Register* (CH Beck 2015).

Roth GH and Kindler P, *The Spirit of Corporate Law: Core Principles of Corporate Law in Continental Europe* (Beck/Hart 2013).

Rządkowski M, '"Piercing the Corporate Veil Doctrine in Poland?" A Comparative Perspective' (2015) 20 Comparative Law Review 55.

Saenger I, 'Conflicts of Interest of Supervisory Board Members in a German Stock Corporation and the Demand for Their Independence: An Investigation in the Context of the Current Corporate Governance Discussion' (2005) 1 Corporate Governance Law Review 147.

Sáez MI and Riaño D, 'Corporate Governance and the Shareholders' Meeting: Voting and Litigation' (2013) 14 European Business Organization Law Review 343.

Samaras I and Athianos S, 'Group Accounting: The Effect of IFRS Adoption. The Case of Greece' (2016) 15 Journal of Accounting and Management Information Systems 661.

Samól K, 'One-Or Two-Tier Board System? A Comparative Analysis of the British and Polish Systems of Corporate Governance' (2016) 13 European Company Law 67.
Sanders P, *Dutch Company Law* (Oyez Publishing 1977).
Sargent N, 'Beyond the Legal Entity Doctrine: Parent-Subsidiary Relations under the West German Konzernrecht' (1985) 10 Canadian Business Law Journal 327.
Schaefer H-B, 'Rule Based Legal Systems as a Substitute for Human Capital: Should Poor Countries Have a More Rule Based Legal System?' (2002) 2001 German Working Papers in Law and Economics 2.
Schäfer H-B and Cooter RD, 'Growth-Oriented Legal Reforms' in Parisi F (ed.), *Production of Legal Rules* (Edward Elgar Publishing 2012).
Scheuch A, 'Konzernrecht: An Overview of the German Regulation of Corporate Groups and Resulting Liability Issues' (2016) 13 European Company Law 191.
Schiessl M, 'The Liability of Corporations and Shareholders for the Capitalization and Obligations of Subsidiaries under German Law' (1985) 7 Northwestern Journal of International Law & Business 480.
Schmidt P-J, 'Disclosure and Auditing: A German Auditor's Perspective' in Hopt KJ and others (eds), *Comparative Corporate Governance, Clarendon, Oxford* (Oxford University Press 1998).
Schroeder U and Jaecks J, 'Report from Germany' (2007) 4 European Company Law 230.
Schutte T, 'Good Governance: Reasonableness and Fairness of Directors and Supervisors' Newsletter, as of 27 August 2015, available at: https://www.russell.nl/Uploaded_files/Zelf/Publicaties/good-governance-reasonableness-and-fairness-of-directors-and-supervisors6588a8pdf, accessed on 30 August 2017.
Scott RE and Triantis GG, 'Incomplete Contracts and the Theory of Contract Design' (2005) 56 Case Western Reserve Law Review 187.
Searjeant G, 'Plc Is Ready to Join Mutuals in Land of the Dodo' Times (21 April 2006).
Shleifer A and Vishny RW, 'A Survey of Corporate Governance' (1997) 52 The Journal of Finance 737.
Shtym T, 'Aktsionerni uhody, pravochyny iz zainteresovannistiu ta znachni pravochyny v aktsionernykh tovarystvakh' (DPhil thesis, Taras Shevchenko National University of Kyiv 2014).
Sjåfjell B, 'Achieving Corporate Sustainability: What Is the Role of the Shareholder?' in Birkmose HS (ed.), *Shareholders' Duties* (Wolters Kluwer 2017).
Sjåfjell B and Anker-Sørensen L, 'Directors' Duties and Corporate Social Responsibility (CSR)' in Birkmose HS, Neville M and Sørensen KE (eds), *Boards of Directors in European Companies: Reshaping and Harmonising Their Organisation and Duties* (Wolters Kluwer Law & Business 2013).
Smits H and Portengen HJ, 'Report from the Netherlands' (2007) 4 European Company Law 128.
Søgaard G, 'Introduction of a Group Definition in the New Accounting Directive: The Impact on Future Accounting Regulation' (2014) 11 European Company Law 232.
Sołtysiński S, 'Corporate Boards in Poland' in Davies PL and others (eds), *Corporate Boards in Law and Practice: A Comparative Analysis in Europe* (1st edn, Oxford University Press 2013).

Sołtysiński S, 'Poland: Corporate Governance of Joint-Stock Companies' in Fleckner AM and Hopt KJ (eds), *Comparative Corporate Governance: A Functional and International Analysis* (Cambridge University Press 2013).

Sørensen KE, 'Duty of Loyalty of Shareholders: A Possible Remedy for Conflicts in SMEs?' in Neville M and Sørensen KE (eds), *Company Law and SMEs* (Thomson Reuters 2010).

Sørensen KE, 'Groups of Companies in the Case Law of the Court of Justice of the European Union' (2016) 27 European Business Law Review 393.

Sørensen KE, 'Shareholders' Duty to Disclose' in Birkmose HS (ed.), *Shareholders' Duties* (Wolters Kluwer 2017).

Spahlinger A and Kortz H, 'Germany' in Baer G and Karen OF (eds), *Financing Company Group Restructurings* (Oxford University Press 2015).

Spindler G, 'Scandals, Regulation, and Supervisory Agencies: The European Perspective' in Hopt KJ (ed.), *Corporate Governance in Context: Corporations, States, and Markets in Europe, Japan, and the US* (Oxford University Press 2005).

Spindler G, 'The Role of Shareholders in Public Companies' in Fleischer H and others (eds), *German and Asian Perspectives on Company Law* (Mohr Siebeck 2016).

Stack G, *Oligarchs Weaponized Cyprus Branch of Ukraine's Largest Bank to Send $5.5 Billion Abroad* OCCPR (19 April 2019), available at: https://www.occrp.org/en/investigations/oligarchs-weaponized-cyprus-eranch-of-ukraines-largest-bank-to-send-5-billion-abroad, accessed on 4 September 2019.

Stark A, 'The Furore over Banker Compensation' in Peters A and Handschin L (eds), *Conflict of Interest in Global, Public and Corporate Governance* (Cambridge University Press 2012).

Statement of the European Corporate Governance Forum on Related Party Transactions for Listed Companies – 10 March 2011 (2011).

Stecher MW, 'Germany' in Stecher MW (ed.), *Protection of Minority Shareholders*, vol 4 (Kluwer Law International 1997).

Stecher MW and others, *Protection of Minority Shareholders*, vol 4 (Kluwer Law International 1997).

Stoljar SJ, *Groups and Entities: An Inquiry into Corporate Theory* (National University Press 1973).

Study on Minority Shareholders Protection, Final Report (Prepared by TGS Baltic 2018).

Sulaiman ANM, 'Responding to Concentrated Ownership: The Related-Party Transaction Provisions of Some Asian Countries' (2007) 3 Corporate Governance Law Review 70.

Tajti T, 'Corporate Governance: An Oversold Elitist Idea of No Interest to or for the Central European Transitory Economies' (2005) 1 Corporate Governance Law Review 21.

Talab HR, 'Transfer Pricing and Its Effect on Financial Reporting: A Theoretical Analysis of Global Tax in Multinational Companies' (2017) 11 International Business Management 921.

Tamowicz P, 'Corporate Governance in Poland' in Mallin CA (ed.), *Handbook on International Corporate Governance: Country Analyses* (Edward Elgar Publishing 2011).

Teichmann C, 'Modernizing the GmbH: Germany's Move in Regulatory Competition' (2010) 7 European Company Law 20.

Teichmann C, 'Towards a European Framework for Cross-Border Group Management' (2016) 13 European Company Law 150.

Teichmann C and Gurman O, 'Directors' Remuneration in Germany' in Van der Elst C (ed.), *Executive Directors' Remuneration in Comparative Corporate Perspective*, vol 11 (Kluwer Law International 2015).

Teubner G, 'Corporate Fiduciary Duties and Their Beneficiaries' in Hopt K and Teubner G (eds), *Corporate Governance and Directors Liabilities* (de Gruyter 1985).

Timmerman L and Doorman A, 'Rights of Minority Shareholders in the Netherlands' in Perakēs E (ed.), *Rights of Minority Shareholders: XVIth Congress of the International Academy of Comparative Law* (Brisbane (Australia) 2002); General and National Reports (Bruylant 2004).

Timmerman V, 'Review of Management Decisions by the Courts, Seen Partly from a Comparative Legal Perspective' in Jitta MJ (ed.), *The Companies and Business Court from a Comparative Law Perspective* (Kluwer 2004).

Timmermans CWA and Timmerman L, 'The Law on Groups of Companies in the Netherlands' in Wymeersch E (ed.), *Groups of Companies in the EEC: a Survey Report to the European Commission on the Law Relating to Corporate Groups in Various Member States* (Walter de Gruyter 1993).

Tkachuk D, 'Publichni ta pryvatni aktsionerni tovarystva: pro zmischennia mezh' Yuryst & Zakon (February 2018), available at: http://uz.ligazakon.ua/ua/magazine_article/EA011255, accessed on 3 September 2019.

Tröger T, 'Corporate Groups: A German's European Perspective' in Fleischer H, Hansen JL and Ringe W-G (eds), *German and Nordic Perspectives on Company Law and Capital Markets Law* (Mohr Siebeck 2015).

Tröger T, 'Germany's Reluctance to Regulate Related Party Transactions: An Industrial Organization Perspective' SAFE Working Paper No. 202, available at SSRN: https://ssrn.com/abstract=3129300, accessed on 7 December 2018.

Tsiura V, 'Pravova pryroda predstavnytskykh povnovazhen organiv i posavodykh osib yurydychnoyi osoby' (2016) Prykarpatskyi yurydychnyi visnyk 54.

Tuijtel MM, 'The Dutch Inquiry Proceedings: A Unique Instrument for Minority Protection from a Comparative Law Perspective' (2005) 2 European Company Law 90.

Ungerer F, *Prozedurale Regulierung und Transparenz von Related Party Transactions in börsennotierten Aktiengesellschaften: eine vergleichende Untersuchung des deutschen und europäischen Aktien-und Kapitalmarktrechts unter besonderer Berücksichtigung von Art. 9c der novellierten Aktionärsrechterichtlinie* (Duncker & Humblot 2019).

'V Opendatabot zyavyvsia poshuk po vlasnykam kompaniy' (2017), available at: https://opendatabot.ua/blog/71-founders, accessed on 29 September 2018.

'V Ukrayini pochav robotu novyi Verkhovnyi Sud' (2017), available at: https://ua.korrespondent.net/ukraine/3918262-v-ukraini-pochav-robotu-novyi-verkhovnyi-sud, accessed on 29 September 2019.

Vaez SA and Banafi M, 'Prediction of Related Party Transactions Using Artificial Neural Network' (2017) 7 International Journal of Economics and Financial Issues 207.
Van Bekkum J and others, 'Corporate Governance in the Netherlands' in Fleckner AM and Hopt KJ (eds), *Comparative Corporate Governance: A Functional and International Analysis* (Cambridge University Press 2013).
Van den Braak S, 'Creditor Protection at the Crossroads of Company and Insolvency Law: The Dutch Example' (2008) 5 European Company Law 229.
Van der Elst C, 'Shareholders Holding the Reins on Remuneration: The European Say on Pay' (2017) 14 European Company Law 114.
Van der Elst C, 'The Duties of Significant Shareholders in Transactions with the Company' in Birkmose HS (ed.), *Shareholders' Duties* (Wolters Kluwer 2017).
Van Galen R, 'The Netherlands' in Baer G and Karen OF (eds), *Financing Company Group Restructurings* (Oxford University Press 2015).
Van Horzen J, 'Netherlands' in Willems M (ed.), *Cash Pooling and Insolvency: A Practical Global Handbook* (Globe Business Publishing Ltd 2012).
Van Zwieten K, 'Related Party Transactions in Insolvency' ECGI – Law Working Paper No. 401/2018, available at SSRN: http://ssrn.com/abstract_id=3173629, accessed on 7 December 2018.
Vandekerckhove K, *Piercing the Corporate Veil* (Wolters Kluwer 2007).
Velasco J, 'Fiduciary Duties and Fiduciary Outs' (2013) 21 George Mason Law Review 157.
Verkerk B, 'Modernizing of Dutch Company Law: Reform of the Law Applicable to the BV and a New Legal Framework for the One-Tier Board Within NVs and BVs' (2010) 7 European Company Law 113.
Vermeulen EM, *The Evolution of Legal Business Forms in Europe and the United States: Venture Capital, Joint Venture and Partnership Structures* (Kluwer Law International 2003).
Vetter J, 'Regelungsbedarf für Related Party Transactions?' (2015) 179 ZHR: Zeitschrift für das gesamte handelsrecht und wirtschaftsrecht 273.
Vetter J and Schwandtner C, 'Cash Pooling under the Revised German Private Limited Companies Act (GmbHG)' (2008) 9 German Law Journal 1155.
Villiers C, 'Mapping Paper: Sustainable Companies UK Report' University of Oslo Faculty of Law Research Paper No. 2013-16 (17 June 2013), available at SSRN: https://ssrn.com/abstract=2280350, accessed on 7 December 2018.
Von Werder A and Talaulicar T, 'Corporate Governance Developments in Germany' in Mallin CA (ed.), *Handbook on International Corporate Governance: Country Analyses* (Edward Elgar Publishing 2011).
Vreeman NL, 'Trading the Straightjacket for a Leotard: Introducing the New Dutch BV Law' (2012) 9 European Company Law 305.
Walton FP, 'The Historical School of Jurisprudence and Transplantations of Law' (1927) 9 Journal of Comparative Legislation and International Law 183.
Wang Q, 'Exit Remedies for Minority Shareholders in Close Companies' (Dphil thesis, University of Groningen 2011).
Warendorf H, Thomas R and Curry-Sumner I, *The Civil Code of the Netherlands* (Kluwer Law International 2013).

Werlauff E, 'Group and Community? The European Court's Development of an Independent Community Law Concept of the Group and Its Significance for National Company Law' (2007) 4 European Company Law 201.

Wiedemann H, *Organverantwortung und Gesellschafterklagen in der Aktiengesellschaft: 296. Sitzung am 16. Oktober 1985 in Düsseldorf (Fassung vom 1. 1. 1989)* (Springer-Verlag 2013).

Wiedemann H, 'The German Law of Affiliated Enterprises' in Hopt KJ (ed.), *Legal and Economic Analyses on Multinational Enterprises: Groups of Companies in European Laws*, vol 2 (Gruyter, De, Rechtswissenschaften 1982).

Williamson OE, 'The Theory of the Firm as Governance Structure: From Choice to Contract' (2002) 16 The Journal of Economic Perspectives 171.

Williamson OE, 'Transaction Cost Economics: The Natural Progression' (2010) 86 Journal of Retailing 215.

Windbichler C, '"Corporate Group Law for Europe": Comments on the Forum Europaeum's Principles and Proposals for a European Corporate Group Law' (2000) 1 European Business Organization Law Review 265.

Winner M, 'Group Interest in European Company Law: An Overview' (2016) 5 Acta Universitatis Sapientiae, Legal Studies 85.

Winter J and others, *Report of the High Level Group of Company Law Experts on a Modern Regulatory Framework for Company Law in Europe* (Office for Official Publications of the European Communities 2002).

Wymeersch E, 'A Status Report on Corporate Governance Rules and Practices in Some Continental European States' in Hopt K (ed.), *Comparative Corporate Governance: The State of the Art and Emerging Research* (Oxford University Press 1998).

Wymeersch E, 'European Corporate Governance Codes and Their Effectiveness' in Belcredi M and Ferrarini G (eds), *Boards and Shareholders in European Listed Companies: Facts, Context and Post-Crisis Reforms* (Cambridge University Press 2013).

Xu G and others, 'Public Governance and Tunneling: Evidence from a Quasi-Experiment in China' Working Paper, available at: http://ied-wbef.hkbu.edu.hk /conference-proceedings/doc/S001-Full.pdf, accessed on 7 December 2018.

Yasui T, 'Corporate Governance of Financial Groups' OECD Corporate Governance Working Papers, available at: http://dx.doi.org/101787/5jlv1m6zq3nx-en, accessed on 7 December 2018.

Yefymenko A, 'Pravochyny iz zainteresovanistiu' (2014) Visnyk Tsentru komertsiynoho prava 2.

Yefymenko A, 'Yurydychni osoby za proektom Tsyvilnoho kodeksu Ukrayiny' (2002) Yurydychnyi zhurnal 53.

Yefymenko A, *Corporate Governance under Ukraine's New Joint Stock Company Law*, available at SSRN: http://ssrn.com/abstract = 1387360, accessed on 7 December 2018.

Zak T, 'Poland' in Loos A (ed.), *Directors 'Liability: A Worldwide Review* (International Bar Association, Netherlands 2006).

Zanuda A, 'Yak Privatbank stav temoyu vyboriv i scho bude pislia nykh' BBC Ukraine (16 April 2019), available at: https://www.bbc.com/ukrainian/features-47913100, accessed on 4 September 2019.
Zasadnyi BA, 'Formuvannia oblikovoyi polityky pidpryyemstva schodo povyazanykh storin' (2015) Visnyk Kyivskoho natsionalnoho universytetu im Tarasa Shevchenka Seriya: Ekonomika 24.
Zlatescu VD and Moroianu-Zlatescu I, 'Le Droit Roumain dans le Système Romano-Germanique' (1991) 43 Revue Internationale de Droit Comparé 829.

Table of Documents and Cases

EU

Germany

Poland

The Netherlands

Ukraine

Index

D

EUROPEAN COMPANY LAW SERIES

1. Steef M. Bartman (ed.), *European Company Law in Accelerated Progress*, 2006 (ISBN 978-90-411-2529-3).
2. Karen Vandekerckhove, *Piercing The Corporate Veil: A Transnational Approach*, 2007 (ISBN 978-90-411-2591-0).
3. Beate Sjåfjell, *Towards a Sustainable European Company Law: A Normative Analysis of the Objectives of EU Law, with the Takeover Directive as a Test Case*, 2009 (ISBN 978-90-411-2768-6).
4. Cornelis de Groot, *Corporate Governance as a Limited Legal Concept*, 2009 (ISBN 978-90-411-2873-7).
5. Adriaan F.M. Dorresteijn, Christoph Teichmann, Erik Werlauff, Tiago Monteiro & Nadia Pocher, *European Corporate Law*, Third Edition, 2017 (ISBN 978-90-411-8593-8).
6. Gert-Jan Vossestein, *Modernization of European Company Law and Corporate Governance: Some Considerations on its Legal Limits*, 2010 (ISBN 978-90-411-2592-7).
7. Catalin Stefan Rusu, *European Merger Control: The Challenges Raised by Twenty Years of Enforcement Experience*, 2010 (ISBN 978-90-411-3259-8).
8. Sabrina Bruno & Eugenio Ruggiero, *Public Companies and the Role of Shareholders: National Models Towards Global Integration*, 2011 (ISBN 978-90-411-3423-3).
9. Hanne S. Birkmose, Mette Neville & Karsten Engsig Sørensen (eds), *The European Financial Market in Transition*, 2012 (ISBN 978-90-411-3360-1).
10. Hanne S. Birkmose, Mette Neville & Karsten Engsig Sørensen (eds), *Boards of Directors in European Companies: Reshaping and Harmonising Their Organisation and Duties*, 2013 (ISBN 978-90-411-4141-5).
11. Christoph Van der Elst, *Executive Directors' Remuneration in Comparative Corporate Perspective*, 2015 (ISBN 978-90-411-5607-5).
12. Hanne S. Birkmose, *Shareholders' Duties*, 2017 (ISBN 978-90-411-6670-8).
13. Alan S. Gutterman, *Sustainability and Corporate Governance: A Practice Guide to Implementing a Sustainability Governance System*, 2018 (ISBN 978-90-411-9975-1).
14. Jan De Bruyne, *Third-Party Certifiers*, 2019 (ISBN 978-94-035-1091-0).
15. Hanne S. Birkmose, Mette Neville & Karsten Engsig Sørensen (eds), *Abuse of Companies*, 2019 (ISBN 978-94-035-0892-4).
16. Ivan Romashchenko, *Related Party Transactions and Corporate Groups: When Eastern Europe Meets the West*, 2020 (ISBN 978-94-035-1701-8).

www.ingramcontent.com/pod-product-compliance
Ingram Content Group UK Ltd.
Pitfield, Milton Keynes, MK11 3LW, UK
UKHW020234290926
15470UKWH00002B/534

9 789403 51701